PRACTICE MAKES PERFECT®

Spanish Vocabulary Building with Suffixes

PRACTICE
MAKES
PERFECT®

Spanish Vocabulary Building with Suffixes

Dorothy Richmond

Mc
Graw
Hill
Education

New York   Chicago   San Francisco   Athens   London   Madrid
Mexico City   Milan   New Delhi   Singapore   Sydney   Toronto

1 2 3 4 5 6 7 8 9 0   QVS/QVS   1 0 9 8 7 6 5 4

ISBN   978-0-07-183528-2
MHID   0-07-183528-8

e-ISBN 978-0-07-183529-9
e-MHID   0-07-183529-6

Library of Congress Control Number 2014933901

Interior design by Village Bookworks, Inc.

McGraw-Hill Education products are available at special quantity discounts to use as premiums and sales promotions or for use in corporate training programs. To contact a representative, please visit the Contact Us pages at www.mhprofessional.com.

This book is printed on acid-free paper.

For Rita Vollbrecht, my favorite cousin and true family treasure

Contents

I ◆ Beginning suffixes 1

◆III◆ Advanced suffixes 213

Acknowledgments

Practice Makes Perfect: Spanish Vocabulary Building with Suffixes represents a labor of love. Many years ago, I discovered the efficiency and power that suffixes bring to the study of Spanish vocabulary. After compiling thousands of words that employ common Spanish suffixes, I turned to several people for assistance as I was writing this book.

Spanish teacher José Fresco, a native of Santa Cruz, Bolivia, answered many questions and always gave excellent advice. In conversations with José, I discovered why he is the favorite Spanish teacher of many students, including my daughter Daisy. Susan Foote, my splendid Spanish student and friend, worked through many sections of this book and offered sound advice and critiques. Dr. James May, professor of classics at St. Olaf College, gave thoughtful attention to the Latin and Greek words used.

My husband, Martin Richmond, M.D., helped me wade through medical terminology. Martin and our daughters, Daisy and Lily, were patient and gave me wide berth while I worked long hours putting this book together. They are my greatest loves.

At McGraw-Hill Education, I was fortunate to work with editor Karen Young, whose support and excellent suggestions were essential throughout the process of organizing and writing this book.

The contributions of these talented and generous people made the preparation of this book a joy, and I am honored to be associated with each of them.

Introduction

Spanish relies on suffixes to denote parts of speech and gender, to modify base words, and to convey nuances of meaning. *Practice Makes Perfect: Spanish Vocabulary Building with Suffixes* will allow you to expand your vocabulary and to gain an appreciation of the language through awareness of its word endings.

Vocabulary building never ends. In one's native language, this is often a source of delight; when learning a new language, however, this task can overwhelm anyone. Familiarity with the logic of Spanish suffixes yields a geometric increase in vocabulary for each new suffix learned.

The dictionary has often been a tool of necessity in vocabulary building, and everyone finds—at least from time to time—that its use can be tedious and frustrating. I have written this book to make the job of increasing vocabulary easier and more interesting, as well as to encourage the ability and confidence to determine the meaning of unfamiliar words by breaking them down into their units of meaning. Not only will this reduce the drudgery of dictionary searches, it will build self-reliance in learning another language.

With a knowledge of basic Spanish words—those included in most first-year courses—and an awareness of Spanish suffixes, you will be able to recognize many unfamiliar words. You will become more confident and less threatened by Spanish literature and conversation, and your use of a dictionary will decrease dramatically.

Using this book

Spanish suffixes contain a wealth of information. A suffix may denote gender, size, quality, status, profession, quantity, type, relationship, habit, style, and much more—and bring all this information and nuance to the base term.

Unfortunately, information on Spanish suffixes tends to be scattered in various text and online sources; typically, only one or two examples are given for a suffix, with little or no analysis. By contrast, *Practice Makes Perfect: Spanish Vocabulary Building with Suffixes* is comprehensive in its scope and detail.

This book presents 150 Spanish suffixes, chosen for their frequency and usage. Some endings are more common than others, but all are used in everyday words, ranging from conversation to newspapers to literature. Each of the suffixes is explained and analyzed, and one or more charts of suffixed words is provided to illustrate the power and semantic range of the suffix. An exercise follows each chart, providing exposure to the suffixed words in ordinary and useful contexts.

Suffixes are arranged alphabetically in three sections: Beginning, Intermediate, and Advanced. These sections reflect the language level of the learner and the material he or she is likely to encounter.

The presentation of a suffix begins with basic information: its form, meaning, English equivalent (if one exists), part of speech, and gender. A paragraph of explanation and analysis follows, including information about how words are formed with the suffix; it often features interesting aspects of the suffix and the words constructed with it.

A chart of suffixed words provides numerous illustrative examples. Included are the English equivalent of the suffixed word, its base word, and the English equivalent of the base word. The charts are by no means exhaustive; in most cases, there are many more suffixed words than can be included in a book of this size. An exercise follows each chart, allowing the student to experience and work with the suffixed words in context. The answer key at the back of the book allows the student to check his or her progress in mastering each suffix.

Most of the suffixed words presented in this book are based on Spanish words. Some, however, are derived from Latin or Greek words, or words from another language; these sources are indicated in the charts. Also noted are special uses of words (for example, colloquial) and uses restricted to a particular country or region.

Appendix A lists 100 common Spanish prefixes, with meanings and examples. No analysis is provided, as Spanish prefixes tend to be either identical or clearly similar to their English counterparts. Appendix B is a synopsis of the 150 Spanish suffixes presented in this book, with meanings and examples.

I hope that this book will enable you to read, write, and speak Spanish with greater confidence and enjoyment.

Abbreviations

The base words for suffixed words are usually Spanish, but they may also be Latin roots or words from another language, such as Greek or English. These languages are indicated in square brackets in the charts.

[ENG.]	English
[FR.]	French
[GER.]	German
[GRK.]	Greek
[ITAL.]	Italian
[LAT.]	Latin
[O.E.]	Old English

Square brackets are also used to indicate grammatical and usage functions.

[ADJ.]	Adjective
[ADV.]	Adverb
[INTERJ.]	Interjection
[M.]	Masculine noun
[F.]	Feminine noun
[M.F.]	Masculine and feminine noun
[PL.]	Plural
[COLLOQ.]	Colloquial
[FAM.]	Familiar
[FIG.]	Figurative

Spanish Vocabulary Building with Suffixes

Beginning suffixes

The 50 suffixes explained and analyzed in this chapter are relatively common, and chances are you are already familiar with many of them. Most are suffixes for nouns, denoting people, profession, and origin, or denoting things to indicate their size or status. They are primarily added to Spanish base words. Even if you're only beginning to learn Spanish, you'll be able to add these suffixed words to your vocabulary and use them with ease.

For some very common suffixes, there are hundreds of words that could be used as examples. The words presented in each chart, therefore, are not exhaustive. The chart is followed by an exercise that allows you to focus on the words in the chart. In fact, there are groups of words that are so common or regularly formed that the example words have been incorporated directly into some exercises, without listing them in charts.

You will encounter many more examples of these suffixes as you progress in your Spanish studies; knowing, for example, that **-ito** often denotes a decrease in the size of the base noun while **-azo** denotes a size increase will save you trips to the dictionary and allow you to become a word detective—and a happier, more independent learner.

 **-a**

MEANING	Resulting object/state/action
ENGLISH EQUIVALENT	—
PART OF SPEECH	Noun
GENDER	Feminine

Thousands of Spanish words end in **-a**. What makes these nouns distinctive is that they are derived from **-ar** verbs; **-er** and **-ir** verbs combine with different suffixes to indicate a resulting object or state. Nouns derived from stem-changing **-ar** verbs show the stem change; for example, **la prueba** *proof, test, quiz* is derived from **probar** *to prove, test.*

Each of the following nouns ending in **-a** represents the resulting object or state of the verb from which it is derived.

NOUN ENDING IN **-a**	ENGLISH EQUIVALENT	BASE WORD	ENGLISH EQUIVALENT
la causa	*cause*	causar	*to cause*
la cena	*dinner*	cenar	*to have dinner*
la cocina	*kitchen*	cocinar	*to cook*
la copia	*copy*	copiar	*to copy*
la cuenta	*bill, sum*	contar	*to count*
la fecha	*date*	fechar	*to date*
la hipoteca	*mortgage*	hipotecar	*to mortgage*
la lágrima	*tear(drop)*	lagrimar	*to cry*
las noticias [PL.]	*news*	noticiar	*to notify*
la plancha	*iron*	planchar	*to iron*
la planta	*plant*	plantar	*to plant*
la pregunta	*question*	preguntar	*to ask*
la prueba	*proof, test, quiz*	probar	*to prove, test*
la renta	*rent*	rentar	*to rent*
la rueda	*wheel*	rodar	*to roll*

EJERCICIO
1·1

Complete each sentence with the correct form of the appropriate noun.

1. Los horticultores y los jardineros saben mucho de las _____.

2. Cuando alguien compra una casa sin suficiente dinero, es necesario obtener una

   _____.

3. Al mediodía comemos el almuerzo y en la noche comemos la

   _____.

4. Después de comer en un restaurante, el mesero le da la _____
   al cliente.

5. Cada mes los compañeros de apartamento pagan la _____
   al propietario.

6. La bicicleta tiene dos _____ y el triciclo tiene tres.

7. El veinticinco de diciembre es la _____ de la Navidad.

8. Típicamente se encuentra el refrigerador, el horno y el lavaplatos en la

   _____ .

9. Se necesita la _____ para quitar las arrugas de la ropa.

10. Después de llorar, usualmente hay _____ en la mejilla.

11. El fumar es la _____ principal del cáncer de pulmón.

12. Los resultados de los exámenes y las _____ son un factor
    importante en determinar la nota final de un estudiante.

13. Los tabloides contienen muchas _____ falsas y sensacionalistas.

14. Para los padres, es importante tener una _____ de los certificados
    de sus niños.

15. Para recibir una respuesta, primero se necesita formular una _____ .

Each of the following nouns ending in **-a** represents the resulting action of the verb from which it is derived.

NOUN ENDING IN **-a**	ENGLISH EQUIVALENT	BASE WORD	ENGLISH EQUIVALENT
la ayuda	*help*	ayudar	*to help*
la burla	*mockery*	burlar	*to mock*
la busca	*search*	buscar	*to search*
la caricia	*caress*	acariciar	*to caress*
la compra	*purchase*	comprar	*to purchase*
la disciplina	*discipline*	disciplinar	*to discipline*
la ducha	*shower*	duchar(se)	*to shower (oneself)*
la espera	*wait*	esperar	*to wait for*
la guarda	*guard, guardianship*	guardar	*to guard*
la obra	*(piece of) work*	obrar	*to work*
la pausa	*pause*	pausar	*to pause*
la práctica	*practice*	practicar	*to practice*
la subasta	*auction*	subastar	*to auction*
la visita	*visit*	visitar	*to visit*

EJERCICIO
1·2

Complete each sentence with the correct form of the appropriate noun.

1. En vez de bañarse, muchas personas prefieren una _____ rápida.

2. Después de trabajar por muchas horas, es bueno tomar una _____ .

3. Después de pasar el día en la zona comercial, una persona típicamente llega a casa con

   unas _____ .

4. En una _____, los compradores pujan por los artículos en vez de pagar un precio establecido.

5. La famosa pintura *Guernica* está incluida en las _____ de arte de Pablo Picasso.

6. Los hombres brutales usan la violencia física y emocional como una forma de _____ para controlar a sus hijos y a sus mujeres.

7. Llegar a un restaurante y averiguar que hay una larga lista de _____ es frustrante, especialmente si tiene mucha hambre.

8. Según el título de este libro, "la _____ hace el maestro."

9. Los niños pequeños necesitan mucha _____ en aprender a hablar, a caminar y a comer.

10. A veces, una _____ afectuosa es el mejor regalo que se puede darle a un amigo triste.

11. En situaciones de divorcio cuando hay niños, la _____ de los niños es una cuestión de suma importancia.

12. La _____ incesante por la perfección es uno de los síntomas del trastorno obsesivo-compulsivo.

13. Se dice que una _____ de un buen amigo es mejor que todo el oro del mundo.

14. Dibujar un bigote en la cara de *La Mona Lisa* es una _____ al mundo de arte y un crimen también.

2 ◆ -able

MEANING	Able to be (acted on)
ENGLISH EQUIVALENT	*-able*
PART OF SPEECH	Adjective
GENDER	Masculine/feminine

The Spanish suffix **-able** is identical to its English counterpart in spelling and meaning: Both mean exactly what they suggest, namely, *able to be (acted on)*. Adjectives with the suffix **-able** are derived from **-ar** verbs; **-er** and **-ir** verbs use the suffix **-ible**, which performs the same function.

ADJECTIVE ENDING IN **-able**	ENGLISH EQUIVALENT	BASE WORD	ENGLISH EQUIVALENT
acabable	*achievable*	acabar	*to finish*
adorable	*adorable*	adorar	*to adore*
aplacable	*appeasable*	aplacar	*to appease*
calculable	*computable*	calcular	*to calculate*
compensable	*able to be compensated*	compensar	*to compensate*
condenable	*reprehensible*	condenar	*to condemn*

▶

ADJECTIVE ENDING IN -able	ENGLISH EQUIVALENT	BASE WORD	ENGLISH EQUIVALENT
conservable	*preservable*	conservar	*to preserve*
cultivable	*arable*	cultivar	*to cultivate*
dudable	*doubtful*	dudar	*to doubt*
evitable	*avoidable*	evitar	*to avoid*
falseable	*forgeable*	falsear	*to falsify, forge*
imputable	*traceable, chargeable*	imputar	*to attribute, charge*

EJERCICIO
2·1

Sinónimos *Provide a synonym for each group of words.*

1. encantador, amable, agradable, precioso _____

2. punible, sancionable, abominable, deplorable _____

3. fértil, productivo, fecundo, labrantío _____

4. atribuible, asignable, achacable _____

5. preservable, salvable, guardable _____

6. computable, conmensurable _____

7. innecesario, preventable _____

8. dudoso, indeciso, dubitativo _____

9. manso, moderado, benigno, apacible _____

10. capaz de ser falsificado _____

11. terminable, finito, limitado _____

12. remunerativo, asalariado, estipendiario _____

ADJECTIVE ENDING IN -able	ENGLISH EQUIVALENT	BASE WORD	ENGLISH EQUIVALENT
mudable	*changeable, fickle*	mudar	*to move, change*
navegable	*navigable*	navegar	*to navigate, sail*
negable	*deniable*	negar	*to deny, refuse*
notable	*prominent, remarkable*	notar	*to observe, notice*
opinable	*questionable, debatable*	opinar	*to think, have an opinion*
palpable	*tangible, obvious*	palpar	*to touch, feel*
pasable	*passable, tolerable*	pasar	*to pass*
penable	*punishable*	penar	*to punish*
penetrable	*penetrable*	penetrar	*to penetrate*
refrenable	*capable of being restrained*	refrenar	*to restrain*
soportable	*manageable, bearable*	soportar	*to support, bear*
vulnerable	*vulnerable, susceptible*	vulnerar	*to damage, violate*

Antónimos *Provide an antonym for each group of words.*

1. ordinario, común, insignificante, sencillo   _____

2. seguro, protegido, fuerte   _____

3. imperceptible, indiscernible, incierto   _____

4. inocente, libre de culpa, sin pecado, perfecto   _____

5. incontrovertible, nada conflictivo, absoluto   _____

6. constante, permanente, invariable, fijo   _____

7. inaccesible, bloqueado, obstruido   _____

8. impermeable, hermético, sellado   _____

9. inaceptable, insufrible, inaguantable   _____

10. confirmado, probado, fiable, veraz   _____

11. inadecuado, inaceptable, insuficiente   _____

12. incontrolable, incontenible   _____

3   -ada

MEANING	Fullness of a measure or vessel
ENGLISH EQUIVALENT	*-ful, -load*
PART OF SPEECH	Noun
GENDER	Feminine

The suffix **-ada** denotes that the suffixed noun is full. The base noun can be a container or receptacle, such as a utensil or truck, or it can be a body part. Usually, the fullness is literal or physical, as in **la cucharada** *spoonful*; however, the meaning can be more figurative, as in **la dedada** *a "pinch," thimbleful*, often used in cooking. While the ending **-ada** is feminine, two common nouns ending in **-ado** also denote fullness of a measure or vessel.

el bocado *mouthful* (from **la boca** *mouth*)
el puñado *handful, fistful* (from **el puño** *fist*)

NOUN ENDING IN **-ada**	ENGLISH EQUIVALENT	BASE WORD	ENGLISH EQUIVALENT
la brazada	*armful*	el brazo	*arm*
la calderada	*cauldronful*	la caldera	*cauldron, boiler*
la capada	*capeful, cloakful*	la capa	*cape, cloak*
la cazolada	*panful*	el cazo	*casserole pot, pan*
la cestada	*basketful*	la cesta	*basket*
la cucharada	*spoonful*	la cuchara	*spoon*
la dedada	*"pinch," thimbleful*	el dedo	*finger*

▶

NOUN ENDING IN -ada	ENGLISH EQUIVALENT	BASE WORD	ENGLISH EQUIVALENT
la hornada	batch	el horno	oven
la narigada	portion inhaled by the nose	la nariz	nose
la panzada	bellyful	la panza	belly
la ponchada	bowlful of punch	el ponche	punch
la pulgada	inch	el pulgar	thumb
la sartenada	panful	la sartén	frying pan
la zurronada	bagful	el zurrón	shepherd's bag, pouch

EJERCICIO
3·1

Complete each sentence with the correct form of the appropriate noun.

1. Cuando preparas la paella, si la receta sugiere sólo un poquito de azafrán, la cantidad requerida es una _____.

2. Las brujas preparan sopa para todo el aquelarre; cuando todo está completo, ellas tienen una _____ de comida.

3. Una yarda tiene treinta y seis _____.

4. La Caperucita Roja va a la casa de su abuelita con una _____ de dulces y otras comidas.

5. El pastor tradicionalmente lleva consigo una _____ de provisiones para el día.

6. La anfitriona tiene una _____ en la mesa para servir la bebida a los muchos invitados que tienen sed.

7. Muchos adictos a la cocaína prefieren una _____ de la droga.

8. La niñera Mary Poppins dice que una _____ de azúcar le ayuda a un niño a tomar la medicina.

9. Antes de llegar los nietos, muchas abuelas hacen varias _____ de galletas.

10. Para hervir una docena de huevos, se necesita una _____ de agua.

11. Después del anuncio de la nueva Miss Universo, la ganadora recibe una corona y una _____ de flores.

12. Cuando fríes huevos y tocino para varias personas para el desayuno, tienes una _____ de comida.

13. Después de este desayuno fabuloso, los comensales tienen una _____ de comida.

14. Se puede decir que Batman tiene una _____ de secretos y poderes.

NOUN ENDING IN -ada	ENGLISH EQUIVALENT	BASE WORD	ENGLISH EQUIVALENT
la barcada	*boatload*	el barco	*boat*
la carretada	*wagonload, cartload*	la carreta	*wagon, cart*
la carretillada	*wheelbarrow load*	la carretilla	*wheelbarrow*
la carretonada	*cartload*	el carretón	*truck, cart*
la esquifada	*boatload*	el esquife	*skiff, small boat*
la furgonada	*boxcar load*	el furgón	*boxcar, freight car*
la lagarada	*(wine)pressful*	el lagar	*(wine)press*
la lanchada	*barge load*	la lancha	*boat, barge*
la palada	*shovelful*	la pala	*spade, shovel*
la paletada	*trowelful*	la paleta	*trowel*
la tonelada	*ton*	el tonel	*barrel*
la vagonada	*train carful*	el vagón	*passenger car*

¿Verdadero o falso? *Indicate whether each statement is true or false, using* **V** *for* **verdadero** *true or* **F** *for* **falso** *false.*

1. _____ Para llenar una parcela de cementerio, el sepulturero necesita muchas paladas de tierra.

2. _____ Una tonelada de agua no pesa mucho.

3. _____ Después de un accidente durante un crucero en 2013, el *Carnival Triumph* tenía una barcada de pasajeros miserables.

4. _____ En su trabajo, el albañil típicamente tiene una carretillada de ladrillos.

5. _____ Hace muchos años, era común ver un burro tirando una carretonada de provisiones para una familia.

6. _____ Hay muchas lagaradas de vino en las viñas de España.

7. _____ Una esquifada de suministros es más que una lanchada de suministros.

8. _____ Una paletada de tierra es una vista muy común a un jardinero.

9. _____ Es muy común ver las furgonadas de carda y las vagonadas de pasajeros en México.

10. _____ Una carretada de flores frescas es una vista triste y fea.

◆ 4 ◆ -ado/-ada

MEANING	Performer of an action, person on whom an action has been performed; result of an action
ENGLISH EQUIVALENT	—
PART OF SPEECH	Noun
GENDER	Masculine/feminine

A noun ending in -**ado** (feminine: -**ada**) may denote a person who performs an action, or a result of an action. These nouns are derived from -**ar** verbs; they are formed by replacing the -**ar** of the infinitive with -**ado**. All of the following nouns are masculine, but if the performer of an action is female, the suffix becomes -**ada**: **el empleado** *male employee*, **la empleada** *female employee*.

The following chart represents persons who perform the action of the base verb or on whom the action is performed.

NOUN ENDING IN -ado	ENGLISH EQUIVALENT	BASE WORD	ENGLISH EQUIVALENT
el abogado	*lawyer, advocate*	abogar	*to advocate, defend*
el adoptado	*adopted person*	adoptar	*to adopt*
el ahijado	*godson*	ahijar	*to adopt*
el chalado [COLLOQ.]	*crazy person, nutcase*	chalar	*to drive crazy*
el convidado	*guest, invited person*	convidar	*to invite*
el criado	*servant*	criar	*to raise, bring up*
el delegado	*delegate, representative*	delegar	*to delegate*
el emigrado	*emigrant*	emigrar	*to emigrate*
el empleado	*employee*	emplear	*to employ*
el enamorado	*lover*	enamorar	*to win the heart of*
el encargado	*person in charge*	encargar	*to put in charge*
el enterrado	*buried person*	enterrar	*to bury*
el enviado	*messenger, envoy*	enviar	*to send*
el invitado	*guest, invited person*	invitar	*to invite*
el licenciado	*university graduate*	licenciar	*to award a degree*

EJERCICIO 4·1

Sinónimos *Provide the synonym(s) for each item, including the article.*

1. el sirviente _____

2. el asesor jurídico _____

3. el jefe _____

4. el graduado _____

5. el representativo _____

6. el hijo no biológico _____

7. el mensajero _____

8. el trabajador _____

9. el loco _____

10. el difunto en el cementerio   _____

11. el amante   _____

12. el expatriado   _____

13. el "hijo" del padrino y de la madrina   _____

14. el huésped   _____ _____

The following chart represents things that are the result of the action of the base verb.

NOUN ENDING IN **-ado**	ENGLISH EQUIVALENT	BASE WORD	ENGLISH EQUIVALENT
el adobado	*pickled meat*	adobar	*to pickle, marinate*
el cercado	*fence, enclosure*	cercar	*to enclose, fence in*
el constipado	*cold (illness)*	constipar(se)	*to catch a cold*
el decorado	*scenery, set*	decorar	*to decorate*
el desagrado	*displeasure, discontent*	desagradar	*to displease*
el estado	*state*	estar	*to be (place, condition)*
el granizado	*slush, iced drink*	granizar	*to hail*
el guisado	*stew, ragout*	guisar	*to cook*
el helado	*ice cream*	helar	*to freeze*
el peinado	*hairstyle, hairdo*	peinar(se)	*to comb (one's hair)*
el teclado	*keyboard*	teclear	*to type*
el tornado	*tornado*	tornar	*to turn, return*

EJERCICIO
4·2

Sinónimos *Provide the synonym for each item, including its article.*

1. el ciclón, el torbellino   _____

2. el escenario, las decoraciones teatrales   _____

3. el descontento   _____

4. el resfriado, el catarro   _____

5. el estofado, la sopa   _____

6. la carne marinada   _____

7. el gelato, el sorbete   _____

8. el hielo triturado   _____

9. el arreglo de pelo   _____

10. el corral, la barricada   _____

11. la situación, la posición   _____

12. la consola, el piano   _____

5 ◆ -al

MEANING	Relating to, like
ENGLISH EQUIVALENT	*-al*
PART OF SPEECH	Adjective
GENDER	Masculine/feminine

The adjective suffix **-al** is common in both Spanish and English and performs the same function in each language: it denotes a characteristic of the base noun (for example, **cerebral** *cerebral*, from **el cerebro** *brain*). Since many of these Spanish adjectives have English cognates, they tend to be easily recognized and used.

ADJECTIVE ENDING IN **-al**	ENGLISH EQUIVALENT	BASE WORD	ENGLISH EQUIVALENT
arsenical	*arsenical*	el arsénico	*arsenic*
astral	*astral*	el astro	*heavenly body, star*
central	*central*	el centro	*center, middle*
cerebral	*cerebral*	el cerebro	*brain*
codal	*elbow-shaped*	el codo	*elbow*
colonial	*colonial*	la colonia	*colony*
cuaresmal	*Lenten*	la Cuaresma	*Lent*
disciplinal	*disciplinary*	la disciplina	*discipline*
elemental	*elemental*	el elemento	*element*
experimental	*experimental*	el experimento	*experiment*
final	*final*	el fin	*end*
horizontal	*horizontal*	el horizonte	*horizon*
intelectual	*intellectual*	el intelecto	*intellect, intelligence*
labial	*labial, of the lips*	el labio	*lip*

EJERCICIO

5·1

Complete each sentence with the appropriate adjective.

1. Una estrella es _____.

2. El período de los cuarenta días antes de la Pascua es _____.

3. Una línea no vertical es _____.

4. Algo muy básico o primario es _____.

5. El medio de algo es _____.

6. Un tipo popular de macarrones en la forma de un codo es _____.

7. El proceso de experimentación es _____.

8. El castigo de un niño es _____.

9. El veredicto judicial es una decisión _____.

10. El sitio de un beso romántico es _____.

11. El período pre-revolucionario es _____.

12. Una persona inteligente es _____ e _____.

13. Un elemento químico cuyo símbolo es "As" (con el número atómico 33) es

_____.

ADJECTIVE ENDING IN -al	ENGLISH EQUIVALENT	BASE WORD	ENGLISH EQUIVALENT
mental	mental	la mente	mind
mundial	worldwide, global	el mundo	world
oriental	oriental	el oriente	orient, east
ornamental	ornamental	el ornamento	ornament
otoñal	autumnal	el otoño	autumn, fall
papal	papal	el Papa	the Pope
parroquial	parochial	la parroquia	parish
personal	personal	la persona	person, human being
poligonal	polygonal	el polígono	polygon
sacerdotal	priestly, of the priesthood	el sacerdote	priest
semanal	weekly	la semana	week
suplemental	supplementary	el suplemento	supplement
terrenal	earthly, mundane	el terreno	ground, terrain
vecinal	neighboring, adjacent	el vecino	neighbor
veinteñal	lasting twenty years	veinte	twenty

EJERCICIO
5·2

Complete each sentence with the appropriate adjective.

1. El tiempo en septiembre y octubre es _____.

2. Una forma geométrica que tiene por los menos tres lados es _____.

3. Una alfombra de Persia o Arabia es _____.

4. Una revista _____, como *Time, ¡Hola!, The New Yorker, Hello!* o *Kerrang!,* sale cada siete días.

5. Un período de dos décadas es _____.

6. Un secreto íntimo es _____.

7. Una decisión del líder de la iglesia católica es _____.

8. Típicamente situada al lado de una iglesia católica, la rectoría es la residencia

_____.

9. Algo que pertenece a una iglesia en particular es _____.

10. Una idea es _____.

11. Algo extra o adicional es _____.

12. Cada octubre el campeonato de béisbol profesional tiene lugar en los Estados Unidos, y se llama la "Serie _____."

13. Muchas personas consideran que una "esposa de trofeo" es _____.

14. Para muchos padres de niños pequeños, el lema "Ubicación, ubicación, ubicación" significa la importancia de una buena escuela _____.

15. Según la religión cristiana, San José es el padre _____ de Jesús.

6 ◆ -ancia

MEANING	Action, result of an action, state
ENGLISH EQUIVALENT	*-ancy*
PART OF SPEECH	Noun
GENDER	Feminine

These nouns denote the action, state, or result of the action of the base **-ar** verb (or, in a few cases, a Latin verb). To form these nouns, the **-ar** ending of the infinitive is replaced by **-ancia**. Since most Spanish nouns with the suffix **-ancia** have English cognates, they tend to be easily recognized.

NOUN ENDING IN -**ancia**	ENGLISH EQUIVALENT	BASE WORD	ENGLISH EQUIVALENT
la ambulancia	*ambulance*	ambular	*to walk around*
la discrepancia	*discrepancy*	discrepar	*to differ, disagree*
la distancia	*distance*	distar	*to be far from*
la estancia	*stay*	estar	*to be (place, state)*
la exuberancia	*exuberance*	exuberare [LAT.]	*to be abundant*
la infancia	*infancy*	in- + fari [LAT.]	*not + to speak*
la intolerancia	*intolerance*	in- + tolerar	*not + to tolerate*
la observancia	*observance*	observar	*to observe*
la perseverancia	*perseverance*	perseverar	*to persevere*
la redundancia	*redundancy*	redundar	*to result*
la relevancia	*relevance*	relevar	*to relieve, substitute*
la vigilancia	*vigilance, surveillance*	vigilar	*to watch over, guard*

EJERCICIO
6·1

Complete each sentence with the correct form of the appropriate noun.

1. La _____ entre New York y Londres es, más o menos, cinco mil seiscientos kilómetros.

2. Después de un ataque cardíaco, el paciente se traslada al hospital por _____.

3. Para la luna de miel, es común tener una _____ de una o dos semanas en un hotel lujoso.

4. El racismo, la discriminación y el odio por los que pertenecen a otra religión, etnia o clase son formas de la _____.

5. El vínculo entre el bebé y sus padres ocurre casi siempre durante la etapa de la

_____.

6. Casi todos los atracos de bancos o tiendas de conveniencia son capturados por la cámara de un sistema de video _____.

7. Existe una gran _____ entre la plataforma política de los demócratas y la de los republicanos en los Estados Unidos.

8. A pesar de su edad avanzada, Nelson Mandela tenía la energía y la

_____ de un hombre de la mitad de su edad.

9. Las expresiones "exactamente el mismo" y "sorpresa inesperada" son ejemplos de la

duplicación o la _____.

10. Para superar los obstáculos que se encuentra durante la vida, se necesita la tenacidad,

la _____ y la confianza en sí mismo.

11. Durante un juicio, los abogados no pueden hacer preguntas que no tienen

_____ en el caso.

12. La _____ de fiestas religiosas incluye la Hanukkah (los judíos), la Navidad (los cristianos), el Ramadán (los musulmanes) y el Día de Bodhi (los budistas).

NOUN ENDING IN -ancia	ENGLISH EQUIVALENT	BASE WORD	ENGLISH EQUIVALENT
la abundancia	abundance	abundar	to be plentiful
la asonancia	assonance	sonar	to seem familiar
la consonancia	accordance	consonar	to harmonize
la constancia	certainty	constar	to be certain
la disonancia	dissonance	disonar	to lack harmony
la importancia	importance	importar	to matter
la repugnancia	repugnance	repugnar	to disgust
la resonancia	resonance, echo	resonar	to reverberate, echo
la tolerancia	tolerance	tolerar	to tolerate
la vagancia	vagrancy	vagar	to wander about

Provide the noun that is related to each group of words. Include its article.

1. la repulsión, la aversión, el asco   _____

2. la profusión, la plétora, el raudal   _____

3. la certeza, la persistencia, el empeño   _____

4. la magnitud, la influencia, la distinción   _____

5. la consentimiento, la misericordia, la benevolencia   _____

6. la repercusión, el eco, la reverberación   _____

7. el paseo, el vagabundeo, la peregrinación   _____

8. la armonía, la melodía, el tono   _____

9. la concordancia, la similitud, la correspondencia   _____

10. la cacofonía, la discordancia, la desarmonía   _____

7   -ano/-ana

MEANING	Citizen, native; adherent, believer
ENGLISH EQUIVALENT	*-an*
PART OF SPEECH	Noun, adjective
GENDER	Masculine/feminine

A word with the suffix **-ano** (feminine: **-ana**) may denote a citizen or native of a country, as well as a person who adheres to a system of beliefs. The suffixed word may be a noun or adjective: **La americana les sirve el café colombiano a los luteranos** *The American woman serves the Colombian coffee to the Lutherans.* Unlike English, Spanish does not capitalize these words.

The words in the following chart represent citizens or natives of a country.

NOUN/ADJECTIVE ENDING IN **-ano**	ENGLISH EQUIVALENT	BASE WORD	ENGLISH EQUIVALENT
(el) americano	*American*	América	*America*
(el) australiano	*Australian*	Australia	*Australia*
(el) boliviano	*Bolivian*	Bolivia	*Bolivia*
(el) camboyano	*Cambodian*	Camboya	*Cambodia*
(el) colombiano	*Colombian*	Colombia	*Colombia*
(el) cubano	*Cuban*	Cuba	*Cuba*
(el) ecuatoriano	*Ecuadorian*	Ecuador	*Ecuador*
(el) italiano	*Italian*	Italia	*Italy*
(el) jordano	*Jordanian*	Jordania	*Jordan*
(el) mexicano/mejicano	*Mexican*	México, Méjico	*Mexico*

NOUN/ADJECTIVE ENDING IN **-ano**	ENGLISH EQUIVALENT	BASE WORD	ENGLISH EQUIVALENT
(el) norcoreano	*North Korean*	Corea del Norte	*North Korea*
(el) paraguayano	*Paraguayan*	Paraguay	*Paraguay*
(el) peruano	*Peruvian*	Perú	*Peru*
(el) surcoreano	*South Korean*	Corea del Sur	*South Korea*
(el) venezolano	*Venezuelan*	Venezuela	*Venezuela*

EJERCICIO

7·1

Complete each sentence with the correct form of the appropriate noun for each person's description.

1. El narcotraficante Pablo Escobar nació en Medellín (aproximadamente 445 kilómetros de Bogotá). Él era _____.

2. La artista Frida Kahlo nació en Coyoacán (aproximadamente 740 kilómetros de la Ciudad de México). Ella era _____.

3. Hugo Chávez nació en Sabaneta y murió en Caracas. Él era _____.

4. La cantante Kylie Minogue nació en Melbourne. Ella es _____.

5. La escritora Isabel Allende nació en Lima. Ella es _____.

6. El presidente Barack Obama nació en Hawái. Él es _____.

7. Fidel Castro nació en Birán (aproximadamente 725 kilómetros de la Habana). Él era

   _____.

8. Che Guevara se murió en La Higuera (aproximadamente 485 kilómetros de La Paz) y a menudo se asocia con este país, pero porque nació en Rosario (más o menos 300 kilómetros de Buenos Aires), él no era _____.

9. Mike Judge, el creador de *Beavis y Butt-head,* nació en Guayaquil. Él es

   _____.

10. El déspota Pol Pot nació en la provincia de Kampong Thom (más o menos 200 kilómetros de Phnom Penh). Él era _____.

11. El presidente Federico Franco nació en Asunción, la capital del país. Él es

    _____.

12. Park Geun-hye, la primera mujer elegida presidenta de su país, nació en Daegu (aproximadamente 236 kilómetros de Seúl). Ella es _____.

13. El famoso dictador Kim Jong-il nació en Rusia, así que aunque vivió por muchos años en Pyongyang y murió (2011) allí, Kim Jong-il no era _____.

14. El rey Husein bin Talal nació y murió en Ammán, la capital del país. Él era

    _____ .

15. El tenor lírico Luciano Pavarotti nació y murió en Módena (aproximadamente 420

    kilómetros de Roma). Él era _____ .

The words in the following chart represent citizens or natives of a continent, city, or area within a country.

NOUN/ADJECTIVE ENDING IN -ano	ENGLISH EQUIVALENT	BASE WORD	ENGLISH EQUIVALENT
(el) aldeano	*villager, of a village*	la aldea	*small village*
(el) alsaciano	*Alsatian*	Alsacia	*Alsace*
(el) californiano	*Californian*	California	*California*
(el) castellano	*Castilian*	Castilla	*Castile*
(el) centroamericano	*Central American*	Centroamérica	*Central America*
(el) jerosolimitano	*(native) of Jerusalem*	Jerusalén	*Jerusalem*
(el) nuevomexicano	*(native) of New Mexico*	Nuevo México	*New Mexico*
(el) romano	*Roman*	Roma	*Rome*
(el) siberiano	*Siberian*	Siberia	*Siberia*
(el) siciliano	*Sicilian*	Sicilia	*Sicily*
(el) sudamericano	*South American*	Sudamérica	*South America*
(el) tejano	*Texan*	Tejas	*Texas*
(el) veneciano	*Venetian*	Venecia	*Venice*

EJERCICIO
7·2

Complete each sentence with the correct form of the appropriate adjective for each description.

1. La actriz Natalie Portman nació en Jerusalén. Ella tiene doble nacionalidad de Israel y de los

   Estados Unidos. Sin embargo, de nacimiento ella siempre es _____ .

2. Steve Jobs, el co-fundador y presidente ejecutivo de Apple, Inc., nació en San Francisco.

   Él era _____ .

3. Los que nacen en Costa Rica, El Salvador, Honduras, Nicaragua o Panamá son

   _____ .

4. Los que nacen en Argentina, Brasil, Colombia, Chile, Perú, Uruguay o Venezuela son

   _____ .

5. Jeff Bezos, el fundador y director ejecutivo de Amazon.com, nació en Albuquerque.

   Él es _____ .

6. Los hermanos y actores Luke y Owen Wilson nacieron en Dallas. Ellos son

   _____ .

7. Las actrices Sophia Loren e Isabella Rossellini nacieron en la capital de Italia. Ellas son

   _____.

8. El explorador Marco Polo nació en la famosa "ciudad de canales" en el noreste de Italia.

   Él era _____.

9. El perro de trabajo originalmente del noreste de Rusia es el husky

   _____.

10. El famoso director (*¡Qué bello es vivir!*) Frank Capra nació en la principal isla italiana.

    Él era _____.

11. El autor Miguel de Cervantes (*Don Quijote de la Mancha*) nació en el área de España
    que incluye Castilla-La Mancha y Madrid en la región central del país. Él era

    _____.

12. Thierry Mugler, el diseñador francés (y favorito de Lady Gaga) nació en Strasbourg,
    la capital y ciudad principal de Alsacia, una región del este de Francia. Él es

    _____.

13. Los que nacen en pueblos o en áreas rurales son _____.

The words in the following chart represent people who adhere to a system of beliefs.

NOUN/ADJECTIVE ENDING IN -ano	ENGLISH EQUIVALENT	BASE WORD	ENGLISH EQUIVALENT
(el) cristiano	*Christian*	Cristo	*Christ*
(el) luterano	*Lutheran*	Lutero	*Luther*
(el) mendeliano	*Mendelian (theorist)*	Mendel	*(Gregor) Mendel*
(el) pagano	*pagan*	paganus [LAT.]	*villager*
(el) presbiteriano	*Presbyterian*	el presbítero	*priest*
(el) puritano	*puritan*	puro	*pure*
(el) republicano	*Republican*	la república	*republic*
(el) vegano	*vegan*	el vegetal	*vegetable*
(el) vegetariano	*vegetarian*	el vegetal	*vegetable*
(el) victoriano	*Victorian*	la reina Victoria	*Queen Victoria*

EJERCICIO 7·3

Complete each sentence with the correct form of the appropriate adjective for each description.

1. Esta persona no come la carne, pero sí come productos lácteos como la leche, el yogur,

   el queso y la mantequilla. Es _____.

2. Esta persona no come ni la carne ni los productos lácteos y se abstiene del consumo o uso

   de productos de origen animal. Es _____.

3. Esta persona cree en Jesúcristo y sus enseñanzas. Es _____.

4. Un presbítero es el líder de los miembros de esta congregación. Ellos son

   _____ .

5. Estas personas son fieles de Martín Lutero. Ellos son _____ .

6. Estas personas viven de acuerdo de los preceptos de los protestantes y consideran especialmente que los placeres y lujos son pecaminosos. Ellos son

   _____ .

7. Estas personas, en el sentido más laxo, no tienen ninguna religión. Ellos son

   _____ .

8. Una casa muy ornamentada, llena de muebles, pinturas, alfombras y millones de cosas

   decorativas es _____ .

9. Los defensores de un gobierno del república son _____ .

10. Un defensor de la teoría de la genética de Gregor Mendel es _____ .

8 ▸ -ante

MEANING	Performer, expert
ENGLISH EQUIVALENT	-ant, -er, -or
PART OF SPEECH	Noun
GENDER	Masculine/feminine

The suffix **-ante** is one of several Spanish endings that denote a person who performs a particular action or job; all are derived from **-ar** verbs. These nouns may refer to both males and females: **el cantante** *the male singer*, **la cantante** *the female singer*.

NOUN ENDING IN -ante	ENGLISH EQUIVALENT	BASE WORD	ENGLISH EQUIVALENT
el amante	*lover*	amar	*to love*
el cantante	*singer*	cantar	*to sing*
el comandante	*commander*	comandar	*to command*
el danzante	*dancer*	danzar	*to dance*
el dibujante	*commercial artist, cartoonist*	dibujar	*to draw*
el gobernante	*ruler, leader*	gobernar	*to govern, rule*
el ignorante	*ignoramus*	ignorar	*to be ignorant of*
el maleante	*crook*	malear	*to corrupt*
el negociante	*businessperson*	negociar	*to do business*
el viajante	*traveler*	viajar	*to travel*

¿Cuál es su profesión o especialidad? *Provide the correct form of the appropriate noun (including its article) to describe the people mentioned in each item.*

1. Barbra Streisand, Madonna y Beyoncé _____

2. Mikhail Baryshnikov, Fred Astaire y Gregory Hines _____

3. Romeo y Julieta, Cleopatra y Mark Antony, Scarlett O'Hara y Rhett Butler _____

4. Lloyd Christmas y Harry Dunne, los protagonistas de la película *Dumb and Dumber* _____

5. Donald Trump, Rupert Murdoch y Warren Buffet _____

6. Charles Ponzi, Bernie Madoff y Captain Hook _____

7. Abraham Lincoln, Margaret Thatcher y Nelson Mandela _____

8. Charles Schulz (*Peanuts*), Gary Larson y James Thurber _____

9. Gulliver (el protagonista de la novela de Jonathan Swift) _____

10. Adolf Hitler, Julio César y Napoleón Bonaparte _____

NOUN ENDING IN **-ante**	ENGLISH EQUIVALENT	BASE WORD	ENGLISH EQUIVALENT
el caminante	*walker*	caminar	*to walk*
el copiante	*copyist, imitator*	copiar	*to copy*
el debutante	*debutante, beginner*	debutar	*to make one's debut*
el delineante	*draftsman*	delinear	*to outline, draft*
el donante	*donor*	donar	*to give*
el estudiante	*student*	estudiar	*to study*
el habitante	*inhabitant, dweller*	habitar	*to live in*
el litigante	*litigant*	litigar	*to dispute, go to court*
el navegante	*navigator*	navegar	*to navigate, sail*
el participante	*participant, entrant*	participar	*to participate*
el protestante	*Protestant*	protestar	*to protest*
el solicitante	*applicant*	solicitar	*to apply for, solicit*
el veraneante	*summer resident, vacationer*	veranear	*to spend the summer*
el visitante	*visitor*	visitar	*to visit*
el votante	*voter*	votar	*to vote*

Provide the noun that is related to each group of words. Include its article.

1. el alumno, el escolar, el universitario _____

2. el peatón, el andarín, el peregrino, el viajero _____

3. la vacacionista, la excursionista, la turista _____

4. el residente, el ocupante, el inquilino   _____

5. el donador, el benefactor, el filántropo   _____

6. el concurrente, el candidato, el copartícipe   _____

7. la electora, la nominadora, la votadora   _____

8. el calvinista, el luterano, el cristiano   _____

9. la novicia, la adolescente, la principiante   _____

10. el dibujante, el diseñador, el cartógrafo   _____

11. la invitada, la convidada, la agasajada   _____

12. el aeronauta, el aviador, el piloto   _____

13. la demandante, la querellante, la pleiteadora, la pleiteante   _____

14. el falseador, el émulo, el copiador   _____

15. la peticionaria, la suplicante, la aspirante, la pretendiente   _____

9 ◆ -ario

MEANING	Book, printed matter, bound collection
ENGLISH EQUIVALENT	*-ary*
PART OF SPEECH	Noun
GENDER	Masculine

The suffix **-ario** is highly specific; it denotes a book or collection of items (printed or online) with a particular function, such as words or data systematically arranged. The most common word with the suffix **-ario** is **el diccionario** *dictionary*; its base noun is **la dicción** *diction*.

Since the Catholic Church plays a large historical role in Spanish culture, many nouns ending in **-ario** are religious in nature.

NOUN ENDING IN **-ario**	ENGLISH EQUIVALENT	BASE WORD	ENGLISH EQUIVALENT
el abecedario	*alphabet book, primer*	a be ce	*a b c*
el anuario	*yearbook, yearly report*	el año	*year*
el calendario	*calendar*	las calendas	*calends*
el comentario	*commentary*	el comento	*comment*
el cuestionario	*questionnaire*	la cuestión	*question*
el diario	*diary*	el día	*day*
el diccionario	*dictionary*	la dicción	*diction*
el glosario	*glossary*	la glosa	*gloss, comment, note*
el horario	*schedule, timetable*	la hora	*hour, time*
el inventario	*inventory*	inventariar	*to inventory, list*
el noticiario	*newsreel, newscast*	la noticia	*news item*
el obituario	*obituary*	el óbito	*death, demise*
el recetario	*recipe book*	la receta	*recipe*
el silabario	*spelling book*	el sílabo	*syllable*
el vocabulario	*vocabulary*	el vocablo	*word*

Complete each sentence with the correct form of the appropriate noun.

1. Cada día, muchas adolescentes escriben sus pensamientos y reflejos en un

   _____.

2. Cada diciembre, un regalo popular para el año que viene es un _____.

3. Después de la muerte de una persona, con frecuencia hay un _____
   en el periódico que contiene información sobre los detalles del funeral.

4. La información que provee detalles sobre todos los artículos que se venden en una tienda

   es un _____.

5. El libro que compila fotos y celebra los talentos de los estudiantes al fin del año escolar

   se llama el _____.

6. Antes de preparar una comida nueva, muchos cocineros consultan un

   _____.

7. Antes de comprar un billete para el tren, primero se necesita consultar el

   _____.

8. Al fin de muchos libros de texto hay listas de información en un

   _____.

9. Para consultar la definición de una palabra, se usa un _____.

10. Para aprender las letras del alfabeto, los niños y sus maestras consultan el

    _____.

11. Se puede consultar y estudiar un _____ para aumentar el número
    de palabras en el hablar.

12. Un tipo de encuesta que consiste en varias preguntas diseñadas para averiguar los deseos

    u opiniones de los participantes se llama el _____.

13. Los presentadores de radio y televisión con frecuencia figuran en más de un

    _____ al día.

14. El uso del _____ en los primeros grados de la escuela elemental
    es fundamental para aprender a escribir y deletrear.

15. Un _____ típicamente contiene varias referencias, opiniones con
    explicaciones para justificarlas y a veces información adicional.

Provide the noun (including its article) that is associated with the following persons.

1. Julia Child, Wolfgang Puck, Rachael Ray _____

2. el agente funerario _____

3. Anne Frank _____

4. Noah Webster _____

5. el gerente de una tienda departamental _____

6. los reporteros y los presentadores de las noticias _____

7. una persona que quiere saber la fecha _____

8. el procurador de información, el encuestador _____

9. el agente de viajes _____

10. un niño aprendiendo a deletrear _____

11. una maestra enseñando las letras del alfabeto _____

12. el que prepara el libro memorial para los futuros graduados _____

13. la persona que quiere aprender muchas nuevas palabras _____

14. la persona que prepara la lista de palabras especializadas para un libro _____

15. el columnista o editorialista para el periódico _____

The following nouns refer to items found in a Catholic church or seminary.

NOUN ENDING IN -ario	ENGLISH EQUIVALENT	BASE WORD	ENGLISH EQUIVALENT
el devocionario	*prayer book*	la devoción	*devotion*
el epistolario	*collection of letters*	la epístola	*letter*
el himnario	*hymnal*	el himno	*hymn*
el maitinario	*book containing matins*	los maitines	*matins*

EJERCICIO
9·3

Complete each sentence with the correct form of the appropriate noun for each type of written work. Include its article where needed.

1. En la Biblia cristiana, la colección de cartas de James, Peter, John, Jude y otros se llama

   _____.

2. En la iglesia, los cantantes necesitan _____ para saber las letras de las canciones.

3. Para aprender, leer y memorizar las varias oraciones, los seminaristas consultan con

   frecuencia _____.

4. Para observar la liturgia que termina al amanecer, los religiosos consultan

   _____.

 # -astro/-astra

MEANING	Step relation, diminutive
ENGLISH EQUIVALENT	*step-*
PART OF SPEECH	Noun
GENDER	Masculine/feminine

The suffix **-astro** (feminine: **-astra**) has two functions. The first, more common use is to denote step relations in a family (for example, **el padrastro** *stepfather*, from **el padre** *father*). The other use is to diminish the status of the base word (for example, **el medicastro** *third-rate doctor, "quack,"* from **el médico** *doctor, physician*).

The nouns in the following chart denote step relations.

NOUN ENDING IN -astro/-astra	ENGLISH EQUIVALENT	BASE WORD	ENGLISH EQUIVALENT
la abuelastra	*step-grandmother*	la abuela	*grandmother*
el abuelastro	*step-grandfather*	el abuelo	*grandfather*
la hermanastra	*stepsister*	la hermana	*sister*
el hermanastro	*stepbrother*	el hermano	*brother*
la hijastra	*stepdaughter*	la hija	*daughter*
el hijastro	*stepson*	el hijo	*son*
la madrastra	*stepmother*	la madre	*mother*
la nietastra	*step-granddaughter*	la nieta	*granddaughter*
el nietastro	*step-grandson*	el nieto	*grandson*
el padrastro	*stepfather*	el padre	*father*

EJERCICIO 10·1

Complete each sentence with the correct form of the appropriate noun for each family member.

Mike es viudo con tres hijos: Greg, Peter y Bobby. Carol es viuda con tres hijas: Marcia, Jan y Cindy. Mike y Carol se casan y forman una familia adoptiva que se llama *La Tribu de los Brady*.

1. Carol es la _____ de Greg.

2. Mike es el _____ de Marcia.

3. Peter es el _____ de Jan.

4. Cindy es la _____ de Bobby.

5. Greg, Peter y Bobby son los _____ de Carol.

6. Marcia, Jan y Cindy son las _____ de Mike.

7. El padre de Carol es el _____ de Greg, Peter y Bobby.

8. La madre de Mike es la _____ de Marcia, Jan y Cindy.

9. Greg, Peter y Bobby son los _____ de los padres de Carol.

10. Marcia, Jan y Cindy son las _____ de los padres de Mike.

The nouns in the following list denote persons or things of diminished status.

NOUN ENDING IN -astro/-astra	ENGLISH EQUIVALENT	BASE WORD	ENGLISH EQUIVALENT
el camastro	*rickety old bed*	la cama	*bed*
el cochastro	*young suckling wild boar*	el cocho	*pig*
el medicastro	*third-rate doctor, "quack"*	el médico	*doctor, physician*
el musicastro	*third-rate musician*	el músico	*musician*
el pinastro	*wild pine*	el pino	*pine tree*
el politicastro	*third-rate politician*	el político	*politician*
la pollastra	*pullet*	el pollo	*chicken*
el pollastro	*cockerel, sly fellow*	el pollo	*chicken*

EJERCICIO 10·2

Provide the correct noun (including its article) for each description.

1. un adolescente sin talento que se piensa el próximo Mick Jagger y que interpreta las canciones frente a una cámara casera _____

2. un puerco joven, un jabalí que todavía mama, un lechón _____

3. un conífero en el bosque que nadie plantó con cuidado _____

4. un tipo astuto, tramposo y furtivo, cuya meta es llevar ventaja de otros _____

5. un profesional que viola el juramento hipocrático de no causar daño _____

6. una polla joven _____

7. un mueble principal en la celda carcelaria _____

11 ◆ -azo

MEANING	Augmentative
ENGLISH EQUIVALENT	—
PART OF SPEECH	Noun
GENDER	Masculine

The suffix **-azo** (and the less common feminine **-aza**) denotes enlargement of a base noun. Sometimes, the augmentation is physical and obvious: **el gatazo** *large cat.* It may, however, be more figurative, at times approaching deprecation: **el maridazo** *doting husband.* Note that **la copa** *wine glass* and **el copo** *snowflake* both yield **el copazo** *large wine glass, large snowflake.* **El plumazo**, from the base term **la pluma** *feather, pen,* may mean *feather pillow* or *elegant stroke of a pen.*

The following nouns ending in **-azo** represent a physical enlargement of the base noun.

NOUN ENDING IN **-azo**	ENGLISH EQUIVALENT	BASE WORD	ENGLISH EQUIVALENT
el animalazo	*large hulking animal*	el animal	*animal*
el bigotazo	*large mustache*	el bigote	*mustache*
el boyazo	*large ox*	el buey	*ox*
el copazo	*large wine glass, goblet*	la copa	*wine glass*
el copazo	*large snowflake*	el copo	*snowflake*
el cuerpazo	*large-framed body*	el cuerpo	*body*
el gatazo	*large cat*	el gato	*cat*
el hombrazo	*hefty fellow*	el hombre	*man*
el perrazo	*big dog*	el perro	*dog*
el playazo	*expansive beach*	la playa	*beach*
el plumazo	*feather pillow*	la pluma	*feather*
el zapatazo	*large shoe, gunboat*	el zapato	*shoe*

Provide the correct form of the appropriate noun (including its article) for each item.

1. Salvador Dalí, Gene Shallit, Snidley Whiplash, Tom Selleck _____

2. un rottweiler, un gran danés, un pastor alemán _____

3. la Costa Amalfitana, la Costa Azul _____

4. Shaquille O'Neal _____

5. un tipo de almohada almohadillado _____

6. el "amigo azul" de Paul Bunyan _____

7. el calzado de un jugador de básquetbol _____

8. el invierno, una tormenta de nieve _____

9. el Hulk, un gigante, William "Refrigerador" Perry _____

10. un león, un tigre, un leopardo, un puma _____

11. el mastodonte _____

12. el vaso de un gigante _____

The following nouns ending in **-azo** represent a figurative enlargement or broadening sense of the base noun.

NOUN ENDING IN **-azo**	ENGLISH EQUIVALENT	BASE WORD	ENGLISH EQUIVALENT
el aceitazo	*thick oil*	el aceite	*oil*
el bombazo	*huge explosion*	la bomba	*bomb*
el exitazo	*terrific success, smash hit*	el éxito	*success*
el gustazo	*great pleasure, relish*	el gusto	*pleasure*
el humazo	*dense smoke*	el humo	*smoke*
el latazo	*big nuisance, bore*	la lata	*bother, pain* [FIG.]
el maretazo	*heavy surge*	la marea	*tide*
el maridazo	*doting husband*	el marido	*husband*
el padrazo	*doting father*	el padre	*father*
el plumazo	*elegant stroke of a pen*	la pluma	*pen*
el terrazo	*landscape (in a painting)*	la tierra	*land*
el vinazo	*strong wine*	el vino	*wine*

Choose the noun in the second column that best matches the term or description in the first column.

1. _____ un tsunami
2. _____ la atmósfera durante un incendio
3. _____ las pinturas de Claude Monet
4. _____ Hiroshima
5. _____ un papá que adora a sus hijos
6. _____ el Cabernet Sauvignon, el Borgoña, el Barbaresco
7. _____ el producto muy viscoso para el coche
8. _____ un hombre complaciente
9. _____ el espectáculo de Broadway *Cats*
10. _____ el egoísta que sólo habla de sí mismo
11. _____ una firma con la rúbrica
12. _____ el tener una comida sabrosísima

a. el aceitazo
b. el bombazo
c. el exitazo
d. el gustazo
e. el humazo
f. el latazo
g. el maretazo
h. el maridazo
i. el padrazo
j. el plumazo
k. el terrazo
l. el vinazo

12 -ción

MEANING	Action, result of an action, state
ENGLISH EQUIVALENT	*-tion*
PART OF SPEECH	Noun
GENDER	Feminine

The Spanish suffix **-ción** corresponds to the English suffix *-tion*, making these nouns easy to recognize and use. There are many, many Spanish nouns with this suffix. In both Spanish and English, the ending denotes an action, the result of an action, or state. With rare exceptions, these nouns are derived from **-ar** verbs. Nouns with the related suffix **-sión** (No. 46) are derived from **-ar**, **-er**, and **-ir** verbs. Note that the plural form omits the accent on **o**: **la acción ~ las acciones**.

NOUN ENDING IN **-ción**	ENGLISH EQUIVALENT	BASE WORD	ENGLISH EQUIVALENT
la acción	*action*	actuar	*to act*
la adoración	*adoration, worship*	adorar	*to adore*
la animación	*animation*	animar	*to animate*
la asociación	*association*	asociar	*to associate*
la celebración	*celebration*	celebrar	*to celebrate*
la condición	*condition*	condicionar	*to make a condition of*
la conversación	*conversation*	conversar	*to talk, converse*

NOUN ENDING IN -ción	ENGLISH EQUIVALENT	BASE WORD	ENGLISH EQUIVALENT
la dicción	*diction*	dictar	*to dictate*
la dominación	*domination*	dominar	*to dominate*
la donación	*donation*	donar	*to donate, give*
la explicación	*explanation*	explicar	*to explain*
la felicitación	*congratulations*	felicitar	*to congratulate*
la frustración	*frustration*	frustrar	*to frustrate*
la infección	*infection*	infectar	*to infect*
la inyección	*injection*	inyectar	*to inject*

EJERCICIO 12·1

¿Verdadero o falso? *Indicate whether each statement is true or false, using* **V** *for* **verdadero** *true or* **F** *for* **falso** *false.*

1. _____ G.I. Joe, Superman y Batman son figuras de acción.

2. _____ La dicción de un orador no es importante.

3. _____ La otitis media es una infección del oído.

4. _____ Típicamente, hay un himno antes de la celebración de la misa.

5. _____ Todo el mundo hace una donación a los miembros del movimiento Hare Krishna en el aeropuerto.

6. _____ Cada domingo millones de cristianos en todo el mundo se reúnen para la adoración de Dios.

7. _____ Pocas personas comprenden la frustración de estar en espera durante una llamada telefónica.

8. _____ A veces, el mejor regalo de un amigo cercano es una conversación buena y larga.

9. _____ Walt Disney es famoso por sus películas de animación.

10. _____ La mayoría de los nuevos padres creen que la vacuna contra la polio es una inyección necesaria.

11. _____ La mayoría de las religiones del mundo no tienen interés en la condición humana.

12. _____ Cuando una persona tiene una explicación de sus acciones es, por definición, inmune a las criticas.

13. _____ De acuerdo con la Asociación Americana del Corazón, el consumo de cigarrillos nunca provoca enfermedades graves.

14. _____ La esclavitud es un ejemplo de una de las peores formas de la dominación del alma humana.

15. _____ Al graduarse de la universidad, los recién graduados típicamente reciben muchas expresiones de felicitación.

NOUN ENDING IN -ción	ENGLISH EQUIVALENT	BASE WORD	ENGLISH EQUIVALENT
la limitación	*limitation*	limitar	*to limit*
la oración	*prayer*	orar	*to pray*
la preparación	*preparation*	preparar	*to prepare*
la revolución	*revolution*	revolver	*to stir*
la separación	*separation*	separar	*to separate*
la situación	*situation*	situar	*to situate, place*
la solución	*solution*	solucionar	*to solve*
la tentación	*temptation*	tentar	*to tempt*
la vindicación	*vindication*	vindicar	*to vindicate*
la violación	*violation*	violar	*to violate*

EJERCICIO 12·2

Choose the translation in the second column that matches the quotation in the first column.

1. _____ La única manera de librarse de la tentación es caer en ella. (Oscar Wilde)

2. _____ La suerte es lo que sucede cuando la preparación y la oportunidad fusionan. (Voltaire)

3. _____ La tristeza de la separación y de la muerte es el más grande de los engaños. (Mahatma Gandhi)

4. _____ No es que no puedan ver la solución. Es que no pueden ver el problema. (G.K. Chesterton)

5. _____ La oración debería ser la llave del día y el cerrojo de la noche. (Thomas Fuller)

6. _____ Los que hacen imposible una revolución pacífica harán inevitable una revolución violenta. (John F. Kennedy)

7. _____ Cobarde: Él que se ve en una situación peligrosa y piensa con las piernas. (Ambrose Bierce)

8. _____ El arte consiste en la limitación. La parte más hermosa de todo cuadro es el marco. (G.K. Chesterton)

9. _____ Toda violación de la verdad no es solamente una especie de suicidio del embustero, sino una puñalada en la salud de la sociedad humana. (Ralph Waldo Emerson)

10. _____ La verdad es generalmente la mejor vindicación ante la difamación. (Abraham Lincoln)

a. *Art consists of limitation. The most beautiful part of every picture is the frame.*

b. *Truth is generally the best vindication against slander.*

c. *Every violation of truth is not only a sort of suicide in the liar, but is a stab at the health of human society.*

d. *Luck is what happens when preparation meets opportunity.*

e. *The only way to get rid of temptation is to yield to it.*

f. *Prayer should be the key of the day and the lock of the night.*

g. *Sorrow over separation and death is perhaps the greatest delusion.*

h. *It isn't that they can't see the solution. It is that they can't see the problem.*

i. *Those who make peaceful revolution impossible will make violent revolution inevitable.*

j. *Coward: One who, in a perilous situation, thinks with his legs.*

13 ◆ -dor/-dora

MEANING	Performer, expert
ENGLISH EQUIVALENT	*-er, -or*
PART OF SPEECH	Noun
GENDER	Masculine/feminine

A noun ending in **-dor** (feminine: **-dora**) represents a person who performs a task related to the base verb. The formation of these nouns is simple: the **-r** of the infinitive is replaced by the suffix **-dor/-dora**. Thus, **matar** *to kill* yields **el matador** *bullfighter, killer,* **morder** *to bite* yields **el mordedor** *biter,* and **escupir** *to spit* yields **el escupidor** *spitter.* An exception is **el veedor** *spy, busybody,* which adds an **e** before the suffix; the base verb is **ver** *to see.* Several Spanish suffixes have the same meaning as **-dor/-dora**. This suffix is distinctive, in that it often indicates that the person possesses or requires physical power and strength, to the point where some nouns with this suffix represent violent brutes.

NOUN ENDING IN **-dor**	ENGLISH EQUIVALENT	BASE WORD	ENGLISH EQUIVALENT
el bateador	*batter*	batear	*to bat*
el boxeador	*boxer*	boxear	*to box*
el cazador	*hunter*	cazar	*to hunt*
el escupidor	*spitter*	escupir	*to spit*
el jugador	*player (game)*	jugar	*to play (a game)*
el luchador	*fighter, wrestler*	luchar	*to fight, wrestle*
el malgastador	*spendthrift, squanderer*	malgastar	*to squander, waste*
el matador	*bullfighter, killer*	matar	*to kill*
el pateador	*kicker (sports)*	patear	*to kick*
el picador	*picador (bullfighter's assistant)*	picar	*to sting, bite*
el toreador	*bullfighter*	torear	*to fight (a bull)*
el veedor	*spy, busybody*	ver	*to see*

EJERCICIO

13·1

Complete each sentence with the correct form of the appropriate noun.

1. Mata Hari, Nathan Hale y Julius y Ethel Rosenberg eran famosos

   _____ que fueron ejecutados por espionaje.

2. Imelda Marcos, conocida por su legendaria colección de zapatos (¡más de tres mil pares!) y su trastorno de compras compulsivas, es un ejemplo clásico de una

   _____ .

3. Orión, el personaje mitológico, y Elmer Fudd, el archienemigo de Bugs Bunny, son famosos

   _____ .

4. David Beckham tal vez es el más famoso _____ de fútbol en el mundo.

5. Hulk Hogan, Dwayne Johnson y André the Giant son ex-_____ .

6. Muhammad Ali, Rocky Marciano y George Foreman son famosos

  _____ .

7. Babe Ruth, Lou Gehrig y Yogi Berra son famosos _____ por sus numerosos jonrones.

8. Adam Vinatieri, Jan Stenerud, George Blanda y Jim Bakken son famosos

  _____, especialmente por sus numerosos goles de campo durante partidos de fútbol americano.

9. Después de masticar tabaco, el _____ expectora el tabaco en una escupidera.

10. Tres participantes en la corrida de toros son el _____,

  el _____ y el _____ .

NOUN ENDING IN **-dor**	ENGLISH EQUIVALENT	BASE WORD	ENGLISH EQUIVALENT
el aborrecedor	*hater*	aborrecer	*to hate, loathe*
el batallador	*battler, fighter*	batallar	*to battle, fight*
el conquistador	*conqueror*	conquistar	*to conquer*
el edificador	*builder*	edificar	*to build*
el explorador	*explorer*	explorar	*to explore*
el malversador	*embezzler*	malversar	*to embezzle*
el mamador	*one who sucks*	mamar	*to suckle*
el mordedor	*biter*	morder	*to bite*
el paleador	*shoveler*	palear	*to shovel, dig*
el peleador	*fighter*	pelear	*to fight*
el saltador	*jumper*	saltar	*to jump*
el saqueador	*looter*	sacar	*to remove, take out*
el secuestrador	*kidnapper*	secuestrar	*to kidnap*
el tirador	*sharpshooter, marksman*	tirar	*to throw, fire (a gun)*
el violador	*violator, rapist*	violar	*to violate, rape*

EJERCICIO
13·2

¿Verdadero o falso? *Indicate whether each statement is true or false, using* **V** *for* **verdadero** *true or* **F** *for* **falso** *false.*

1. _____ El neoyorquino Bernie Madoff es uno de los peores malversadores en la historia reciente.

2. _____ Un edificador trabaja en el campo de la construcción.

3. _____ Un buen tirador no necesita preocuparse por la seguridad de su rifle.

4. _____ Los violadores y secuestradores son criminales violentos.

5. _____ No hay saltadores de altura en las Olimpiadas.

6. _____ El aborrecedor es un hombre feliz y tranquilo.

7. _____ Los tiburones, las serpientes de cascabel y los pitbull son famosos por ser mordedores.

8. _____ Un batallador o peleador necesita tener mucho coraje.

9. _____ El mamador bebe la leche materna.

10. _____ Dora la Exploradora es la sobrina del explorador Cristóbal Colón.

11. _____ El conquistador Hernán Cortés nació en España.

12. _____ El sepulturero que trabaja en el cementerio es un paleador.

13. _____ Después de un desastre natural como un huracán, con frecuencia hay problemas adicionales con los saqueadores.

14 ◆ -ente/-enta

MEANING	Performer, expert
ENGLISH EQUIVALENT	*-ent, -ant, -er-, -or*
PART OF SPEECH	Noun
GENDER	Masculine/feminine

A noun with the suffix **-ente** (in some cases, **-enta**) represents a person who performs a task related to the base verb. The suffixed nouns in the following charts are derived from **-er** and **-ir** verbs (just as words ending with **-ante** are derived from **-ar** verbs (see No. 8). Most nouns ending in **-ente** may be masculine or feminine (for example **el creyente / la creyente** *believer*). In a handful of cases, however, the ending changes to **-enta** to denote females; these nouns are marked by an asterisk (*). The Spanish language has evolved as a result of advances in women's rights and roles; whereas **la presidenta** once meant *the president's wife*, it now usually refers to the president herself.

NOUN ENDING IN **-ente**	ENGLISH EQUIVALENT	BASE WORD	ENGLISH EQUIVALENT
el adquirente	*purchaser*	adquirir	*to acquire, buy*
el asistente*	*assistant*	asistir	*to assist*
el compareciente	*person appearing in court*	comparecer	*to appear in court*
el contendiente	*contestant, litigant*	contender	*to contend, litigate*
el contribuyente	*contributor, taxpayer*	contribuir	*to contribute, pay taxes*
el correspondiente	*correspondent*	corresponder	*to correspond*
el creyente	*believer*	creer	*to believe*
el dependiente*	*shop assistant, salesperson*	depender	*to be dependent on*
el distribuyente	*distributor*	distribuir	*to distribute*
el doliente	*sick person, mourner*	doler	*to hurt*

EJERCICIO
14·1

Provide the correct masculine form of the appropriate noun (including its article) for each description.

1. Tú vendes artículos en una tienda. _____

2. Tú sufres de una enfermedad. _____

3. Tú ayudas a la jefa. _____

4. Tú compras algo. _____

5. Tú pagas los impuestos. _____

6. Tú eres deísta y crees en Dios. _____

7. Tú escribes una carta a un amigo. _____

8. Tú compareces ante el tribunal. _____

9. Tú eres litigante en un caso legal. _____

10. Tú repartes artículos y bienes a otros. _____

NOUN ENDING IN -ente	ENGLISH EQUIVALENT	BASE WORD	ENGLISH EQUIVALENT
el maldiciente	*malcontent, curser*	maldecir	*to curse, insult*
el oyente	*listener, hearer*	oír	*to hear*
el presidente*	*president*	presidir	*to preside over*
el pretendiente	*suitor, candidate*	pretender	*to try, pretend*
el recipiente	*recipient*	recibir	*to receive*
el regente*	*regent*	regir	*to govern, rule*
el residente	*resident*	residir	*to reside*
el respondiente	*respondent*	responder	*to respond, answer*
el sirviente*	*servant, server*	servir	*to serve*
el sobreviviente	*survivor*	sobrevivir	*to survive*

EJERCICIO
14·2

Provide the correct masculine form of the appropriate noun (including its article) for each description.

1. Tú vives en una casa. _____

2. Tú eres el líder de un país. _____

3. Tú escuchas un discurso. _____

4. Tú recibes un regalo. _____

5. Tú no mueres después de un accidente. _____

6. Tú sirves la comida al dueño de la casa. _____

7. Tú contestas una pregunta. _____

8. Tú estás enojado y maldices mucho. _____

9. Tú estás enamorado y cortejas a una mujer. _____

10. Tú eres administrador de una escuela. _____

Ladies' night! As previously noted, the majority of nouns ending in **-ente** may be either masculine or feminine, depending on context and the modifying articles and adjectives, if any. The nouns in the following chart, however, use the suffix **-enta** to refer specifically to women.

NOUN ENDING IN **-enta**	ENGLISH EQUIVALENT	BASE WORD	ENGLISH EQUIVALENT
la asistenta	*assistant*	asistir	*to assist*
la dependienta	*shop assistant, saleswoman*	depender	*to be dependent on*
la presidenta	*president, First Lady*	presidir	*to preside over*
la regenta	*regent, wife of the regent*	regir	*to govern, rule*
la sirvienta	*servant, server, maid*	servir	*to serve*

EJERCICIO
14·3

Provide the correct feminine form of the appropriate noun (including its article) for each description.

1. Marta vende artículos en una tienda. _____

2. Carlota sirve la comida o limpia la casa. _____

3. Ana es administradora de una escuela. _____

4. Raquel es la líder de un país. _____

5. Juanita ayuda al jefe. _____

15 ◆ -era

MEANING	Container, vessel
ENGLISH EQUIVALENT	—
PART OF SPEECH	Noun
GENDER	Feminine

Several everyday words in Spanish have the suffix **-era**, denoting containers or vessels. A related suffix, **-ero** (No. 17), is less common. While nouns with the suffix **-era** are feminine, the base noun may be either masculine or feminine.

Many of the following nouns ending in **-era** are not as common as those in Exercise 15-2.

NOUN ENDING IN -era	ENGLISH EQUIVALENT	BASE WORD	ENGLISH EQUIVALENT
la cajonera	chest of drawers	el cajón	drawer
la caldera	soup kettle	el caldo	broth, soup
la carbonera	coal bin	el carbón	coal
la cartera	briefcase	la carta	letter, card
la escalera	staircase	la escala	scale
la gorrinera	pigsty	el gorrín	(suckling) pig
la leñera	woodshed	la leña	firewood
la mantequera	butter dish	la manteca	butter, lard
la pecera	fishbowl, aquarium	el pez	fish
la pistolera	holster	la pistola	pistol, gun
la polvera	powder case, compact	el polvo	powder, dust
la pulsera	bracelet	el pulso	pulse
la regadera	watering can	el riego	irrigation, watering
la salsera	gravy boat	la salsa	gravy
la sopera	soup tureen	la sopa	soup
la tortera	cake pan	la torta	cake

EJERCICIO
15·1

Provide the correct noun (including its article) that names the container for the item(s) listed.

1. el agua para las plantas en el jardín _____

2. la madera para quemar en la chimenea _____

3. las camisetas, los calcetines, la ropa interior _____

4. el arma del policía _____

5. los documentos de un hombre de negocios _____

6. los cerdos en la granja _____

7. el pez de colores _____

8. el antebrazo, la muñeca _____

9. el líquido para echar sobre las patatas _____

10. el caldo, la sopa o el guiso (para preparar) _____

11. el caldo, la sopa o el guiso (para servir) _____

12. el carbón _____

13. los polvos, el colorete, la sombra de ojos _____

14. los peldaños, los escalones _____

15. el pastel, la torta, la tarta _____

16. la mantequilla, la margarina _____

Many nouns ending in -**era** are very common; several are presented in the following exercise rather than in a chart.

¡**Resuélvelo!** *Match each of the following nouns ending in* -**era** *with its English equivalent. The base word for each noun ending in* -**era** *is provided for you.*

1. _____ la bañera (el baño)	a.	*milk pitcher*
2. _____ la cafetera (el café)	b.	*hatbox*
3. _____ la coctelera (el cóctel)	c.	*salad bowl*
4. _____ la cucarachera (la cucaracha)	d.	*soap dish*
5. _____ la cuchillera (el cuchillo)	e.	*breadbasket*
6. _____ la chocolatera (el chocolate)	f.	*liquor cabinet*
7. _____ la ensaladera (la ensalada)	g.	*bathtub*
8. _____ la gasolinera (la gasolina)	h.	*mousetrap*
9. _____ la guantera (el guante)	i.	*cocktail shaker*
10. _____ la jabonera (el jabón)	j.	*dog kennel*
11. _____ la joyera (la joya)	k.	*coffeepot*
12. _____ la lechera (la leche)	l.	*knife case, scabbard*
13. _____ la licorera (el licor)	m.	*jewelry box*
14. _____ la panera (el pan)	n.	*punch bowl*
15. _____ la papelera (el papel)	o.	*cockroach trap*
16. _____ la perrera (el perro)	p.	*teapot, teakettle*
17. _____ la ponchera (el ponche)	q.	*glove compartment, glove box*
18. _____ la ratonera (el ratón)	r.	*clock case, watch case*
19. _____ la relojera (el reloj)	s.	*chocolate pot*
20. _____ la sombrerera (el sombrero)	t.	*tobacco pouch*
21. _____ la tabaquera (el tabaco)	u.	*gas station*
22. _____ la tetera (el té)	v.	*wastebasket*

16 ◆ -ería

MEANING	Store, shop
ENGLISH EQUIVALENT	—
PART OF SPEECH	Noun
GENDER	Feminine

The common suffix **-ería** is used to denote a specific type of store or shop. The base noun is typically the main article that is sold, handled, or manufactured. Formation generally consists in omitting the final vowel of the base noun and adding **-ería**; if the base noun ends in a consonant, **-ería** is added directly to the noun. For example, **la fruta** *fruit* yields **la frutería** *fruit stand* and **el reloj** *watch, clock* yields **la relojería** *clock shop*.

The following chart contains the names of a variety of stores and shops.

NOUN ENDING IN **-ería**	ENGLISH EQUIVALENT	BASE WORD	ENGLISH EQUIVALENT
la cafetería	*cafeteria, coffee shop*	el café	*coffee*
la calcetería	*hosier's shop*	el calcetín	*sock*
la carnicería	*butcher shop*	la carne	*meat*
la droguería	*drugstore*	la droga	*drug*
la dulcería	*candy store*	el dulce	*candy, sweet*
la especiería	*spice shop*	la especia	*spice*
la ferretería	*hardware store*	el fierro [LAT. AM.]	*iron, metal bar*
la floristería	*flower shop*	la flor	*flower*
la frutería	*fruit stand*	la fruta	*fruit*
la juguetería	*toy shop*	el juguete	*toy*
la licorería	*liquor store*	el licor	*liquor*
la mueblería	*furniture store*	el mueble	*piece of furniture*
la pastelería	*pastry shop*	el pastel	*pastry, cake*
la pescadería	*fish market*	el pescado	*fish (prepared)*
la relojería	*clock shop*	el reloj	*watch, clock*
la tabaquería	*tobacco shop*	el tabaco	*tobacco*
la vaquería	*dairy store*	la vaca	*cow*
la verdulería	*vegetable stand*	la verdura	*vegetable*

EJERCICIO
16·1

¿Qué tipo de tienda? *Provide the name of the store where each of the following item(s) can be bought.*

1. la aspirina _____

2. el sofá, la silla, la mesa _____

3. el capuchino _____

4. la tarta, la torta, el pan dulce _____

5. el caramelo, el chicle, el chocolate _____

6. la paprika, el cilantro, la sal y la pimienta _____

7. la cerveza, el ron, el vodka, el ginebra _____

8. el salmón, la langosta, las ostras, la trucha _____

9. la crema, la mantequilla, el helado _____

10. el filete, las chuletas de cordero, la hamburguesa _____

11. la zanahoria, el apio, el coliflor, el brócoli _____

12. los cigarrillos, los cigarros _____

13. la rosa, la violeta, el lirio, la margarita, la amarilis _____

14. la muñeca, la pelota, el rompecabezas, el barco
pequeño para el baño _____

15. las pantimedias _____

16. el martillo, la sierra _____

The nouns in the following exercise represent stores and shops commonly found in shopping areas. Most of the base nouns should be familiar to you.

EJERCICIO

16·2

¡Resuélvelo! *Match each of the following nouns ending in* **-ería** *with its English equivalent. The base word for each noun ending in* **-ería** *is provided for you.*

1. _____ la barbería (la barba)   a. *dairy store*

2. _____ la guantería (el guante)   b. *shoe store*

3. _____ la huevería (el huevo)   c. *bakery*

4. _____ la joyería (la joya)   d. *hat shop*

5. _____ la lechería (la leche)   e. *clothing store*

6. _____ la librería (el libro)   f. *egg shop*

7. _____ la panadería (el pan)   g. *barbershop*

8. _____ la papelería (el papel)   h. *wine shop*

9. _____ la peluquería (el pelo)   i. *bookstore*

10. _____ la platería (la plata)   j. *jewelry store*

11. _____ la pollería (el pollo)   k. *silversmith's (shop)*

12. _____ la ropería (la ropa)   l. *hair salon, beauty shop*

13. _____ la sombrerería (el sombrero)   m. *tortilla shop*

14. _____ la tortillería (la tortilla)   n. *glove shop*

15. _____ la vinatería (el vino)   o. *stationery shop*

16. _____ la zapatería (el zapato)   p. *poultry shop*

17 ▸ -ero

MEANING	Container, vessel, collection
ENGLISH EQUIVALENT	—
PART OF SPEECH	Noun
GENDER	Masculine

The suffix -**ero** (and its more common feminine form, -**era**; see No. 15) denotes a container or holder for the base noun.

NOUN ENDING IN -ero	ENGLISH EQUIVALENT	BASE WORD	ENGLISH EQUIVALENT
el alfiletero	*pincushion, needle case*	el alfiler	*pin*
el arenero	*sandbox*	la arena	*sand*
el brasero	*brazier, coal pan*	la brasa	*red-hot coal*
el cenicero	*ashtray*	la ceniza	*ash*
el costurero	*sewing basket*	la costura	*sewing, needlework*
el harinero	*flour bin*	la harina	*flour*
el hormiguero	*anthill*	la hormiga	*ant*
el paragüero	*umbrella stand*	el paraguas	*umbrella*
el pastillero	*pillbox*	la pastilla	*pill, tablet*
el pimentero	*pepper shaker*	la pimienta	*pepper*
el salero	*saltshaker*	la sal	*salt*
el servilletero	*napkin ring*	la servilleta	*napkin*

EJERCICIO
17·1

Provide the correct noun (including its article) that names the container or holder for the item(s) listed.

1. el condimento blanco que es muy común _____

2. el condimento negro que es muy común _____

3. lo que se necesita para protegerse cuando está lloviendo _____

4. el ingrediente más importante cuando se prepara el pan _____

5. la medicina, las píldoras _____

6. las agujas y los alfileres, nada más _____

7. las tijeras, los alfileres, las agujas, el hilo _____

8. el residuo de un cigarrillo o un cigarro _____

9. las palas y los baldes de niños jugando en un parque _____

10. el carbón, la brasa _____

11. los insectos que frecuentemente invaden un picnic _____

12. un pedazo de tela para proteger la ropa durante la comida _____

The base word for the nouns in the following exercise are very common, so their meanings should be easy to determine.

¡Resuélvelo! *Match each of the following nouns ending in* **-ero** *with its English equivalent. The base word for each noun ending in* **-ero** *is provided for you.*

1. _____ el azucarero (el azúcar)   a. *key chain*

2. _____ el basurero (la basura)   b. *fruit bowl*

3. _____ el cervecero (la cerveza)   c. *spoon rack*

4. _____ el cochero (el coche)   d. *sugar bowl*

5. _____ el cucharero (la cuchara)   e. *locker*

6. _____ el florero (la flor)   f. *garbage pail*

7. _____ el frutero (la fruta)   g. *vase*

8. _____ el gatero (el gato)   h. *towel rack*

9. _____ el lapicero (el lápiz)   i. *set of beer mugs*

10. _____ el llavero (la llave)   j. *garage*

11. _____ el ropero (la ropa)   k. *pencil case*

12. _____ el toallero (la toalla)   l. *cat carrier*

 18 ◆ -ero/-era

MEANING	Worker, professional
ENGLISH EQUIVALENT	-er, -man, -person
PART OF SPEECH	Noun
GENDER	Masculine/feminine

Nouns with the suffix **-ero** (feminine: **-era**) may represent people in particular professions or occupations. The base noun may signify what the person works with (for example, **el cartero** *mailman, letter carrier* works with **la carta** *letter*) or where the person works (for example, **el cocinero** *cook* works in **la cocina** *kitchen*).

NOUN ENDING IN **-ero**	ENGLISH EQUIVALENT	BASE WORD	ENGLISH EQUIVALENT
el banquero	*banker*	el banco	*bank*
el barbero	*barber*	la barba	*beard*
el basurero	*garbage collector*	la basura	*garbage*
el carnicero	*butcher*	la carne	*meat*

▶

NOUN ENDING IN **-ero**	ENGLISH EQUIVALENT	BASE WORD	ENGLISH EQUIVALENT
◄ el cartero	*mailman, letter carrier*	la carta	*letter*
el casero	*landlord*	la casa	*house*
el cervecero	*brewer*	la cerveza	*beer*
el chispero	*blacksmith*	la chispa	*spark*
el cochero	*coachman, driver*	el coche	*car*
el cocinero	*cook*	la cocina	*kitchen*
el droguero	*druggist*	la droga	*drug*
el florero	*florist*	la flor	*flower*
el fontanero	*plumber*	la fontana	*fountain*
el granjero	*farmer*	la granja	*farm*
el guerrero	*warrior, fighter*	la guerra	*war*
el lechero	*milkman*	la leche	*milk*
el librero	*bookseller*	el libro	*book*

EJERCICIO
18·1

Provide the noun (including its article) that names the worker whose job involves the items listed. Give both the masculine and feminine forms.

1. la prescripción, los medicamentos, las píldoras _____ _____

2. la crema, la mantequilla, los productos lácteos _____ _____

3. el dinero, la cuenta de cheques, las inversiones _____ _____

4. la rosa, el tulipán, la margarita, el lirio _____ _____

5. el filete, la hamburguesa, el jamón, la chuleta de cordero _____ _____

6. el correo, el paquete, los sellos _____ _____

7. la vaca, el cerdo, la cosecha, el establo, el tractor _____ _____

8. la limusina, el camión, el carro, el taxi _____ _____

9. el pelo del hombre, el bigote, las tijeras, la navaja _____ _____

10. el fregadero, el lavabo, el agua _____ _____

11. la batalla, el ejército, las fuerzas aéreas, la marina _____ _____

12. la habitación, el apartamento, la vivienda, la renta _____ _____

13. la comida, los ingredientes, el horno, la receta _____ _____

14. el licor de malta, la cebada, el lúpulo _____ _____

15. las cosas sin valor, la chatarra, la bazofia, los tiliches _____ _____

16. la novela, el tomo, las publicaciones, la revista _____ _____

17. la herradura, el hierro, el fuego, el martillo _____ _____

NOUN ENDING IN -ero	ENGLISH EQUIVALENT	BASE WORD	ENGLISH EQUIVALENT
el marinero	*sailor*	la marina	*seacoast, navy*
el mensajero	*messenger*	el mensaje	*message*
el mesero	*waiter*	la mesa	*table*
el panadero	*baker*	el pan	*bread*
el peluquero	*hairdresser*	el pelo	*hair*
el perrero	*dog catcher*	el perro	*dog*
el pistolero	*gunman, gangster*	la pistola	*pistol, gun*
el platero	*silversmith*	la plata	*silver*
el prisionero	*prisoner*	la prisión	*prison*
el relojero	*clockmaker, watchmaker*	el reloj	*clock, watch*
el tendero	*store owner, shopkeeper*	la tienda	*store, shop*
el tesorero	*treasurer*	el tesoro	*treasure*
el tilichero	*peddler*	los tiliches	*trinkets, junk*
el torero	*bullfighter*	el toro	*bull*
el vaquero	*cowboy, cowherd*	la vaca	*cow*
el zapatero	*shoemaker*	el zapato	*shoe*

¿A o B? *Choose the best completion for each sentence.*

1. _____ El perrero está en busca del _____.

    a. canino   b. felino

2. _____ El mesero trabaja en _____.

    a. el hospital   b. el restaurante

3. _____ La tendera trabaja en _____.

    a. la bodega   b. la escuela

4. _____ El torero es popular en _____.

    a. la India   b. España

5. _____ El marinero trabaja en _____.

    a. la tierra   b. el mar

6. _____ La tesorera trabaja con _____.

    a. la comida   b. el dinero

7. _____ El platero es fabricante de _____.

    a. la joyería   b. la ropa

8. _____ El panadero usa mucha _____.

    a. carne   b. harina

9. _____ El prisionero vive en _____.

   a. la cárcel   b. la Abadía de Westminster

10. _____ La mensajera entrega _____.

    a. la información   b. el vino

11. _____ El pistolero es _____.

    a. un santo   b. un criminal

12. _____ La relojera trabaja con _____.

    a. el Rolex   b. el Rolodex

13. _____ El vaquero monta _____.

    a. en bicicleta   b. a caballo

14. _____ La peluquera trabaja en _____.

    a. el salón de belleza   b. la ropería

15. _____ El zapatero trabaja con _____.

    a. los calcetines   b. las botas

16. _____ El tilichero vende _____.

    a. las cosas preciosas   b. las cosas de poco valor

19 ◆ -eta

MEANING	Diminutive
ENGLISH EQUIVALENT	—
PART OF SPEECH	Noun
GENDER	Feminine

The suffix **-eta** is one of many Spanish noun endings that mark diminutives; see its masculine counterpart, **-ete** (No. 20). The suffixed noun may be a physically diminutive form of the base noun, or it may involve a figurative twist; for example, **la vela** *sail, awning* yields **la veleta** *weathervane.*

NOUN ENDING IN **-eta**	ENGLISH EQUIVALENT	BASE WORD	ENGLISH EQUIVALENT
la aleta	*small wing or fin*	el ala [F.]	*wing*
la avioneta	*light aircraft*	el avión	*airplane*
la buseta	*small bus, minibus*	el autobús	*bus*
la cajeta	*small box*	la caja	*box*
la camioneta	*van*	el camión	*truck*
la camiseta	*T-shirt*	la camisa	*shirt*

▶

NOUN ENDING IN -eta	ENGLISH EQUIVALENT	BASE WORD	ENGLISH EQUIVALENT
◄ la capeta	*short cape*	la capa	*cape, cloak*
la caseta	*hut, (telephone) booth*	la casa	*house*
la cazoleta	*small pan*	el cazo	*saucepan*
la coleta	*pigtail, pony-tail (hair)*	la cola	*tail*
la cuarteta	*quatrain*	el cuarto	*fourth, fourth part*
la faldeta	*short skirt, miniskirt*	la falda	*skirt*
la hacheta	*hatchet*	el hacha [F.]	*axe*
la historieta	*comic strip*	la historia	*story*
la isleta	*small island, islet*	la isla	*island*

Complete each sentence with the correct form of the appropriate noun.

1. Un "mini-Batman" lleva una _____ negra.

2. Una "mini–Lizzie Borden" mata a sus padres con una _____.

3. *Doonesbury*, *Dilbert* y *Beetle Bailey* son títulos de _____ populares.

4. Para las familias con muchos niños, un SUV no es bastante; ellos necesitan una

    _____.

5. Pippi Longstocking es famosa por sus _____ que sobresalen de la cabeza.

6. El Cessna, el Beechcraft y el Piper son _____ populares para vuelos no comerciales.

7. Muchos comediantes en vivo clásicos como Bob Hope y Rodney Dangerfield siempre se vestían en chaqueta y corbata, mientras que el cómico Louis C.K. siempre lleva jeans y una

    _____ negra.

8. Superman se cambia la ropa en una _____ telefónica.

9. El pez no puede nadar sin _____.

10. Para hervir un poco de agua se necesita una _____.

11. La diseñadora de moda británica Mary Quant adquirió fama en la década de 1960 con

    la creación de la _____.

12. La _____ es una forma de transporte pública, pero no para muchas personas.

13. Muchos recién casados quieren pasar una semana o dos aislados en una

    _____ en medio de la nada.

14. Una _____ es un poema de cuatro versos. Un ejemplo es el clásico "Las rosas son rojas / y las violetas azules / la miel es dulce / pero no tan dulce como tú."

NOUN ENDING IN -eta	ENGLISH EQUIVALENT	BASE WORD	ENGLISH EQUIVALENT
la lengüeta	*tongue of a shoe*	la lengua	*tongue*
la libreta	*notebook, bank book*	el libro	*book*
la manteleta	*shawl*	el mantel	*tablecloth*
la opereta	*operetta*	la ópera	*opera*
la paleta	*palette*	la pala	*shovel*
la papeleta	*ballot, certificate*	el papel	*paper*
la peineta	*ornamental comb*	el peine	*comb*
la tarjeta	*card*	la tarja	*signboard*
la tijereta	*small scissors*	las tijeras	*scissors*
la tineta	*small tub*	la tina	*(bath)tub*
la toalleta	*napkin, small towel*	la toalla	*towel*
la veleta	*weathervane*	la vela	*sail, awning*
la vinagreta	*vinaigrette*	el vinagre	*vinegar*

Complete each sentence with the correct form of the appropriate noun.

1. Se usa una _____ para limpiar las comisuras de la boca.

2. Se encuentra una _____ en el zapato.

3. Para saber de qué lado sopla el viento, se mira la _____.

4. Después de recibir un regalo, es importante enviarle al donante una

    _____ de agradecimiento.

5. Se usa una _____ para cortarse las uñas.

6. Antes de pintar un cuarto, los dueños de la casa consideran la _____
    de colores que les parecen buenos.

7. *H.M.S. Pinafore, Los Piratas de Penzance* y *El Mikado* de Gilbert y Sullivan son famosas

    y clásicas _____.

8. Para calentarse en una noche fría, una mujer puede llevar una _____.

9. Una persona muy pequeña sólo necesita una _____ para bañarse.

10. Para votar, el votante necesita una _____.

11. Al abrir una cuenta de ahorros, muchos bancos le dan al cliente una

    _____ de ahorros.

12. Se sirven muchas ensaladas con una salsa _____.

13. La _____ es para adornar el cabello.

20 ▸ -ete

MEANING	Diminutive
ENGLISH EQUIVALENT	—
PART OF SPEECH	Noun
GENDER	Masculine

The relatively uncommon suffix **-ete** is one of many Spanish word endings that mark diminutives. Sometimes, the diminutive size is physical; for example, **el toro** *bull* yields **el torete** *small bull, young bull*. It may also be figurative or related to status; for example, **el color** *color* yields **el colorete** *rouge, blush*. The related feminine suffix **-eta** (No. 19) has the same function and meaning, differing only in gender. Note especially **el banquete** *banquet*, derived from **el banco** *bench, pew*. Originally, **el banquete** was a snack eaten informally on a bench. Over time, the meaning evolved to its meaning today: a formal and elaborate feast.

NOUN ENDING IN **-ete**	ENGLISH EQUIVALENT	BASE WORD	ENGLISH EQUIVALENT
el arete	*earring*	el aro	*hoop*
el banquete	*banquet*	el banco	*bench, pew*
el barrilete	*keg*	el barril	*barrel*
el brazalete	*bracelet*	el brazo	*arm*
el caballete	*sawhorse, artist's easel*	el caballo	*horse*
el clarinete	*clarinet*	el clarín	*bugle*
el colorete	*rouge, blush*	el color	*color*
el gorrete	*small cap*	la gorra	*(baseball) cap*
el guantelete	*gauntlet*	el guante	*glove*
el juguete	*toy*	el juego	*game*
el mollete	*muffin*	la molla	*doughy part of bread*
el paquete	*package, parcel*	la paca	*bale, bundle*
el sombrerete	*little hat/cap*	el sombrero	*hat*
el soplete	*blowtorch, blowpipe*	el soplo	*gust, puff*
el templete	*small temple or shrine*	el templo	*temple*
el tenderete	*(market) stall*	la tienda	*store, shop*
el torete	*small bull, young bull*	el toro	*bull*
el zaguanete	*small entrance or vestibule*	el zaguán	*entrance hall*

EJERCICIO 20·1

¿Qué es esto? *Provide the correct noun (including its article) for each group or description.*

1. el instrumento musical de Benny Goodman, Artie Shaw y Kenny G _____

2. lo que lleva un jugador de Tee ball en la cabeza _____

3. lo que soporta las pinturas de un artista _____

4. la posesión importante de un niño _____

5. lo que lleva una mujer en las orejas _____

6. lo que lleva una mujer en la muñeca _____

7. lo que se aplica una mujer en las mejillas _____

8. según la leyenda, cada comida del rey Enrique VIII _____

9. una comida popular para el desayuno _____

10. lo que contiene la cerveza para muchas fiestas universitarias _____

11. el hijo de una vaca _____

12. lo que se arroja al declararse listo para una lucha _____

13. lo que lleva una persona con una cabeza muy pequeña _____

14. lo que se recibe del cartero _____

15. una entrada pequeña _____

16. lo que se usa por el platero para fundir el metal _____

17. la tienda temporario en una feria de arte _____

18. donde se puede adorar un ídolo _____

21 ◆ -eza

MEANING	State, abstract concept
ENGLISH EQUIVALENT	*-ness, -ity*
PART OF SPEECH	Noun
GENDER	Feminine

A Spanish noun with the suffix **-eza** denotes a state relating to its base adjective. Nearly all of these nouns are formed regularly, taking into account standard orthographic changes (**c** > **qu**, **g** > **gu**, and **z** > **c** before **e** or **i**). If the base word ends in a vowel, the vowel is replaced by **-eza**; if the base word ends in a consonant, **-eza** is added directly to the noun.

NOUN ENDING IN **-eza**	ENGLISH EQUIVALENT	BASE WORD	ENGLISH EQUIVALENT
la agudeza	*acuteness, smartness*	agudo	*acute, sharp*
la bajeza	*baseness*	bajo	*base, low, short*
la belleza	*beauty, loveliness*	bello	*beautiful, lovely*
la certeza	*certainty*	cierto	*certain, true*
la dureza	*hardness*	duro	*hard*
la franqueza	*candor, frankness*	franco	*candid, frank*
la gentileza	*courtesy, kindness*	gentil	*pleasant, kind*
la graseza	*fattiness*	graso	*greasy, fatty, oily*
la lindeza	*loveliness*	lindo	*lovely, pretty*
la llaneza	*straightforwardness*	llano	*flat, straightforward*
la majeza	*boldness, flamboyance*	majo	*free, nonchalant*
la presteza	*quickness, promptness*	presto	*quick, prompt*
la rudeza	*roughness, coarseness*	rudo	*coarse, crude*
la sutileza	*subtlety*	sutil	*subtle*
la terneza	*tenderness, softness*	tierno	*tender*

Complete each sentence with the correct form of the appropriate noun. Include its article where needed.

1. Tú estás a dieta, y por eso estás preocupado con _____ de la comida.

2. Tú eres abogado, y por eso es necesario tener razón y también tener _____ y _____ en el tribunal.

3. Eres carpintero, y por eso es necesario considerar _____ de la madera para asegurar buena calidad de la construcción de los muebles.

4. Tú eres Batman, y por eso _____ tiene mucha importancia porque necesitas llegar al lugar del crimen lo antes posible.

5. Eres concursante en el espectáculo de Miss Universo, y por eso quieres más que nada proyectar a los jueces _____ y _____.

6. Durante una entrevista, es importante tener una actitud de _____ y _____.

7. Una persona completamente descortés está afectado con _____ y _____.

8. Una madre llena de amor por su bebé tiene mucha _____ y _____.

9. Una persona muy egoísta y liberal con sus sentimientos está afectada con _____.

10. Una persona con mucho tacto, discernimiento y discreción tiene el don de _____.

The following nouns ending in **-eza** represent a state of being.

NOUN ENDING IN **-eza**	ENGLISH EQUIVALENT	BASE WORD	ENGLISH EQUIVALENT
la flaqueza	*thinness*	flaco	*thin*
la grandeza	*greatness, grandeur*	grande	*great, big*
la guapeza	*good looks*	guapo	*handsome*
la largueza	*length, broadness*	largo	*long*
la limpieza	*cleanliness*	limpio	*clean*
la maleza	*weeds, underbrush*	malo	*bad, evil*
la naturaleza	*nature, temperament*	natural	*natural*
la nobleza	*nobility*	noble	*noble*
la pobreza	*poverty*	pobre	*poor*
la pureza	*purity*	puro	*pure*
la rareza	*rarity, rareness*	raro	*rare*
la riqueza	*richness, wealth*	rico	*rich*

NOUN ENDING IN -eza	ENGLISH EQUIVALENT	BASE WORD	ENGLISH EQUIVALENT
la torpeza	*clumsiness*	torpe	*clumsy*
la tristeza	*sadness*	triste	*sad*
la viveza	*liveliness, vivacity*	vivo	*alive*

EJERCICIO
21·2

Provide the correct noun (including its article) for the characteristic or concern associated with the person(s) described in each item.

1. una persona muy deprimida _____

2. una persona anoréxica _____

3. un santo, la virgen María _____

4. una persona sin dinero _____

5. Donald Trump, una persona que ama el dinero _____

6. un borracho que no anda bien _____

7. un jardinero en un jardín descuidado _____

8. el ama de llaves que quiere una casa perfecta _____

9. una persona con un ego enorme _____

10. un hombre muy honrado _____

11. una persona en busca del diamante perfectísimo _____

12. Adonis, un hombre muy atractivo _____

13. un bailarín flamenco, una persona con mucho carisma _____

14. una persona interesada en la esencia o personalidad de algo o alguien _____

15. una persona interesada en la medida de longitud _____

22 ▶ -ible

MEANING	Able to be (acted on)
ENGLISH EQUIVALENT	*-ible, -able*
PART OF SPEECH	Adjective
GENDER	Masculine/feminine

The Spanish suffix **-ible** is identical to its English counterparts in spelling and meaning: They mean exactly what they suggest, namely, *able to be (acted on)*. Nearly all of the adjectives with the **-ible** suffix are derived from **-er** and **-ir** verbs. An exception is **ostensible** *appearing to be true*, which derives from **ostentar** *to show, flaunt*. Usually, the suffix **-ible** is added directly to stem of the base verb; sometimes, however, slight orthographic changes are made (for example, **admitir** *to admit, allow* yields **admisible** *admissible, acceptable*). Since most of these Spanish adjectives have English cognates, they tend to be easily recognized and used.

ADJECTIVE ENDING IN **-ible**	ENGLISH EQUIVALENT	BASE WORD	ENGLISH EQUIVALENT
aborrecible	*hateful, despicable*	aborrecer	*to hate, despise*
admisible	*admissible, acceptable*	admitir	*to admit, allow*
audible	*audible*	audire [LAT.]	*to hear*
bebible	*drinkable*	beber	*to drink*
comible	*edible, fit to eat*	comer	*to eat*
comprimible	*compressible*	comprimir	*to compress*
concebible	*conceivable*	concebir	*to conceive, imagine*
convertible	*convertible*	convertir	*to convert, change*
rompible	*breakable*	romper	*to break*
vendible	*saleable, marketable*	vender	*to sell*

EJERCICIO

22·1

Complete each sentence with the correct form of the appropriate adjective.

1. Una hamburguesa, cubierta de gusanos, cucarachas y mugre, no es

   _____.

2. El vinagre, mezclado con la gasolina y la leche cuajada, no es _____.

3. Un silbato ultrasónico para perros no es _____ para la mayoría
   de los humanos.

4. Las pruebas obtenidas de manera ilegal no son _____ en los
   tribunales.

5. El cristal y otras cosas muy frágiles son _____.

6. En la novela *Casino Royale* por Ian Fleming, James Bond conduce un coche

   _____, el Bentley Mark VI (un coche que no existe en realidad).

7. En una tienda, los artículos rotos, quemados y/o cubiertos de lodo, sin importar el precio,

   no son _____.

8. Para muchas personas, no es _____ que un hombre quiera cinco
   esposas.

9. La violación de una mujer es un acto _____.

10. Las cosas en el compactador de basura son _____.

ADJECTIVE ENDING IN **-ible**	ENGLISH EQUIVALENT	BASE WORD	ENGLISH EQUIVALENT
absorbible	*absorbable*	absorber	*to absorb*
comprensible	*understandable*	comprender	*to understand*
creíble	*believable, credible*	creer	*to believe*
deducible	*deducible*	deducir	*to deduce, infer*
definible	*definable, definite*	definir	*to define*
discutible	*questionable, debatable*	discutir	*to argue, discuss*
imponible	*taxable*	imponer	*to impose, tax*
increíble	*incredible*	in- + creer	*not + to believe*
leíble	*legible, readable*	leer	*to read*
movible	*movable*	mover	*to move*
ostensible	*appearing to be true*	ostentar	*to show, flaunt*
permisible	*permissible*	permitir	*to permit, allow*
producible	*producible*	producir	*to produce*
risible	*laughable, absurd*	reír	*to laugh*
sorbible	*able to be sipped*	sorber	*to sip*
unible	*able to be joined*	unir	*to unite, join*

¿Verdadero o falso? *Indicate whether each statement is true or false, using* **V** *for* **verdadero** *true or* **F** *for* **falso** *false.*

1. _____ Para varias operaciones, se realiza la incisión para que las suturas estén bajo la piel y últimamente desaparezcan y sean absorbibles.

2. _____ En un vuelo de una aerolínea comercial, es permisible tener una pistola, unos fósforos, una gran selección de navajas, unas tijeras y una espada samurái en su equipaje de mano.

3. _____ Los formularios de impuestos son completamente comprensibles—"claro como el agua" para todos.

4. _____ Las contribuciones caritativas en general (pero no tu boda y luna de miel) son deducibles de impuestos.

5. _____ Un mentiroso compulsivo es creíble.

6. _____ Es importante que la escritura de una maestra de escuela elemental sea leíble.

7. _____ El embarazo típico dura un período de tiempo definible (nueve meses, más o menos).

8. _____ Una malteada de chocolate, una Coca-Cola y muchos otros refrescos son sorbibles.

9. _____ El agua y el aceite son fácilmente unibles.

10. _____ No importa la escala salarial o el sueldo, cada centavo que gane una persona es imponible.

11. _____ Después de un fracaso, a menudo se dice "Sí no fuera tan trágica, la situación sería risible."

12. _____ En la política, parece que todo es discutible y, con demasiada frecuencia, no se hace nada y la economía y la gente sufren.

13. _____ El propósito ostensible para la cooperación en la política es siempre el verdadero propósito.

14. _____ La energía producible es de gran interés por los científicos y los astrónomos.

15. _____ Para entrar en el escáner de CT, se recuesta en una cama movible que se desliza dentro de la máquina.

16. _____ Es increíble y maravilloso que Diana Nyad, a los 64 años, nadara de la Habana, Cuba hasta Key West, Florida entre el 31 de agosto y el 2 de septiembre 2013.

23 -ico/-ica

MEANING	Relating to, like
ENGLISH EQUIVALENT	*-ic, -ical*
PART OF SPEECH	Adjective
GENDER	Masculine/feminine

The adjectival suffix **-ico** (feminine: **-ica**) is one of the more common endings indicating that someone or something is like, or related to, a base noun. English counterparts often end in *-ic/ -ical*, and many of the Spanish adjectives in the following charts have English cognates. As a rule, if the base noun ends with a vowel, the vowel is replaced by **-ico/-ica**; if the base noun ends in a consonant, **-ico/-ica** is added directly to the noun. Note that the stress in these suffixed adjectives is on the antepenultimate syllable, thus requiring an accent mark.

ADJECTIVE ENDING IN -ico	ENGLISH EQUIVALENT	BASE WORD	ENGLISH EQUIVALENT
asmático	*asthmatic*	el asma [F.]	*asthma*
básico	*basic*	la base	*base*
católico	*Catholic*	kata- + holos [GRK.]	*about + whole*
dramático	*dramatic*	el drama	*drama*
evangélico	*evangelical*	el evangelio	*gospel*
metálico	*metallic*	el metal	*metal*
pacífico	*peaceful*	la paz	*peace*
panorámico	*panoramic*	el panorama	*panorama*
patriótico	*patriotic*	la patria	*fatherland*
psíquico	*psychic*	la psique	*psyche*
sádico	*sadistic*	Sade	*Marquis de Sade*
satánico	*satanic(al)*	Satanás, Satán	*Satan*
semítico	*Semitic*	el/la semita	*Semite*
telefónico	*telephonic*	el teléfono	*telephone*
tóxico	*toxic*	la toxina	*toxin*

Complete each sentence with the correct form of the appropriate adjective.

1. Las obras de Shakespeare son _____.

2. Los niños que necesitan un nebulizador en casa y un inhalador portátil son

   _____.

3. Los presidentes, los primeros ministros y otros líderes del mundo que claramente aman

   sus países son _____.

4. Superman se cambia la ropa en una cabina _____.

5. Si alguien está muy sereno y calmo, está _____.

6. Algo absolutamente malo, como un acto del diablo, es _____.

7. El Papa es el líder de la iglesia _____.

8. El arsénico, el mercurio, el veneno y el cianuro son _____.

9. Las clases en la escuela elemental (la lectura, la escritura y la aritmética) son muy

   _____.

10. Se encuentran los mensajes _____ de Mateo, Marcos, Lucas y Juan
    en el Nuevo Testamento.

11. Se dice que una persona con percepción extrasensorial (en inglés, ESP) es

    _____.

12. Un efecto secundario de tomar antibióticos es un sabor _____
    en la boca.

13. Los idiomas _____ incluyen el hebreo, el árabe y el arameo.

14. Un hombre a quien le gusta torturar a otros es _____.

15. Es difícil escalar una montaña, pero una recompensa es la vista

    _____.

ADJECTIVE ENDING IN -ico	ENGLISH EQUIVALENT	BASE WORD	ENGLISH EQUIVALENT
analítico	*analytical*	el análisis	*analysis*
angélico	*angelic*	el ángel	*angel*
bíblico	*Biblical*	la Biblia	*Bible*
caótico	*chaotic*	el caos	*chaos*
científico	*scientific*	la ciencia	*science*
clásico	*classic(al)*	la clase	*class, kind*
cósmico	*cosmic*	el cosmos	*cosmos*
cúbico	*cubic(al)*	el cubo	*cube*
enérgico	*energetic*	la energía	*energy*

ADJECTIVE ENDING IN -ico	ENGLISH EQUIVALENT	BASE WORD	ENGLISH EQUIVALENT
enfático	*emphatic*	la énfasis	*emphasis*
específico	*specific*	la especie	*species*
estratégico	*strategic*	la estrategia	*strategy*
fantástico	*fantastic*	la fantasía	*fantasy*
frenético	*frenetic, frenzied*	el frenesí	*frenzy*
galáctico	*galactic*	la galaxia	*galaxy*
mágico	*magic(al)*	el mago	*magician, wizard*
telepático	*telepathic*	la telepatía	*telepathy*
titánico	*huge, Titanic*	Titán	*Titan*
trágico	*tragic*	la tragedia	*tragedy*
único	*unique*	uno	*one*

EJERCICIO
23·2

¿Verdadero o falso? *Indicate whether each statement is true or false, using* **V** *for* **verdadero** *true or* **F** *for* **falso** *false.*

1. _____ Los estudios científicos tienden a ser muy analíticos y específicos.

2. _____ Un niño angélico siempre dice "¡No!" y nunca dice "Por favor."

3. _____ La guerra involucra muchos planes estratégicos.

4. _____ La esclavitud en cualquier forma es trágica.

5. _____ Un psíquico tiene poderes telepáticos.

6. _____ La vida de una madre que tiene niños pequeños raramente incluye un día frenético.

7. _____ Se dice que cada copo de nieve es único.

8. _____ Los ateístas creen las historias bíblicas.

9. _____ La entrega del Premio Nobel es un logro titánico para el recipiente.

10. _____ Un templo, una sinagoga, una iglesia, una mezquita u otro lugar sagrado casi siempre está caótico.

11. _____ Después de cinco tazas de café, una persona usualmente se siente muy enérgica.

12. _____ J.R.R. Tolkien escribió la saga fantástica de Harry Potter y su mundo mágico.

13. _____ Usualmente, pero no siempre, un grito es más enfático que un susurro.

14. _____ El ruido galáctico (también llamado el ruido cósmico) consiste en la radiación radioeléctrica no identificada que viene de más allá de la atmósfera terrestre.

15. _____ Originalmente llamado el "cubo mágico," el juguete clásico en forma cúbica vendido por Ideal Toy Corporación desde 1980 es el popular Rubik's Cube.

MEANING	State, quality		
ENGLISH EQUIVALENT	*-ity*		
PART OF SPEECH	Noun		
GENDER	Feminine		

Many of the Spanish nouns ending in **-idad** have English cognates ending in *-ity*. The suffix **-idad** generally denotes the state or quality of the base adjective.

NOUN ENDING IN **-idad**	ENGLISH EQUIVALENT	BASE WORD	ENGLISH EQUIVALENT
la adversidad	*adversity*	adverso	*adverse, calamitous*
la atrocidad	*atrocity*	atroz	*atrocious*
la castidad	*chastity*	casto	*chaste*
la densidad	*density*	denso	*dense*
la fecundidad	*fertility*	fecundo	*fertile*
la ferocidad	*fierceness, ferocity*	feroz	*fierce, ferocious*
la humanidad	*humanity*	humano	*human*
la infinidad	*infinity*	infinito	*infinite*
la mortalidad	*mortality*	mortal	*mortal*
la probabilidad	*probability*	probable	*probable*
la prosperidad	*prosperity*	próspero	*prosperous*
la relatividad	*relativity*	relativo	*relative, relating*
la superioridad	*superiority*	superior	*superior, better*
la utilidad	*utility, usefulness*	útil	*useful*
la veracidad	*truthfulness, veracity*	veraz	*truthful*
la virilidad	*virility, manliness*	viril	*virile, manly*

EJERCICIO

24·1

Complete each sentence with the correct form of the appropriate noun(s).

1. Es difícil contemplar la _____ de los cielos.

2. Los sacerdotes jesuitas profesan votos de la pobreza, la _____ y la obediencia.

3. La famosa navaja suiza (*Swiss Army knife*) es conocida por su _____.

4. El aligátor, el león y el tiburón son conocidos por su _____.

5. Albert Einstein es famoso por su Teoría de la _____.

6. Herbert Morrison, el locutor de radio, es famoso por su emotiva descripción del accidente del dirigible Hindenburg (6 mayo 1937) y especialmente por su exclamación, "Oh, la _____."

7. La _____ de tener gemelos fraternales es aproximadamente 3%, para gemelos idénticos es .03%.

8. Michelle Duggar, una madre de 19 hijos (incluidos dos pares de gemelos fraternales), es famosa por su _____.

9. La _____ de un líquido es igual a la masa del líquido entre el volumen que ocupa.

10. En el juicio ante el tribunal, la _____ de un testigo es crucial.

11. El egocéntrico, el esnob o la persona que cree que es más inteligente que el resto del mundo tiene un complejo de _____.

12. Un hombre macho se preocupa por su _____.

13. El holocausto es un ejemplo clásico de una _____.

14. Por la pobreza y la falta de educación y atención médica, Somalia tiene una de las tasas más elevadas del mundo de la _____ infantil.

15. Victor Hugo escribió, "La _____ hace a hombres, y la _____ hace a monstruos."

NOUN ENDING IN -idad	ENGLISH EQUIVALENT	BASE WORD	ENGLISH EQUIVALENT
la casualidad	*coincidence, chance*	casual	*casual, informal*
la conformidad	*compliance, approval*	conformista	*similar, in agreement*
la espiritualidad	*spirituality*	espiritual	*spiritual*
la eternidad	*eternity*	eterno	*eternal*
la fragilidad	*fragility*	frágil	*fragile*
la integridad	*integrity*	íntegro	*upright, honorable*
la posibilidad	*possibility*	posible	*possible*
la productividad	*productivity*	productivo	*productive*
la proximidad	*proximity, closeness*	próximo	*close, near*
la realidad	*reality*	real	*real*
la severidad	*severity, harshness*	severo	*severe, strict*
la tenacidad	*tenacity, toughness*	tenaz	*tenacious, persistent*
la vanidad	*vanity*	vano	*vain, shallow*
la velocidad	*velocity, speed*	veloz	*fast, quick*
la visibilidad	*visibility*	visible	*visible*

EJERCICIO
24·2

¿Verdadero o falso? *Indicate whether each statement is true or false, using V for* **verdadero** *true or F for* **falso** *false.*

1. _____ La proximidad de su casa a una buena escuela es muy importante a muchos padres de niños pequeños.

2. _____ Si una persona nunca fuma cigarrillos ni toma el alcohol, come solamente la comida sana y duerme al menos ocho horas cada noche, puede vivir por toda la eternidad.

3. _____ La abeja es conocida por su productividad.

4. _____ Los asesinos en serie son hombres de una gran integridad personal.

5. _____ Dracón, el legislador de Atenas y un hombre muy cruel, es recordado por la severidad de sus castigos, así que de ahí viene el término "medidas draconianas."

6. _____ Es imposible calcular la velocidad de cerdos voladores porque no existen.

7. _____ La conformidad es importante para una banda de marcha.

8. _____ La visibilidad del candidato político no es muy importante.

9. _____ Una persona psicótica tiende a vivir en su propia realidad.

10. _____ La posibilidad del infierno convirtiéndose en hielo no existe.

11. _____ "Vanidad de vanidades, ¡todo es vanidad!" es del Libro de Eclesiastés.

12. _____ Los narcisistas sufren de una fragilidad del ego.

13. _____ Es por la pura casualidad que estás pensando en alguien y de repente suena el teléfono y oyes su voz al otro extremo de la línea.

14. _____ La Madre Teresa, Mahatma Gandhi y Nelson Mandela son conocidos por su espiritualidad.

15. _____ Para alcanzar el éxito en la vida, en cualquier forma o carrera, la tenacidad es crucial.

25 ◆ -ificar

MEANING	To make (like)
ENGLISH EQUIVALENT	*-ify*
PART OF SPEECH	Verb

The suffix -**ificar** is unusual, because verbs rarely form a specific group with a suffix. A Spanish verb ending in -**ificar** corresponds to an English verb ending in *-ify*; as a result, these words are easy to recognize and use. Verbs with the suffix -**ificar** are regular, with the single orthographic change of **c** to **qu** before **e** when conjugated (for example, present tense **yo clasifico** *I classify* and preterit **yo clasifiqué** *I classified*).

The following verbs ending in -**ificar** are based on nouns.

VERB ENDING IN -**ificar**	ENGLISH EQUIVALENT	BASE WORD	ENGLISH EQUIVALENT
calificar	*to qualify, grade*	la calidad	*quality*
clasificar	*to classify*	la clase	*class, kind*
cosificar	*to treat as an object*	la cosa	*thing*
crucificar	*to crucify*	la cruz	*cross*
cuantificar	*to quantify*	la cantidad	*quantity*
dosificar	*to ration, dispense*	la dosis	*dose, dosage*
gasificar	*to gasify*	el gas	*gas*
glorificar	*to glorify*	la gloria	*glory, heaven*
orificar	*to fill a tooth*	el oro	*gold*
osificar	*to become hard(ened)*	os [LAT.]	*bone*
pacificar	*to pacify*	la paz	*peace*
santificar	*to sanctify, make holy*	el santo	*saint*

Complete each sentence with the correct form of the appropriate verb.

1. Cada vez que necesito tomar la medicina, tengo que _____ las píldoras de la botella.

2. Los padres tratan de _____ a su bebé cuando llora.

3. Es imposible _____ las estrellas en el cielo o los granos de arena de la playa.

4. Cuando tengo una caries, el dentista me _____ el diente cariado.

5. Él me trata como un objeto y estoy harto de esto. Él me _____ .

6. Necesito ordenar mi biblioteca, pero estoy muy cansado. Mañana voy a

   _____ los libros por tema.

7. Los miembros de casi cada religión _____ a su Dios.

8. Los maestros establecen un criterio para _____ a los estudiantes y les asignan el grado para el curso.

9. Para los cristianos es importante _____ el domingo.

10. En el proceso de _____ la madera, la madera se convierte en monóxido de carbono e hidrógeno.

11. El proceso de _____ una sustancia ocurre cuando se endurece hasta que sea similar a un hueso.

12. Según la Biblia, los asesinos de Jesucristo lo _____ en una cruz.

The following verbs ending in **-ificar** are based on adjectives.

VERB ENDING IN **-ificar**	ENGLISH EQUIVALENT	BASE WORD	ENGLISH EQUIVALENT
amplificar	*to amplify*	amplio	*large, ample*
beatificar	*to beatify*	beato	*blessed, devout*
certificar	*to certify*	cierto	*certain*
diversificar	*to diversify*	diverso	*diverse*
especificar	*to specify*	específico	*specific*
falsificar	*to falsify*	falso	*false*
fortificar	*to fortify*	fuerte	*strong, forceful*
intensificar	*to intensify*	intenso	*intense*
justificar	*to justify*	justo	*just, fair*
petrificar	*to petrify*	pétreo	*stony, of stone*
purificar	*to purify*	puro	*pure*
rectificar	*to rectify*	recto	*straight, right*
simplificar	*to simplify*	simple	*simple*
solidificar	*to solidify*	sólido	*solid*
tipificar	*to categorize*	típico	*typical, customary*
unificar	*to unify*	unido	*united*

Provide the verb ending in -ificar that is most closely related to each group of words.

1. facilitar, reducir, hacer más simple _____

2. corregir, reformar, enmendar, hacer más correcto _____

3. aumentar, acentuar, fortalecer, hacer más intenso _____

4. manipular, representar falsamente, engañar _____

5. fortalecer, robustecer, hacer más fuerte _____

6. igualar, conjuntar, agrupar, hacer más unido _____

7. endurecer, coagular, cohesionar, hacer más sólido _____

8. hacer más venerable, hacer más beato _____

9. hacer más grande, hacer más fuerte _____

10. fosilizar, osificar, calcificar, hacer rocoso _____

11. autentificar, asegurar, afirmar, hacer cierto _____

12. limpiar, higienizar, purgar, hacer puro _____

13. variar, diferenciar, cambiar, hacer diverso _____

14. precisar, detallar, determinar, hacer específico _____

15. defender, acreditar, razonar, hacer justo _____

26 ◆ -illa

MEANING	Diminutive
ENGLISH EQUIVALENT	*-ette*
PART OF SPEECH	Noun
GENDER	Feminine

The suffix **-illa** (masculine: **-illo**; see No. 27) is a common diminutive ending. The suffix may denote the diminished physical size of the base noun or its diminished status or function, sometimes circuitously; for example, **la rueda** *wheel, roller* yields **la rodilla** *knee*—the knee is a little roller in the leg.

The following nouns ending in **-illa** represent a physical diminution of their base nouns.

NOUN ENDING IN **-illa**	ENGLISH EQUIVALENT	BASE WORD	ENGLISH EQUIVALENT
la cadenilla	*small chain*	la cadena	*chain*
la cajetilla	*cigarette packet*	la cajeta	*small box*
la camilla	*stretcher, cot*	la cama	*bed*
la carretilla	*wheelbarrow*	la carreta	*cart, wagon*

▶

NOUN ENDING IN -illa	ENGLISH EQUIVALENT	BASE WORD	ENGLISH EQUIVALENT
la cocinilla	*kitchenette*	la cocina	*kitchen*
la cortinilla	*thin curtain, lace curtain*	la cortina	*curtain*
la escobilla	*whisk broom, brush*	la escoba	*broom*
la frutilla	*small fruit*	la fruta	*fruit*
la gavetilla	*small desk drawer*	la gaveta	*desk drawer*
la mariposilla	*small moth*	la mariposa	*butterfly, moth*
la mesilla	*side table, end table, nightstand*	la mesa	*table*
la sabanilla	*small sheet, napkin*	la sábana	*bedsheet*
la saetilla	*small arrow or dart*	la saeta	*arrow, dart*
la tortilla	*tortilla, omelet*	la torta	*cake*
la zapatilla	*slipper, sports shoe*	el zapato	*shoe*

EJERCICIO
26·1

¿Qué es esto? *Provide the correct noun (including its article) for each description.*

1. la fresa, la uva _____

2. donde se prepara la comida en un apartamento pequeño _____

3. el contenedor del relleno de un taco _____

4. donde el paciente se acuesta en la ambulancia _____

5. el calzado deportivo de Adidas o Nike _____

6. el paquete de los Marlboros o los Camels _____

7. una flecha pequeña _____

8. donde se pone la lámpara al lado de la cama _____

9. lo que se usa para transportar tierra _____

10. un insecto nocturnal que revolotea cerca de la luz _____

11. donde se guardan las plumas en el escritorio _____

12. lo que se usa para barrer un área pequeña _____

13. lo que cubre una ventana pequeña _____

14. lo que cubre el colchón de una cama pequeña _____

15. una sucesión de vínculos pequeños _____

The following nouns ending in **-illa** represent a figurative, sometimes delightfully creative, diminution of their base nouns.

NOUN ENDING IN **-illa**	ENGLISH EQUIVALENT	BASE WORD	ENGLISH EQUIVALENT
la barbilla	*point of the chin*	la barba	*beard*
la bombilla	*lightbulb*	la bomba	*bomb*
la cerilla	*earwax*	la cera	*wax*
la colilla	*cigarette butt*	la cola	*tail*
la estampilla	*postage stamp*	la estampa	*print, engraving*
la felpilla	*chenille*	la felpa	*plush, thick fabric*
la gacetilla	*gossip column*	la gaceta	*gazette, newspaper*
la gargantilla	*choker, small necklace*	la garganta	*throat*
la lanilla	*nap (of cloth), flannel*	la lana	*wool*
la manecilla	*hour hand on clock*	la mano	*hand*
la mantequilla	*butter*	la manteca	*lard*
la papadilla	*loose flesh on the throat*	la papada	*double chin, jowls*
la pastilla	*small portion, pill*	la pasta	*paste, dough*
la plumilla	*nib, fountain pen*	la pluma	*pen*
la rodilla	*knee*	la rueda	*wheel, roller*
la semilla	*seed*	el semen	*seed*

¿Verdadero o falso? *Indicate whether each statement is true or false, using* **V** *for* **verdadero** *true or* **F** *for* **falso** *false.*

1. _____ La felpilla es muy suave al tacto.

2. _____ No hay muchas calorías en la mantequilla.

3. _____ Los jardineros plantan millones de semillas en la primavera.

4. _____ Se encuentra la cerilla en la oreja.

5. _____ La papadilla se encuentra en el abdomen.

6. _____ Se encuentran las colillas en el cenicero.

7. _____ La rodilla es una parte de la pierna.

8. _____ Se encuentra la bombilla en la lámpara.

9. _____ Se encuentra la gacetilla en una novela.

10. _____ La manecilla es una parte del reloj.

11. _____ Se pone la estampilla en el sobre.

12. _____ La barbilla se encuentra bajo la boca.

13. _____ Se usa la gargantilla alrededor del cuello.

14. _____ Se encuentra la pastilla en el botiquín.

15. _____ Se encuentra la plumilla en el extremo del bolígrafo.

27 ▸ -illo

MEANING	Diminutive
ENGLISH EQUIVALENT	—
PART OF SPEECH	Noun
GENDER	Masculine

The suffix **-illo** (feminine: **-illa**; see No. 26) denotes smallness, either physical or figurative. Many of the nouns in the following charts are simply smaller versions of their base nouns (for example, **el librillo** *booklet, small book*, from **el libro** *book*), but sometimes the meaning shifts slightly (for example, **el cigarrillo** *cigarette*, from **el cigarro** *cigar*). Some of these nouns exhibit linguistic elasticity in their derivation; for example, **el véspero** *vesper, evening star* yields **el vespertillo** *bat* (the nocturnal mammal).

The following nouns ending in **-illo** represent a physical diminution of their base nouns.

NOUN ENDING IN **-illo**	ENGLISH EQUIVALENT	BASE WORD	ENGLISH EQUIVALENT
el balconcillo	*small balcony*	el balcón	*balcony*
el banquillo	*small bench*	el banco	*bench*
el bolsillo	*pocket*	el bolso	*bag*
el cachorrillo	*small puppy*	el cachorro	*puppy*
el cervatillo	*fawn*	el ciervo	*deer*
el cigarrillo	*cigarette*	el cigarro	*cigar*
el dragoncillo	*little dragon*	el dragón	*dragon*
el jaboncillo	*small bar of soap*	el jabón	*soap*
el librillo	*booklet, small book*	el libro	*book*
el perrillo	*small dog*	el perro	*dog*
el platillo	*saucer, small dish*	el plato	*plate, dish*
el plieguecillo	*folded half-sheet of paper*	el pliego	*sheet of paper*
el torillo	*little bull*	el toro	*bull*
el zarandillo	*small sieve*	la zaranda	*sifter, sieve*

EJERCICIO
27·1

Complete each sentence with the correct form of the appropriate noun.

1. En el baño de la habitación de un hotel se encuentra el _____.

2. James Bond fuma los _____ (¡uno tras otro!).

3. El niño de una vaca es el _____.

4. Bambi es un _____.

5. Una mini-Julieta le pregunta, "Romeo, Romeo, ¿dónde estás, Romeo?" de su

   _____.

6. En comparación con la novela *Guerra y paz* de León Tolstói, la obra *De ratones y hombres*

   de John Steinbeck es un _____.

7. Un mini-Enrique VIII come su banquete mientras está sentado en su

   _____.

8. Muchos hombres guardan la cartera en el _____ trasero.

9. Un mini-Beowulf muere luchando contra un _____.

10. Los extraterrestres viajan a la Tierra en un _____ volante.

11. Una mini-cocinero tamiza la harina con un _____.

12. Para escribir una nota corta, se necesita sólo un _____.

13. La cría de un chihuahua o de un pequinés es un _____, o dicho

de otra manera, un _____.

The following nouns ending in **-illo** represent a figurative, sometimes delightfully creative, diminution of their base nouns.

NOUN ENDING IN **-illo**	ENGLISH EQUIVALENT	BASE WORD	ENGLISH EQUIVALENT
el bocadillo	sandwich, snack	el bocado	mouthful, bite
el dedillo	fingertip	el dedo	finger
el farolillo	paper or Chinese lantern	el farol	lantern, streetlight
el flequillo	bangs	el fleco	fringe
el hornillo	camping stove	el horno	oven, furnace
el humillo	thin smoke, vapor	el humo	smoke
el nudillo	knuckle	el nudo	knot
el panecillo	roll	el pan	bread
el pasillo	hallway, aisle	el paso	walkway, path
el pecadillo	peccadillo, slight fault	el pecado	sin
el puntillo	petty point	el punto	point, period
el tinterillo	pen pusher, pencil pusher	la tinta	ink
el tornillo	screw	el torno	lathe, potter's wheel
el vespertillo	bat (animal)	el véspero	vesper, evening star

EJERCICIO

27·2

¿Verdadero o falso? *Indicate whether each statement is true or false, using* **V** *for* **verdadero** *true or* **F** *for* **falso** *false.*

1. _____ A los vespertillos les encantan comer los mosquitos.

2. _____ Algunas personas que siguen una dieta estricta llevan un registro de cada comida o bocadillo que comen, sin importar que sea pequeño.

3. _____ Todo el mundo luce bien con flequillo.

4. _____ A menudo, en un restaurante se sirve la ensalada con un panecillo.

5. _____ Para usar un tornillo, se necesita un destornillador—a veces un destornillador plano, a veces un destornillador de estrella.

6. _____ El asesinato es un pecadillo.

7. _____ Muchas personas creen que presionar los nudillos obsesivamente puede causar la artritis o resultar en otra discapacidad de las manos.

8. _____ Durante las celebraciones del Año Nuevo chino, se ven muchas grandes decoraciones, incluyendo farolillos y dragoncillos.

9. _____ Donde hay humillo, siempre hay incendio.

10. _____ Se usa el dedillo para tocar la pantalla táctil.

11. _____ Doctor Frankenstein usa varios hornillos en sus laboratorios.

12. _____ El tinterillo tiene trabajo fascinante y excitante.

13. _____ El Pentágono, la sede del Departamento de Defensa de los Estados Unidos, que está cerca de Washington, D.C., es un edificio enorme que tiene muchos kilómetros de pasillos.

 **28 ◆ -ín**

MEANING	Diminutive
ENGLISH EQUIVALENT	—
PART OF SPEECH	Noun
GENDER	Masculine

The suffix **-ín** may denote smallness, either in physical size or status (for example, **el violín** *violin*, from **la viola** *viola*). The suffix may also denote a useless or undesirable product of the base noun (for example, **el serrín** *sawdust*, from **la sierra** *saw*, and **el herrín** *rust*, from **el hierro** *iron*).

In the following nouns ending in -**ín**, the diminutive nature tends to be physical.

NOUN ENDING IN -ín	ENGLISH EQUIVALENT	BASE WORD	ENGLISH EQUIVALENT
el balín	pellet, buckshot	la bala	bullet
el banderín	small flag	la bandera	flag
el bolín	boccie or lawn bowling ball	la bola	ball
el botín	ankle boot	la bota	boot
el botiquín	medicine chest, first-aid kit	la botica	pharmacy
el cajetín	tiny box	la caja	box
el calabacín	zucchini	la calabaza	gourd, pumpkin
el calcetín	sock	la calceta	stocking
el camarín	alcove, boudoir	la cámara	room, chamber
el espadín	small dress sword, rapier	la espada	sword
el fajín	sash	la faja	large belt, girdle
el maletín	overnight case, briefcase	la maleta	suitcase
el sillín	saddle, bicycle seat	la silla	chair
el violín	violin	la viola	viola

¡Resuélvelo! *Provide the correct noun (including its article) for each description.*

1. un contenedor para los vendajes, el peróxido, las pinzas, etc. _____

2. donde se guarda una sortija de diamantes _____

3. el asiento en que te sientas cuando montas en bicicleta o a caballo _____

4. el instrumento musical de Isaac Stern, Joshua Bell y Anne-Sophie Mutter _____

5. la ropa para un día se lleva aquí cuando viajas _____

6. una verdura popular como ingrediente del pan _____

7. lo que te pones antes de ponerte los zapatos deportivos _____

8. el proyectil cuando se usa una carabina de aire comprimido _____

9. el calzado cuando no hay mucha nieve _____

10. un arma suficientemente pequeña como para esconder en el abrigo _____

11. la banda que distingue las candidatas por la corona de Miss Universo _____

12. lo que se ve con frecuencia en el Día de la Independencia _____

13. un cuarto pequeño para una conversación privada _____

14. el proyectil para jugar a la petanca _____

In the following nouns ending in **-ín**, the diminutive status tends to be figurative.

NOUN ENDING IN **-ín**	ENGLISH EQUIVALENT	BASE WORD	ENGLISH EQUIVALENT
el batín	*dressing gown*	la bata	*bathrobe*
el cafetín	*small coffeehouse*	el café	*café*
el camisolín	*dickey, shirtfront*	la camisa	*shirt*
el collarín	*priest's collar, surgical collar*	el collar	*collar*
el copetín	*cocktail, aperitif*	la copa	*alcoholic drink*
el faldellín	*underskirt, petticoat*	la falda	*skirt*
el herrín	*rust*	el hierro	*iron*
el labrantín	*small farmer*	el labrador	*laborer, farmer*
el langostín	*prawn*	la langosta	*lobster*
el llavín	*latchkey*	la llave	*key*
el magín	*fancy, imagination, mind*	el mago	*magician, wizard*
el malandrín	*rascal, scoundrel*	el malandar	*wild hog*
el pilotín	*pilot's apprentice*	el piloto	*pilot*
el pizarrín	*slate pencil*	la pizarra	*slate, blackboard*
el serrín	*sawdust*	la sierra	*saw*
el verdín	*pond scum, mold*	el verde	*the color green*

Match each noun in the second column with its description in the first column.

1. _____ un marisco popular

2. _____ el whisky escocés y soda

3. _____ lo que se necesita para abrir la puerta de la casa

4. _____ ropa sartorial que distingue un sacerdote

5. _____ un niño travieso

6. _____ un hombre con una granja pequeña

7. _____ lo que está en el suelo del carpintero

8. _____ donde se sirven las bebidas con expreso

9. _____ un aprendiz que quiere ser piloto

10. _____ lo que se lleva debajo de un vestido

11. _____ lo que se lleva debajo de un suéter con escote en V

12. _____ el producto de la oxidación del hierro

13. _____ de donde viene una idea creativa

14. _____ la ropa como un kimono

15. _____ el alga de estanque encima del agua

16. _____ un utensilio para escribir en la sala de clase

a. el batín

b. el cafetín

c. el camisolín

d. el collarín

e. el copetín

f. el faldellín

g. el herrín

h. el labrantín

i. el langostín

j. el llavín

k. el magín

l. el malandrín

m. el pilotín

n. el pizarrín

o. el serrín

p. el verdín

29 ◆ -ina

MEANING	Diminutive; female counterpart
ENGLISH EQUIVALENT	*-ine*
PART OF SPEECH	Noun
GENDER	Feminine

The suffix **-ina** may denote smallness, either physical (for example, **la filmina** *slide, transparency,* from **el filme** *film*) or figurative (for example, **la neblina** *mist, haze,* from **la niebla** *fog*). It may also denote the female counterpart of the base noun (for example, **la heroína** *heroine,* from **el héroe** *hero*). This latter use may also be applied to personal names (for example, **Carolina** *Caroline,* from **Carlos** *Charles*).

NOUN ENDING IN -ina	ENGLISH EQUIVALENT	BASE WORD	ENGLISH EQUIVALENT
la bronquina [COLLOQ.]	*dispute, quarrel*	la bronca	*quarrel, ruckus*
la chocolatina	*chocolate bar*	el chocolate	*chocolate*
la escarlatina	*scarlet fever*	la escarlata	*the color scarlet*
la filmina	*slide, transparency*	el filme	*film*
la llantina	*sobbing*	el llanto	*crying*
la marina	*shore, seacoast, navy*	el mar	*sea*
la neblina	*mist, haze*	la niebla	*fog*
la oficina	*office*	el oficio	*job, trade*
la palomina	*pigeon dung*	la paloma	*pigeon, dove*
la piscina	*swimming pool, fish pond*	piscis [LAT.]	*fish*
la sonatina	*sonatina, short sonata*	la sonata	*sonata*
la sordina	*mute, piano damper*	el sordo	*deaf person*
la turbina	*turbine*	el turbo	*turbo mode, turbocharger*

EJERCICIO

29·1

¿Verdadero o falso? *Indicate whether each statement is true or false, using* **V** *for* **verdadero** *true or* **F** *for* **falso** *false.*

1. _____ Se nada en la piscina.

2. _____ La escarlatina no es una enfermedad seria.

3. _____ Se encuentra la sordina en el piano.

4. _____ Los científicos miran muchas filminas.

5. _____ Los burócratas no trabajan en una oficina.

6. _____ Beethoven es famoso por varias sonatas y sonatinas.

7. _____ Es agradable tener una bronquina durante una cena formal.

8. _____ Se encuentra la palomina en las aceras y los parques.

9. _____ Es agradable escuchar la llantina de un bebé con cólicos.

10. _____ Hay turbinas de gas, de vapor, de agua y de aire.

11. _____ Está húmedo cuando hay neblina.

12. _____ A casi todo el mundo le gusta una chocolatina, pero las personas que tienen una alergia a las nueces no pueden comer la chocolatina con almendras.

13. _____ La marina está en la tierra adentro.

NOUN ENDING IN -ina	ENGLISH EQUIVALENT	BASE WORD	ENGLISH EQUIVALENT
Agustina	*Augustine*	Agustín	*Augustine*
Angelina	*Angelina*	ángel	*angel*
la bailarina	*ballerina*	el bailarín	*male ballet dancer*
Carolina	*Caroline*	Carlos	*Charles*
Cristina	*Christine*	Cristo	*Christ*
la gallina	*hen*	el gallo	*rooster*
Geraldina	*Geraldine*	Geraldo	*Gerald*
Guillermina	*Wilhelmina*	Guillermo	*William*
la heroína	*heroine*	el héroe	*hero*
Josefina	*Josephine*	José	*Joseph*
la madrina	*godmother, sponsor*	la madre	*mother*
la reina	*queen*	el rey	*king*
Serafina	*Serafina*	el serafín	*angel, seraph*
Tomasina	*Thomasina*	Tomás	*Thomas*

EJERCICIO
29·2

Provide the correct noun(s) (including the article, where appropriate) for each description.

1. la madre de un pollito _____

2. una danzante _____

3. Elizabeth o Victoria de la familia real inglesa _____

4. una mujer muy valiente _____

5. la hada que le da a Cenicienta los zapatos de cristal _____

6. dos nombres de mujer que significan "ángel" _____

_____

7. la forma femenina de Carlos _____

8. la forma femenina de Tomás _____

9. la forma femenina de Guillermo _____

10. la cantante famosa cuyo apellido es Aguilera _____

11. la forma femenina de José _____

12. la forma femenina de Agustín _____

13. la forma femenina de Geraldo _____

30 ◆ -ino

MEANING	Diminutive; place where
ENGLISH EQUIVALENT	—
PART OF SPEECH	Noun
GENDER	Masculine

The suffix **-ino** usually denotes smallness (for example, **el ansarino** *gosling*, from **el ánsar** *goose, gander*). The suffix may, however, denote the place where the action of the base verb occurs (for example, **el molino** *mill*, from **moler** *to grind*). The related feminine suffix -ina (No. 29) is more common, but similar in function.

NOUN ENDING IN **-ino**	ENGLISH EQUIVALENT	BASE WORD	ENGLISH EQUIVALENT
el ansarino	*gosling*	el ánsar	*goose, gander*
el camino	*road, path*	caminar	*to walk*
el casino	*casino, social club*	la casa	*house, home*
el cebollino	*chives*	la cebolla	*onion*
el colino	*small plot of cabbage*	la col	*cabbage*
el michino	*kitty, pussycat*	el micho	*cat, puss*
el molino	*mill*	moler	*to grind*
el padrino	*godfather, best man*	el padre	*father*
el palomino	*young pigeon*	la paloma	*pigeon*
el pollino [COLLOQ.]	*ass, idiot*	el pollo [COLLOQ.]	*young lad*
el porrino	*tender leek plant*	el puerro	*leek*
el vellocino	*fleece*	el vello	*fuzz, soft hair*

EJERCICIO
30·1

Complete each sentence with the correct form of the appropriate noun.

1. Típicamente se encuentra el _____ de boda junto al novio durante la ceremonia.

2. El hijito de Mamá Ganso es el _____.

3. Un pájaro joven que se suele encontrar en las ciudades grandes es un

   _____.

4. El _____ dice "¡miau!" y le gusta jugar con ovillos.

5. Un textil de _____ es suave y muy caliente.

6. Se prepara el chucrut (*sauerkraut*) de la cosecha del _____.

7. Si quiere cocinar con el puerro muy tierno, hay que hallar el _____.

8. Se usa el _____, una hierba aromática, para sazonar los guisos.

9. Se puede decir que un joven que se comporta muy tontamente es un

   _____.

10. Un poema popular, bien conocido y frecuentemente citado, es "El _____ no elegido."

11. La máquina que muele el harina es el _____.

12. En un _____ se encuentran los juegos como la ruleta, el blackjack, el póquer y las máquinas tragamonedas.

31 ◆ -ísimo/-ísima

MEANING	Superlative
ENGLISH EQUIVALENT	—
PART OF SPEECH	Adjective
GENDER	Masculine/feminine

The most common superlative ending for Spanish adjectives is -**ísimo** (feminine: -**ísima**). Adjectives with this suffix may assume a range of nuances: *very, extremely, really, extraordinarily, super,* and more. Typical formation consists in omitting the vowel (if there is one) at the end of an adjective and adding the suffix (for example, **claro** *clear* yields **clarísimo** *extremely clear*). Common exceptions follow.

1. If the base adjective ends in -**ble**, **i** is added between the **b** and the **l** (for example, **amable** *kind, nice* yields **amabilísimo** *extremely kind*).

2. Since this suffix begins in accented **í**, standard orthographic changes apply: **c** > **qu** (**rico** yields **riquísimo**), **z** > **c** (**feliz** yields **felicísimo**), and **g** > **gu** (**largo** yields **larguísimo**).

3. If the base adjective ends in -**io**, the **i** is also omitted before the suffix -**ísimo** is added (**sucio** yields **sucísimo**).

The following adjectives ending in -**ísimo** exhibit orthographic changes.

ADJECTIVE ENDING IN -ísimo	ENGLISH EQUIVALENT	BASE WORD	ENGLISH EQUIVALENT
amabilísimo	*extremely kind*	amable	*kind, nice*
felicísimo	*extremely happy*	feliz	*happy*
ferventísimo	*extremely fervent*	ferviente	*fervent*
jovencísimo	*extremely young*	joven	*young*
larguísimo	*extremely long*	largo	*long*
nobilísimo	*most noble*	noble	*noble*
notabilísimo	*most notable*	notable	*notable*
poquísimo	*extremely small*	poco	*small (amount)*
probabilísimo	*extremely likely*	probable	*probable, likely*
riquísimo	*extremely rich*	rico	*rich*
sucísimo	*extremely filthy*	sucio	*dirty*
valentísimo	*most valiant*	valiente	*valiant*
venerabilísimo	*most venerable*	venerable	*venerable*

EJERCICIO
31·1

Complete each sentence with the correct form of the appropriate adjective.

1. Un billonario es _____.

2. Una persona con una sonrisa enorme está _____.

3. El pelo de Lady Godiva es _____.

4. Muchos católicos creen que el Papa es _____.

5. Un infante de tres días es _____.

6. Un grano de arena es _____.

7. Una persona que quiere algo entusiastamente está _____.

8. Madre Teresa era _____.

9. Se dice que un guerrero muy honrado es _____ y

   _____.

10. Una persona extremadamente famosa es _____.

11. La posibilidad que el sol vaya a aparecer mañana es _____.

12. Un cuarto que nunca se limpia por nadie está _____.

The adjectives in the following exercise are formed regularly. If the base adjective ends in a vowel, the vowel is replaced by -**ísimo**; if the base adjective ends in a consonant, -**ísimo** is added directly to the adjective.

EJERCICIO
31·2

¡Resuélvelo! *Provide the correct form of the adjective ending in -**ísimo** for each English equivalent. The base word for each adjective in -**ísimo** is provided for you.*

ADJECTIVE ENDING IN -ísimo	ENGLISH EQUIVALENT	BASE WORD	ENGLISH EQUIVALENT
1. _____	*most blessed*	beato	*blessed, devout*
2. _____	*extremely beautiful*	bello	*fair, beautiful*
3. _____	*extremely good*	bueno	*good*
4. _____	*extremely clear*	claro	*clear*
5. _____	*extremely thin*	delgado	*thin, slim*
6. _____	*extremely delicate*	delicado	*delicate, dainty*
7. _____	*most excellent*	excelente	*excellent*
8. _____	*extremely ugly*	feo	*ugly*
9. _____	*huge*	grande	*big, large*

10. _____	*very handsome*	guapo	*handsome*
11. _____	*very beautiful*	hermoso	*beautiful*
12. _____	*most illustrious*	ilustre	*illustrious*
13. _____	*very important*	importante	*important*
14. _____	*squeaky clean*	limpio	*clean*
15. _____	*extremely bad*	malo	*bad*
16. _____	*a huge amount of*	mucho	*much, a lot*
17. _____	*very pale, ashen*	pálido	*pale*
18. _____	*extremely small*	pequeño	*small*
19. _____	*extremely holy*	santo	*holy, blessed*
20. _____	*extremely tranquil*	tranquilo	*tranquil, calm*

32 ◆ -ismo

MEANING	System, doctrine, attitude, way of life
ENGLISH EQUIVALENT	*-ism*
PART OF SPEECH	Noun
GENDER	Masculine

Although the suffix **-ismo** may confer a specific meaning on a base noun or adjective, its basic function can be reduced to expanding from a particular. For example, **el vándalo** *vandal* yields **el vandalismo** *vandalism*, which encompasses all vandals and their illicit actions.

Each of the following nouns ending in **-ismo** represents a way of life, a personal philosophy, or a personal characteristic.

NOUN ENDING IN **-ismo**	ENGLISH EQUIVALENT	BASE WORD	ENGLISH EQUIVALENT
el alcoholismo	*alcoholism*	el alcohol	*alcohol*
el egoísmo	*egoism*	el ego	*ego, self*
el esnobismo	*snobbery, snobbishness*	el esnob	*snob*
el feísmo	*cult of the hideous*	feo	*ugly*
el hipnotismo	*hypnotism*	la hipnosis	*hypnosis*
el idealismo	*idealism*	el ideal	*ideal*
el idiotismo	*ignorance*	el idiota	*idiot*
el machismo	*chauvinism*	el macho	*male*
el magnetismo	*magnetism*	el magneto	*magnet*
el materialismo	*materialism*	el material	*material*
el narcisismo	*narcissism*	Narciso	*Narcissus*
el narcotismo	*drug addiction*	el narcótico	*narcotic*
el tabaquismo	*addiction to smoking*	el tabaco	*tobacco*
el terrorismo	*terrorism*	el terror	*terror*
el vandalismo	*vandalism*	el vándalo	*vandal*

Provide the correct noun(s) (including the article) for the description of each type of activity.

1. Fuma los cigarrillos y la marihuana todo el día. _____

2. Consuma drogas como la heroína y la cocaína todo el día. _____

3. Toma el ron, la tequila o el vino todo el día. _____

4. Cree que los hombres son superiores a las mujeres. _____

5. Va de compras todo el día porque no puede tener suficientes cosas. _____

6. Le encanta la estupidez. _____

7. Le encanta todo lo que sea repugnante, disforme y desagradable. _____

8. Le encanta influir o dirigir por el mesmerismo. _____

9. Le encanta hablar de sí mismo. _____
_____

10. Cree que es mejor que los otros y los mira don desdén. _____

11. Usa la violencia y la intimidación para alcanzar sus objetivos políticos. _____

12. Destruye intencionalmente y maliciosamente la propiedad de otra persona. _____

13. Siempre cree que lo mejor está por venir. _____

14. Tiene atracción muy fuerte a otra persona. _____

The following nouns ending in **-ismo** represent organized systems or doctrines based on religion, politics, or nationality.

NOUN ENDING IN **-ismo**	ENGLISH EQUIVALENT	BASE WORD	ENGLISH EQUIVALENT
el argentinismo	*Argentinism*	Argentina	*Argentina*
el ateísmo	*atheism*	el ateo	*atheist*
el catolicismo	*Catholicism*	el católico	*Catholic*
el conservadurismo	*conservatism*	conservativo	*conservative*
el deísmo	*deism*	dios	*god*
el despotismo	*despotism*	el déspota	*despot*
el españolismo	*devotion to Spain*	España	*Spain*
el judaísmo	*Judaism*	el judío	*Jew*
el mejicanismo	*Mexicanism*	Méjico	*Mexico*
el mormonismo	*Mormonism*	el mormón	*Mormon*
el nacionalismo	*nationalism*	nacional	*national*
el obrerismo	*labor movement*	el obrero	*laborer*
el paganismo	*paganism*	el pagano	*pagan*
el patriotismo	*patriotism*	la patria	*native land*
el teísmo	*theism*	theos [GRK.]	*god*

Provide the correct noun(s) (including the article) for the description of each type of activity.

1. Le encantan Madrid, Barcelona y Toledo. _____

2. Le encantan Guadalajara, Juárez y el Distrito Federal. _____

3. Le encantan Buenos Aires, Córdoba y Rosario. _____

4. Le encantan las enseñanzas de Iván el Terrible, Pol Pot y Tamerlane. _____

5. Lucha por los derechos de los trabajadores. _____

6. No cree en Dios en ninguna forma. _____

7. Practica la misma religión que el Papa del Vaticano. _____

8. Cree en el Dios de Abraham, Isaac y Jacob, como se describe en la Torá. _____

9. Su religión es la de los wicanos y unas brujas. _____

10. Cree en el Dios de la Iglesia de los Santos de los Últimos Días. _____

11. En la política, es el contrario del liberalismo. _____

12. Le encanta su propio país. _____

13. Cree en Dios. _____

_____

33 ◆ -ista

MEANING	Performer, expert
ENGLISH EQUIVALENT	*-ist*
PART OF SPEECH	Noun
GENDER	Masculine/feminine

Most Spanish suffixes that denote persons have different masculine and feminine forms (for example, **-ero/-era** and **-dor/-dora**). The suffix **-ista**, however, may be masculine or feminine (for example, **el/la dentista** *dentist*), and the gender of the person is determined from context or by the gender of a modifying article or adjective. Nouns ending in **-ista** are usually derived from nouns, but some are derived from adjectives.

The following nouns ending in **-ista** represent persons in the arts and humanities, or who perform specific jobs.

NOUN ENDING IN -ista	ENGLISH EQUIVALENT	BASE WORD	ENGLISH EQUIVALENT
el acuarelista	*watercolor artist*	la acuarela	*watercolor*
el artista	*artist*	el arte	*art*
el clarinetista	*clarinetist*	el clarinete	*clarinet*
el dentista	*dentist*	el diente	*tooth*
el flautista	*flutist*	la flauta	*flute*
el florista	*florist*	la flor	*flower*
el inversionista	*investor*	la inversión	*investment*
el licorista	*liquor dealer, liquor seller*	el licor	*liquor*
el maquinista	*machinist*	la máquina	*machine*
el paisajista	*landscape painter*	el paisaje	*landscape, scenery*
el percusionista	*percussionist*	la percusión	*percussion*
el periodista	*journalist*	el periódico	*newspaper*
el pianista	*pianist*	el piano	*piano*
el violinista	*violinist*	el violín	*violin*
el vocabulista	*a student of vocabulary*	el vocablo	*word*

EJERCICIO
33·1

Provide the correct noun (including its article) for each person's description.

1. Toca un instrumento de Stradivarius o Amati. _____

2. Toca un instrumento de Steinway, Kawai o Yamaha. _____

3. Toca la batería, el xilófono, el timbal, la pandereta y el címbalo. _____

4. Toca el instrumento preferido de Benny Goodman, Artie Shaw, Woody Allen y Mitch Blatt. _____

5. Toca el instrumento preferido de Sir James Galway y Jean-Pierre Rampal. _____

6. Vende los lirios, las margaritas, las rosas y las violetas. _____

7. Vende el vino, la cerveza, el ron, la vodka y el whisky. _____

8. Escribe artículos para el *New York Times*. _____

9. Es un cliente de Goldman Sachs, Deutsche Bank o Credit Suisse. _____

10. Usa varias herramientas, incluyendo el torno, la perforadora y el martillo. _____

11. Atende a los pacientes que tienen la gingivitis o una enfermedad de las encías. _____

12. Trabaja con muchas listas de palabras. _____

13. Es escultor, pintor o ceramista. _____

14. Pinta escenas exteriores, especialmente las del campo. _____

15. Pinta con colores diluidos en agua sobre papel o cartulina. _____

The following nouns ending in **-ista** represent persons with particular orientations, talents, or political or religious leanings.

NOUN ENDING IN **-ista**	ENGLISH EQUIVALENT	BASE WORD	ENGLISH EQUIVALENT
el andinista	*mountain climber*	los Andes	*the Andes*
el bautista	*one who baptizes*	bautizar	*to baptize*
el budista	*Buddhist*	Buda	*Buddha*
el capitalista	*capitalist*	el capital	*capital*
el carterista	*pickpocket*	la cartera	*wallet*
el ciclista	*cyclist*	el ciclo	*cycle*
el comunista	*communist*	común	*common*
el cuentista	*storyteller*	el cuento	*short story, tale*
el deportista	*sportsman*	el deporte	*sport*
el fatalista	*fatalist*	fatal	*fatal*
el optimista	*optimist*	óptimo	*ideal, optimal*
el pacifista	*pacifist*	la paz	*peace*
el perfeccionista	*perfectionist*	la perfección	*perfection*
el pesimista	*pessimist*	pésimo	*dreadful, disastrous*
el terrorista	*terrorist*	el terror	*terror*

EJERCICIO

33·2

Provide the correct noun (including its article) for each person's description.

1. Le encanta montar en bicicleta. _____

2. Le encanta ver siempre lo bueno de las cosas. _____

3. Tiende a fijarse en lo negativo. _____

4. Le encanta robar a las personas inocentes, especialmente a los turistas. _____

5. Le disgustan la guerra y todo lo relacionado con el combate. _____

6. El Dalái Lama es su líder espiritual. _____

7. Le encanta subir a las montañas. _____

8. Cree que la vida es predeterminada. _____

9. Le encantan los escritos de Karl Marx y Vladimir Lenin. _____

10. Un escritor como Aesop, Homer o Mamá Ganso. _____

11. El clérigo que celebra la entrada a la comunidad cristiana. _____

12. Cree que un error de cualquier clase no es aceptable. _____

13. Un financista o empresario como Gordon Gekko, el protagonista de la película *Wall Street*. _____

14. Le encanta jugar al fútbol, al béisbol o al baloncesto, por ejemplo. _____

15. Es un fanático que trata de alcanzar un gol político usando la violencia. _____

34 ◆ -ita

MEANING	Diminutive
ENGLISH EQUIVALENT	—
PART OF SPEECH	Noun
GENDER	Feminine

The suffix **-ita** (masculine: **-ito**; see No. 35) denotes smallness. Most nouns with this suffix, but not all, are derived from feminine nouns.

The following nouns ending in **-ita** represent living beings, their body parts, or their characteristics transferred to animals, including people, and things.

NOUN ENDING IN **-ita**	ENGLISH EQUIVALENT	BASE WORD	ENGLISH EQUIVALENT
la chiquita	*little girl*	la chica	*girl*
la hormiguita	*tiny little ant*	la hormiga	*ant*
la manecita	*small hand, clock hand*	la mano	*hand*
la patita	*small foot*	la pata	*foot, paw*
la pollita [COLLOQ.]	*"chick," girl*	el pollo	*chicken*
la ramita	*sprig, twig*	la rama	*branch*
la señorita	*Miss, young lady*	la señora	*Mrs., lady*
la sortijita	*little ring, ringlet*	la sortija	*ring, curl (hair)*
las trencitas [PL.]	*braids, plaits*	la trenza	*braided hair, tresses*
la vaquita	*small cow*	la vaca	*cow*
la viejecita	*little old woman*	la vieja	*elderly woman*
la viudita	*little widow*	la viuda	*widow*

EJERCICIO 34·1

Complete each sentence with the correct form of the appropriate noun.

1. En su niñez, la gallina es una _____.

2. En su niñez, la hija de un toro es una _____.

3. En su niñez, la mujer es una _____.

4. En su adolescencia, la mujer es una _____.

5. Se puede decir que una mujer anciana es una _____.

6. Esta misma mujer anciana, después de la muerte de su esposo, es una

   _____.

7. Un insecto joven que invade los picnics es una _____.

8. Los peinados populares entre las jóvenes incluyen las _____ como Pippi Longstocking.

9. El pelo del caniche destaca por sus rizos y las _____.

10. Al extremo de una pierna pequeña de un animal, típicamente se encuentra una

    _____.

11. Al extremo de un brazo menudo y delgado, típicamente se encuentra una

_____.

12. Después de una tormenta se encuentran muchas _____ sobre el terreno en un parque.

The following nouns ending in -**ita** represent inanimate objects or temporal concepts.

NOUN ENDING IN -**ita**	ENGLISH EQUIVALENT	BASE WORD	ENGLISH EQUIVALENT
la bolita	*little ball, bead*	la bola	*ball*
la cajita	*small box*	la caja	*box*
la caperucita	*little hood or cap*	la caperuza	*pointed hood or cap*
la cunita	*little cradle*	la cuna	*cradle*
la espadita	*small sword*	la espada	*sword*
la nochecita	*nightfall, dusk*	la noche	*night*
la notita	*short note*	la nota	*note*
la ollita	*small pot*	la olla	*pot*
la pajita	*drinking straw*	la paja	*straw*
la palabrita	*brief word*	la palabra	*word*
la pesita	*small weight*	el peso	*weight*
la velita	*little candle*	la vela	*candle*

EJERCICIO
34·2

¿Verdadero o falso? *Indicate whether each statement is true or false, using* **V** *for* **verdadero** *true or* **F** *for* **falso** *false.*

1. _____ Muchas personas prefieren beber una malteada con una pajita.

2. _____ El gigante guarda los zapatos en cajitas.

3. _____ Muchas personas encienden una velita en la iglesia en memoria de alguien especial.

4. _____ Después de recibir un regalo, una notita de agradecimiento siempre es apreciada.

5. _____ Cuando una persona reza el rosario, cada bolita o cuenta del rosario representa un ave María y las cuentas más grandes representan un padrenuestro.

6. _____ Los hijos adultos de Hércules duermen en una cunita.

7. _____ A veces a la nochecita se puede ver los murciélagos volando por encima.

8. _____ El elogio típico es poco más que una palabrita o dos.

9. _____ El enemigo de la Caperucita Roja es el Lobo Feroz.

10. _____ La ollita de fondue típicamente contiene queso o chocolate caliente.

11. _____ Una tonelada es una pesita.

12. _____ El arma preferida de un guerrero diminuto puede ser una espadita.

35 ◆ -ito

MEANING	Diminutive
ENGLISH EQUIVALENT	—
PART OF SPEECH	Noun
GENDER	Masculine

The suffix **-ito** (feminine: **-ita**; see No. 34) may denote physical smallness, especially if affixed to nouns representing animals. The suffix may also connote softness or sweetness, thereby creating familiar and endearing terms. Note, for example, **el corazoncito** *dear little heart.*

The following words ending in **-ito** represent living beings or terms of endearment for them.

NOUN ENDING IN **-ito**	ENGLISH EQUIVALENT	BASE WORD	ENGLISH EQUIVALENT
el abuelito	*grandpa*	el abuelo	*grandfather*
el amiguito	*little friend, buddy*	el amigo	*friend*
el burrito	*little donkey*	el burro	*donkey, burro*
el caballito	*little horse*	el caballo	*horse*
el cerdito	*piglet*	el cerdo	*pig*
el conejito	*little rabbit, bunny*	el conejo	*rabbit*
el gatito	*kitten, kitty*	el gato	*cat*
el halconcito	*small falcon or hawk*	el halcón	*falcon, hawk*
el hijito	*little child, sonny*	el hijo	*son*
el huerfanito	*little orphan*	el huérfano	*orphan*
el pajarito	*little bird/birdie*	el pájaro	*bird*
el patito	*duckling*	el pato	*duck*
el perrito	*little dog, puppy*	el perro	*dog*
el pobrecito	*poor little person*	el pobre	*poor person*
el viejecito	*little old man*	el viejo	*old man*

EJERCICIO
35·1

Complete each sentence with the correct form of the appropriate noun.

1. El hijo de Eeyore (el amigo de Pooh) es un _____.

2. El hijo de Lassie o Benji es un _____.

3. El hijo de Lucifer (*Cinderella*) o Garfield es un _____.

4. El hijo de Wilbur (*La telaraña de Charlotte*) es un _____.

5. El hijo de Seabiscuit, Flicka o Secretariat es un _____.

6. El hijo de Bugs Bunny es un _____.

7. El hijo de Donald, Daisy o Daffy es un _____.

8. El hijo de Tweety o un loro es un _____.

9. La cría de un tipo de ave predadora es un _____.

10. El personaje Oliver (de *Oliver Twist* por Charles Dickens) es un _____.

11. Un chico favorecido por su papá es llamado un _____.

12. Se refiere con cariño al padre del papá o de la mamá como el _____.

13. Se refiere a un chico sin dinero y también patético como un _____.

14. Frecuentemente se refiere a un anciano como el _____.

15. Bashful, Doc, Sleepy, Sneezy, Dopey, Grumpy y Happy son los siete

_____ de Blancanieves.

The following nouns ending in **-ito** represent inanimate objects or terms of endearment.

NOUN ENDING IN **-ito**	ENGLISH EQUIVALENT	BASE WORD	ENGLISH EQUIVALENT
el adiosito	*saying ta-ta/bye-bye*	el adiós	*saying good-bye*
el besito	*little kiss*	el beso	*kiss*
el cajoncito	*small drawer, desk drawer*	el cajón	*drawer*
el cochecito	*baby carriage, pram*	el coche	*car, carriage*
el corazoncito	*dear little heart*	el corazón	*heart*
el corralito	*playpen*	el corral	*yard, barnyard*
el granito	*small grain, pimple*	el grano	*grain*
el momentito	*tiny bit of time*	el momento	*moment*
el pedacito	*small bit, tiny piece*	el pedazo	*piece*
el poquito	*tiny amount*	el poco	*small amount*
el puentecito	*small bridge, footbridge*	el puente	*bridge*
el ratito	*little while*	el rato	*short time, awhile*
el regalito	*little gift*	el regalo	*gift, present*
el saltito	*little hop or leap*	el salto	*jump, leap*
el traguito	*short swig, nip*	el trago	*swallow, gulp*

EJERCICIO
35·2

Complete each sentence with the correct form of the appropriate noun.

1. En muchas casas, el bebé juega en el _____.

2. Con frecuencia una madre le da muchos _____ a la cara de su precioso bebé.

3. Cuando una madre pasea por el parque, frecuentemente su bebé está durmiendo en

el _____.

4. Cuando vas a una fiesta, es cortés comprar un _____ para los anfitriones.

5. Al salir de la casa de un buen amigo, en vez de decirle el adiós formal, se puede decirle

más informalmente un _____.

6. Muchos adolescentes sufren del acné y tienen unos _____ en la cara y la espalda.

7. Cuando una persona quiere perder peso, es importante hacer más ejercicio y comer menos comida, optando por _____ de comida en vez de, por ejemplo, una pizza entera.

8. Cuando una persona quiere perder diez libras en una semana, sólo puede comer un _____ cada día (o no comer en absoluto).

9. Muchos escritorios tienen varios _____ para contener y organizar los lápices, las plumas, los clips y los papelitos.

10. En un parque, se necesita un _____ para pasar al otro lado de un estanque.

11. Si el estanque es muy pequeño, es posible cruzarlo simplemente por dar un _____.

12. Una calculadora puede sumar o restar números dentro de un _____.

13. La persona que posterga todo siempre le dice a la persona que le pide algo, "mañana" o "en un _____."

14. La persona que abstiene totalmente de tomar las bebidas alcohólicas no toma siquiera un _____ ni del vino ni de la cerveza.

15. El hijito del "Hombre de hojalata" (de *El maravilloso Mago de Oz*) no tiene un _____.

36 ◆ -ivo/-iva

MEANING	Characterized by a tone/manner
ENGLISH EQUIVALENT	*-ive*
PART OF SPEECH	Adjective
GENDER	Masculine/feminine

Because many Spanish adjectives ending in **-ivo/-iva** have English cognates ending in *-ive*, they tend to be easily recognized and used.

The following adjectives ending in **-ivo/-iva** are derived from verbs and denote tone or manner.

ADJECTIVE ENDING IN **-ivo**	ENGLISH EQUIVALENT	BASE WORD	ENGLISH EQUIVALENT
abusivo	*abusive*	abusar	*to abuse*
administrativo	*administrative*	administrar	*to administer, manage*
admirativo	*admiring, full of admiration*	admirar	*to admire*
declarativo	*declarative*	declarar	*to declare, state*
defensivo	*defensive*	defender	*to defend*

ADJECTIVE ENDING IN **-ivo**	ENGLISH EQUIVALENT	BASE WORD	ENGLISH EQUIVALENT
descriptivo	*descriptive*	describir	*to describe*
digestivo	*digestive*	digerir	*to digest, take in*
educativo	*educational*	educar	*to educate*
ejecutivo	*executive*	ejecutar	*to execute, carry out*
evocativo	*evocative*	evocar	*to evoke*
evolutivo	*evolutionary*	evolucionar	*to evolve*
exclamativo	*exclamatory*	exclamar	*to exclaim, cry out*
exclusivo	*exclusive*	excluir	*to exclude*
expansivo	*expansive*	expansionar	*to expand*
expeditivo	*expeditious, prompt*	expedir	*to expedite, dispatch*

Complete each sentence with the correct form of the appropriate adjective.

1. Una oración _____ es una frase que informa objetivamente.

2. Una oración _____ es una frase que expresa emociones.

3. Se vomita del tracto _____.

4. Se necesita una invitación para asistir a una fiesta _____.

5. Charles Darwin, el naturalista y geólogo inglés, es más conocido por sus estudios

   _____.

6. El objetivo _____ de cada escuela buena es que cada estudiante
   aprenda mucho.

7. Un hombre que golpea a su mujer y le grita a ella es un esposo _____.

8. Algunas personas mantienen una pistola cargada en casa como arma

   _____ contra los ladrones.

9. Cada madre orgullosa tiene una expresión _____ al ver a su niño
   perfecto.

10. Un relato no verdaderamente _____ del verdadero acontecimiento
    es una mentira.

11. La sensación olfativa tiene una gran capacidad _____ y puede
    transportarse a otro tiempo y lugar.

12. En una corporación, muchos empleados quieren ser promovidos al nivel

    _____ o _____.

13. Todas las personas que esperan el reembolso de impuestos esperan que sea un proceso

    _____.

ADJECTIVE ENDING IN -ivo	ENGLISH EQUIVALENT	BASE WORD	ENGLISH EQUIVALENT
ilustrativo	*serving as an example*	ilustrar	*to illustrate*
imaginativo	*imaginative*	imaginar	*to imagine*
imperativo	*obligatory*	imperar	*to command, prevail*
inclusivo	*inclusive*	incluir	*to include*
indicativo	*indicative*	indicar	*to indicate*
interrogativo	*interrogative*	interrogar	*to interrogate, question*
nutritivo	*nutritious*	nutrir	*to nourish, feed*
ofensivo	*offensive*	ofender	*to offend*
representativo	*representative*	representar	*to represent*
repulsivo	*repulsive*	repulsar	*to reject*
restrictivo	*restrictive*	restringir	*to restrict, limit*
sedativo	*sedative*	sedar	*to sedate*
subjuntivo	*subjunctive*	sub- + jungere [LAT.]	*under + to yoke*

EJERCICIO
36·2

¿Verdadero o falso? *Indicate whether each statement is true or false, using* **V** *for* **verdadero** *true or* **F** *for* **falso** *false.*

1. _____ Una persona con muchas ideas creativas es imaginativa.

2. _____ Un ojo amoratado es ilustrativo de la violencia doméstica.

3. _____ Un hombre repulsivo y ofensivo es un esposo magnífico.

4. _____ Muchas personas creen que la comida de McDonald's no tiene valor nutritivo.

5. _____ La segregación racial es muy inclusiva.

6. _____ Las drogas tranquilizantes tienen un efectivo sedativo.

7. _____ Hacer lo correcto es imperativo para las personas con sólidos principios morales.

8. _____ El gobierno representativo es esencial para una democracia.

9. _____ Un ego enorme y la falta de amigos son señales indicativos de un narcisista.

10. _____ Una oración interrogativa es, en realidad, una pregunta.

11. _____ Todas las frases en la forma subjuntiva son verdaderas.

12. _____ No existan reglas restrictivas en los aeropuertos.

37 ◆ -ívoro/-ívora

MEANING	Person/animal that eats
ENGLISH EQUIVALENT	*-ivore, -ivorous*
PART OF SPEECH	Noun, adjective

Words with the suffix **-ívoro/-ívora** denote eaters and their eating habits. These words may function as nouns or adjectives, depending on context.

NOUN/ADJECTIVE ENDING IN **-ívoro**	ENGLISH EQUIVALENT	BASE WORD	ENGLISH EQUIVALENT
(el) carnívoro	*carnivore, carnivorous*	la carne	*meat, flesh*
(el) frugívoro	*frugivore, fruit-eating*	fructus [LAT.]	*fruit*
(el) granívoro	*granivore, grain-eating*	el grano	*grain*
(el) herbívoro	*herbivore, herbivorous*	la hierba	*grass*
(el) insectívoro	*insectivore, insect-eating*	el insecto	*insect*
(el) omnívoro	*omnivore, omnivorous*	omnis [LAT.]	*all*
(el) piscívoro	*piscivore, fish-eating*	piscis [LAT.]	*fish*

EJERCICIO 37·1

¿Quién prefiere estas comidas? *Provide the correct noun (including its article) to name those who eat the items mentioned in each group.*

1. la manzana, la naranja, la pera, el melocotón _____

2. el salmón, el atún, la trucha, el esturión _____

3. las plantas, las verduras, las hortalizas _____

4. el filete, el tocino, la chuleta de cordero _____

5. la mosca, la hormiga, el escarabajo _____

6. la langosta, el plátano, la lechuga, la hamburguesa _____

7. el cereal, el trigo, la avena, la cebada _____

EJERCICIO 37·2

¿Verdadero o falso? *Indicate whether each statement is true or false, using **V** for* **verdadero** *true or **F** for* **falso** *false.*

1. _____ El vegetariano es carnívoro.

2. _____ El cerdo es omnívoro.

3. _____ La mosca de la fruta es frugívora.

4. _____ El vegetariano estricto es piscívoro.

5. _____ El búfalo es herbívoro.

6. _____ La araña es insectívora.

7. _____ El americano típico es insectívoro.

8. _____ El animal herbívoro está contento en la pastura.

9. _____ El caballo es granívoro.

10. _____ La mayoría de los niños de dos años de edad son omnívoros.

11. _____ Una persona piscívora se niega a comer el pescado.

12. _____ Varios murciélagos son frugíferos.

13. _____ Los pájaros no son granívoros.

38 ◆ -lento/-lenta

MEANING	Relating to, like, full of
ENGLISH EQUIVALENT	*-lent*
PART OF SPEECH	Adjective
GENDER	Masculine/feminine

An adjective with the suffix **-lento/-lenta** is affixed to a base noun to denote a characteristic of a person or thing.

ADJECTIVE ENDING IN **-lento**	ENGLISH EQUIVALENT	BASE WORD	ENGLISH EQUIVALENT
corpulento	*fat, fleshy*	el cuerpo	*body*
flatulento	*flatulent*	el flato	*flatus*
fraudulento	*fraudulent*	el fraude	*fraud*
friolento	*sensitive to the cold*	el frío	*cold*
pulverulento	*dusty, powdery*	el polvo	*dust, powder*
purulento	*pus-filled*	pus/puris [LAT.]	*pus*
sanguinolento	*bloody, bleeding*	sanguis [LAT.]	*blood*
suculento	*succulent, juicy*	el suco	*sap, juice*
vinolento	*fond of wine, boozy* [COLLOQ.]	el vino	*wine*
violento	*violent*	la violencia	*violence*
virolento	*pockmarked*	la viruela	*smallpox*
virulento	*virulent, ferocious*	el virus	*virus*

*Provide the correct form of the appropriate adjective ending in **-lento/-lenta** for each description.*

1. una persona a quien no le gustan las situaciones que involucran las bajas temperaturas, especialmente el invierno _____

2. una fruta muy jugosa, como la naranja, la uva, la toronja, la piña y la pera _____

3. un hombre que le golpea a su esposa _____

4. una persona que pesa más de trescientas libras _____

5. un quiste enorme que se ha infectado _____

6. el esquema Ponzi como los negocios de Bernie Madoff _____

7. un ataque de una enfermedad terminal que progresa rápidamente _____

8. una herida que se resulta de un ataque con un cuchillo _____

9. una persona que es intolerante a la lactosa pero que bebe una malteada _____

10. un hombre a quien le gusta mucho el Merlot, el Cabernet y el Chardonnay _____

11. una atmósfera donde es necesario cambiar los filtros de aire con frecuencia _____

12. una persona que ha sufrido de varicela o viruela _____

39 ▸ -manía

MEANING	Mania, madness
ENGLISH EQUIVALENT	*-mania*
PART OF SPEECH	Noun
GENDER	Feminine

Because almost all Spanish nouns ending in **-manía** have English cognates, they tend to be easily recognized and used. Many of these nouns are based on Greek roots; *-mania* itself is based on the Greek name of a goddess of madness. Some of these nouns are derived from Spanish words, as indicated in the following chart; for example, **la ninfa** *nymph* yields **la ninfomanía** *nymphomania*.

NOUN ENDING IN -manía	ENGLISH EQUIVALENT	BASE WORD	ENGLISH EQUIVALENT
la anglomanía	*Anglomania*	Anglii [LAT.]	*the English*
la bibliomanía	*bibliomania*	biblion [GRK.]	*book*
la cleptomanía	*kleptomania*	kleptes [GRK.]	*thief*
la dipsomanía	*craving for alcohol*	dipsa [GRK.]	*thirst*
la erotomanía	*delusion of being desired*	Eros	*Eros*
la lipemanía	*melancholia*	lipos [GRK.]	*fat*
la megalomanía	*megalomania*	megas [GRK.]	*great, large*
la melomanía	*love of music*	melos [GRK.]	*song, melody*
la monomanía	*obsession*	monos [GRK.]	*single, alone*
la ninfomanía	*nymphomania*	la ninfa	*nymph*
la piromanía	*pyromania*	la pira	*pyre*
la toxicomanía	*drug addiction*	el tóxico	*poison*

EJERCICIO

39·1

Mania is an excessive or unreasonable enthusiasm for something (or someone). Provide the correct noun (including its article) to name the mania most related to the item(s) listed.

1. los libros, las novelas _____

2. el fuego, el incendio provocado _____

3. las canciones, las melodías, la música _____

4. el vino, la cerveza, el vodka, el ron, la ginebra _____

5. la cocaína, le heroína, la marihuana, el crack _____

6. la familia real británica, el Rolls Royce, el programa *Downton Abbey* _____

7. la tristeza, la depresión _____

8. el robo, el hurto crónico _____

9. (por parte de una mujer) la pasión sexual, el coito _____

10. el amor romántico, la ilusión de ser deseado, las fantasías _____

11. el delirio de grandeza, de poder, de riqueza o de omnipotencia _____

12. la obsesión con una sola idea, el entusiasmo exagerada por un tópico _____

40 ▸ -mente

MEANING	In a manner pertaining to
ENGLISH EQUIVALENT	-ly
PART OF SPEECH	Adverb

Just as nearly all English adverbs end in -*ly*, most Spanish adverbs end in -**mente**. These adverbs, which modify verbs, adjectives, and other adverbs, are derived from adjectives. If the base adjective ends in -**o**, the **o** changes to **a** before -**mente**; for example, **exacto** *exact* yields **exactamente** *exactly*. All other adjectives simply add -**mente** to form an adverb; for example, **feliz** *happy* yields **felizmente** *happily*.

The following adverbs ending in -**mente** are derived from adjectives that do not end in -**o**.

ADVERB ENDING IN -**mente**	ENGLISH EQUIVALENT	BASE WORD	ENGLISH EQUIVALENT
actualmente	*presently, nowadays*	actual	*present, present-day*
alegremente	*cheerfully*	alegre	*cheerful*
culpablemente	*guiltily*	culpable	*guilty, culpable*
difícilmente	*with difficulty*	difícil	*difficult*
felizmente	*happily*	feliz	*happy*
frecuentemente	*frequently, often*	frecuente	*frequent*
neutralmente	*neutrally*	neutral	*neutral*
notablemente	*notably*	notable	*notable*
valientemente	*valiantly, bravely*	valiente	*valiant, brave*
vehementemente	*vehemently*	vehemente	*vehement*

EJERCICIO
40·1

¡Resuélvelo! *Match each of the following adverbs ending in* -**mente** *with the English equivalent of its base word.*

1. _____ actualmente   a. *difficult*

2. _____ alegremente   b. *frequent*

3. _____ culpablemente   c. *cheerful*

4. _____ difícilmente   d. *neutral*

5. _____ felizmente   e. *notable*

6. _____ frecuentemente   f. *present-day*

7. _____ neutralmente   g. *vehement*

8. _____ notablemente   h. *brave*

9. _____ valientemente   i. *guilty*

10. _____ vehementemente   j. *happy*

¡Resuélvelo! *Provide the correct form of the adverb ending in -***mente** *for each English equivalent. The base word for each adverb ending in -***mente** *is provided for you.*

ADVERB ENDING IN -**mente**	ENGLISH EQUIVALENT	BASE WORD	ENGLISH EQUIVALENT
1. _____	*apparently*	aparente	*apparent*
2. _____	*elegantly*	elegante	*elegant*
3. _____	*evidently*	evidente	*evident*
4. _____	*easily*	fácil	*easy*
5. _____	*finally*	final	*final*
6. _____	*horribly*	horrible	*horrible*
7. _____	*mentally*	mental	*mental*
8. _____	*naturally*	natural	*natural*
9. _____	*normally*	normal	*normal*
10. _____	*probably*	probable	*probable*
11. _____	*sadly*	triste	*sad*
12. _____	*usually*	usual	*usual*

The following adverbs ending in -**mente** have base adjectives that end in -**o**.

ADVERB ENDING IN -**mente**	ENGLISH EQUIVALENT	BASE WORD	ENGLISH EQUIVALENT
afortunadamente	*fortunately, luckily*	afortunado	*fortunate, lucky*
ciegamente	*blindly*	ciego	*blind*
cuidadosamente	*carefully*	cuidadoso	*careful*
desgraciadamente	*unfortunately*	desgraciado	*unfortunate*
estupendamente	*wonderfully*	estupendo	*wonderful, great*
exactamente	*exactly*	exacto	*exact*
heroicamente	*heroically*	heroico	*heroic*
justamente	*precisely, fairly*	justo	*just, fair, right*
nuevamente	*again, anew*	nuevo	*new*
pragmáticamente	*pragmatically*	pragmático	*pragmatic*
relativamente	*relatively*	relativo	*relative, comparative*
tranquilamente	*quietly, calmly*	tranquilo	*quiet, calm*

¡Resuélvelo! *Match each of the following adverbs ending in* **-mente** *with its English equivalent.*

1. _____ relativamente		a.	*luckily*
2. _____ heroicamente		b.	*blindly*
3. _____ estupendamente		c.	*carefully*
4. _____ tranquilamente		d.	*unfortunately*
5. _____ afortunadamente		e.	*wonderfully*
6. _____ nuevamente		f.	*exactly*
7. _____ ciegamente		g.	*heroically*
8. _____ cuidadosamente		h.	*precisely, fairly*
9. _____ exactamente		i.	*again, anew*
10. _____ desgraciadamente		j.	*pragmatically*
11. _____ justamente		k.	*relatively*
12. _____ pragmáticamente		l.	*quietly, calmly*

¡Resuélvelo! *Complete the following chart by providing the correct form for (1) the adverb ending in* **-mente** *or (2) the adjective as base word for each English equivalent.*

ADVERB ENDING IN **-mente**	ENGLISH EQUIVALENT	BASE WORD	ENGLISH EQUIVALENT
1. _____	*absolutely*	absoluto	*absolute*
2. claramente	*clearly*	_____	*clear*
3. _____	*directly*	directo	*direct*
4. enfáticamente	*emphatically*	_____	*emphatic*
5. _____	*fabulously*	fabuloso	*fabulous*
6. lentamente	*slowly*	_____	*slow*
7. _____	*in an evil manner*	malo	*bad, evil*
8. necesariamente	*necessarily*	_____	*necessary*
9. _____	*obviously*	obvio	*obvious*

ADVERB ENDING IN -mente	ENGLISH EQUIVALENT	BASE WORD	ENGLISH EQUIVALENT
10. perfectamente	*perfectly*	_____	*perfect*
11. _____	*precisely*	preciso	*precise*
12. rápidamente	*rapidly, fast*	_____	*rapid, fast*
13. _____	*surely, very likely*	seguro	*sure, certain*
14. trágicamente	*tragically*	_____	*tragic*

-o

MEANING	Resulting object/action
ENGLISH EQUIVALENT	—
PART OF SPEECH	Noun
GENDER	Masculine

These nouns ending in **-o** are derived from **-ar** verbs; **-er** and **-ir** verbs generally do not yield nouns ending in **-o** that have the same set of meanings. In fact, these suffixed nouns have the same form as the **-ar** verb's first-person singular (**yo**) form in the present indicative (for example, **yo trabajo** *I work* ~ **el trabajo** *work, labor, job*). Note that if the **-ar** base verb is a stem-changing verb, the change occurs in the noun as well as in the verb (for example, **yo almuerzo** *I eat lunch* ~ **el almuerzo** *lunch, luncheon*).

The following nouns ending in **-o** represent objects or outcomes that result from the actions of the base verbs.

NOUN ENDING IN -o	ENGLISH EQUIVALENT	BASE WORD	ENGLISH EQUIVALENT
el abrigo	*overcoat, shelter*	abrigar	*to shelter, protect*
el almuerzo	*lunch, luncheon*	almorzar	*to eat lunch*
el aumento	*increase, raise (salary)*	aumentar	*to increase*
el comienzo	*beginning*	comenzar	*to begin*
el cuento	*tale, story*	contar	*to tell (a story)*
el desayuno	*breakfast*	desayunar	*to eat breakfast*
el ejército	*army*	ejercitar	*to train, drill*
el fracaso	*failure*	fracasar	*to fail, be unsuccessful*
el gobierno	*government*	gobernar	*to govern, rule*
el hado	*fate, destiny*	hadar	*to predict, foretell*
el juego	*game*	jugar	*to play (a game)*
el pago	*payment*	pagar	*to pay (for)*
el silencio	*silence, rest (music)*	silenciar	*to silence*
el vómito	*vomit*	vomitar	*to vomit*
el voto	*vote, ballot*	votar	*to vote*
el vuelo	*flight*	volar	*to fly*

¿Qué es esto? *Provide the correct noun (including its article) for each description.*

1. la primera comida del día   _____

2. una comida ligera, tomada hacia el mediodía   _____

3. la ausencia de ruidos y sonidos   _____

4. el opuesto del final de un proceso   _____

5. una historia, la que puede ser verdadera o no   _____

6. lo que llevas cuando hace mucho frío   _____

7. lo que recibes después de trabajar por una o dos semanas   _____

8. lo que quieres después de trabajar por un año   _____

9. el destino, el futuro predeterminado   _____

10. lo que un productor de una nueva película quiere evitar   _____

11. lo que el ciudadano responsable emite el día de una elección   _____

12. lo que se echa a veces por consecuencia de la náusea   _____

13. lo que esperas al bordar un avión   _____

14. el ajedrez, el béisbol, el fútbol o el baloncesto   _____

15. los soldados que protegen el país y preservan la seguridad de la nación   _____

16. lo que representa el presidente o el primer ministro de un país   _____

The following nouns ending in **-o** represent actions expressed by the base verbs.

NOUN ENDING IN -o	ENGLISH EQUIVALENT	BASE WORD	ENGLISH EQUIVALENT
el abrazo	*embrace, hug*	abrazar	*to embrace, hug*
el atajo	*shortcut*	atajar	*to take a shortcut*
el atraco	*holdup, robbery*	atracar	*to hold up, rob*
el auxilio	*aid, help, relief*	auxiliar	*to aid, help, assist*
el ayuno	*fast, abstinence*	ayunar	*to fast*
el beso	*kiss*	besar	*to kiss*
el castigo	*punishment*	castigar	*to punish*
el desarrollo	*development*	desarrollar	*to develop*
el estudio	*study, learning*	estudiar	*to study*
el grito	*shout, scream*	gritar	*to shout, scream*
el odio	*hatred*	odiar	*to hate*
el paso	*step, walk*	pasar	*to pass, go across*
el regreso	*return*	regresar	*to return*
el saludo	*greeting, wave*	saludar	*to greet, welcome*
el sueño	*dream, sleepiness*	soñar	*to dream*
el trabajo	*work, labor, job*	trabajar	*to work, labor*

Complete each sentence with the correct form of the appropriate noun.

1. Al ver un ratón, muchas personas dan un _____ de horror.

2. "Lo contrario del amor no es el _____ , sino la indiferencia," escribió Elie Wiesel, superviviente de los campos de concentración nazis.

3. Lao Tsu, filósofo chino, escribió, "Un viaje de mil millas comienza con un solo

   _____ ."

4. Para perder peso rápidamente, muchas personas optan por hacer un

   _____ y deciden no comer nada.

5. "Hola," "¿cómo estás?" y "buenos días" son ejemplos de _____ básicos.

6. Cuando los novios se ven, es común que den _____ y

   _____ el uno al otro.

7. Los _____ ocurren frecuentemente durante la fase de los movimientos oculares rápidos (MOR)—REM en inglés.

8. Los padres nuevos deben tener expectativas apropiadas al _____ mental, emocional, socio y físico del niño.

9. Darle una nalgada a un niño es una forma de _____ corporal.

10. La ecología es el _____ de la relación entre los organismos y su medio ambiente.

11. Una película de horror clásica se llama *El _____ de los muertos vivientes*.

12. De vez en cuando, un maratonista toma un _____ en un intento de ganar la carrera.

13. Después de graduarse de la universidad, muchos graduados tratan de encontrar

    _____ en un área que les interesa y que utiliza sus habilidades.

14. Unas personas esconden su dinero en el colchón por temor de un

    _____ del banco.

15. Después de un catástrofe natural, la Cruz Roja aporta _____ a las víctimas.

42 ▸ -o/-a

MEANING	Performer, professional
ENGLISH EQUIVALENT	*-ist, -er*
PART OF SPEECH	Noun
GENDER	Masculine/feminine

Each of these nouns ending in -o (feminine: -a) is derived from a science, occupation, or calling and denotes the person who practices it. The base nouns generally end in **-ía** or **-ia**; exceptions are **la física** *physics*, **la medicina** *medicine*, and **la química** *chemistry*. The formation consists in replacing **-ía** or **-ia** with **-o**, or with **-a** if the person is female. All of these suffixed nouns have an accent on the antepenultimate syllable.

NOUN ENDING IN -o	ENGLISH EQUIVALENT	BASE WORD	ENGLISH EQUIVALENT
el astrónomo	*astronomer*	la astronomía	*astronomy*
el biólogo	*biologist*	la biología	*biology*
el coreógrafo	*choreographer*	la coreografía	*choreography*
el filósofo	*philosopher*	la filosofía	*philosophy*
el fotógrafo	*photographer*	la fotografía	*photography*
el gastrónomo	*gourmet*	la gastronomía	*gastronomy*
el médico	*physician, doctor*	la medicina	*medicine*
el polígamo	*polygamist*	la poligamia	*polygamy*
el pornógrafo	*pornographer*	la pornografía	*pornography*
el psicólogo	*psychologist*	la psicología	*psychology*
el sociólogo	*sociologist*	la sociología	*sociology*
el teólogo	*theologian*	la teología	*theology*

EJERCICIO 42·1

Complete each sentence with the correct form of the appropriate noun for each profession.

1. Sócrates, Plato y Aristóteles son _____.

2. Christiaan Barnard, Mehmet Oz y Jack Kevorkian son _____.

3. Bob Fosse, Alvin Ailey y Martha Graham son _____.

4. Ansel Adams, Diane Arbus y Richard Avedon son _____.

5. Nicolaus Copernicus y Galileo Galilei son _____.

6. Martin Luther, John Calvin y C.S. Lewis son _____.

7. Larry Flint y Bob Guccione son _____.

8. Brigham Young, Joseph Smith, Jr. y Warren Jeffs son _____.

9. Sigmund Freud, B.F. Skinner y William James son _____.

10. Max Weber, Karl Marx y Herbert Spencer son _____.

11. Anthony Bourdain, Jamie Oliver y Guy Fieri son _____.

12. Gregor Mendel, Louis Pasteur y Joseph Lister son _____.

NOUN ENDING IN -o	ENGLISH EQUIVALENT	BASE WORD	ENGLISH EQUIVALENT
el astrólogo	*astrologer*	la astronomía	*astronomy*
el bígamo	*bigamist*	la bigamia	*bigamy*
el calígrafo	*calligrapher*	la caligrafía	*calligraphy*
el cartógrafo	*cartographer, mapmaker*	la cartografía	*cartography*
el físico	*physicist*	la física	*physics*
el ginecólogo	*gynecologist*	la ginecología	*gynecology*
el misántropo	*misanthrope*	la misantropía	*misanthropy*
el mitólogo	*mythologist*	la mitología	*mythology*
el monógamo	*monogamist*	la monogamia	*monogamy*
el neurólogo	*neurologist*	la neurología	*neurology*
el oftalmólogo	*ophthalmologist*	la oftalmología	*ophthalmology*
el patólogo	*pathologist*	la patología	*pathology*
el químico	*chemist*	la química	*chemistry*
el radiólogo	*radiologist*	la radiología	*radiology*
el toxicólogo	*toxicologist*	la toxicología	*toxicology*

EJERCICIO
42·2

Provide the correct noun (including its article) for each person's description.

1. el especialista de los ojos   _____

2. la adolescente que estudia el zodiaco   _____

3. el hombre que prepara mapas   _____

4. la profesora que estudia los escritos de Homer, Sophocles y Virgil   _____

5. un hombre con dos esposas   _____

6. una mujer con un esposo   _____

7. el médico que estudia los rayos X   _____

8. la médica que cuida a las mujeres embarazadas y atiende partos   _____

9. el hombre que odia a todos   _____

10. la médica que estudia el cerebro, la médula espinal y los nervios periféricos   _____

11. el médico que examina los cuerpos y los cadáveres   _____

12. el científico que estudia las partículas subatómicas   _____

13. la científica que analiza la composición de la materia en un laboratorio   _____

14. el científico que estudia los venenos virulentos   _____

15. la maestra que tiene escritura bella   _____

43 ◆ -ón/-ona

MEANING	Augmentative; pejorative
ENGLISH EQUIVALENT	—
PART OF SPEECH	Noun
GENDER	Masculine/feminine

The suffix **-on** (feminine: **-ona**) is one of several augmentative Spanish endings. It may denote an increase in physical size, but it may also have a pejorative connotation, of the "too much of a good thing" sort; for example, **la comedia** *comedy* yields **el comedión** *long and/or tedious comedy*.

The following nouns ending in **-ón** reflect the suffix's augmentative denotation.

NOUN ENDING IN **-ón**	ENGLISH EQUIVALENT	BASE WORD	ENGLISH EQUIVALENT
el avispón	*hornet*	la avispa	*wasp*
el balón	*soccer ball*	la bola	*ball*
el barcón	*big boat*	el barco	*boat*
el bolsón	*large purse, tote bag*	la bolsa	*purse, bag*
el cajón	*drawer, crate*	la caja	*box*
el camón	*large bed*	la cama	*bed*
el cestón	*big basket*	la cesta	*basket*
el cortezón	*thick bark/rind/crust*	la corteza	*bark, rind, crust*
el cortinón	*large curtain*	la cortina	*curtain*
el culebrón	*large snake*	la culebra	*snake*
el gigantón	*enormous giant*	el gigante	*giant*
el goterón	*large raindrop*	la gota	*(rain)drop*
el hombretón	*hefty fellow*	el hombre	*man*
el manchón	*big dirty spot or stain*	la mancha	*spot, stain*
el moscón	*big fly, pest* [COLLOQ.]	la mosca	*fly*
el narigón	*big nose*	la nariz	*nose*
el platón	*platter, large dish*	el plato	*dish*
el portón	*gate, large door*	la puerta	*door*
el rodeón	*long detour*	el rodeo	*detour, roundabout way*
el sillón	*overstuffed chair*	la silla	*chair*
el tazón	*mug, big cup*	la taza	*cup*
el zapatón	*big shoe, overshoe*	el zapato	*shoe*

EJERCICIO 43·1

¡Resuélvelo! *Provide the correct form of the appropriate noun (including its article) for each group.*

1. un yate, un crucero _____

2. la entrada de un castillo _____

3. el calzado de la talla 15EEE _____

4. el pitón, la boa, la anaconda, la cobra _____

5. Jimmy Durante, Cyrano de Bergerac, Pinocho _____

6. la pelota de fútbol _____

7. el exterior de un roble, una secoya o cualquier árbol enorme _____

8. un titán, el antagonista de "Jack y las habichuelas mágicas" _____

9. el protagonista del libro *La metamorfosis* de Franz Kafka, un tábano _____

10. el contenedor para un café con leche _____

11. donde duerme un gigantón _____

12. una ruta muy indirecta _____

13. la decoración de una ventana grande en un castillo _____

14. el producto clásico y grande de Louis Vuitton, una mochila _____

15. Oliver Hardy, John Candy, William "Refrigerador" Perry _____

16. la lluvia en el relato del Arca de Noé _____

17. la cosa en que se sirve la comida para un grupo grande _____

18. algo grande para contener mucha ropa sucia _____

19. donde se pone la ropa interior en el dormitorio _____

The following nouns ending in -**ón** express a figurative increase of size or degree; some express a pejorative connotation.

NOUN ENDING IN -ón	ENGLISH EQUIVALENT	BASE WORD	ENGLISH EQUIVALENT
el barbón	*full-bearded man*	la barba	*beard*
el botellón	*drinking session*	la botella	*bottle*
el calenturón	*violent fever*	la calentura	*fever*
el caserón	*big run-down house*	la casa	*house*
el cocherón	*roundhouse*	el coche	*train car*
el comedión	*long and/or tedious comedy*	la comedia	*comedy*
el hambrón	*chronically hungry person*	el hambre	*hunger*
el hombrón	*lusty man, he-man*	el hombre	*man*
el memorión	*phenomenal memory*	la memoria	*memory*
la mujerona	*stout or lusty woman*	la mujer	*woman*
el novelón	*third-rate novel, pulp novel*	la novela	*novel*
el panzón	*big-bellied person*	la panza	*belly*
el paredón	*thick wall*	la pared	*wall*
el pavón	*peacock*	el pavo	*turkey*
la solterona	*spinster*	la soltera	*unmarried woman*
el vocejón	*harsh voice*	la voz	*voice*

¿Verdadero o falso? *Indicate whether each statement is true or false, using* **V** *for* **verdadero** *true or* **F** *for* **falso** *false.*

1. _____ El memorión es una calidad importante para un abogado.

2. _____ Abraham Lincoln era un barbón.

3. _____ Elizabeth Taylor era una solterona.

4. _____ El calenturón es un síntoma común de la influenza.

5. _____ La Casa Blanca en Washington, D.C., es un caserón.

6. _____ Un hambrón está muy feliz cuando asiste a un bufé.

7. _____ *Hamlet* es un comedión.

8. _____ Al panzón, con frecuencia, le gusta mucho la cerveza y los alimentos grasos.

9. _____ Mae West es un ejemplo clásico de una mujerona.

10. _____ Los universitarios nunca asistan al botellón porque prefieren estudiar todas las noches.

11. _____ Un paredón es importante para una prisión federal.

12. _____ Muchas personas consideran *Los puentes del condado de Madison* un novelón.

13. _____ Tradicionalmente un cocherón es circular.

14. _____ El pavón es un símbolo de la belleza, la inmortalidad, el orgullo y la paz.

15. _____ El vocejón es bienvenido a la Ópera Metropolitana de Nueva York.

44 ◆ -or/-ora

MEANING	Performer, professional
ENGLISH EQUIVALENT	*-or*
PART OF SPEECH	Noun
GENDER	Masculine/feminine

This is one of several Spanish suffixes denoting a person who performs an action. Since nearly all of these nouns are derived from verbs and nearly all of them have English cognates, they are easy to recognize and use. Note that most of these nouns actually end in **-tor**, even if the stem of the base verb does not include the letter **t**.

NOUN ENDING IN -or	ENGLISH EQUIVALENT	BASE WORD	ENGLISH EQUIVALENT
el actor	*actor*	actuar	*to act*
el autor	*author*	augere [LAT.]	*to originate, produce*
el compositor	*composer*	componer	*to compose*
el confesor	*confessor*	confesar	*to confess*
el director	*director*	dirigir	*to direct, manage*
el editor	*editor*	editar	*to edit*
el escritor	*writer*	escribir	*to write*
el escultor	*sculptor*	esculpir	*to sculpt, carve*
el inspector	*inspector*	inspeccionar	*to inspect*
el instructor	*instructor*	instruir	*to instruct, teach*
el inventor	*inventor*	inventar	*to invent*
el pastor	*shepherd, pastor*	pascere [LAT.]	*to lead to pasture*
el pintor	*painter*	pintar	*to paint*
el profesor	*professor*	profesar	*to profess, practice*
el rector	*rector, headmaster*	regere [LAT.]	*to rule, guide*

EJERCICIO

44·1

¿Cuál es su profesión? *Provide the correct form of the appropriate noun(s) (including the article) for each group.*

1. Pablo Picasso, Rembrandt, Vincent Van Gogh, Renoir _____

2. Daniel Day-Lewis, George Clooney, Sir Laurence Olivier, Jude Law _____

3. Thomas Edison, George Washington Carver, Johannes Gutenberg, Benjamin Franklin _____

4. Ludwig van Beethoven, Antonio Vivaldi, Frederic Chopin, Manuel de Falla _____

5. Steven Spielberg, Tim Burton, Pedro Almodóvar, Alfred Hitchcock _____

6. Auguste Rodin, Constantin Brancusi, Henry Moore, Jean (Hans) Arp _____

7. Leo Tolstoi, Victor Hugo, H.L. Mencken, David Sedaris _____

   _____

8. el sacerdote que escucha los pecados del confeso _____

9. el principal de una escuela privada _____

10. un maestro en la universidad _____

    _____

11. el empleado de un periódico que redacta los artículos _____

12. el líder de una iglesia protestante _____

NOUN ENDING IN -or	ENGLISH EQUIVALENT	BASE WORD	ENGLISH EQUIVALENT
el auditor	*auditor*	auditar	*to audit*
el conductor	*conductor*	conducir	*to drive, guide*
el consultor	*consultant, adviser*	consultar	*to consult*
el contralor	*comptroller*	controlar	*to control, regulate*
el ejecutor	*executor*	ejecutar	*to execute, carry out*
el expositor	*speaker, exhibitor*	exponer	*to explain, exhibit*
el lector	*reader*	leer	*to read*
el mentor	*mentor, tutor*	Mentor [GRK.]	*Mentor (advisor to Telemachus)*
el opositor	*opponent*	oponer	*to oppose*
el seductor	*seducer, charmer*	seducir	*to seduce, tempt, charm*

EJERCICIO

44·2

Provide the correct feminine form of the appropriate noun (including its article) for each description.

1. la chofer de coche, taxi, autobús u otro medio de transporte _____

2. una persona que siempre tiene un punto de vista diferente _____

3. una persona que asesora a corporaciones en el área de marketing _____

4. una persona que guía a los estudiantes y les ayuda a tener éxito en sus clases _____

5. una mujer que fascina y atrae a los hombres _____

6. una mujer que habla en frente de un gran grupo de personas _____

7. una persona que lee libros o periódicos, con frecuencia a otra persona _____

8. una persona que inspecciona las declaraciones de impuestos _____

9. una persona que supervisa el desempeño de los detalles de un testamento y distribuye el patrimonio _____

10. la persona encargada de administrar los asuntos financieros de las corporaciones _____

45 ◆ -oso/-osa

MEANING	Possessing, full of
ENGLISH EQUIVALENT	-ous, -y, -ful
PART OF SPEECH	Adjective
GENDER	Masculine/feminine

The Spanish suffix **-oso/-osa** is commonly used to indicate that a person or thing possesses a good deal of the base noun. Since many of these adjectives have English cognates, they tend to be easy to recognize and use. If the base noun ends in a vowel, the vowel is usually replaced with the **-oso/-osa** ending; if the base noun ends in a consonant, the **-oso/-osa** ending is added directly to the noun. The base noun may undergo a slight spelling change (for example, **el temor** *fear* yields **temeroso** *fearful*), but the stem is still recognizable.

The following adjectives ending in **-oso/-osa** relate to emotions and sentiments.

ADJECTIVE ENDING IN **-OSO**	ENGLISH EQUIVALENT	BASE WORD	ENGLISH EQUIVALENT
celoso	*jealous*	el celo	*jealousy*
codicioso	*covetous, greedy*	la codicia	*greed*
dudoso	*doubtful*	la duda	*doubt*
gozoso	*joyful*	el gozo	*joy, delight*
jubiloso	*jubilant, joyous*	el júbilo	*jubilation, joy*
lastimoso	*pitiful, woeful*	la lástima	*pity, shame*
lloroso	*tearful, weepy*	el lloro	*crying, weeping*
mocoso	*snot-nosed, bratty*	el moco	*mucus*
nervioso	*nervous*	el nervio	*nerve*
odioso	*hateful, heinous*	el odio	*hatred, hate*
pomposo	*pompous*	la pompa	*pomp*
rencoroso	*spiteful, resentful*	el rencor	*rancor, resentment*
respetuoso	*respectful*	el respeto	*respect*
temeroso	*fearful*	el temor	*fear*

EJERCICIO
45·1

Complete each sentence with the correct form of the appropriate adjective.

1. Según la Biblia, el apóstol Tomás se rehusó a creer que Jesucristo resucitó. Esto es el origen

   de la expresión el "_____ Tomás."

2. Un chico con maneras terribles que le contesta mal a su maestra es un niño

   _____.

3. Una persona tímida está _____ con frecuencia.

4. Cuando una persona quiere lo que otra persona tiene, se dice que esta persona se siente

   _____ o _____.

5. Desgraciadamente, un niño con cólicos está _____ mucho del tiempo.

6. Antes de dar un discurso, un orador con frecuencia se siente _____.

7. Usualmente, una graduación es una ocasión _____ y

    _____.

8. El asesinato y la violación son ejemplos de crímenes _____.

9. Según la Biblia (y en particular, según el cuarto mandamiento), es importante ser

    _____ con sus padres.

10. Un padre que no le hace caso a sus niños es un padre _____.

11. Al descubrir que su esposo está teniendo un lío, ella se siente vengativa y

    _____.

12. El narcisista habla con frecuencia en un estilo _____.

The following adjectives ending in **-oso/-osa** are frequently used to describe situations.

ADJECTIVE ENDING IN **-OSO**	ENGLISH EQUIVALENT	BASE WORD	ENGLISH EQUIVALENT
doloroso	*sorrowful, painful*	el dolor	*pain*
escandaloso	*scandalous*	el escándalo	*scandal*
espantoso	*frightening, hideous*	el espanto	*fright, terror*
fabuloso	*fabulous*	la fábula	*fable*
lujoso	*luxurious*	el lujo	*luxury*
maravilloso	*wonderful, marvelous*	la maravilla	*wonder, marvel*
milagroso	*miraculous*	el milagro	*miracle*
misterioso	*mysterious*	el misterio	*mystery*
pegajoso	*sticky*	la pega (< el pegamento)	*glue*
peligroso	*dangerous*	el peligro	*danger*
ventajoso	*advantageous*	la ventaja	*advantage*
ventoso	*windy*	el viento	*wind*

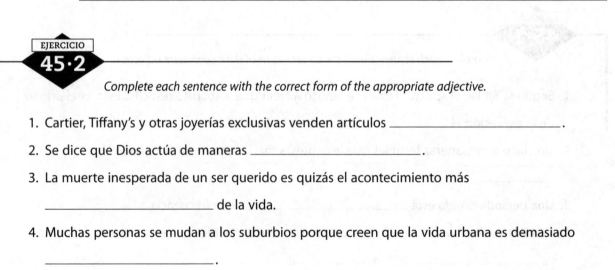

EJERCICIO
45·2

Complete each sentence with the correct form of the appropriate adjective.

1. Cartier, Tiffany's y otras joyerías exclusivas venden artículos _____.

2. Se dice que Dios actúa de maneras _____.

3. La muerte inesperada de un ser querido es quizás el acontecimiento más

    _____ de la vida.

4. Muchas personas se mudan a los suburbios porque creen que la vida urbana es demasiado

    _____.

5. El objetivo de Halloween es proveer una noche con elementos _____ pero igualmente divertidos.

6. Cuando una persona busca trabajo, es importante poseer las calificaciones necesarias para una posición, y también es muy _____ tener buenas conexiones.

7. A veces una coincidencia es tan impresionante que parece _____.

8. Cuando el presidente de un país tiene una aventura amorosa, muchas personas creen que es una situación absolutamente _____.

9. Se debe lavar el arroz antes de cocinarlo, porque si no lo hace, el resultado puede ser un montón de arroz _____.

10. No se debe usar pesticidas en los días _____ porque los químicos venenosos se pueden dispersar por los áreas donde hay niños, mascotas y otros seres vivos.

11. Durante el Festival de Cannes, además de mostrar películas, hay muchas fiestas

_____ y _____.

The following adjectives ending in **-oso/-osa** reflect a wide range of meanings.

ADJECTIVE ENDING IN **-OSO**	ENGLISH EQUIVALENT	BASE WORD	ENGLISH EQUIVALENT
carnoso	*fleshy, meaty*	la carne	*flesh, meat*
cuidadoso	*careful*	el cuidado	*care*
humoso	*smoky*	el humo	*smoke*
mantecoso	*buttery, fatty, greasy*	la manteca	*lard, fat*
mentiroso	*lying, deceitful*	la mentira	*lie*
perezoso	*lazy, slothful*	la pereza	*sloth, laziness*
poderoso	*powerful*	el poder	*power*
pulgoso	*flea-ridden*	la pulga	*flea*
sabroso	*tasty, delicious*	el sabor	*taste, flavor*
venenoso	*poisonous*	el veneno	*poison*

EJERCICIO
45·3

Complete each sentence with the correct form of the appropriate adjective.

1. La cobra es una serpiente _____ y una mordedura de esta serpiente es una emergencia medical.

2. No puede creer nada de lo que dice un hombre _____.

3. Muchas personas consideran que el presidente de los Estados Unidos es el hombre más _____ del mundo.

4. Un queso _____, como el Brie o el Camembert, tiene un sabor suave.

5. Un perro _____ casi ciertamente está miserable.

6. Una bomba o una granada de mano requiere tratamiento _____.

7. Una persona tiene derecho a esperar una comida _____ en un restaurante de cinco estrellas.

8. La manzana, la naranja, la uva y la sandía son ejemplos de frutas

_____.

9. La ambliopía, o "ojo _____," ocurre cuando un ojo no puede ver tan bien como el otro.

10. Una ciudad grande como Londres, Los Ángeles o Beijing tiene unas áreas

_____ y mugrientas.

-sión

MEANING	Action, result of an action, state
ENGLISH EQUIVALENT	-sion
PART OF SPEECH	Noun
GENDER	Feminine

Spanish nouns ending in **-sión** are derived from verbs. The typical formation is to replace the **-ar**, **-er**, or **-ir** ending of the infinitive and the final consonant of its stem with the ending **-sión**. Very rarely does a Spanish noun ending in **-sión** have an English counterpart ending in **-tion** (an exception is **la distorsión** *distortion*); the English ending is almost always *-sion*, which makes these nouns easy to recognize and use.

NOUN ENDING IN **-sión**	ENGLISH EQUIVALENT	BASE WORD	ENGLISH EQUIVALENT
la accesión	*consent, accession*	acceder	*to accede*
la ascensión	*ascension*	ascender	*to ascend*
la aspersión	*aspersion, sprinkling*	asperjar	*to sprinkle*
la confusión	*confusion*	confundir	*to confuse, confound*
la decisión	*decision, resolution*	decidir	*to decide*
la depresión	*depression*	deprimir	*to depress*
la distorsión	*distortion*	distorsionar	*to distort, twist*
la expansión	*expansion*	expansionar	*to expand*
la fusión	*fusion*	fusionar	*to fuse*
la incisión	*incision*	incidere [LAT.]	*to cut into*
la invasión	*invasion*	invadir	*to invade*
la inversión	*investment*	invertir	*to invest*

Definiciones *Provide the correct noun (including its article) for each description.*

1. el estado psíquico que se caracteriza por una gran tristeza sin causa aparente _____

2. la subida a un lugar más alto, por ejemplo, la de Cristo a los cielos _____

3. la determinación acerca de algo ante las opciones posibles _____

4. el uso de unos fondos con la intención de ganar más dinero a lo largo del tiempo _____

5. la falta de claridad y orden en cualquier situación _____

6. el aumento de algo para ocupar más espacio _____

7. la entrada por la fuerza, frecuentemente durante una guerra, para ocupar el área _____

8. la dispersión de un líquido en finas gotas _____

9. un corte poco profundo hecho en un cuerpo en preparación para la cirugía _____

10. la representación falsa de algo _____

11. el proceso de la unión de dos (o más de dos) cosas para formar una sola entidad _____

12. el logro de una position de poder, por ejemplo, de un monarca _____

NOUN ENDING IN **-sión**	ENGLISH EQUIVALENT	BASE WORD	ENGLISH EQUIVALENT
la extensión	*extension*	extender	*to extend, spread out*
la oclusión	*occlusion*	ocluir	*to occlude*
la percusión	*percussion*	percutir	*to strike, tap*
la persuasión	*persuasion*	persuadir	*to persuade, convince*
la posesión	*possession*	poseer	*to possess, own*
la precisión	*precision*	precisar	*to specify*
la progresión	*progression*	progresar	*to progress*
la propulsión	*propulsion*	propulsar	*to propel, drive*
la repulsión	*repulsion*	repulsar	*to reject, repulse*
la suspensión	*suspension*	suspender	*to suspend*
la televisión	*television*	televisar	*to televise*
la transfusión	*transfusion*	transfundir	*to transfuse*
la transgresión	*transgression*	transgredir	*to transgress, sin*
la transmisión	*transmission*	transmitir	*to transmit, broadcast*
la visión	*vision*	videre [LAT.]	*to see*

Complete each sentence with the correct form of the appropriate noun.

1. La _____ de drogas narcóticas es ilegal.

2. Una persona que se ha hecho mueble (*couch potato*) permanece en el sillón, mirando la _____ muchas horas al día.

3. El optómetro y el oftalmólogo son especialistas en la _____.

4. Muchos estudiantes universitarios de primer año esperan que la universidad sea una _____ de su experiencia en la escuela secundaria, cuando no tenían que lavar la ropa ni limpiar el dormitorio ellos mismos.

5. En una orquesta la sección de los instrumentos de _____ incluye los tambores, el xilófono, la pandereta, los platillos y el gong.

6. Los veleros utilizan el viento como su fuente principal de _____.

7. Muchas personas donan sangre para los que necesitan una _____ de sangre.

8. Quizás el aspecto más importante del Internet es la _____ de información.

9. La _____ es un proceso destinado a cambiar las creencias o las actitudes de otra persona o de un grupo de personas.

10. Según la iglesia católica, después de la confesión sincera del penitente ante el sacerdote, Dios perdonará cualquier pecado o _____.

11. La _____ es un sentimiento muy fuerte del desagrado o el asco intenso.

12. Se necesita seguir avanzando cada día—por poco que sea—para tener un sentido de la _____ en la vida.

13. El Puente Golden Gate en San Francisco es un puente colgante que depende de la _____ del tablero por muchos cables de acero.

14. La _____ de la medición es de suma importancia en la carpintería.

15. En la medicina, una obstrucción de un vaso sanguíneo es una _____.

47 ▸ -teca

MEANING	Repository
ENGLISH EQUIVALENT	—
PART OF SPEECH	Noun
GENDER	Feminine

Very few Spanish nouns end in -**teca**, although **la biblioteca** *library* and **la discoteca** *record library, discotheque* may be familiar to you. These nouns denote a place where items are collected or stored.

NOUN ENDING IN -teca	ENGLISH EQUIVALENT	BASE WORD	ENGLISH EQUIVALENT
la biblioteca	*library*	biblion [GRK.]	*book*
la discoteca	*record library, discotheque*	el disco	*record*
la filmoteca	*film library*	el filme	*film*
la fototeca	*photo library*	la foto	*photo*
la hemeroteca	*newspaper library*	hemera [GRK.]	*day*
la pinacoteca	*place for storing paintings*	la pintura	*painting*
la videoteca	*video library*	el video	*video*

EJERCICIO 47·1

¿Dónde se guarda? *Provide the correct noun (including its article) that names the repository for each group of items.*

1. las obras maestras de Rembrandt, Picasso y Renoir _____

2. las colecciones de Ansel Adams, Diane Arbus y Annie Leibovitz _____

3. las publicaciones de Victor Hugo, John Steinbeck y Jane Austen _____

4. las copias del *New York Times, London Telegraph* y *Herald Sun* _____

5. los productos de YouTube _____

6. las producciones de Steven Spielberg, Alfred Hitchcock y David Lean _____

7. las colecciones de Bruce Springsteen, los Rolling Stones y los Beatles _____

48 ▶ -triz

MEANING	Female performer/professional
ENGLISH EQUIVALENT	*-ess*
PART OF SPEECH	Noun
GENDER	Feminine

No men allowed! These Spanish nouns ending in **-triz** represent women with specific occupations or roles. In English, the suffix *-ess* denotes such a woman, although the tendency has been toward genderless naming. In Spanish, however, the male/female distinction continues, and **-triz** is an example. Most of these nouns are formed by adding **-triz** to the stem of the base verb; the thematic vowel of **-ar** verbs is often retained before the suffix (for example, **adorar** *to adore, worship* yields **la adoratriz** *cloistered nun*).

NOUN ENDING IN **-triz**	ENGLISH EQUIVALENT	BASE WORD	ENGLISH EQUIVALENT
la actriz	*actress*	actuar	*to act*
la adoratriz	*cloistered nun*	adorar	*to adore, worship*
la cantatriz	*female singer*	cantar	*to sing*
la emperatriz	*empress*	el emperador	*emperor*
la fregatriz	*kitchen maid*	fregar	*to scrub, swab, mop*
la institutriz	*governess*	instituir	*to instruct, teach*
la meretriz	*prostitute*	merere [LAT.]	*to earn*
la protectriz	*protectress*	proteger	*to protect*
la saltatriz	*ballerina*	saltar	*to jump, leap*

EJERCICIO
48·1

¿Cuál es su profesión? *Choose the noun in the second column that best matches the group in the first column.*

1. _____ Lady Gaga, Barbra Streisand, Madonna

2. _____ Maria von Trapp, Jane Eyre, Miss Clavel (*Madeline*)

3. _____ Anna Pavlova, Margot Fonteyn

4. _____ Fantine (*Les Misérables*), Heidi Fleiss

5. _____ Meryl Streep, Jennifer Lawrence, Dame Judi Dench

6. _____ Alice Nelson (*Brady Bunch*), Prissy (*Gone with the Wind*)

7. _____ Santa Teresa de Ávila, Santa Clara de Asís

8. _____ Catalina la Grande, Michiko de Japón

9. _____ Nuestra Señora de Guadalupe, Juno de Grecia

a. la actriz

b. la adoratriz

c. la cantatriz

d. la emperatriz

e. la fregatriz

f. la institutriz

g. meretriz

h. la protectriz

i. la saltatriz

Provide the correct feminine form of the noun (including its article) for the masculine form(s) given.

1. el emperador _____

2. el protector _____

3. el saltante, el saltador _____

4. el actor _____

5. el fregador _____

6. el adorador _____

7. el institutor _____

8. el cantor, el cantante _____

9. el merecedor _____

49 ◆ -udo/-uda

MEANING	Possessing a great deal of; augmentative
ENGLISH EQUIVALENT	—
PART OF SPEECH	Adjective
GENDER	Masculine/feminine

The suffix **-udo/-uda** indicates that a person or thing possesses a good deal of the base noun (for example, **un hombre peludo** *a hairy man*). This suffix is often attached to names of specific body parts. The base noun may be masculine or feminine, but the adjective ending in **-udo/-uda** corresponds to the gender of the noun it modifies: **Marta es bocuda** *Marta has a big mouth*.

The following adjectives ending in **-udo/-uda** are based on nouns that name specific human body parts.

ADJECTIVE ENDING IN **-udo**	ENGLISH EQUIVALENT	BASE WORD	ENGLISH EQUIVALENT
barbudo	*full-bearded*	la barba	*beard*
barrigudo	*big-bellied, pot-bellied*	la barriga	*belly, bulge*
bigotudo	*heavily mustached*	el bigote	*mustache*
bocudo	*having a big mouth*	la boca	*mouth*
cabezudo	*having a big head*	la cabeza	*head*
caderudo	*having large hips*	la cadera	*hip*
cejudo	*having bushy eyebrows*	la ceja	*eyebrow*
cornudo	*horned*	el cuerno	*horn*
dentudo	*having big teeth*	el diente	*tooth*

▶

ADJECTIVE ENDING IN -udo	ENGLISH EQUIVALENT	BASE WORD	ENGLISH EQUIVALENT
espaldudo	*broad-shouldered*	la espalda	*back*
huesudo	*bony, big-boned*	el hueso	*bone*
juanetudo	*having bunions*	el juanete	*bunion*
nalgudo	*having big buttocks*	la nalga	*buttock*
narizudo	*having a big nose*	la nariz	*nose*
orejudo	*big-eared, long-eared*	la oreja	*ear (external)*
pantorrilludo	*thick-calved*	la pantorrilla	*calf of the leg*
panzudo	*having a big belly*	la panza	*belly*
papudo	*double-chinned*	el papo	*double chin, jowls*
peludo	*hairy, hirsute*	el pelo	*hair*
rodilludo	*having fat knees*	la rodilla	*knee*

EJERCICIO
49·1

*Match the adjective ending in -**udo** with the English equivalent of its base word.*

1. _____ barbudo
2. _____ barrigudo
3. _____ bigotudo
4. _____ bocudo
5. _____ cabezudo
6. _____ caderudo
7. _____ cornudo
8. _____ cejudo
9. _____ dentudo
10. _____ espaldudo
11. _____ huesudo
12. _____ juanetudo
13. _____ nalgudo
14. _____ narizudo
15. _____ orejudo
16. _____ pantorrilludo
17. _____ panzudo
18. _____ papudo
19. _____ peludo
20. _____ rodilludo

a. *hip*
b. *belly*
c. *hair*
d. *bone*
e. *knee*
f. *nose*
g. *back*
h. *beard*
i. *calf of the leg*
j. *ear (external)*
k. *double chin, jowls*
l. *mouth*
m. *mustache*
n. *horn*
o. *belly, bulge*
p. *tooth*
q. *buttock*
r. *head*
s. *eyebrow*
t. *bunion*

The following adjectives ending in **-udo/-uda** are based on nouns other than those that name specific human body parts.

ADJECTIVE ENDING IN -udo	ENGLISH EQUIVALENT	BASE WORD	ENGLISH EQUIVALENT
carnudo	*fleshy*	la carne	*flesh, meat*
ceñudo	*frowning*	el ceño	*brow, frown*
felpudo	*plushy, downy*	la felpa	*plush*
lanudo	*woolly, fleecy*	la lana	*wool*
mantudo	*masked, in disguise*	el manto	*cloak, cape, mantle*
molletudo	*chubby-cheeked*	la molla	*flab, fat*
patudo	*having big feet, paws*	la pata	*animal's hoof or paw*
picudo	*pointy-beaked*	el pico	*beak, bill*
talludo	*tall, lanky*	el tallo	*stem, stalk*
tetudo	*having large breasts*	la teta	*teat, breast*
tozudo	*obstinate, stubborn*	la toza	*block of wood, stump*
zancudo	*long-legged*	el zanco	*stilt*
zapatudo	*wearing big shoes*	el zapato	*shoe*

EJERCICIO
49·2

¡Resuélvelo! *Provide the base word that is related to each description or group. Then provide the masculine singular form of the appropriate adjective ending in -udo for the base word.*

	BASE WORD	ADJECTIVE ENDING IN -udo
1. un tucán, un pelicano, un frailecillo	_____	_____
2. una persona altísima, una supermodelo	_____	_____
3. la oveja, la alpaca, la vicuña	_____	_____
4. una persona que siempre está infeliz	_____	_____
5. un bebé saludable, un querubín	_____	_____
6. las nalgas, los brazos gordos	_____	_____
7. un niño que siempre dice "¡No!"	_____	_____
8. bolas de algodón, un abrigo de visón, un edredón	_____	_____
9. una persona con pies enormes	_____	_____
10. una mamífera que produce leche	_____	_____
11. el "pie" de un elefante, un Clydesdale o un mastodonte	_____	_____

50 ◆ -uno/-una

MEANING	Relating to, like, resembling
ENGLISH EQUIVALENT	—
PART OF SPEECH	Adjective
GENDER	Masculine/feminine

The suffix -**uno**/-**una** is unique among adjective suffixes meaning *relating to, like, resembling*: It has a specialized use in reference to animals. While the suffix is not restricted solely to the animal kingdom, it is usually the suffix of choice where animals are concerned, and far less so for humans and things.

The following adjectives ending in -**uno**/-**una** denote characteristics of specific animals.

ADJECTIVE ENDING IN -**uno**	ENGLISH EQUIVALENT	BASE WORD	ENGLISH EQUIVALENT
abejuno	*pertaining to bees*	la abeja	*bee*
boyuno	*bovine, pertaining to cattle*	el buey	*ox*
caballuno	*equine, pertaining to horses*	el caballo	*horse*
cabrituno	*pertaining to a young goat*	el cabrito	*kid, young goat*
carneruno	*ovine, pertaining to sheep*	el carnero	*sheep, ram*
cervuno	*cervine, pertaining to deer*	el ciervo	*deer, stag, hart*
conejuno	*pertaining to rabbits*	el conejo	*rabbit*
corderuno	*pertaining to lambs*	el cordero	*lamb*
gatuno	*feline, pertaining to cats*	el gato	*cat*
lebruno	*pertaining to hares, harelike*	el liebre	*hare*
lobuno	*pertaining to wolves, wolfish*	el lobo	*wolf*
osuno	*pertaining to bears, bearish*	el oso	*bear*
ovejuno	*ovine, pertaining to sheep*	la oveja	*sheep, ewe*
perruno	*canine, pertaining to dogs*	el perro	*dog*
porcuno	*porcine, pertaining to pigs*	el puerco	*pig, hog*
vacuno	*bovine, pertaining to cows*	la vaca	*cow*
zorruno	*pertaining to foxes*	el zorro	*fox*

EJERCICIO
50·1

¡**Resuélvelo!** *Provide the base word that names the animal represented by each description or group. Then provide the masculine singular form of the appropriate adjective ending in* -**uno** *for the base word.*

	BASE WORD	ADJECTIVE ENDING IN -**uno**
1. Smokey, Yogi, Fozzie, Baloo	_____	_____
2. Harvey, Bugs, un símbolo de la Pascua	_____	_____
3. Secretariat, Flicka, Pegasus	_____	_____
4. Lassie, Checkers, Rin Tin Tin	_____	_____
5. Akela (*The Jungle Book*), el antagonista en "La Caperucita Roja"	_____	_____

6. Dolly (el primer mamífero clonado) _____ _____

7. Bambi, Faline, Ena _____ _____

8. Tod, Swiper (el antagonista de Dora la Exploradora) _____ _____

9. Porky, Arnold Ziffel, Babe, Wilbur _____ _____

10. Elsie, la causa del gran problema de Mrs. O'Leary _____ _____

11. Garfield, Morris, Mr. Bigglesworth, Figaro _____ _____

12. el animalito de Mary en la rima popular de Mamá Ganso _____ _____

The following adjectives ending in **-uno/-una** do not specifically refer to animals (other than humans).

ADJECTIVE ENDING IN **-uno**	ENGLISH EQUIVALENT	BASE WORD	ENGLISH EQUIVALENT
alguno	*relating to something*	algo	*something*
bajuno	*base, low, vile*	el bajo	*deep place*
boquiconejuno	*hare-lipped*	la boca + el conejo	*mouth + rabbit*
hombruno	*mannish, manly*	el hombre	*man*
machuno	*macho, very manly*	el macho	*male, he-man*
montuno	*of the mountain, wild*	el monte	*mountain*
moruno	*Moorish*	el moro	*Moor, Arab*

EJERCICIO
50·2

¡Resuélvelo! *Provide the base word(s) represented by each description or group. Then provide the masculine singular form of the appropriate adjective(s) ending in* **-uno** *for each base word.*

	BASE WORD	ADJECTIVE ENDING IN **-uno**
1. Everest, Kilimanjaro, McKinley	_____	_____
2. Death Valley, el Mar Muerto	_____	_____
3. Otelo, un musulmán de la península ibérica	_____	_____
4. el paladar deformado	_____	_____
5. una cosa	_____	_____
6. Arnold Schwarzenegger, Ernest Hemingway, Gen. George S. Patton	_____	_____

Intermediate suffixes

This second group of suffixes produces many useful words that you are likely to encounter at the intermediate level of learning Spanish. While several of the suffixes in Part I denote size, profession, or origin, the 50 suffixes in Part II have much more specific meanings, ranging from landing type to ruler to madness and murder. Quite a few adjectives are also included in this section, and many of the suffixed words have base words that you may not be familiar with; some of these base words, in fact, are Latin or Greek.

Not only are the suffixed words themselves more complex than those in Part I, but so are the exercises that follow each chart. This will prepare you to recognize and use these suffixes in conversation and outside reading. As a result, you will be able to determine the meaning of "new" words by analyzing them—and not turning to the dictionary. You're on your way to becoming an independent learner.

51 ◆ -ada

MEANING	Blow, strike, swift movement; resulting action
ENGLISH EQUIVALENT	—
PART OF SPEECH	Noun
GENDER	Feminine

The suffix **-ada** may denote the swift movement of an object, generally resulting in a blow or strike; for example, **el puño** *fist* yields **la puñada** *punch, blow with the fist*. Some of the suffixed nouns represent swift movement without a resulting blow; for example, **el ojo** *eye* yields **la ojeada** *glance*. A related suffix, **-azo** (No. 62), also indicates force.

The base noun for each of the following nouns ending in **-ada** is a human, a body part, or a related article; see, for example, **la mangonada** *push with the arm*.

NOUN ENDING IN -ada	ENGLISH EQUIVALENT	BASE WORD	ENGLISH EQUIVALENT
la brazada	*(swimming) stroke (of arm)*	el brazo	*arm*
la cabezada	*nod, headshake*	la cabeza	*head*
la corazonada	*hunch, presentiment*	el corazón	*heart*
la gargantada	*liquid ejected from the throat*	la garganta	*throat*
la gaznatada	*violent blow on windpipe*	el gaznate	*windpipe*
la hombrada	*manly deed*	el hombre	*man*
la lengüetada	*lick, licking*	la lengua	*tongue*
la mangonada	*push with the arm*	la manga	*sleeve*
la morrada	*head butt*	la morra	*top of head*
la muchachada	*childish prank*	el muchacho	*boy, lad*
la nalgada	*slap on the buttocks*	la nalga	*buttock*
la ojeada	*glance*	el ojo	*eye*
la palmada	*slap*	la palma	*palm of the hand*
la patada	*kick with the foot*	la pata	*foot, paw*
la pernada	*kick with the leg*	la pierna	*leg*
la puñada	*punch, blow with the fist*	el puño	*fist*
la rodillada	*shove with the knee*	la rodilla	*knee*
la uñada	*fingernail scratch*	la uña	*fingernail*
la zancada	*long stride*	la zanca	*shank, long leg*

EJERCICIO
51·1

Provide the correct form of the appropriate noun(s) (including the article) to name the action indicated by each item.

1. un niño travieso _____

2. una persona muy intuitiva _____

3. un boxeador _____

4. un experto en jiujitsu _____

   _____

5. una mujer furiosa a su novio _____

   _____

6. un jugador de fútbol _____

_____

7. una persona que ataque la tráquea de otra persona _____

8. una persona muy brusca en una cola larga _____

9. una persona muy alta _____

10. una persona que responde con la cabeza _____

11. una persona que vomita violentamente _____

12. una persona comiendo un cono de helado _____

13. la acción de alguien muy macho _____

14. un nadador en la piscina _____

The base noun for each of the following nouns ending in **-ada** is an animal, a body part of an animal, or an inanimate object.

NOUN ENDING IN **-ada**	ENGLISH EQUIVALENT	BASE WORD	ENGLISH EQUIVALENT
la azadada	*blow with spade or hoe*	la azada	*spade, hoe*
la badajada	*stroke of the clapper*	el badajo	*bell clapper*
la coleada	*swish of a tail*	la cola	*tail*
la cuchillada	*stab wound*	el cuchillo	*knife*
la escobada	*sweep of a broom*	la escoba	*broom*
la fumada	*whiff of smoke, puff, drag*	el fumar	*smoking*
la galopada	*lunge or race at a gallop*	el galope	*gallop*
la mazada	*blow with mace or club*	la maza	*mace, war club*
la palotada	*stroke with a drumstick*	el palote	*drumstick*
la panderada	*stroke with a tambourine*	la pandereta	*tambourine*
la puñalada	*stab*	el puñal	*dagger*
la tijeretada	*to cut with scissors, clip*	las tijeras	*scissors*

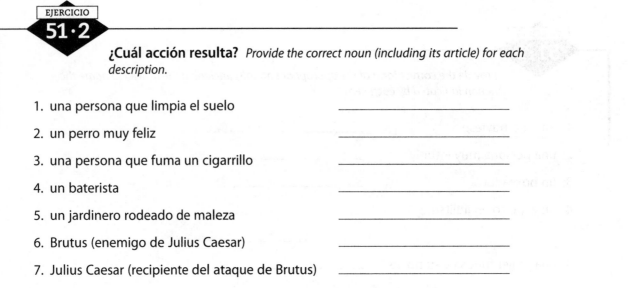

EJERCICIO
51·2

¿Cuál acción resulta? *Provide the correct noun (including its article) for each description.*

1. una persona que limpia el suelo _____

2. un perro muy feliz _____

3. una persona que fuma un cigarrillo _____

4. un baterista _____

5. un jardinero rodeado de maleza _____

6. Brutus (enemigo de Julius Caesar) _____

7. Julius Caesar (recipiente del ataque de Brutus) _____

8. un campanero _____

9. un caballo fogoso _____

10. una persona que corta el papel _____

11. un guerrero _____

52 ▸ -ada

MEANING	Group, collection; flock, drove; amount
ENGLISH EQUIVALENT	—
PART OF SPEECH	Noun
GENDER	Feminine

The suffix **-ada** may denote a group of animals. Many of the base words are probably familiar to you.

NOUN ENDING IN **-ada**	ENGLISH EQUIVALENT	BASE WORD	ENGLISH EQUIVALENT
la animalada	*pack of animals*	el animal	*animal*
la arañada	*collection of spiders*	la araña	*spider*
la borregada	*large flock of lambs*	el borrego	*young lamb*
la boyada	*drove of oxen*	el buey	*ox*
la burrada	*drove of asses*	el burro	*ass, donkey*
la caballada	*group of horses*	el caballo	*horse*
la carnerada	*flock of sheep*	el carnero	*male sheep, ram*
la cerdada	*herd of swine*	el cerdo	*pig, hog*
la gatada	*group of cats*	el gato	*cat*
la mulada	*drove of mules*	el mulo	*mule*
la novillada	*drove of young bulls*	el novillo	*young bull*
la pavada	*flock of turkeys*	el pavo	*turkey*
la perrada	*pack of dogs*	el perro	*dog*
la torada	*drove of bulls*	el toro	*bull*
la vacada	*herd of cattle*	la vaca	*cow*

EJERCICIO

52·1

Provide the correct form of the appropriate noun (including its article) for each group.

1. Charlotte (*La telaraña de Charlotte*) y sus hijas _____

2. Flicka, Secretariat y Trigger _____

3. Babe, Arnold Ziffel y Wilbur (*La telaraña de Charlotte*) _____

4. Babe (el amigo de Paul Bunyan) y sus amigos _____

5. Elsie, Bessie y Flossie _____

6. Lassie, Benji, Clifford y Toto   _____

7. Morris, Garfield, Felix y Fluffy   _____

8. Ferdinand, Manzanito y Bodacious   _____

9. los amigos jóvenes de Ferdinand, Manzanito y Bodacious   _____

10. el títere Lamb Chop y sus amigos   _____

11. "Tom" y sus amigos antes del día de Acción de Gracias   _____

12. Eeyore, Nestor y Benjamín   _____

Each of the following nouns ending in **-ada** has as its base word something other than an animal.

NOUN ENDING IN **-ada**	ENGLISH EQUIVALENT	BASE WORD	ENGLISH EQUIVALENT
la armada	*navy, fleet, squadron*	el arma [F.]	*weapon, arm, force*
la cotonada	*cotton goods*	el cotón	*cotton fabric*
la década	*decade, ten years*	deka [GRK.]	*ten*
la endécada	*eleven years*	hendeka [GRK.]	*eleven*
la invernada	*winter season*	el invierno	*winter*
la mesada	*monthly pay*	el mes	*month*
la millonada	*huge sum of money, fortune*	el millón	*million*
la obrada	*day's work*	la obra	*(piece of) work*
la otoñada	*autumn season*	el otoño	*autumn, fall*
la palabrada	*verbiage*	la palabra	*word*
la peonada	*gang of laborers*	el peón	*laborer*
la riñonada	*kidney stew*	el riñón	*kidney*
la uvada	*glut of grapes*	la uva	*grape*
la veranada	*summer season*	el verano	*summer*

EJERCICIO
52·2

¿Verdadero o falso? *Indicate whether each statement is true or false, using* **V** *for* **verdadero** *true or* **F** *for* **falso** *false.*

1. _____ Típicamente hace frío en la invernada.

2. _____ Una década dura veinte años.

3. _____ La riñonada es un plato popular con los niños.

4. _____ Cada persona que compra un billete de lotería espera ganar una millonada.

5. _____ Las hojas de muchos árboles cambian de color en la otoñada.

6. _____ Se puede ver muchas uvadas en las viñas de Italia.

7. _____ Las personas en una armada no saben nadar.

8. _____ El adolescente típico está muy feliz después de recibir la mesada.

9. _____ Una endécada dura once años.

10. _____ La obrada de un mulo o un buey en la granja es muy fácil.

11. _____ Los locutores de radio son famosos por su palabrada.

12. _____ En la India hay varias fábricas de cotonadas.

13. _____ Tradicionalmente, la veranada es un tiempo cuando los niños no asisten a la escuela.

14. _____ El jefe de la peonada nunca demanda mucho trabajo.

53 ▸ -ado/-ada

MEANING	Relating to, like
ENGLISH EQUIVALENT	—
PART OF SPEECH	Adjective
GENDER	Masculine/feminine

The suffix **-ado/-ada** is one of several Spanish suffixes meaning *relating to, like*, and numerous adjectives share this suffix. All of the words in the following charts are derived from nouns. The formation of these words is generally straightforward: If the base noun ends in a vowel, the vowel is replaced by **-ado**; if the base noun ends in a consonant, **-ado** is added directly to the noun.

The following adjectives ending in **-ado/-ada** denote colors, shapes, and flavors.

ADJECTIVE ENDING IN **-ado**	ENGLISH EQUIVALENT	BASE WORD	ENGLISH EQUIVALENT
anisado	*aniseed-flavored*	el anís	*anise, aniseed*
azafranado	*saffron-colored*	el azafrán	*saffron*
colorado	*red-colored*	el color	*color*
cuadrado	*square-shaped*	el cuadro	*square*
irisado	*iridescent*	el iris	*iris*
leonado	*tawny, lion-colored*	el león	*lion*
limonado	*lemon-colored*	el limón	*lemon*
nevado	*snow-covered, snow-white*	la nieve	*snow*
nublado	*cloudy, overcast*	la nube	*cloud*
ovalado	*egg-shaped, oval-shaped*	el óvalo	*oval*
rosado	*pink, rosy*	la rosa	*rose, the color pink*
triangulado	*triangle-shaped*	el triángulo	*triangle*

EJERCICIO
53·1

Complete each sentence with the correct form of the appropriate adjective.

1. Los signos de fiebre incluyen la cara _____ y la frente caliente.

2. Una forma geométrica con tres lados es _____.

3. Una forma geométrica con cuatro lados es _____.

4. Un día gris, sin sol, está _____.

5. El arroz en la paella está _____.

6. Se puede decir que un tono del amarillo es _____.

7. El plumaje de un pavo real y una marea negra son _____.

8. Un huevo es _____.

9. Los licores Pernod y Aguardiente son _____.

10. A los esquiadores alpinos les encantan una montaña _____.

11. El cabello _____ es de color rubio oscuro.

12. Se puede producir el vino _____ de una mezcla del vino tinto y el vino blanco, pero eso es infrecuente y es despreciado por los mejores enólogos.

The following adjectives ending in **-ado/-ada** denote feelings, appearances, and characteristics of humans, other animals, and inanimate objects.

ADJECTIVE ENDING IN **-ado**	ENGLISH EQUIVALENT	BASE WORD	ENGLISH EQUIVALENT
avergonzado	*ashamed, embarrassed*	la vergüenza	*shame*
cruzado	*crossed, crossbred*	la cruz	*cross*
destinado	*destined*	el destino	*destination*
enojado	*angry*	el enojo	*anger*
estrellado	*starry, star-filled*	la estrella	*star*
frustrado	*frustrated*	frustratio [LAT.]	*deception, disappointment*
jorobado	*hunchbacked, curved*	la joroba	*hump*
letrado	*learned, lettered*	la letra	*letter, handwriting*
pesado	*heavy*	el peso	*weight*
rayado	*striped, streaked*	la raya	*stripe, streak*
rizado	*curly*	rizar	*to curl*
vertebrado	*vertebrate*	la vértebra	*vertebra, spine*

EJERCICIO
53·2

Complete each sentence with the correct form of the appropriate adjective.

1. Cuasimodo, el campanero de Notre Dame (de la famosa novela de Victor Hugo),

   es _____.

2. La cebra es un animal _____.

3. El labradoodle (parte labrador y parte caniche) es un ejemplo de un perro

   _____.

4. "Una tonelada de ladrillos" es una expresión que describe algo muy

   _____.

5. Después de cometer un *faux pas*, una persona usualmente se siente

_____.

6. La famosa pintura *La noche* _____ por Vincent van Gogh está expuesto en el Museo de Arte Moderno de Nueva York.

7. Un animal _____ tiene una columna espinal.

8. Cuando el coche no arranca o algo no funciona como debe funcionar, una persona casi

ciertamente está _____ y _____.

9. Un graduado de la universidad de Oxford es un hombre educado y

_____.

10. En la peluquería, una permanente crea un peinado _____.

11. Después de muchos años de trabajo intenso en la escuela secundaria y en la universidad,

el buen graduado está _____ a tener un futuro brillante.

54 ▸ -aje

MEANING	Landing
ENGLISH EQUIVALENT	—
PART OF SPEECH	Noun
GENDER	Masculine

The suffix **-aje** is rare because of its specific meaning: it denotes a landing. **-Aje** may also denote a collection/set (No. 103) or fee/toll (No. 104).

NOUN ENDING IN **-aje**	ENGLISH EQUIVALENT	BASE WORD	ENGLISH EQUIVALENT
el alunizaje	*moon landing*	alunizar	*to land on the moon*
el arribaje	*harbor entry*	arribar	*to arrive at port*
el aterraje	*landfall, landing* (*nautical*)	aterrar	*to reach land* (*nautical*)
el aterrizaje	*landing* (*aerial*)	aterrizar	*to land* (*aerial*)

EJERCICIO
54·1

Complete each sentence with the appropriate noun.

1. El primer _____ ocurrió el 20 de julio 1969, cuando Neil Armstrong, Buzz Aldrin y Michael Collins llegaron a la luna.

2. Al ver la tierra, los exploradores y piratas por igual esperan un _____ seguro.

3. Durante un vuelo, todos los pasajeros y el piloto del avión esperan un

_____ seguro.

4. Al entrar en el puerto, el capitán del crucero espera un _____ seguro.

 **-ante**

MEANING	Relating to, like; doing
ENGLISH EQUIVALENT	*-ant, -ing*
PART OF SPEECH	Adjective
GENDER	Masculine/feminine

The suffix **-ante** confers the characteristic of the base verb on a person, place, or thing. The base verb is an **-ar** verb; a related suffix **-ente** (No. 71) produces adjectives from **-er** and **-ir** verbs. Since the English translation of a suffixed word is frequently a word ending in *-ing*, it is important not to confuse the word with the English present progressive, which ends in *-ing*, as in *I am studying*. The ambiguous English sentence *They are fascinating women* may be expressed in two very different sentences in Spanish: **Ellas son mujeres fascinantes** and **Ellos están fascinando a las mujeres**.

ADJECTIVE ENDING IN **-ante**	ENGLISH EQUIVALENT	BASE WORD	ENGLISH EQUIVALENT
abundante	*abundant, plentiful*	abundar	*to be plentiful*
agravante	*aggravating*	agravar	*to aggravate*
alarmante	*alarming*	alarmar	*to alarm, alert*
ambulante	*traveling, ambulatory*	ambular	*to walk around, wander*
aplastante	*overwhelming, crushing*	aplastar	*to crush, flatten*
brillante	*brilliant, shining, sparkling*	brillar	*to shine*
colgante	*hanging*	colgar	*to hang*
espumante	*sparkling, bubbly*	espumar	*to foam, froth, sparkle*
fascinante	*fascinating, exciting*	fascinar	*to fascinate*
flagrante	*flagrant*	flagrar	*to flame, blaze*

EJERCICIO
55·1

Complete each sentence with the correct form of the appropriate adjective.

1. Algunas personas que han pasado por una muerte clínica y han sobrevivido reportan que

vieron una luz _____ .

2. La champaña es un vino _____ .

3. Guillermo tiene el hábito _____ de interrumpir a sus colegas.

4. Decir que se sorprende un ladrón "con las manos en la masa" es como decir que se sorprende un criminal en _____ delito.

5. Un nómada, por definición, es una persona _____.

6. Un puente _____ (o de suspensión) es un puente con varios cables aéreos que soportan la carretera.

7. Por varios años, la conductora de televisión Barbara Walters ha revelado su "Lista de diez personas más _____ del año."

8. Un gran banquete tiene comida _____.

9. Una mayoría _____ de habitantes de Inglaterra hablan inglés.

10. Antes de las elecciones presidenciales, los anuncios políticos aumentan a un ritmo _____ y los televidentes se sienten cada vez más frustrados y aburridos.

ADJECTIVE ENDING IN -ante	ENGLISH EQUIVALENT	BASE WORD	ENGLISH EQUIVALENT
flamante	brand-new	flamear	to blaze, flare up
interesante	interesting	interesar	to interest
parlante	talking, spoken	parlar	to chatter, talk a lot
participante	participating	participar	to participate
penetrante	penetrating, acute	penetrar	to penetrate
saltante	outstanding, noteworthy	saltar	to jump, leap
sobrante	remaining, left over	sobrar	to remain, be left over
susurrante	whispering	susurrar	to whisper
triunfante	triumphant	triunfar	to succeed, win
vacilante	vacillating, unsteady	vacilar	to vacillate
vibrante	vibrant, full of life	vibrar	to vibrate, be thrilled
vigilante	vigilant	vigilar	to watch, guard

EJERCICIO
55·2

Complete each sentence with the correct form of the appropriate adjective.

1. En las Olimpiadas, las mujeres _____ no compiten directamente contra los hombres.

2. Un _____ coche usualmente viene con una garantía de tres o cuatro años, mientras que un coche usado típicamente se vende "tal cual."

3. Algo aburrido, por definición, no es _____.

4. La característica más _____ de Cyrano de Bergerac o de Pinocho es su nariz enorme.

5. Una persona paranoica siempre está _____ y atenta al peligro de cualquier forma.

6. Un signo de advertencia de la inflamación de la garganta es una voz

_____ y la incapacidad de hablar en voz alta.

7. Después del cambio de aceite de un vehículo, es ilegal tirar el aceite

_____ por el desagüe.

8. Al ganar la medalla de oro, el atleta olímpico se siente _____.

9. Jamaica—donde el idioma oficial es el inglés—es el único país caribeño no

hispano_____.

10. Muchos judíos consideran que las enseñanzas de la Torá son profundas y

_____.

11. Una persona insegura y llena de dudas es una persona cuya confianza en sí misma está

_____.

12. Varias ciudades grandes, como São Paulo, Londres, Tokio y Nueva York, son famosas por

su _____ vida nocturna.

56 ◆ -anza

MEANING	Quality, state, condition; process
ENGLISH EQUIVALENT	*-ance*
PART OF SPEECH	Noun
GENDER	Feminine

A noun ending in **-anza** is derived from **-ar** verbs and denotes the quality, state, condition, or process of the base verb, that is, it represents the result of the action of the base verb. For example, **probar** *to prove, test* yields **la probanza** *proof.* Note that two of the following suffixed nouns—**las andanzas** *adventures, endeavors* and **las finanzas** *finances*—are plural; these words are rarely used in the singular.

NOUN ENDING IN **-anza**	ENGLISH EQUIVALENT	BASE WORD	ENGLISH EQUIVALENT
la adivinanza	*guess, riddle*	adivinar	*to guess*
la alabanza	*praise, glory*	alabar	*to praise*
la alianza	*alliance, wedding ring*	aliar	*to ally, combine*
las andanzas [PL.]	*adventures, endeavors*	andar	*to walk, go, travel*
la añoranza	*homesickness, yearning*	añorar	*to long for, miss*
la balanza	*balance, scales*	balancear	*to balance, swing, rock*
la cobranza	*collection*	cobrar	*to collect*
la confianza	*confidence, trust*	confiar	*to trust*
la crianza	*raising, rearing*	criar	*to raise, rear (children)*
la desconfianza	*distrust*	desconfiar	*to distrust*
la desemejanza	*dissimilarity*	desemejar	*to be dissimilar/unlike*
la desesperanza	*hopelessness, despair*	desesperar	*to despair, lose hope*

Complete each sentence with the correct form of the appropriate noun.

1. Si no pagas tus deudas, seguramente vas a recibir una llamada de una agencia de

   _____.

2. La responsabilidad más importante de cualquier padre o madre es la

   _____ de sus niños.

3. Es imposible tener _____ en una persona que te miente con frecuencia o que no respeta los sentimientos tuyos.

4. Durante el primer semestre, muchos universitarios experimentan la

   _____ por el hogar.

5. Una _____ clásica es ¿Por qué cruzó el pollo la carretera?

6. El objetivo principal del Secretario de Estado es forjar las _____ entre países.

7. Una persona que sufre de depresión grave tiene una sensación de

   _____.

8. La novela más famosa y popular de Miguel de Cervantes Saavedra describe las

   _____ de Don Quiote y de su fiel acompañante Sancho Panza.

9. Cuando una persona está a dieta y monitorea su peso cada día, es importante usar la

   misma _____ todos los días.

10. Promover la diversidad es alentar el reconocimiento de la individualidad y de la

    _____ de todas las personas en una comunidad determinada.

11. En casi cada servicio religioso, los fieles cantan himnos de _____ a Dios.

12. Al descubrir un cónyuge infiel, es natural tener sentimientos de traición, de desilusión

    y de _____.

NOUN ENDING IN **-anza**	ENGLISH EQUIVALENT	BASE WORD	ENGLISH EQUIVALENT
la enseñanza	*teaching, instruction*	enseñar	*to teach*
la fianza	*bail, bond, security*	fiar	*to give credit, trust*
las finanzas [PL.]	*finances*	financiar	*to fund, finance*
la holganza	*idleness, leisure*	holgar	*to be idle*
la labranza	*cultivation, tilling*	labrar	*to cultivate*
la matanza	*killing, slaughter*	matar	*to kill*
la mudanza	*move (residential)*	mudarse	*to move, change residence*
la ordenanza	*ordinance, law*	ordenar	*to put in order, arrange*
la probanza	*proof*	probar	*to prove, test*
la pujanza	*strength, vigor*	pujar	*to struggle*

▶

NOUN ENDING IN -anza	ENGLISH EQUIVALENT	BASE WORD	ENGLISH EQUIVALENT
la semejanza	*similarity, resemblance*	semejar	*to resemble*
la tardanza	*delay*	tardar	*to be late*
la templanza	*temperance*	templar	*to moderate, temper*
la venganza	*revenge, vengeance*	vengar	*to avenge*

EJERCICIO
56·2

¿Verdadero o falso? *Indicate whether each statement is true or false, using* **V** *for* **verdadero** *true or* **F** *for* **falso** *false.*

1. _____ En vez de ir directamente a la cárcel, a veces los acusados reciben libertad provisional con la fianza antes de la iniciación del juicio.

2. _____ Nadie siente nunca el estrés durante la preparación para la mudanza.

3. _____ Después de un accidente grave, la tardanza de la ambulancia es horrible.

4. _____ Los recién casados no necesitan preocuparse por las finanzas porque ellos pueden vivir del amor.

5. _____ El filósofo Plato fue impresionado por las enseñanzas de Sócrates y, a su vez, el estudiante Aristóteles fue impresionado por las enseñanzas de Plato.

6. _____ Después de ganar la lotería, muchas personas creen que pueden vivir la vida de holganza.

7. _____ La semejanza entre los gemelos idénticos es increíble.

8. _____ Carrie Nation es una de las personas más famosas del movimiento por la templanza (la lucha contra el alcohol) durante los primeros años del siglo veinte.

9. _____ Una ordenanza es una ley aprobada por un consejo municipal.

10. _____ Cuando una persona siente rabia y quiere venganza, probablemente esta persona necesita hablar con un confidente o un psicólogo sensato.

11. _____ La organización internacional PETA está en favor de la matanza de animales para el uso de pieles naturales.

12. _____ Unas de las funciones de la labranza es destruir las malas hierbas.

57 ▷ -arca

MEANING	Ruler
ENGLISH EQUIVALENT	*-arch*
PART OF SPEECH	Noun
GENDER	Masculine/feminine

The suffix **-arca** denotes a ruler (or no ruler at all, as in the case of **el anarca** *anarchist*). Almost all of the Spanish nouns with this suffix have English cognates, so they are easily recognized and used. The Spanish ending **-arca** is typically *-arch* in English and, with the exceptions of **el patriarca** *patriarch* and **la matriarca** *matriarch*, may denote either a male or a female, for example, **el/la monarca** *monarch*. Examples are **el monarca Augusto de Roma** and **la monarca Victoria del Reino Unido.**

NOUN ENDING IN **-arca**	ENGLISH EQUIVALENT	BASE WORD	ENGLISH EQUIVALENT
el anarca	*anarchist*	an- [GRK.]	*without*
el jerarca	*leader, high priest*	hieros [GRK.]	*sacred*
la matriarca	*matriarch*	mater [LAT.]	*mother*
el monarca	*monarch*	monos [GRK.]	*single, alone*
el oligarca	*oligarch, one of few rulers*	oligos [GRK.]	*few, little*
el patriarca	*patriarch*	pater [LAT.]	*father*
el pentarca	*one of five joint rulers*	pente [GRK.]	*five*
el tetrarca	*one of four joint rulers*	tetra [GRK.]	*four*

EJERCICIO
57·1

¿Quién es esto? *Complete each sentence with the correct form of the appropriate noun that names each leader.*

1. La líder de una familia es la _____.

2. El líder de una familia es el _____.

3. En un gobierno con sólo una reina, la líder es la _____.

4. Uno de cuatro líderes de un gobierno es un _____.

5. Uno de cinco líderes de un gobierno es un _____.

6. Uno de los líderes de un gobierno que tiene dos o tres personas que dirigen el gobierno

   es un _____.

7. El sacerdote principal o un arzobispo es el _____.

8. Una persona que piensa que ni el gobierno ni sus líderes son necesarios es un

   _____.

58 ◆ -ario/-aria

MEANING	Relating to, like	
ENGLISH EQUIVALENT	*-ary*	
PART OF SPEECH	Adjective	
GENDER	Masculine/feminine	

The suffix **-ario/-aria** may be used to create an adjective; the base word may be a verb, noun, or adjective. (See No. 59 for the use of **-ario/-aria** as a noun suffix, and No. 9 for the use of **-ario** as a noun suffix.) Since many of these suffixed adjectives have English cognates, they tend to be easily recognized and used.

ADJECTIVE ENDING IN **-ario**	ENGLISH EQUIVALENT	BASE WORD	ENGLISH EQUIVALENT
arbitrario	*arbitrary*	arbitrar	*to arbitrate, referee*
centenario	*centenary, century-old*	ciento	*one hundred*
contrario	*contrary, opposite*	contra	*against*
estacionario	*stationary, fixed*	la estación	*station*
hereditario	*hereditary*	heredar	*to inherit*
honorario	*honorary*	el honor	*honor*
literario	*literary*	la letra	*letter*
necesario	*necessary*	necesitar	*to need*
ordinario	*ordinary, common, coarse*	el orden	*order*
primario	*primary, essential*	primo	*prime*
rutinario	*routine*	la rutina	*routine*
sanitario	*sanitary*	sano	*healthy*
semanario	*weekly*	la semana	*week*
visionario	*visionary*	la visión	*vision*
voluntario	*voluntary*	la voluntad	*will, willpower*

EJERCICIO
58·1

*Complete each sentence with either **es** or **no es** OR **son** or **no son** to create a true statement.*

1. Algo que no se mueve _____ estacionario.

2. La reina de Inglaterra _____ ordinaria.

3. Una decisión seria y difícil _____ arbitraria.

4. El objetivo primario de cualquier aerolínea _____ servirles a los pasajeros la comida más exquisita posible.

5. Las obras de Miguel de Cervantes Saavedra _____ literarias.

6. La cloaca _____ sanitaria.

7. Algo muy aburrido probablemente _____ rutinario.

8. El servicio militar en Israel _____ voluntario.

9. Una persona que tiene cien años _____ centenaria.

10. Un título honorario de una universidad _____ tan bueno como el título autentico.

11. Los tabloides *The Enquirer* y *Weekly World News* _____ semanarios.

12. El color de los ojos _____ hereditario.

13. Henry Ford, Isaac Newton, Thomas Edison y Charles Darwin _____ nombres de visionarios e inventores.

14. Una persona que siempre defiende la posición contraria, especialmente durante una cena con unos invitados, _____ popular.

15. La esposa de trofeo típica cree que un anillo de compromiso con diamante enorme _____ necesario.

In the following chart, **canario** *of the Canary Islands* has nothing to do with canaries. Rather, its Latin root refers to the large dogs that inhabited the island, so many of them that Mauretanian king Juba II named the island **Canaria**!

ADJECTIVE ENDING IN -ario	ENGLISH EQUIVALENT	BASE WORD	ENGLISH EQUIVALENT
bancario	*relating to banking*	bancar	*to pay for*
canario	*of the Canary Islands*	canis [LAT.]	*dog*
coronario	*coronary, of the heart*	la corona	*crown*
diario	*daily*	el día	*day*
funerario	*relating to a funeral*	el funeral	*funeral*
millonario	*millionaire*	millón	*million*
nonagenario	*ninety-year-old*	nonaginta [LAT.]	*ninety*
planetario	*planetary*	el planeta	*planet*
plenario	*plenary, full*	pleno	*full*
secundario	*secondary*	segundo	*second*
sedentario	*sedentary*	sedente	*seated*
suplementario	*supplementary*	el suplemento	*supplement*
terciario	*tertiary, third in order*	el tercio	*third, third part*
universitario	*of the university*	la universidad	*university*

EJERCICIO 58·2

¿Verdadero o falso? *Indicate whether each statement is true or false, using* **V** *for* **verdadero** *true or* **F** *for* **falso** *false.*

1. _____ La sala de redacción de un periódico diario es un lugar muy tranquilo.

2. _____ Una vida sedentaria contribuye a la mala salud.

3. _____ Hay muchos trabajadores nonagenarios porque cien años es la edad de jubilación en la mayoría de los países del mundo.

4. _____ La mayoría de los estudiantes en casi todas las escuelas secundarias se gradúan.

5. _____ Muchas nuevas empresas necesitan un préstamo bancario para iniciarse.

6. _____ La educación terciaria es más o menos sinónima de la educación universitaria.

7. _____ El bypass coronario es un procedimiento médico común para los adolescentes.

8. _____ Una sesión plenaria es una reunión para todos los miembros de una conferencia.

9. _____ Una mujer que aspira a ser esposa de trofeo necesita un esposo millonario.

10. _____ Los padres de quintillizos necesitan mucha ayuda suplementaria.

11. _____ El ritual funerario ocurre antes de la muerte de una persona.

12. _____ El archipiélago Canario es una comunidad autónoma de España.

59 ◆ -ario/-aria

MEANING	Person/thing possessing a characteristic
ENGLISH EQUIVALENT	*-ary*
PART OF SPEECH	Noun
GENDER	Masculine/feminine

The suffix -**ario**/-**aria** may denote a person or thing that has the essential characteristic of the base word. (See No. 58 for the use of -**ario**/-**aria** as an adjective suffix, and No. 9 for the use of -**ario** as a noun suffix.)

NOUN ENDING IN -**ario**	ENGLISH EQUIVALENT	BASE WORD	ENGLISH EQUIVALENT
el actuario	*actuary*	actus [LAT.]	*public business*
el adversario	*adversary*	adverso	*adverse*
el beneficiario	*beneficiary*	el beneficio	*to benefit*
el boticario	*apothecary, druggist*	la botica	*drugstore*
el canario	*canary*	canis [LAT.]	*dog*
el centenario	*100-year anniversary*	ciento	*one hundred*
el contrario	*opposite*	contra	*against*
el diario	*diary, daily newspaper*	el día	*day*
el dignatario	*dignitary*	digno	*worthy*
el honorario	*fee, honorarium*	el honor	*honor*
el millonario	*millionaire*	millón	*million*
el misionario	*missionary*	la misión	*mission*

¿Verdadero o falso? *Indicate whether each statement is true or false, using* **V** *for* **verdadero** *true or* **F** *for* **falso** *false.*

1. _____ Hay más billonarios que millonarios en el mundo.

2. _____ Los adversarios de Batman incluyen el Riddler, el Joker, Catwoman y el Pingüino.

3. _____ Anne Frank es conocida por su diario.

4. _____ En 2039 conmemoraremos el centenario del estallido de la Segunda Guerra Mundial.

5. _____ Es necesario designar a un beneficiario cuando se compra una póliza de seguro de vida.

6. _____ Un misionario raramente es religioso.

7. _____ Un actuario típicamente no es bueno en matemáticas.

8. _____ Un Marxista sostiene que el capitalismo es la fuente de todos los males, pero los capitalistas piensan lo contrario.

9. _____ Cuando un dignatario de una nación visita otro país, usualmente se aloja en un hotel económico y sucio.

10. _____ Un boticario trabaja en una farmacia.

11. _____ Cuando un ex-presidente ofrece un discurso, típicamente recibe un honorario de más o menos cincuenta dólares.

12. _____ Los mineros llevaban canarios a las minas de carbón para detectar la acumulación del gas metano, porque sabían que cuando el canario moría, ellos tenían que salir inmediatamente de la mina.

NOUN ENDING IN **-ario**	ENGLISH EQUIVALENT	BASE WORD	ENGLISH EQUIVALENT
el nonagenario	*person in his nineties*	nonaginta [LAT.]	*ninety*
el notario	*notary (public)*	notar	*to note*
el ordinario	*the commonplace*	el orden	*order*
el planetario	*planetarium*	el planeta	*planet*
el rosario	*rosary*	la rosa	*rose*
el sanitario	*health officer, toilet*	sano	*healthy*
el secretario	*secretary*	el secreto	*secret*
el semanario	*weekly publication*	la semana	*week*
el seminario	*seminary, seminar*	el semen	*semen, seed*
el universitario	*university student*	la universidad	*university*
el visionario	*visionary*	la visión	*vision*
el voluntario	*volunteer*	la voluntad	*will, willpower*

Complete each sentence with either **es** *or* **no es** *OR* **son** *or* **no son** *to create a true statement.*

1. Un planetario _____ un modelo o representación del sistema solar.

2. Un voluntario _____ un asalariado (una persona que recibe un salario).

3. Si tú oyes que una nonagenaria está embarazada, _____ una mentira.

4. *Time, OK!, People* y *The Economist* _____ semanarios.

5. El ordinario _____ similar a la mediocridad o la banalidad.

6. Un universitario que tiene doce años _____ un prodigio.

7. En el bosque, el sanitario con frecuencia _____ un hoyo en la tierra.

8. El rosario _____ un rezo de devoción para los católicos.

9. Una buena secretaria jurídica _____ necesaria para un prominente bufete de abogados.

10. Un seminario _____ para aquellos que quieren ser sacerdotes o ministros.

11. Los autoproclamados visionarios, especialmente los que tienen programas de televisión muy tarde de noche, _____ honestos.

12. _____ necesario que un notario público tenga una estampilla de goma.

60 ▸ -asma, -asmo

MEANING	Result of an action, condition; being
ENGLISH EQUIVALENT	*-asm*
PART OF SPEECH	Noun
GENDER	Masculine

The suffix **-asma** or **-asmo** is ultimately derived from Greek and denotes a condition or the result of an action. The suffixed words are of Latin or Greek origin and are masculine, whether they end in **-asma** or **-asmo**. (In general, nouns ending in **-asma** are derived from Latin nouns and nouns ending in **-asmo** are derived directly from Greek words.)

NOUN ENDING IN -asma, -asmo	ENGLISH EQUIVALENT	BASE WORD	ENGLISH EQUIVALENT
el citoplasma	cytoplasm	kytos + plasma [GRK.]	vessel + something formed
el entusiasmo	enthusiasm	enthousiazein [GRK.]	to be inspired by a god
el espasmo	spasm	spasmos [GRK.]	spasm, convulsion
el fantasma	ghost	phantasma [LAT.]	apparition
el marasmo	stagnation, atrophy (medical)	marasmos [GRK.]	wasting away, decay
el miasma	miasma	miasma [LAT.]	noxious vapors
el orgasmo	orgasm	orgasmos [GRK.]	swelling, excitement
el plasma	plasma (biology)	plasma [GRK.]	something formed
el protoplasma	protoplasm	protos + plasma [GRK.]	first + something formed
el sarcasmo	sarcasm	sarkasmos [GRK.]	sneer, jest, mockery

EJERCICIO
60·1

Complete each sentence with the correct form of the appropriate noun.

1. Uso de la ironía humillante es un ejemplo del _____.

2. El interés intenso es el _____.

3. Un espíritu, una aparición o un poltergeist es un _____.

4. Una contracción muscular e involuntaria es un _____.

5. El clímax de la excitación sexual es el _____.

6. La emanación de un olor horrible que se desprende de aguas estancadas es el

   _____.

7. El enflaquecimiento extremado del cuerpo humano es el _____.

8. El líquido incoloro de la sangre es el _____.

9. El contenido vivo de una célula, rodeado por una membrana plasmática, es el

   _____.

10. El material dentro de la célula viva, excluso el núcleo, es el _____.

61 ◆ -aza

MEANING	Augmentative; depreciative
ENGLISH EQUIVALENT	—
PART OF SPEECH	Noun
GENDER	Masculine

The suffix -**aza**, like its more common related suffix -**azo** (No. 11), may indicate an enlargement or exaggeration of the base word. The augmentation may reflect an increase in physical size (for example, **la pernaza** *thick/big leg*, from **la pierna** *leg*). However, the suffix -**aza** may convey an unpleasant connotation (for example, **la sangraza** *filthy blood*, from **la sangre** *blood*).

NOUN ENDING IN -**aza**	ENGLISH EQUIVALENT	BASE WORD	ENGLISH EQUIVALENT
la barbaza	*long and shaggy beard*	la barba	*beard*
la barcaza	*barge*	la barca	*small boat*
la bocaza	*large/wide mouth*	la boca	*mouth*
la carnaza	*abundance of meat*	la carne	*meat*
la hilaza	*yarn, coarse thread*	el hilo	*thread*
la madraza	*doting mother*	la madre	*mother*
la manaza	*large hand*	la mano	*hand*
la pajaza	*straw refuse*	la paja	*straw*
la pernaza	*thick/big leg*	la pierna	*leg*
la sangraza	*filthy blood*	la sangre	*blood*
la terraza	*terrace*	la tierra	*land, earth*
la trapaza	*fraud, deceitful trick*	trapacear	*to cheat, swindle*

EJERCICIO
61·1

Complete each sentence with the correct form of the appropriate noun.

1. Una madre indulgente es una _____.

2. Santa Claus es famoso por su _____ blanca.

3. Se teje un suéter con _____.

4. Es difícil reparar los relojes si alguien tiene una _____.

5. La _____ transporta carga, típicamente por canales y ríos.

6. Un payaso usualmente tiene una _____ en su rostro.

7. Un vampiro extremadamente vil prefiere beber la _____.

8. Se encuentra la _____ en el suelo del establo de caballos.

9. A los animales carnívoros les encanta la _____.

10. Se puede gozar del aire fresco en la _____ de la casa.

11. Las personas con _____ no deben llevar pantalones ajustados.

62 ◆ -azo

MEANING	Blow, strike, swift movement; resulting action
ENGLISH EQUIVALENT	—
PART OF SPEECH	Noun
GENDER	Masculine

A noun with the suffix **-azo** may denote the swift movement of an object and may be translated *blow*, *strike*, *hit*, *shove*, *slam*, and so forth. (See the related suffix **-ada** in No. 51.) Nouns ending in **-azo** are compact and tidy, compared to the English phrase that is usually necessary to express them.

The following nouns ending in **-azo** feature a broad range of ways to whack or poke somene.

NOUN ENDING IN -azo	ENGLISH EQUIVALENT	BASE WORD	ENGLISH EQUIVALENT
el alazo	*strike with the wings*	el ala [F.]	*wing*
el chinelazo	*blow with a slipper*	la chinela	*slipper*
el palazo	*whack or blow with a shovel*	la pala	*shovel*
el patinazo	*skid, blunder*	el patín	*skate*
el picazo	*jab, peck*	el pico	*beak, bill*
el portazo	*door slam*	la puerta	*door*
el pretinazo	*strike with a belt*	la pretina	*belt, leather strap*
el tablazo	*strike with a board*	la tabla	*board*
el tacazo	*strike with a billiard cue*	el taco	*billiard cue*
el tijeretazo	*cut or snip with a scissors*	la(s) tijera(s)	*scissors*
el timbrazo	*sharp ring of a bell*	el timbre	*bell*

EJERCICIO
62·1

Provide the correct form of the appropriate noun(s) (including the article) to describe the result of likely action by the people mentioned in each item.

1. la Cenicienta (*Cinderella*) _____

2. un pájaro _____

   _____

3. un jugador del billar _____

4. un niño que entra y sale de la casa muy rápidamente _____

5. una costurera como Betsy Ross _____

6. un carpintero _____

7. un hombre abusivo con un cinturón _____

8. un campanero como Cuasimodo _____

9. un sepulturero _____

10. un conductor o un taxista _____

¡La violencia! A noun ending in **-azo** often denotes or refers to a violent act.

NOUN ENDING IN -azo	ENGLISH EQUIVALENT	BASE WORD	ENGLISH EQUIVALENT
el balazo	*gunshot, bullet wound*	la bala	*bullet*
el botonazo	*thrust with fencing foil*	el botón	*tip of foil*
el culatazo	*kick of a gun*	la culata	*butt of a gun*
el escopetazo	*gunshot wound*	la escopeta	*shotgun*
el estacazo	*blow with a stake*	la estaca	*stake, stick*
el gatillazo	*click of a trigger*	el gatillo	*gun trigger*
el golpazo	*violent blow, heavy thump*	el golpe	*hit, blow*
el latigazo	*whipping, lashing*	el látigo	*whip*
el pistoletazo	*pistol shot*	la pistola	*pistol*
el porrazo	*blow, knock, fall*	la porra	*stick, nightstick*
el puñetazo	*blow with a fist, punch*	el puño	*fist*
el varazo	*whack with a pole*	la vara	*pole, rod, staff*

EJERCICIO

62·2

Provide the correct noun ending in -azo for each of the following base words. Include the article.

1. el gatillo _____

2. la culata _____

3. la pistola _____

4. la bala _____

5. la escopeta _____

6. el puño _____

7. el botón _____

8. la porra _____

9. la estaca _____

10. el látigo _____

11. la vara _____

12. el golpe _____

The nouns in the following exercise are based on nouns that should be familiar to you; the base nouns are provided in parentheses.

¡Resuélvelo! *Match each of the following nouns ending in* **-azo** *with its English equivalent. The base word for each noun ending in* **-azo** *is provided for you.*

1. _____ el botellazo (la botella)   a. *slap with an open hand or glove*

2. _____ el codazo (el codo)   b. *stroke of a pen*

3. _____ el guantazo (el guante)   c. *blow with a ball*

4. _____ el librazo (el libro)   d. *blow with a shoe*

5. _____ el martillazo (el martillo)   e. *blow with a bottle*

6. _____ el pelotazo (la pelota)   f. *shove with an elbow*

7. _____ el plumazo (la pluma)   g. *slamming of a window*

8. _____ el rodillazo (la rodilla)   h. *blow with a hammer*

9. _____ el ventanazo (la ventana)   i. *blow with a book*

10. _____ el zapatazo (el zapato)   j. *shove with the knee*

63 ▸ -cial

MEANING	Relating to, like
ENGLISH EQUIVALENT	*-cial, -tial*
PART OF SPEECH	Adjective
GENDER	Masculine/feminine

Most Spanish adjectives ending in **-cial** have English cognates, so they tend to be easy to recognize and use. The suffix **-cial** is identical in function to the suffix **-al** in No. 5. The base words for this suffix end in **-c**, **-t**, or **-z**. For ease of pronunciation and to maintain the original **s** sound of the **c** and **z**, the ending **-al** becomes **-cial**.

ADJECTIVE ENDING IN **-cial**	ENGLISH EQUIVALENT	BASE WORD	ENGLISH EQUIVALENT
artificial	*artificial, man-made*	el artificio	*artifice, craft, trick*
comercial	*commercial, relating to trade*	el comercio	*trade, commerce*
consecuencial	*resulting, consequential*	la consecuencia	*consequence*
crucial	*crucial*	la cruz	*cross*
esencial	*essential*	la esencia	*essence*
especial	*special, particular*	la especie	*species, kind, sort*
existencial	*existential*	la existencia	*existence*
exponencial	*exponential*	el exponente	*exponent*
judicial	*judicial*	el juicio	*judgment*
palacial	*palatial*	el palacio	*palace*
parcial	*partial*	la parte	*part*
penitencial	*penitential*	la penitencia	*penance, punishment*

Complete each sentence with the correct form of the appropriate adjective.

1. Una casa enorme y espléndida es _____.

2. Algo que no es natural, pero que es hecho por el hombre, es _____.

3. Algo absolutamente necesario es _____ o

_____.

4. Algo que se trata de un exponente es _____.

5. Algo que es el resulto o efecto de una acción es _____.

6. Una decisión del juez es _____.

7. Algo que no es común o general es _____.

8. Algo que se trata del sacramento de la reconciliación es _____.

9. Algo que tiene como el objetivo principal las ganancias financieras es

_____.

10. Un eclipse que no es completo es _____.

11. Lo que se trata de la existencia es _____.

ADJECTIVE ENDING IN -cial	ENGLISH EQUIVALENT	BASE WORD	ENGLISH EQUIVALENT
perjudicial	*harmful, detrimental*	el perjuicio	*damage, loss*
policial	*of the police*	la policía	*police (department)*
presencial	*on-site, in-person*	la presencia	*presence*
providencial	*fortunate*	la providencia	*providence, precaution*
provincial	*provincial*	la provincia	*province*
racial	*racial*	la raza	*race, lineage*
residencial	*residential*	la residencia	*residence, domicile*
social	*social*	el socio	*partner, member*
superficial	*superficial, shallow*	la superficie	*surface, area*
sustancial	*substantial, solid*	la sustancia	*substance*
tangencial	*tangential*	la tangente	*tangent*
torrencial	*torrential, overpowering*	el torrente	*torrent*

¿Verdadero o falso? *Indicate whether each statement is true or false, using* **V** *for* **verdadero** *true or* **F** *for* **falso** *false.*

1. _____ Un testigo presencial vale más que un reportero de un crimen.

2. _____ Típicamente, una persona superficial es bien educada.

3. _____ Las tensiones raciales son la causa de varias disputas.

4. _____ Una fiesta es un evento social.

5. _____ Cualquier callejón de Nueva York es un exclusivo enclave residencial.

6. _____ Según la Biblia, Noé y su familia, en el arca llena de animales, pasaron cuarenta días y noches en una lluvia torrencial.

7. _____ Un terremoto siempre es bienvenido y providencial.

8. _____ Una investigación policial típicamente ocurre después de un crimen.

9. _____ La contaminación del aire es perjudicial para el medio ambiente.

10. _____ Se puede ver una reducción sustancial del peso de una persona que ha perdido cien libras.

11. _____ Un comento tangencial es bien conectado al punto original.

12. _____ Londres, Nueva York y Paris son ciudades muy provinciales.

64 ◆ -cidio

MEANING	Murder, killing
ENGLISH EQUIVALENT	*-cide*
PART OF SPEECH	Noun
GENDER	Masculine

Detectives and forensics fans, this one's for you! Most of the Spanish nouns with the suffix **-cidio** have English cognates, so they tend to be easily recognized and used. The base word for most of these suffixed nouns is a Latin root that may be familiar to you, since many of these roots are found in common English words.

NOUN ENDING IN **-cidio**	ENGLISH EQUIVALENT	BASE WORD	ENGLISH EQUIVALENT
el conyugicidio	*murder of one's spouse*	el cónyuge	*spouse*
el deicidio	*deicide, murder of a god*	dios	*god*
el excidio	*destruction, depopulation*	ex [LAT.]	*out of*
el feticidio	*killing of a fetus*	el feto	*fetus*
el filicidio	*murder of one's child*	filius [LAT.]	*son*
el fratricidio	*fratricide, murder of a brother*	frater [LAT.]	*brother*
el genocidio	*genocide*	genus [LAT.]	*race, species*
el homicidio	*homicide, murder*	homo [LAT.]	*human*
el infanticidio	*infanticide, killing of an infant*	el infante	*infant*
el magnicidio	*murder of an important person*	magnus [LAT.]	*great*
el matricidio	*matricide, murder of one's mother*	mater [LAT.]	*mother*
el parricidio	*patricide, murder of one's father*	parus [LAT.]	*relative*
el regicidio	*regicide, murder of a king*	rex [LAT.]	*king*
el suicidio	*suicide*	sui [LAT.]	*of oneself*
el tiranicidio	*tyrannicide, murder of a tyrant*	el tirano	*tyrant*
el uxoricidio	*uxoricide, murder of one's wife*	uxor [LAT.]	*wife*

EJERCICIO

64·1

Provide the correct noun (including its article) for each description.

1. el asesinato del hermano _____

2. el asesinato de o el esposo o la esposa _____

3. el asesinato de la esposa _____

4. el asesinato de un bebé _____

5. el asesinato de un niño no nacido _____

6. el asesinato del padre _____

7. el asesinato de la madre _____

8. el asesinato del hijo o de la hija _____

9. el asesinato de un ser divino _____

10. el asesinato del rey _____

11. el asesinato del déspota _____

12. el asesinato de una persona importante _____

13. el asesinato en masa de una raza _____

14. el asesinato de otra persona _____

15. el asesinato de sí mismo _____

16. la ruina y destrucción de un pueblo _____

65 ▸ -culo, -cula

MEANING	Diminutive; result of an action
ENGLISH EQUIVALENT	*-c(u)le*
PART OF SPEECH	Noun
GENDER	Masculine/feminine

The suffix -**culo** (less commonly, -**cula**) often denotes a very small object (for example, **el taber-náculo** *tabernacle*, from **la taberna** *hut, booth*). Many of the nouns formed with this suffix are taken directly from Latin. The suffix -**(c)ulo** may also denote the result of an action; suffixed nouns with this meaning are derived from verbs (for example, **el obstáculo** *obstacle* is derived from the Latin verb **obstare** *to stand before, block*). Note that the stress in these nouns falls on the antepenultimate syllable, which is accented.

Each of the following nouns ending in -**culo** or -**cula** is a diminutive of the base word.

NOUN ENDING IN -culo, -cula	ENGLISH EQUIVALENT	BASE WORD	ENGLISH EQUIVALENT
el artículo	*article, item, knuckle*	artus [LAT.]	*joint*
el círculo	*circle, club*	circulus [LAT.]	*circle, hoop*
el cubículo	*cubicle*	cubiculum [LAT.]	*bedroom*
el edículo	*small building*	aedificium [LAT.]	*building*
el folículo	*follicle*	follis [LAT.]	*bellows, inflated ball*
el minúsculo	*lowercase letter*	minus [LAT.]	*less*
la molécula	*molecule, minute particle*	moles [LAT.]	*mass, barrier*
el pedículo	*foot-like structure, tumor base*	pes/pedis [LAT.]	*foot*
la película	*film, movie*	pellicula [LAT.]	*small skin*
el pináculo	*pinnacle*	pinna [LAT.]	*peak, point*
el signáculo	*seal, signet*	el signo	*sign, mark, symbol*
el tabernáculo	*tabernacle*	la taberna	*hut, booth*
el testículo	*testicle*	el teste	*testis*
el ventrículo	*ventricle, cavity of a body organ*	venter/ventris [LAT.]	*belly*
el versículo	*short verse, Bible verse*	versus [LAT.]	*verse, line of writing*

EJERCICIO
65·1

Complete each sentence with the correct form of the appropriate noun.

1. Vamos al cine para ver una _____.

2. El _____ es una forma geométrica básica.

3. Otro nombre para un edificio pequeño es un _____.

4. Todos los días se puede leer innumerables _____ en el *Guardian*, el *New York Times* y el *Daily Telegraph*.

5. Se puede leer innumerables _____ en la Biblia.

6. El punto más alto de una montaña es el _____.

7. El estómago, como otras cavidades dentro de un órgano del cuerpo, es un

   _____.

8. Un vendedor telefónico trabaja a menudo en un _____.

9. No es correcto comenzar una oración con un _____.

10. En una iglesia católica, se puede encontrar las hostias consagradas en el

    _____.

11. La _____ se compone de dos átomos o más, y es la mínima porción de una sustancia química.

12. El órgano que produce el esperma en el hombre es el _____.

13. El órgano situado en la piel de que emerge el pelo es el _____.

14. El sello o señal en lo escrito es un _____.

15. Algunos pólipos y tumores tienen un _____ y otros, no.

The following nouns ending in **-culo** denote the result of the action of the base verb.

NOUN ENDING IN **-culo**	ENGLISH EQUIVALENT	BASE WORD	ENGLISH EQUIVALENT
el obstáculo	*obstacle*	obstare [LAT.]	*to stand before, block*
el oráculo	*oracle, font of wisdom*	orare [LAT.]	*to plead, pray*
el receptáculo	*receptacle, vessel*	recipere [LAT.]	*to hold, contain*
el ridículo	*the ridiculous, embarrassment*	ridere [LAT.]	*to laugh*
el tentáculo	*tentacle*	tentar	*to feel, grope*
el vehículo	*vehicle*	vehere [LAT.]	*to carry*
el vínculo	*link, tie, bond*	vincular	*to tie, bind*

EJERCICIO
65·2

Provide the noun that is related to each group of words. Include its article.

1. el profeta, el vidente, el adivino _____

2. el automóvil, el autobús, el transporte _____

3. la burla, el sarcasmo, la risa _____

4. el contenedor, el recipiente, el depósito _____

5. la conexión, la relación, el lazo _____

6. la barricada, la fortaleza, la obstrucción _____

7. el tentador, la garra, la pinza _____

66 ▸ -dor

MEANING	Device, machine, appliance
ENGLISH EQUIVALENT	—
PART OF SPEECH	Noun
GENDER	Masculine

A noun with the suffix **-dor** denotes a device, machine, or appliance that performs a specific function. Each of these nouns is directly derived from a verb, usually an **-ar** verb; note that the **a** of the infinitive ending is retained before the suffix **-dor** (for example, **calentar** *to heat* yields **el calentador** *heater*). This retention of the infinitive's thematic vowel is nearly universal, so that **-er** base verbs retain the **e** and **-ir** base verbs retain the **i**. A related suffix, **-dora** (No. 67), has the same meaning and differs only in gender.

NOUN ENDING IN **-dor**	ENGLISH EQUIVALENT	BASE WORD	ENGLISH EQUIVALENT
el abridor	*opener*	abrir	*to open*
el acondicionador	*air conditioner*	acondicionar	*to air-condition*
el asador	*grill, spit, rotisserie*	asar	*to roast*
el borrador	*eraser*	borrar	*to erase*
el calentador	*heater*	calentar	*to heat*
el congelador	*freezer*	congelar	*to freeze, congeal*
el contestador	*answering machine*	contestar	*to answer*
el despertador	*alarm clock*	despertar	*to awaken, rouse*
el destornillador	*screwdriver*	destornillar	*to unscrew*
el destripador	*seam ripper*	destripar	*to rip open, gut*
el humidificador	*humidifier*	humidificar	*to humidify*

EJERCICIO
66·1

Complete each sentence with the appropriate noun to name the item that would be used in each situation.

1. Se usa _____ para eliminar un error hecho con un lápiz.

2. Se usa _____ cuando el aire está seco en la casa.

3. Se usa _____ cuando hace demasiado calor en la casa.

4. Se usa _____ para recibir mensajes de teléfono.

5. Se usa _____ para levantarse a una hora específica.

6. Se usa _____ para elevar la temperatura en la casa cuando hace frío.

7. Se usa _____ para guardar el helado y los cubitos de hielo.

8. Se usa _____ del portón de garaje para entrar en y salir del garaje.

9. Se usa _____ para apretar y aflojar tornillos.

10. Se usa _____ para cocinar la carne afuera.

11. Se usa _____ para separar la costura cuando hay un error.

NOUN ENDING IN **-dor**	ENGLISH EQUIVALENT	BASE WORD	ENGLISH EQUIVALENT
el incinerador	*incinerator*	incinerar	*to incinerate, cremate*
el mezclador	*mixer*	mezclar	*to mix*
el ordenador	*computer*	ordenar	*to arrange, put in order*
el ordeñador	*milking machine*	ordeñar	*to milk*
el purificador	*purifier*	purificar	*to purify, cleanse*
el radiador	*radiator*	radiar	*to radiate*
el rallador	*grater (cheese, etc.)*	rallar	*to grate*
el refrigerador	*refrigerator*	refrigerar	*to refrigerate*
el rociador	*sprayer*	rociar	*to spray*
el secador	*hair dryer*	secar	*to dry*
el tostador	*toaster*	tostar	*to toast*

Provide the appropriate noun (including its article) to name the appliance that would be used in each situation.

1. Se usa _____ para guardar la leche y el queso.

2. Se usa _____ para quemar y destruir la evidencia de un crimen.

3. Se usa _____ para enviar un correo electrónico y para navegar la red.

4. Se usa _____ para obtener la leche de la vaca.

5. Se usa _____ después de lavarse el pelo.

6. Se usa _____ para cortar el queso en tiras pequeñas o para separar la piel del limón.

7. Se usa _____ para calentar el pan, usualmente en la mañana para acompañar los huevos.

8. Se usa _____ para matar los virus y las bacterias y para remover los parásitos e impurezas del agua.

9. Se usa _____ para combinar los ingredientes antes de cocer el pan.

10. Se usa _____ para calentar un cuarto (especialmente en una casa vieja).

11. Se usa _____ para aplicar una aspersión de agua, de fertilizante o de pesticida en plantas.

67 ▸ -dora

MEANING	Device, machine, appliance
ENGLISH EQUIVALENT	—
PART OF SPEECH	Noun
GENDER	Feminine

A noun with the suffix -**dora** denotes a device, machine, or appliance that performs a specific function. Each of these nouns is derived from a verb. If the base verb is an -**ar** verb, the **a** is retained before the suffix (for example, **aspirar** *to inhale, suck* yields **la aspiradora** *vacuum cleaner*). If the base verb is an -**er** verb, the **e** is retained before the suffix (for example, **expender** *to sell, retail* yields **la máquina expendedora** *vending machine*). If the base verb is an -**ir** verb, the **i** is retained before the suffix (for example, **batir** *to beat, whip* yields **la batidora** *food mixer*).

NOUN ENDING IN **-dora**	ENGLISH EQUIVALENT	BASE WORD	ENGLISH EQUIVALENT
la aspiradora	*vacuum cleaner*	aspirar	*to inhale, suck*
la batidora	*food mixer*	batir	*to beat, whip*
la calculadora	*calculator*	calcular	*to calculate*
la computadora	*computer*	computar	*to compute, calculate*
la copiadora	*photocopier*	copiar	*to copy*
la cosechadora	*harvester, combine*	cosechar	*to harvest, reap*
la cribadora	*sifter*	cribar	*to sift*
la cultivadora	*cultivator*	cultivar	*to cultivate, grow*
la grabadora	*tape recorder*	grabar	*to record, engrave*
la grapadora	*stapler*	grapar	*to staple*
la lavadora	*washing machine*	lavar	*to wash*
la licuadora	*blender*	licuar	*to blend, liquefy*
la máquina expendedora	*vending machine*	expender	*to sell, retail*
la secadora	*clothes dryer*	secar	*to dry*
la segadora de césped	*lawnmower*	segar	*to mow, reap*
la trilladora	*threshing machine*	trillar	*to thresh*

EJERCICIO
67·1

Complete each sentence with the appropriate noun (including its article) to name the item used in each of the following situations.

1. Se usa _____ para limpiar la ropa.

2. Se usa _____ para cortar la hierba.

3. Se usa _____ para hacer un smoothie.

4. Se usa _____ para recordar la voz.

5. Se usa _____ para sumar, sustraer, multiplicar y dividir los números.

6. Se usa _____ para extraer la humedad de la ropa.

7. Se usa _____ para combinar los ingredientes para un pastel.

8. Se usa _____ para comprar los tentempiés en la oficina.

9. Se usa _____ para limpiar la alfombra.

10. Se usa _____ para separar el grano de la paja.

11. Se usa _____ para sujetar firmemente los papeles.

12. Se usa _____ para preparar la harina para un pastel.

13. Se usa _____ para preparar la tierra antes de plantar.

14. Se usa _____ para duplicar documentos y otros papeles.

15. Se usa _____ para acceder a información desde Internet y navegar la red.

16. Se usa _____ para cortar el heno y colocar el material cortado en filas.

68 ◆ -ecto

MEANING	Person; result of an action; abstract concept
ENGLISH EQUIVALENT	-ect
PART OF SPEECH	Noun
GENDER	Masculine

Many Spanish nouns with the suffix -ecto have English cognates, so they tend to be easy to recognize and use. The base word for many of these suffixed nouns has a Latin or Greek root and is often a verb. Some nouns ending in -ecto function as adjectives (see No. 115). An especially interesting noun with this suffix is **el insecto** *insect*, from the Latin verb **insectare** *to cut (into)*, a reference to an insect's notched body.

NOUN ENDING IN -ecto	ENGLISH EQUIVALENT	BASE WORD	ENGLISH EQUIVALENT
el arquitecto	*architect*	tekton [GRK.]	*builder*
el defecto	*defect, flaw*	deficere [LAT.]	*to fail, disappoint*
el efecto	*effect*	efectuar	*to carry out*
el electo	*elect, person chosen*	elegir	*to elect, choose*
el insecto	*insect*	insectare [LAT.]	*to cut (into)*
el intelecto	*intellect, understanding*	intelligere [LAT.]	*to understand*
el pluscuamperfecto	*pluperfect tense*	plus (quam) perfectum [LAT.]	*more (than) perfect*
el prospecto	*prospectus, information sheet*	prospectare [LAT.]	*to look out over*
el recto	*rectum, straight intestine*	regere [LAT.]	*to straighten*
el respecto	*relation*	respectere [LAT.]	*to look back*

EJERCICIO
68·1

¿Verdadero o falso? *Indicate whether each statement is true or false, using* **V** *for* **verdadero** *true or* **F** *for* **falso** *false.*

1. _____ El arquitecto Frank Lloyd Wright creó lo que llegó a conocerse como el "estilo de la pradera."

2. _____ La araña es un insecto.

3. _____ El talón de Aquiles fue su defecto y, últimamente, su perdición.

4. _____ Una persona lógica comprende la relación entre causa y efecto.

5. _____ Todos los políticos son hombres y mujeres de gran intelecto y de carácter noble.

6. _____ El colon y el recto forman parte del intestino grueso.

7. _____ Con respecto a determinar la paternidad de un infante, a veces es necesario realizar una prueba de ADN.

8. _____ Es importante seguir las instrucciones en el prospecto incluido en el envase de cada medicamento.

9. _____ La frase "Habíamos comido la pizza" es un ejemplo del pluscuamperfecto.

10. _____ La primera cosa que hace el electo es dar un discurso de concesión.

NOUN ENDING IN -ecto	ENGLISH EQUIVALENT	BASE WORD	ENGLISH EQUIVALENT
el afecto	*affection, fondness*	afectar	*to affect*
el aspecto	*aspect, appearance*	aspicere [LAT.]	*to look at*
el desafecto	*disaffection, dislike*	desafectar	*to lose affection*
el desperfecto	*imperfection, flaw*	des- + perficere [LAT.]	*not + to complete*
el dialecto	*dialect*	dialektos [GRK.]	*talk, conversation*
el insurrecto	*insurgent, rebel*	insurgere [LAT.]	*to rise up, revolt*
el prefecto	*prefect, magistrate*	praeficere [LAT.]	*to put in front*
el proyecto	*project, plan*	proicere [LAT.]	*to throw forth*
el trayecto	*trajectory, route, journey*	traicere [LAT.]	*to throw across*

EJERCICIO

68·2

Sinónimos *Provide the synonym for each group of words. Include its article.*

1. el idioma, la germanía, la lengua, la habla _____

2. el magistrado, el jefe, el funcionario _____

3. el daño, el detrimento, el defecto, la avería _____

4. el rebelde, el activista, el agitador, el insurgente _____

5. el plan, el esquema, el propósito _____

6. la apariencia, la facha, la traza _____

7. la aversión, la animosidad, la malquerencia _____

8. el viaje, el itinerario, la distancia _____

9. el cariño, el aprecio, la estima, el apego _____

69 ▸ -ejo

MEANING	Diminutive; pejorative
ENGLISH EQUIVALENT	—
PART OF SPEECH	Noun
GENDER	Masculine

The suffix **-ejo** generally denotes physical smallness of the base word (for example, **el anillo** *ring* yields **el anillejo** *small ring*). It may, however, have a derogatory implication (for example, **el caballo** *horse* yields **el caballejo** *small horse, pony, nag*). These are unusual words; as a result, they have real verbal punch.

NOUN ENDING IN -ejo	ENGLISH EQUIVALENT	BASE WORD	ENGLISH EQUIVALENT
el anillejo	*small ring*	el anillo	*ring*
el animalejo	*very small animal*	el animal	*animal*
el arbolejo	*small tree*	el árbol	*tree*
el arenalejo	*small sandy place*	la arena	*sand, sandy ground*
el atabalejo	*small kettledrum*	el atabal	*kettledrum*
el azoguejo	*small marketplace*	el azogue	*marketplace*
el castillejo	*small castle*	el castillo	*castle*
el diablejo	*scamp, little devil*	el diablo	*devil, demon, fiend*
el librejo	*little book, pamphlet*	el libro	*book*
el lugarejo	*small village*	el lugar	*place, spot, village*
el zagalejo	*young lad or shepherd*	el zagal	*lad, youth, shepherd*

EJERCICIO
69·1

Provide the correct noun (including its article) for each description.

1. una playa pequeña _____

2. un pueblo pequeño _____

3. la decoración para un dedo pequeño _____

4. un pastor joven _____

5. una zona comercial pequeña _____

6. el panfleto o el folleto _____

7. un tambor pequeño _____

8. un demonio pequeño _____

9. una criatura muy pequeña _____

10. una casa pequeña para el rey _____

11. un bonsái o un pino pequeño _____

NOUN ENDING IN -ejo	ENGLISH EQUIVALENT	BASE WORD	ENGLISH EQUIVALENT
el barrilejo	*small barrel*	el barril	*barrel*
el bozalejo	*small muzzle*	el bozal	*muzzle*
el caballejo	*small horse, pony, nag*	el caballo	*horse*
el camellejo	*small camel*	el camello	*camel*
el collarejo	*small collar, necklace*	el collar	*collar, necklace*
el cordelejo	*small rope*	la cuerda	*cord, string, rope*
el marmolejo	*small marble column*	el mármol	*marble*
el martillejo	*small hammer*	el martillo	*hammer*
el puñalejo	*small dagger*	el puñal	*dagger*
el telarejo	*small loom*	el telar	*loom*
el vallejo	*small valley*	el valle	*valley, vale, glen*

Provide the correct noun (including its article) for each description.

1. un aparato, usualmente de correas, que se pone _____
   a los perros para que no muerdan ni ladren

2. una gargantilla u otra decoración pequeña llevada _____
   alrededor del cuello

3. una herramienta pequeña del carpintero que sirve _____
   para golpear clavos

4. una máquina pequeña para tejer _____

5. un arma pequeña de acero que sólo hiere al víctima _____
   con la punta

6. un recipiente pequeño de madero o metal que sirve _____
   principalmente para conservar líquidos de varios tipos

7. una parcela pequeña de terreno entre montes o alturas _____

8. un dromedario pequeño _____

9. una columna pequeña de piedra preciosa _____

10. la transportación de un vaquero pequeño _____

11. una cuerda de hilos delicados _____

70 ◆ -encia

MEANING	Result of an action, state
ENGLISH EQUIVALENT	*-ence, -ency*
PART OF SPEECH	Noun
GENDER	Feminine

Almost all Spanish nouns with the suffix **-encia** have English cognates; they denote a state or the result of an action of the verbs from which they are derived. Most of these suffixed nouns have **-er** or **-ir** verbs as their base words. If a noun ending in **-encia** is derived from an **-ar** verb, it is usually a verb whose infinitive ends in **-enciar** (for example, **agenciar** *to bring about, effect*).

NOUN ENDING IN **-encia**	ENGLISH EQUIVALENT	BASE WORD	ENGLISH EQUIVALENT
la agencia	*agency*	agenciar	*to bring about, effect*
la coincidencia	*coincidence*	coincidir	*to coincide*
la conciencia	*conscience*	concienciar	*to create awareness in*
le deficiencia	*deficiency*	deficere [LAT.]	*to fail, disappoint*
la diferencia	*difference*	diferir	*to differ*

▶

NOUN ENDING IN **-encia**	ENGLISH EQUIVALENT	BASE WORD	ENGLISH EQUIVALENT
la evidencia	*evidence*	evidenciar	*to show*
la existencia	*existence*	existir	*to exist*
la independencia	*independence*	in- + depender	*not + to depend*
la obediencia	*obedience*	obedecer	*to obey*
la preferencia	*preference*	preferir	*to prefer*
la presidencia	*presidency*	presidir	*to preside over*
la residencia	*residence*	residir	*to reside*

EJERCICIO

70·1

Complete each sentence with the correct form of the appropriate noun.

1. El 16 de septiembre (México), el 4 de julio (Estados Unidos) y el primero de enero (Haití)

   son días de _____ .

2. Cuando dos acontecimientos que no parecen estar relacionados ocurren al mismo tiempo,

   se dice que es una _____ .

3. A las mujeres de más de cuarenta años que tienen una _____ por
   los hombres jóvenes se les llama "puma."

4. Cuando una persona quiere comprar una casa o un condominio, probablemente va

   a contactar una _____ de bienes raíces.

5. Muchos sacerdotes y monjas, en particular los jesuitas, profesan votos de la pobreza,

   la castidad y la _____ .

6. Para probar la culpabilidad de un acusado, el abogado del demandante necesita mucha

   _____ del presunto delito.

7. El cargo político más elevado en los Estados Unidos es la _____ .

8. La _____ oficial del primer ministro de Inglaterra es 10 Downing
   Street.

9. Muchos filósofos discuten y a veces tratan de demostrar la _____
   de Dios.

10. Se dice que el sociópata es un individuo completamente absorbido en sí mismo, es sin

    _____ y no tiene remordimientos.

11. Las varias causas de la osteoporosis incluyen una _____ del calcio
    y la vitamina D, una vida sedentaria y una condición tiroidea.

12. La _____ entre una bombilla de 5 vatios en una lámpara (similar
    a una velita) y una bombilla de 180 vatios en una cabina bronceadora (similar al sol
    mediterráneo) es enorme.

NOUN ENDING IN -encia	ENGLISH EQUIVALENT	BASE WORD	ENGLISH EQUIVALENT
la afluencia	*affluence*	afluir	*to flow, flock in*
la conferencia	*conference*	conferir	*to confer*
la deferencia	*deference*	deferir	*to defer*
la dependencia	*dependence*	depender (de)	*to depend (on)*
la descendencia	*descent*	descender	*to descend*
la divergencia	*divergence*	divergir	*to diverge*
la influencia	*influence*	influir	*to influence*
la insistencia	*insistence*	insistir	*to insist*
la opulencia	*opulence*	opulentare [LAT.]	*to make rich, enrich*
la presencia	*presence*	presenciar	*to witness, be present*
la resistencia	*resistance*	resistir	*to resist*
la reverencia	*reverence*	reverenciar	*to revere*
la tendencia	*tendency*	tendere [LAT.]	*to stretch, aim*

EJERCICIO

70·2

Sinónimos y antónimos *Provide the correct noun (including its article) for each description.*

1. sinónimo de la veneración y la admiración _____

2. antónimo de la ascensión _____

3. sinónimo de la inclinación y la propensión _____

4. antónimo de la ausencia _____

5. sinónimo de la bifurcación _____

6. antónimo de la falta, la ausencia, la escasez _____

7. sinónimo de la reunión, la convención, el foro _____

8. antónimo de la independencia _____

9. sinónimo del ultimátum, la imploración, la necesidad _____

10. antónimo de la impotencia y la incapacidad _____

11. sinónimo de la batalla, la contención, la obstrucción _____

12. antónimo de la pobreza y la miseria _____

13. sinónimo de la obediencia, la conformidad, la sumisión _____

71 ◆ -ente

MEANING	Relating to, like; doing
ENGLISH EQUIVALENT	*-ent, -ing*
PART OF SPEECH	Adjective
GENDER	Masculine/feminine

Adjectives with the suffix **-ente** are derived from **-er** and **-ir** verbs. (The related suffix **-ante** (No. 55) is used to form adjectives derived from **-ar** verbs.) Both of these endings indicate that the person, place, or thing described exhibits a quality directly relating to the base verb. Since the English equivalent *-ing* may be used to translate the Spanish gerund as a progressive form, it is important not to confuse the two functions in Spanish: **Juan está corriendo** *John is running* ~ **Tengo agua corriente** *I have running water.*

ADJECTIVE ENDING IN **-ente**	ENGLISH EQUIVALENT	BASE WORD	ENGLISH EQUIVALENT
absorbente	*absorbent, absorbing*	absorber	*to absorb*
abstinente	*abstinent, abstemious*	abstenerse	*to refrain from*
atrayente	*appealing, attractive*	atraer	*to attract*
correspondiente	*corresponding, relevant*	corresponder	*to correspond*
corriente	*current, running* (water)	correr	*to run*
deprimente	*depressing*	deprimir	*to depress*
diferente	*different*	diferir	*to differ, be different*
doliente	*aching, suffering*	doler	*to hurt, be painful*
durmiente	*sleeping*	dormir	*to sleep*
emergente	*emergent, emerging*	emerger	*to emerge* (from water)
existente	*existing, existent*	existir	*to exist*
influyente	*influential*	influir	*to influence*

EJERCICIO 71·1

¿Verdadero o falso? *Indicate whether each statement is true or false, using* **V** *for* **verdadero** *true or* **F** *for* **falso** *false.*

1. _____ El interior de una prisión es un ambiente deprimente.

2. _____ Es importante que una toalla de papel sea absorbente.

3. _____ Panamá es el país más influyente del mundo.

4. _____ El canal de cable CNN emite noticias corrientes las 24 horas al día.

5. _____ Al recibir el beso vivificante del príncipe, la Bella Durmiente gira la cabeza y vomita.

6. _____ Una persona doliente está sufriendo.

7. _____ Todos los sacerdotes católicos son abstinentes.

8. _____ Hay inquietudes existentes aun en las mejores familias.

9. _____ Al comparecer ante el juez, es importante traer todos los documentos correspondientes al caso.

10. _____ Para comprar una casa, se necesita presentar una oferta atrayente a los vendedores.

11. _____ La lujuria (deseo sexual) no es diferente del amor.

12. _____ La isla de Truk en el Pacífico Sur es una potencia mundial emergente.

ADJECTIVE ENDING IN **-ente**	ENGLISH EQUIVALENT	BASE WORD	ENGLISH EQUIVALENT
luciente	*bright, shining, brilliant*	lucir	*to light, light up*
reincidente	*recidivist, relapsing*	reincidir	*to relapse, backslide*
reluciente	*shining, gleaming (teeth)*	relucir	*to shine, glitter*
repelente	*repellent, repulsive*	repeler	*to repel*
residente	*resident*	residir	*to reside*
resistente	*resistant, tough, strong*	resistir	*to resist*
rugiente	*roaring, bellowing*	rugir	*to roar*
siguiente	*following*	seguir	*to follow, continue*
sorprendente	*astonishing, surprising*	sorprender	*to surprise*
teniente	*miserly, mean*	tener	*to have, hold*
viviente	*living*	vivir	*to live*
yacente	*lying down, reclining*	yacer	*to lie down*

EJERCICIO
71·2

Complete each sentence with the correct form of the appropriate adjective.

1. El león es _____.

2. Una persona durmiendo en la cama está _____.

3. Si hoy es lunes, el día _____ es martes.

4. Un criminal que prefiere el mundo de la delincuencia y continúa entrar y salir de la prisión es un delincuente _____.

5. Una persona cuyo corazón funciona y que respira es un ser _____.

6. Un reloj que puedes llevar cuando estás nadando es _____ al agua.

7. Una participante en un concurso de belleza necesita tener una sonrisa blanca y _____.

8. Un hombre miserable y mezquino es _____.

9. Antes de ir de campamento, es importante tener una tienda de campaña _____ al agua.

10. Albert Einstein y Stephen Hawking son hombres _____ debido a su aptitud intelectual.

11. Un médico _____ tiene el título de médico, pero todavía tiene que ejercer la medicina bajo vigilancia.

12. Una bombilla de 50,000 vatios ciertamente es _____.

72 ◆ -eño/-eña

MEANING	Relating to, like; citizen, native
ENGLISH EQUIVALENT	-y
PART OF SPEECH	Adjective, noun
GENDER	Masculine/feminine

The suffix **-eño** (feminine: **-eña**) may denote a similarity to or origination from the base noun. An adjective with this suffix may be based on a geographical entity and function as a noun or an adjective: **La brasileña lee el periódico hondureño** *The Brazilian woman reads the Honduran newspaper.* Note that, unlike in English, adjectives that refer to geographical entities are not capitalized in Spanish.

The following words ending in **-eño/-eña** are used only as adjectives.

ADJECTIVE ENDING IN -eño	ENGLISH EQUIVALENT	BASE WORD	ENGLISH EQUIVALENT
caribeño	*Caribbean*	el Caribe	*the Caribbean (Sea)*
costeño	*coastal*	la costa	*coast, shore*
galgueño	*like a greyhound*	el galgo	*greyhound*
guijarreño	*pebbly, gravelly*	el guijarro	*pebble*
halagüeño	*flattering*	el halago	*flattery*
hogareño	*home-loving*	el hogar	*home, household*
marfileño	*of or like ivory*	el marfil	*ivory*
marmoleño	*of or like marble*	el mármol	*marble*
navideño	*relating to Christmas*	la Navidad	*Christmas*
risueño	*smiling, cheerful*	la risa	*laughter*
roqueño	*rocky*	la roca	*rock*
trigueño	*swarthy, dark-skinned*	el trigo	*wheat*

EJERCICIO 72·1

Complete each sentence with the correct form of the appropriate adjective.

1. Una mujer que está muy feliz mucho del tiempo tiene una cara

   _____.

2. Un perro delgado que es muy utilizado en las carreras de perros es

   _____.

3. Durante la última parte de diciembre, muchos cristianos en el mundo entero decoran un

   árbol _____.

4. Los colmillos del elefante son _____.

5. Una persona que siempre prefiere estar en casa es _____.

6. *El beso* por Auguste Rodin, *La Piedad* por Miguel Ángel y *La Venus de Milo* por Alejandro de

   Antioquía son tres de las más famosas esculturas _____.

7. Una persona servil y obsequiosa es _____.

8. Amalfi (Italia), Miami Beach (Florida) y Río de Janeiro (Brasil) son famosas ciudades

   _____.

9. Antigua, Barbuda y las Bahamas son islas _____.

10. Los animales como el alce y la cabra montés pueden vivir en las montañas y en otras áreas

   _____.

11. Muchos caminos en las áreas rurales son _____.

12. Una persona que toma el sol cada día o que pasa mucho tiempo en una cama de

   bronceado tiene la piel _____.

The following words ending in **-eño/-eña** may function as adjectives or nouns.

ADJECTIVE/NOUN ENDING IN **-eño**	ENGLISH EQUIVALENT	BASE WORD	ENGLISH EQUIVALENT
(el) brasileño	*Brazilian*	Brasil	*Brazil*
(el) gibraltareño	*(native) of Gibraltar*	Gibraltar	*Gibraltar*
(el) guadalajareño	*(native) of Guadalajara*	Guadalajara	*Guadalajara*
(el) guayaquileño	*(native) of Guayaquil*	Guayaquil	*Guayaquil*
(el) hondureño	*Honduran*	Honduras	*Honduras*
(el) isleño	*(native) of an island*	la isla	*island*
(el) limeño	*(native) of Lima*	Lima	*Lima*
(el) lugareño	*villager, of a village*	el lugar	*place, village*
(el) madrileño	*(native) of Madrid*	Madrid	*Madrid*
(el) nicaragüeño	*Nicaraguan*	Nicaragua	*Nicaragua*
(el) norteño	*northerner, of the north*	el norte	*north*
(el) panameño	*Panamanian*	Panamá	*Panama*
(el) puertorriqueño	*Puerto Rican*	Puerto Rico	*Puerto Rico*
(el) salvadoreño	*Salvadoran*	El Salvador	*El Salvador*
(el) sureño	*southerner, of the south*	el sur	*south*

EJERCICIO
72·2

Complete each sentence with the correct form of the appropriate noun.

1. El _____ vive en la capital de España.

2. La _____ vive en Managua, la capital.

3. Los _____ viven en São Paulo, la ciudad más grande del país.

4. Las _____ viven en Tegucigalpa, la capital.

5. El _____ vive en San Juan, la capital.

6. La _____ vive en San Salvador, la capital.

7. Los _____ viven en Colón, Tocumen, San Miguelito y la ciudad de Panamá.

8. Las _____ viven en la capital del estado mexicano de Jalisco.

9. Los _____ viven en la ciudad más poblada y más grande de Ecuador.

10. El _____ vive en el sur más extremo de la Península Ibérica.

11. La _____ vive en la capital del Perú.

12. Los _____ viven en las aldeas, los pueblos y las áreas rurales.

13. Los _____ son habitantes de Aruba, Maui y Bora Bora.

14. Los _____ son habitantes de Groenlandia, Noruega y el Canadá.

15. En los Estados Unidos, los _____ son habitantes de Texas, Louisiana, Mississippi, Alabama y Florida.

73 -eo

MEANING	Action
ENGLISH EQUIVALENT	*-ing*
PART OF SPEECH	Noun
GENDER	Masculine

The suffix **-eo** denotes action, as do several other Spanish suffixes. This suffix is distinctive in that its base verbs end in **-ear**.

NOUN ENDING IN **-eo**	ENGLISH EQUIVALENT	BASE WORD	ENGLISH EQUIVALENT
el besuqueo	*slobbery kissing*	besuquear	*to smother with kisses*
el blanqueo	*whitening, bleaching*	blanquear	*to bleach, whiten*
el bloqueo	*blockade*	bloquear	*to block*
el cabeceo	*nod, bob of the head*	cabecear	*to shake one's head*
el campaneo	*bell ringing*	campanear	*to ring bells*
el careo	*confrontation*	carear	*to bring face to face*
el ceceo	*lisp, lisping*	cecear	*to lisp*
el deletreo	*spelling*	deletrear	*to spell*
el devaneo	*delirium, frenzy*	devanear	*to rave, talk nonsense*
el empleo	*employment, job*	emplear	*to employ*
el escopeteo	*gunfire, shooting*	escopetear	*to shoot at with a gun*
el fisgoneo	*snooping, prying*	fisgonear	*to pry (into)*
el lavoteo	*hurried washing*	lavotear(se)	*to wash (oneself) hurriedly*
el paladeo	*tasting, relishing*	paladear	*to savor, taste*
el papeleo	*paperwork*	papelear	*to rummage through papers*

Provide the correct noun (including its article) for each of the following situations.

1. una persona con un rifle _____

2. el cliente de un terapeuta del habla _____

3. una mujer en el lavadero con una botella de Clorox _____

4. una persona psicótica _____

5. un adolescente en su primera cita romántica _____

6. Cuasimodo, el jorobado de Notre Dame _____

7. un gastrónomo o glotón _____

8. un muñeco bobblehead _____

9. una persona que tiene trabajo _____

10. el escritorio de una secretaria _____

11. una persona que no puede contener la furia al volante _____

12. un voyeur _____

13. la maestra de ortografía _____

14. la persona que toma una ducha rápida _____

15. una persona que se encuentra en un área de la cual no puede salir _____

NOUN ENDING IN **-eo**	ENGLISH EQUIVALENT	BASE WORD	ENGLISH EQUIVALENT
el pareo	*pairing up, matching*	parear	*to pair, match*
el parqueo	*parking*	aparcar	*to park*
el paseo	*walk, stroll, ride*	pasear	*to go for a walk or ride*
el pataleo	*kicking, stamping*	patalear	*to kick or stamp one's feet*
el recreo	*recess, break, playtime*	recrear	*to entertain, amuse*
el repiqueteo	*pealing, ringing*	repiquetear	*to ring out*
el revoloteo	*fluttering, flitting about*	revolotear	*to flutter, flit about*
el salteo	*assault, highway robbery*	saltear	*to rob on the highway*
el tartamudeo	*stuttering, stammering*	tartamudear	*to stutter, stammer*
el tecleo	*typing, keying*	teclear	*to type, play (piano)*
el traqueteo	*rattling, shaking*	traquetear	*to rattle, shake*
el zapateo	*tap, tapping*	zapatear	*to tap, tap-dance*

EJERCICIO
73·2

Complete each sentence with the correct form of the appropriate noun.

1. Cada día los niños en la escuela primaria tienen un período de _____ en el patio o en un parque.

2. Match.com se especializa en el _____ de personas.

3. El _____ es un robo que ocurre en la carretera.

4. El estacionamiento es para el _____.

5. En un jardín que está en plena floración, se puede ver el _____ de las mariposas, las abejas, las mariquitas y otros insectos.

6. Es maravilloso observar el _____ de un pianista profesional.

7. Muchas personas van al parque para dar un _____ y admirar la naturaleza.

8. La película británica *El discurso del rey,* que ganó el premio Oscar a la mejor película en

   2011, se relata la vida del rey George VI y su _____.

9. Gregory Hines, Bill "Bojangles" Robinson y Fred Astaire son bailarines famosos que son

   conocidos especialmente por su habilidad para el _____.

10. No debes acercarte a un caballo salvaje porque el _____ puede ser peligroso.

11. Las personas que sufren tinnitus sienten el campanilleo, el rugido, el zumbido o el

    _____ que ocurre dentro de la cabeza.

12. En los días de las calles adoquinadas, se oía el _____ de los coches tirados por caballos.

74 ◆ -ero/-era

MEANING	Relating to, like; able to be (acted on)
ENGLISH EQUIVALENT	*-y, -able*
PART OF SPEECH	Adjective
GENDER	Masculine/feminine

The suffix **-ero** may denote a characteristic of a base noun (for example, **casero** *homemade*, from **la casa** *house, home*). If the base word is a verb, the suffix **-ero** conveys the sense that the action of the verb is able to be performed (for example, **bebedero** *drinkable*, from **beber** *to drink*). If the base word is a verb, the **-r** of the infinitive ending is dropped and **d** is added before the suffix.

ADJECTIVE ENDING IN **-ero**	ENGLISH EQUIVALENT	BASE WORD	ENGLISH EQUIVALENT
aduanero	*relating to customs*	la aduana	*customs*
azucarero	*relating to sugar*	el azúcar	*sugar*
bananero	*relating to bananas*	la banana	*banana*
bebedero	*drinkable*	beber	*to drink*
caminero	*relating to the road*	el camino	*toad*
carbonero	*relating to coal*	el carbón	*coal, carbon*
casero	*homemade*	la casa	*house, home*
faldero	*fond of women*	la falda	*skirt*
guerrero	*warlike, argumentative*	la guerra	*war*
hacendero	*industrious*	hacer	*to do, make*
harinero	*made of flour, relating to flour*	la harina	*flour*
lastimero	*sad, doleful, miserable*	la lástima	*shame, pity*
llevadero	*bearable, tolerable*	llevar	*to carry, bear*
maderero	*of wood, timber*	la madera	*wood*
mañanero	*of the morning*	la mañana	*morning*

EJERCICIO 74·1

Complete each sentence with the correct form of the appropriate noun.

1. Un hombre que es aficionado a las mujeres es _____.

2. Una mujer que trabaja mucho es _____.

3. La leche, la cerveza y la gaseosa son _____.

4. Una situación triste es _____.

5. Una situación tolerable es _____.

6. En vez de ir a un restaurante, muchas personas prefieren una comida

   _____.

7. El departamento del control de pasaportes es _____.

8. Muchos mineros trabajan en la industria _____.

9. El famoso leñador Paul Bunyan trabaja en la industria _____.

10. Los países de Brasil, India y Tailandia, donde se cultivan mucha caña de azúcar, son líderes

    en la industria _____.

11. Los países de India, Brasil y Ecuador, donde se cultivan muchos plátanos y bananas, son

    líderes en la industria _____.

12. Los tres modos principales de transporte son el aéreo, el ferroviario y el

    _____.

13. Lo contrario de una civilización pacífica es una civilización _____.

14. Se necesita un molino _____ para preparar el ingrediente principal del pan.

15. Para muchas personas, el ritual _____ incluye ducharse, cepillarse los dientes, vestirse, tomar el café y leer el periódico.

ADJECTIVE ENDING IN **-ero**	ENGLISH EQUIVALENT	BASE WORD	ENGLISH EQUIVALENT
noticiero	*news-bearing*	la noticia	*piece of news*
ovejero	*relating to sheep*	la oveja	*sheep, ewe*
pendenciero	*quarrelsome*	la pendencia	*quarrel, dispute*
perecedero	*perishable*	perecer	*to perish*
playero	*relating to the beach*	la playa	*beach*
sensiblero	*sentimental*	sensible	*sensitive*
taquillero	*relating to the box office*	la taquilla	*ticket office, box office*
traicionero	*treacherous*	la traición	*treachery*
verdadero	*true, real, sincere*	la verdad	*truth*
zapatero	*relating to shoes*	el zapato	*shoe*

EJERCICIO
74·2

¿Verdadero o falso? *Indicate whether each statement is true or false, using* **V** *for* **verdadero** *true or* **F** *for* **falso** *false.*

1. _____ Cada productor de un espectáculo de Broadway espera un éxito taquillero.

2. _____ La fruta plástica es elegante y perecedera.

3. _____ Un pastor trabaja en la industria ovejera.

4. _____ El viaje de Odiseo, de Troy hasta Ítaca, fue traicionero.

5. _____ Un Congreso pendenciero tiene mucho éxito.

6. _____ Al planificar sus vacaciones, especialmente en el invierno cuando hace mucho frío, muchas personas buscan un destino playero.

7. _____ Blancanieves y los siete enanitos son líderes en la industria zapatera.

8. _____ Thomas Reuters es una de las agencias noticieras más grandes del mundo.

9. _____ Una mentira verdadera es una contradicción conceptual, similar a un triángulo cuadrado.

10. _____ Una persona que se pone sensiblera está imbuida de nostalgia.

75 ▸ -és/-esa

MEANING	Citizen, native; relating to
ENGLISH EQUIVALENT	-ese
PART OF SPEECH	Noun, adjective
GENDER	Masculine/feminine

The suffix **-és** (feminine: **-esa**) is one of several Spanish suffixes that denote geographical origin. Words with these suffixes can function as nouns or adjectives: **El holandés sirve el queso a la japonesa** *The Dutch man serves cheese to the Japanese woman.* Unlike in English, these words are not capitalized in Spanish. Since the gender is inherent in the suffix, it is unnecessary to include a noun for *male* or *female*. In the masculine plural, the accent is omitted: **el polonés ~ los poloneses**.

The base word for each of the following words ending in **-és/-esa** is the name of a country.

NOUN/ADJECTIVE ENDING IN **-és**	ENGLISH EQUIVALENT	BASE WORD	ENGLISH EQUIVALENT
(el) danés	*Danish, Dane*	Dinamarca	*Denmark*
(el) escocés	*Scottish, Scot*	Escocia	*Scotland*
(el) finlandés	*Finnish, Finn*	Finlandia	*Finland*
(el) francés	*French, native of France*	Francia	*France*
(el) groenlandés	*(native) of Greenland*	Groenlandia	*Greenland*
(el) holandés	*Dutch, native of Holland*	Holanda	*Holland*
(el) inglés	*English, native of England*	Inglaterra	*England*
(el) irlandés	*Irish, native of Ireland*	Irlanda	*Ireland*
(el) japonés	*Japanese, native of Japan*	Japón	*Japan*
(el) libanés	*Lebanese, native of Lebanon*	Líbano	*Lebanon*
(el) luxemburgués	*(native) of Luxembourg*	Luxemburgo	*Luxembourg*
(el) neozelandés	*(native) of New Zealand*	Nueva Zelanda	*New Zealand*
(el) nepalés	*Nepalese, native of Nepal*	Nepal	*Nepal*
(el) polonés	*Polish, Pole*	Polonia	*Poland*
(el) portugués	*Portuguese, native of Portugal*	Portugal	*Portugal*
(el) tailandés	*Thai, native of Thailand*	Tailandia	*Thailand*

EJERCICIO 75·1

Complete each sentence with the correct form of the appropriate adjective for each person's description.

1. Van Morrison nació en Belfast. Él es _____.

2. Una habitante de Lisboa es _____.

3. Un hombre de Katmandú es _____.

4. Lech Walesa vive en Warsaw. Él es _____.

5. Coco Chanel nació en Saumur, Francia. Ella era _____.

6. Søren Kierkegaard nació en Copenhague. Él era _____.

7. Amy Winehouse nació en Londres. Ella era _____.

8. Los habitantes de Beirut son _____.

9. Un habitante de Ámsterdam es _____.

10. Yoko Ono nació en Tokio. Ella es _____.

11. Una habitante de Helsinki es _____.

12. Los niños que nacen en Edimburgo son _____.

13. Las niñas que nacen en Wellington son _____.

14. Una mujer de Luxemburgo es _____.

15. Un hombre de Bangkok es _____.

16. Una niña que nace en Nuuk es _____.

The base word for each of the following words ending in **-és/-esa** is the name of a city or province, the former name of a country (for example, **Siam**), or a geographical feature.

NOUN/ADJECTIVE ENDING IN **-és**	ENGLISH EQUIVALENT	BASE WORD	ENGLISH EQUIVALENT
(el) aragonés	*Aragonese, native of Aragon*	Aragón	*Aragon*
(el) barcelonés	*(native) of Barcelona*	Barcelona	*Barcelona*
(el) berlinés	*(native) of Berlin*	Berlín	*Berlin*
(el) burgués	*(someone) of or from the middle class*	el burgo	*borough*
(el) hamburgués	*(native) of Hamburg*	Hamburgo	*Hamburg*
(el) leonés	*(native) of Leon*	León	*Leon*
(el) lisbonés	*(native) of Lisbon*	Lisboa	*Lisbon*
(el) milanés	*Milanese, native of Milan*	Milán	*Milan*
(el) montañés	*(someone) of or from the mountain*	la montaña	*mountain*
(el) neoescocés	*(native) of Nova Scotia*	Nueva Escocia	*Nova Scotia*
(el) pequinés	*Pekingese, native of Peking*	Pequín	*Peking*
(el) salamanqués	*(native) of Salamanca*	Salamanca	*Salamanca*
(el) siamés	*Siamese, native of Siam*	Siam	*Siam*
(el) vienés	*Viennese, native of Vienna*	Viena	*Vienna*

EJERCICIO
75·2

Complete each sentence with the correct form of the appropriate adjective for each person's description.

1. Un hombre de la capital de Portugal es _____.

2. Una mujer de la capital de Alemania es _____.

3. Una mujer de una ciudad principal de china es _____.

4. Yul Brynner en la película *El rey y yo* es _____.

5. Las mujeres de Aragón son _____.

6. Los hombres y las mujeres que no son ricos ni pobres son _____.

7. Johann Strauss era _____.

8. El personaje principal de la novela picaresca de Lazarillo de Tormes es

_____.

9. Un hombre de los Alpes es _____.

10. Una niña de Hamburgo es _____.

11. Los hombres de León son _____.

12. Un niño que nació en Barcelona es _____.

13. Los que viven en Milán, donde vivía Leonardo da Vinci por mucho de su vida, son

_____.

14. Una mujer de Halifax es _____.

76 ▸ -estre

MEANING	Relating to, like
ENGLISH EQUIVALENT	*-estrian, -estrial*
PART OF SPEECH	Adjective
GENDER	Masculine

The uncommon suffix **-estre** denotes a characteristic of the base word. The next time you run into a coyote, think **silvestre** *wild, uncivilized*. Adjectives with the suffix **-estre** may be masculine or feminine: **el hombre silvestre / la mujer silvestre**.

ADJECTIVE ENDING IN -**estre**	ENGLISH EQUIVALENT	BASE WORD	ENGLISH EQUIVALENT
alpestre	*alpine*	los Alpes	*the Alps*
campestre	*rural, bucolic*	el campo	*country, field*
ecuestre	*equestrian, related to horseback riding*	equus [LAT.]	*horse*
pedestre	*pedestrian, prosaic*	pes/pedis [LAT.]	*foot*
silvestre	*wild, uncivilized*	la selva	*jungle, forest*
terrestre	*terrestrial*	la tierra	*earth, land*

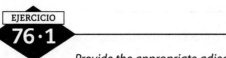

EJERCICIO 76·1

Provide the appropriate adjective that is related to each description or group.

1. Tarzan, Jane y Cheeta _____

2. una cadena de montañas situada en la Europa _____
Central que incluye Mont Blanc

3. una granja, un establo con vacas y caballos, unas gallinas y un gallo _____

4. la princesa Ana de Inglaterra, Roy Rogers, el Llanero Solitario y su amigo Toro (*Tonto*) _____

5. el mundo, la geografía, la cartografía, la topografía _____

6. un paseo por el parque, una caminata en el bosque, la ambulación en general _____

-fobia

MEANING	Fear, aversion
ENGLISH EQUIVALENT	*-phobia*
PART OF SPEECH	Noun
GENDER	Feminine

Since most Spanish nouns with the suffix **-fobia** have English cognates, they tend to be easily recognized and used. English *ph* appears as Spanish **f**; **el telefóno** *telephone*, **el elefante** *el elephant*, and **la acrofobia** *acrophobia, fear of heights* are examples.

NOUN ENDING IN **-fobia**	ENGLISH EQUIVALENT	BASE WORD	ENGLISH EQUIVALENT
la acrofobia	*acrophobia, fear of heights*	akros [GRK.]	*highest (point)*
la aerofobia	*aerophobia, fear of flying*	aer/aeros [GRK.]	*air*
la agorafobia	*agoraphobia, fear of open places*	agora [GRK.]	*open space*
la androfobia	*androphobia, dread of men*	aner/andros [GRK.]	*man*
la anglofobia	*Anglophobia, hatred of the English*	Anglii [LAT.]	*the English*
la claustrofobia	*claustrophobia, fear of small spaces*	claustrum [LAT.]	*enclosure, prison*
la clerofobia	*aversion to clerics*	clericus [LAT.]	*priest*
la fotofobia	*photophobia, fear of light*	phos/photos [GRK.]	*light*
la hemafobia	*aversion to blood*	haima [GRK.]	*blood*
la hidrofobia	*hydrophobia, dread of water*	hydor/hydros [GRK.]	*water*
la homofobia	*aversion to homosexuals*	homos [GRK.]	*same*
la xenofobia	*xenophobia, fear of strangers*	xenos [GRK.]	*stranger, foreigner*

EJERCICIO
77·1

¿De qué sufre esta persona? *Provide the correct noun (including its article) for each description.*

1. Jorge se niega a entrar en una cueva o en cualquier espacio pequeño. Él sufre de

_____ .

2. Paco se desmaya a la vista de la sangre. El pobrecito sufre de _____ .

3. Al vampiro le encanta la vista de la sangre, pero tiene miedo de la luz y por eso su trabajo es nocturnal. Él tiene _____.

4. Griselda odia a los hombres con todo su corazón. Ella tiene _____.

5. Marcos tiene una fuerte aversión a los clérigos—no le importa la religión. Pobre Marcos sufre de _____.

6. Juanita tiene un gran miedo de las alturas. Ella sufre de _____.

7. Adolfo odia a los ingleses con un sentimiento irracional. Adolfo sufre de

_____.

8. David Bowie, Kate Winslet y Whoopi Goldberg reportan que tienen miedo de volar. Estos pobrecitos sufren de _____.

9. El dictador de Zimbabwe, Robert Mugabe, es un homófobo notorio. Él sufre de

_____.

10. Luisa tiene una aversión a los ríos y los lagos y no quiere estar cerca de ellos; nunca viaja en barco. Ella sufre de _____.

11. Daniela tiene un miedo irracional de los espacios y lugares abiertos. Ella sufre de

_____.

12. Lucas tiene un miedo irracional de los extraños y de las personas desconocidas. Él sufre

de _____.

78 ◆ -fono

MEANING	Sound
ENGLISH EQUIVALENT	-phone
PART OF SPEECH	Noun
GENDER	Masculine

The Greek word for *sound* is **phonos**. Since most Spanish words with the suffix **-fono** have English cognates ending in *-phone*, they tend to be easily recognized and used. In Spanish, these words have stress on the antepenultimate syllable (for example, **el micrófono** *microphone*).

NOUN ENDING IN **-fono**	ENGLISH EQUIVALENT	BASE WORD	ENGLISH EQUIVALENT
el dictáfono	*Dictaphone*	dictare [LAT.]	*to say often*
el gramófono	*gramophone, phonograph*	gramma [GRK.]	*letter*
el homófono	*homophone*	homos [GRK.]	*same*
el megáfono	*megaphone*	megas [GRK.]	*great*

▶

NOUN ENDING IN **-fono**	ENGLISH EQUIVALENT	BASE WORD	ENGLISH EQUIVALENT
el micrófono	*microphone*	mikros [GRK.]	*small*
el saxófono	*saxophone*	Sax [GRK.]	*(Adolphe) Sax*
el teléfono	*telephone*	tele [GRK.]	*far away*
el vibráfono	*vibraphone*	vibrare [GRK.]	*to vibrate*
el xilófono	*xylophone*	xylon [GRK.]	*wood*

EJERCICIO 78·1

Complete each sentence with the appropriate noun.

1. Un instrumento musical de percusión que tiene láminas que se afinan según las notas musicales y que se toca con mazas es el _____.

2. Charlie Parker, John Coltrane y Kenny G. son famosos por su habilidad para tocar el _____.

3. Las palabras ingleses *there, their* y *they're* son ejemplos del _____.

4. El _____ es un término antiguo para el tocadiscos.

5. Millones de personas llevan un _____ celular a todas partes.

6. El aparato utilizado por los cantantes y por los maestros de ceremonias para que sean oídos por la audiencia es un _____.

7. Un dispositivo en forma de embudo que se usa por la policía y las animadoras para amplificar y dirigir la voz es un _____.

8. Una máquina que graba las palabras habladas para que se pueda escucharlas y transcribirlas más tarde es un _____.

9. El _____ es un instrumento musical similar al xilófono que tiene un motor eléctrico que produce un efecto de vibrato.

79 ◆ -icio

MEANING	Result of an action, attribute, abstract noun
ENGLISH EQUIVALENT	*-ice*
PART OF SPEECH	Noun
GENDER	Masculine

Spanish words with the suffix **-icio** are abstract nouns, implying the result of an action if the base word is a verb, or an attribute if the base word is an adjective. Since many of these suffixed words are common and many have English cognates, they tend to be easily recognized and used.

NOUN ENDING IN **-icio**	ENGLISH EQUIVALENT	BASE WORD	ENGLISH EQUIVALENT
el beneficio	*benefit, profit*	beneficiar	*to benefit*
el edificio	*building*	edificar	*to build*
el ejercicio	*exercise, practice*	ejercer	*to exercise, practice*
el indicio	*indication, sign*	indicar	*to indicate, point out*
el juicio	*judgment, opinion*	juzgar	*to judge*
el novicio	*novice, beginner*	nuevo	*new*
el oficio	*profession, trade, office*	oficiar	*to officiate*
el perjuicio	*damage, harm*	perjudicar	*to harm, slander*

EJERCICIO
79·1

¿Qué o quién es esto? *Provide the noun that is related to each group of words. Include its article.*

1. un principiante, una persona nueva en algún arte o disciplina _____

2. un domicilio, una estructura, la manifestación del diseño de un arquitecto _____

3. el trabajo, el puesto, la posición en una oficina o en una corporación _____

4. la donación, el regalo, la ventaja _____

5. el signo, la señal, la implicación, la prueba _____

6. el daño, el sufrimiento, el impedimento _____

7. la opinión, la intuición, la percepción _____

8. el práctico, la disciplina, el entrenamiento _____

NOUN ENDING IN **-icio**	ENGLISH EQUIVALENT	BASE WORD	ENGLISH EQUIVALENT
el precipicio	*precipice, cliff*	precipitar(se)	*to fall, plunge*
el prejuicio	*prejudice*	prejuzgar	*to prejudge*
el sacrificio	*sacrifice*	sacrificar	*to sacrifice*
el servicio	*service, dinner set*	servir	*to serve, help*
el solsticio	*solstice*	sol + stare [LAT.]	*sun + to stand*
el suplicio	*torture, torment*	suplicar	*to beg, entreat*
el vicio	*vice*	viciar	*to corrupt, be corrupted*
el vitalicio	*life insurance policy*	vital	*vital, full of life*

¿Qué es esto? *Provide the noun that is related to each group of words. Include its article.*

1. la corrupción, la depravación, la degeneración   _____

2. la discriminación, la parcialidad, la intolerancia   _____

3. la dispensa, la indulgencia, la ayuda, los platos y vasos   _____

4. la tortura, el tormento, el sufrimiento, el martirio   _____

5. la escarpa, el sobresalir, la roca escarpada   _____

6. la renuncia, la abnegación, la privación, la inmolación   _____

7. el veintiuno de junio o de diciembre   _____

8. la póliza de seguro de vida   _____

80 ◆ -ico

MEANING	Diminutive
ENGLISH EQUIVALENT	—
PART OF SPEECH	Noun
GENDER	Masculine

The suffix **-ico** is an infrequently used diminutive. It usually denotes physical smallness (for example, **el saltico** *short hop, small leap*, from **el salto** *hop, jump*). It may also convey an endearing quality (for example, **el santico** *little saint, good child*, from **el santo** *saint*).

NOUN ENDING IN **-ico**	ENGLISH EQUIVALENT	BASE WORD	ENGLISH EQUIVALENT
el angélico	*little angel, darling child*	el ángel	*angel*
el asnico	*little donkey*	el asno	*donkey, ass*
el corecico	*small hide/skin*	el cuero	*leather, animal hide*
el corpecico	*small body*	el cuerpo	*body*
el liebratico	*young hare*	la liebre	*hare*
el patico	*duckling*	el pato	*duck*
el saltico	*short hop, small leap*	el salto	*hop, jump*
el santico	*little saint, good child*	el santo	*saint*
el sillico	*chamber pot*	la silla	*chair*
el tontico	*little dolt*	el tonto	*idiot, dimwit*
el ventanico	*small window*	la ventana	*window*
el villancico	*Christmas carol*	el villano	*villager, rustic person*
el zatico	*small bit of bread*	el zato	*small piece of bread*

Provide the correct noun(s) (including the article) for each description.

1. su madre dice "cuac cuac" _____

2. una canción que celebra la Navidad _____

3. un burro pequeño _____

4. un niño bueno, un amorcito _____

  _____

5. un pedazo pequeño de pan _____

6. un idiota _____

7. la piel de un animal pequeño _____

8. el inodoro pequeño _____

9. la vidriera pequeña _____

10. un organismo pequeño _____

11. un brinco muy pequeño _____

12. un conejo pequeño _____

81 ◆ -ida

MEANING	Action, result of an action
ENGLISH EQUIVALENT	—
PART OF SPEECH	Noun
GENDER	Feminine

The suffix **-ida** is combined with verbs to denote an action or the result of an action. A related suffix, **-ido** (No. 129), is more common. You are probably familiar with several of the following nouns, such as **la comida** *food, meal* and **la bebida** *drink, beverage.*

NOUN ENDING IN -ida	ENGLISH EQUIVALENT	BASE WORD	ENGLISH EQUIVALENT
la acogida	*welcome*	acoger	*to welcome*
la bebida	*drink, beverage*	beber	*to drink*
la comida	*food, meal*	comer	*to eat*
la corrida	*run, sprint, bullfight*	correr	*to run*
la despedida	*farewell, leave-taking*	despedir	*to say good-bye*
la herida	*injury, wound*	herir	*to hurt, wound*
la huida	*flight, escape*	huir	*to flee, run away*
la mordida	*bite (mouth)*	morder	*to bite*
la parida	*one who has just given birth*	parir	*to give birth*
la partida	*departure*	salir	*to leave, depart*
la sacudida	*shake, shock, jolt*	sacudir	*to shake, jar, jolt*
la salida	*exit, egress*	salir	*to leave, go out*

¿Qué o quién es esto? *Provide the correct noun (including its article) for each description.*

1. lo que quieres al llegar a un restaurante _____

2. lo que quiere cada prisionero _____

3. lo que ocurre cuando una persona coge y aprieta algo con los dientes _____

4. lo que quieres al abordar un avión _____

5. lo que buscas cuando termina la película en el cine _____

6. la madre con su recién nacido _____

7. lo que recibes de un buen anfitrión al llegar a una fiesta _____

8. lo que recibes de un buen anfitrión al salir de una fiesta _____

9. lo que recibes cuando un bárbaro te golpea _____

10. lo que quieres cuando tienes mucha sed _____

11. lo que te sientes cuando hay turbulencia en el avión _____

12. la fiesta brava (un evento con toros en una plaza cerrada) _____

82 ▶ -ido/-ida

MEANING	Relating to, like
ENGLISH EQUIVALENT	*-id*
PART OF SPEECH	Adjective
GENDER	Masculine/feminine

The suffix **-ido** (feminine: **-ida**) is common in Spanish. It is used to form the regular past participles of **-er** and **-ir** verbs, and it can be found in both nouns and adjectives. In the following chart of adjectives, there are two important features.

1. Many of these suffixed adjectives are derived directly from Latin. In fact, Latin, Spanish, and English share many cognates among these words.

2. The antepenultimate syllable is always stressed, and therefore it bears an accent.

ADJECTIVE ENDING IN **-ido**	ENGLISH EQUIVALENT	BASE WORD	ENGLISH EQUIVALENT
ácido	*acid*	acidus [LAT.]	*sharp, sour*
árido	*arid*	aridus [LAT.]	*dry, parched*
cándido	*candid, naive*	candidus [LAT.]	*white, honest*
estólido	*emotionless*	stolidus [LAT.]	*dull, stolid, slow* ▶

ADJECTIVE ENDING IN **-ido**	ENGLISH EQUIVALENT	BASE WORD	ENGLISH EQUIVALENT
estúpido	stupid, dense	stupidus [LAT.]	dull, foolish
fétido	fetid, foul-smelling	fetidus [LAT.]	fetid, stinking
flácido	flaccid, flabby	flaccidus [LAT.]	flaccid, flabby
frígido	frigid, extremely cold	frigidus [LAT.]	frigid, cold
gélido	icy	gelidus [LAT.]	icy cold
grávido	laden, full	gravidus [LAT.]	loaded
hórrido	horrid, hideous	horridus [LAT.]	rough, frightful
insípido	spiritless	in- + sapidus [LAT.]	not + tasty
lánguido	languid, listless	languidus [LAT.]	faint, listless
límpido	crystal clear	limpidus [LAT.]	clear
líquido	liquid	liquidus [LAT.]	liquid, fluid
lívido	livid, enraged	lividus [LAT.]	bluish black, malicious
lúcido	lucid, coherent	lucidus [LAT.]	light, bright, clear
pálido	pale, wan	pallidus [LAT.]	pale, colorless
plácido	placid, calm	placidus [LAT.]	peaceful, calm
rábido	rabid, raging, violent	rabidus [LAT.]	rabid, mad, furious
rápido	rapid, fast	rapidus [LAT.]	rapid, swift
sólido	solid	solidus [LAT.]	solid, whole, entire
sórdido	sordid, squalid, filthy	sordidus [LAT.]	dirty, unclean, filthy
tímido	timid, shy	timidus [LAT.]	fearful, afraid
tórrido	torrid, scorching, hot	torridus [LAT.]	scorching hot
translúcido	translucent, semitransparent	translucere [LAT.]	to shine through
túmido	swollen	tumidus [LAT.]	swollen
válido	valid	validus [LAT.]	strong, effective

EJERCICIO

82·1

¿Verdadero o falso? *Indicate whether each statement is true or false, using* **V** *for* **verdadero** *true or* **F** *for* **falso** *false.*

1. _____ Se encuentra el tórrido triángulo amoroso regularmente en las telenovelas.

2. _____ Los desiertos Gobi, Sahara y Kalahari son áridos.

3. _____ Una persona lívida está de buen humor.

4. _____ La Antártida tiene un clima frígido y gélido.

5. _____ El vinagre es líquido y ácido.

6. _____ Una frutería con mucha fruta fétida es muy atractiva y tentadora.

7. _____ Para tener y operar un coche se necesita una licencia de conducir válida.

8. _____ Es divertido viajar con una persona insípida, lánguida, estólida y estúpida.

9. _____ Muchos niños son cándidos y tímidos.

10. _____ Un filósofo es un pensador lúcido.

11. _____ Nueva York es una ciudad plácida.

12. _____ El hielo es sólido y translúcido.

13. _____ Los tabloides, como *The National Enquirer* y *The Daily Mirror,* cubren los detalles sórdidos de las celebridades.

14. _____ Una persona grávida de desesperanza está deprimida.

15. _____ El guepardo (el chita) es el animal terrestre más rápido.

16. _____ Un abdomen flácido tiene mucho tono muscular.

17. _____ El cielo límpido es de un color azul pálido.

83 ◆ -ífero/-ífera

MEANING	Bearing, producing
ENGLISH EQUIVALENT	*-iferous*
PART OF SPEECH	Adjective
GENDER	Masculine/feminine

The suffix -**ífero** (feminine: -**ífera**) and its English counterpart, *-iferous*, denote the characteristic of bearing or producing. The suffix is derived from the Latin verb **ferre** *to carry, bear.* An adjective ending in -**ífero** has a base noun; if the noun ends in a vowel, the vowel is omitted and -**ífero** is added directly to the word.

ADJECTIVE ENDING IN -**ífero**	ENGLISH EQUIVALENT	BASE WORD	ENGLISH EQUIVALENT
astrífero	*starry (poetry)*	el astro	*heavenly body*
aurífero	*gold-producing*	aurum [LAT.]	*gold*
conchífero	*shell-bearing*	la concha	*shell*
conífero	*coniferous, cone-bearing*	el cono	*cone*
coralífero	*coral-bearing*	el coral	*coral*
florífero	*flower-bearing*	la flor	*flower*
fructífero	*fruit-bearing, fruitful*	fructus [LAT.]	*fruit*
fumífero	*smoking, emitting smoke (poetry)*	fumus [LAT.]	*smoke*
gumífero	*gum- or rubber-producing*	la goma	*rubber, gum*
lactífero	*milk-producing*	lac/lactis [LAT.]	*milk*
lanífero	*wool-bearing*	la lana	*wool*
lucífero	*shining, light-bearing*	la luz	*light*

EJERCICIO 83·1

Complete each sentence with the correct form of the appropriate adjective.

1. La oveja es _____.

2. Un mineral que produce el oro es _____.

3. Durante el proceso de la elección del nuevo Papa, millones de personas miran fijamente

   a la chimenea _____ con la esperanza de ver el humo blanco.

4. Las plantas que producen flores son _____.

5. La vaca es _____.

6. Es importante proteger los arrecifes _____ a lo largo de las costas del Caribe.

7. El abeto, el pino y la pícea son árboles _____.

8. La playa que se caracteriza por una abundancia de conchas es

_____.

9. Un árbol _____ produce el caucho.

10. El manzano y el peral son árboles _____.

11. Una de las pinturas más conocidas del pintor Vincent van Gogh se llama *La noche estrellada*. Un sinónimo de "estrellado" es _____.

ADJECTIVE ENDING IN -ífero	ENGLISH EQUIVALENT	BASE WORD	ENGLISH EQUIVALENT
melífero	*honey-producing*	la miel	*honey*
mortífero	*lethal, death-producing*	la muerte	*death*
nectarífero	*nectar-bearing*	el néctar	*nectar*
nubífero	*cloud-bearing (poetry)*	la nube	*cloud*
odorífero	*odoriferous*	el olor	*odor*
palmífero	*palm-bearing*	la palma	*palm (botany)*
pestífero	*foul smelling, pestiferous*	la peste	*plague, pestilence*
pomífero	*apple-bearing*	pomum [LAT.]	*apple*
salífero	*salt-bearing (chemistry)*	la sal	*salt*
sanguífero	*blood-producing*	sanguis [LAT.]	*blood*
soporífero	*sleep-inducing*	el sopor	*drowsiness*
sudorífero	*sweat-producing*	el sudor	*sweat, perspiration*

EJERCICIO

83·2

¿**Verdadero o falso?** *Indicate whether each statement is true or false, using* **V** *for* **verdadero** *true or* **F** *for* **falso** *false.*

1. _____ El manzano (el árbol de manzanas) es pomífero.

2. _____ El cuerpo contiene dos tipos de glándulas sudoríferas—las endócrinas y las exócrinas—y sus secreciones pueden causar un olor problemático.

3. _____ Un olmo (*elm*) afligido con la plaga de grafiosis es nectarífero.

4. _____ La grafiosis es mortífera para los olmos.

5. _____ El abeto, el pino y la pícea son árboles palmíferos.

6. _____ A Drácula le encantan los cuellos sanguíferos.

7. _____ La cafeína es soporífera.

8. _____ La cloaca tiene un olor pestífero.

9. _____ La abeja es melífera.

10. _____ Es bueno beber el agua salífera.

11. _____ Los compuestos odoríferos como el metano, el etano y los gases de la combustión de tu coche son elementos esenciales de los perfumes de Estée Lauder.

84 ▸ -iforme

MEANING	Shaped, in the form of, like
ENGLISH EQUIVALENT	*-iform*
PART OF SPEECH	Adjective
GENDER	Masculine/feminine

The Spanish suffix **-iforme** and its English counterpart, *-iform*, have the same general meaning. The English suffix, however, is more closely connected to the concept of shape, while the Spanish suffix may also mean *like* (for example, **carniforme** *flesh-like*). Generally speaking, if the base word ends in a vowel, the vowel is omitted before **-iforme** is added; if the base word ends in a consonant, **-iforme** is added directly to the word.

The following adjectives ending in **-iforme** represent easily recognized physical shapes.

ADJECTIVE ENDING IN **-iforme**	ENGLISH EQUIVALENT	BASE WORD	ENGLISH EQUIVALENT
aliforme	*wing-shaped*	el ala [F.]	*wing*
arboriforme	*tree-shaped*	el árbol	*tree*
coniforme	*cone-shaped, conical*	el cono	*cone*
conquiforme	*shell-shaped*	la concha	*shell*
corniforme	*horn-shaped*	el cuerno	*horn*
cruciforme	*cross-shaped*	la cruz	*cross*
cuadriforme	*square-shaped*	el cuadrado	*square*
cuneiforme	*wedge-shaped*	la cuña	*wedge*
dendriforme	*tree-shaped*	dendron [GRK.]	*tree*
fungiforme	*mushroom-shaped*	el fungo	*fungus*
lotiforme	*lotus-shaped*	el loto	*lotus*
periforme	*pear-shaped*	la pera	*pear*
pisciforme	*fish-shaped*	piscis [LAT.]	*fish*
ramiforme	*branch-shaped*	la rama	*branch*
reniforme	*kidney-shaped*	el riñón	*kidney*

EJERCICIO 84·1

Provide the correct adjective(s) for each description.

1. la forma del símbolo de la Cruz Roja _____

2. una forma popular para piscinas y mesas de centro _____

3. la forma de un pedazo de pizza _____

4. la forma de una zanahoria o de lo que produce el pino _____

5. la forma ubicua que se encuentra en la playa _____

6. la forma de un pez _____

7. lo que se encuentra en la cabeza del rinoceronte o el antílope _____

8. la forma de la parte del pájaro que le permite volar _____

9. la forma de un champiñón o un hongo _____

10. la forma geométrica que tiene cuatro lados iguales y cuatro ángulos rectos _____

11. la forma de la flor sagrada para los budistas que simboliza la pureza _____

12. la forma de lo que se ve en todas partes de un bosque _____

_____

13. la forma del "brazo" de un árbol _____

The following adjectives ending in -**iforme** do not represent obvious or recognizable physical shapes.

ADJECTIVE ENDING IN -**iforme**	ENGLISH EQUIVALENT	BASE WORD	ENGLISH EQUIVALENT
baciliforme	*bacilliform*	el bacilo	*bacillus, bacterium*
biforme	*biform*	bi- [LAT.]	*twice*
carniforme	*flesh-like*	la carne	*flesh, meat*
coleriforme	*resembling cholera*	la cólera	*cholera*
deiforme	*godlike*	deus [LAT.]	*god*
estratiforme	*arranged in layers*	el estrato	*stratum, layer*
filiforme	*threadlike*	filum [LAT.]	*thread*
gaseiforme	*in the form of gas*	el gas	*gas*
semiforme	*semi-formed*	semi- [LAT.]	*half*
triforme	*triform*	tres/tria [LAT.]	*three*
uniforme	*uniform, standard*	unus [LAT.]	*one*

EJERCICIO

84·2

Complete each sentence with the correct form of the appropriate adjective.

1. Algo que tiene tres partes es _____ .

2. Algo que se parece a una deidad es _____ .

3. Algo que tiene las cualidades del microbio o microorganismo es

_____ .

4. Algo que tiene varios hilos es _____.

5. Algo que es doble es _____.

6. Algo que es parcialmente constituido es _____.

7. Una enfermedad con síntomas como las náuseas, los vómitos y las diarreas puede ser

_____.

8. Algo que está ordenado en capas o estratos es _____.

9. Algo que conforme a una norma es _____.

10. Algo en la forma de gas es _____.

11. Algo con cualidades como la carne es _____.

 **-il**

MEANING	Relating to, like; able to be (acted on)
ENGLISH EQUIVALENT	*-ile, -able, -ible*
PART OF SPEECH	Adjective
GENDER	Masculine/feminine

Words with the suffix **-il** are usually based on a noun or verb, although in rare cases, an adjective may be the base word (for example, **femenil** *feminine, womanly*, from **femenino** *feminine*). Since you are probably familiar with most of the base words, the adjectives in the following chart should be relatively easy to recognize and use. These adjectives do not change form with respect to gender; the plural form ends in **-iles: el servicio abogadil ~ los servicios abogadiles**.

ADJECTIVE ENDING IN **-il**	ENGLISH EQUIVALENT	BASE WORD	ENGLISH EQUIVALENT
abogadil	*like a lawyer*	el abogado	*lawyer*
aceitunil	*olive-colored*	la aceituna	*olive*
becerril	*relating to cows*	el becerro	*calf*
borreguil	*relating to lambs*	el borrego	*young lamb*
concejil	*public, of the municipal council*	el concejo	*municipal council*
estudiantil	*relating to students*	el estudiante	*student*
fabril	*industrial, manufacturing*	la fábrica	*factory*
febril	*feverish, febrile*	la fiebre	*fever*
femenil	*feminine, womanly*	femenino	*feminine*
grácil	*graceful*	la gracia	*grace*
infantil	*infantile, like a child*	el infante	*infant*
juvenil	*juvenile, relating to youth*	el joven	*young person*

Provide the correct adjective for each description.

1. como un bebé, un neonato o una persona muy inmadura _____

2. como un cordero, una oveja joven o el títere Lamb Chop _____

3. como Perry Mason, Judith Sheindlin o Atticus Finch _____

4. como Bessie, Elsie, Flossie o cualquier vaca _____

5. como un universitario, un escolar o un discípulo _____

6. como una persona con síntomas de la influenza o un resfriado _____

7. como el color verde oscuro mezclado con el color amarillo _____

8. como una mujer muy fina y afeminada _____

9. como un sector del gobierno de un pueblo o ciudad _____

10. como un muchacho, un adolescente o una persona antes de cumplir la mayoría de edad _____

11. como la industria o la producción de máquinas _____

12. como una bailarina o una persona muy agraciada _____

ADJECTIVE ENDING IN -il	ENGLISH EQUIVALENT	BASE WORD	ENGLISH EQUIVALENT
libreril	*relating to books*	el libro	*book*
manzanil	*relating to apples*	la manzana	*apple*
monjil	*nun-like, prudish*	la monja	*nun*
móvil	*movable*	mover	*to move (an object)*
muchachil	*youthful, like a child*	el muchacho	*young boy, lad*
mujeril	*womanly*	la mujer	*woman*
portátil	*portable*	portar	*to carry, bear*
señoril	*lordly, haughty*	el señor	*lord, master*
servil	*servile*	servir	*to serve*
tornátil	*changeable, fickle*	tornar	*to turn, change*
varonil	*manly*	el varón	*man, male*
versátil	*versatile*	versar	*to turn, go round*
volátil	*volatile, capable of flying*	volar	*to fly*

Provide the appropriate adjective(s) for each description.

1. como un hombre muy macho _____

2. como algo ligero, que se puede transportar fácilmente de un lugar a otro _____

_____

3. como una mujer católica, religiosa y beata   _____

4. como alguien obsequiosa y sumisa, a quien le gusta servir   _____

5. como la fruta famosa del jardín de Edén   _____

6. como un chico, un niño o un joven   _____

7. como algo que se cambia fácilmente   _____

  _____

8. como el negocio de la publicación   _____

9. como una persona femenina   _____

10. como un hombre elegante, majestuoso, agosto y noble   _____

11. como algo inestable, transitorio, mercurial o no permanente   _____

86 ▸ -illa

MEANING	Diminutive; depreciative
ENGLISH EQUIVALENT	—
PART OF SPEECH	Noun
GENDER	Feminine

The common suffix **-illa** denotes diminution, usually physical, of the base noun. Some of these suffixed nouns, however, reflect decreased status or a figurative reduction of some type. A related suffix, **-illo/-illa** (No. 87), is more frequently used.

All of the following nouns ending in **-illa** have a disparaging connotation.

NOUN ENDING IN **-illa**	ENGLISH EQUIVALENT	BASE WORD	ENGLISH EQUIVALENT
la colilla	*cigarette butt*	la cola	*tail*
la cosilla	*miserable little thing*	la cosa	*thing*
la dudilla	*sneaking doubt*	la duda	*doubt*
la figurilla	*insignificant little person*	la figura	*figure, person*
la gacetilla	*gossipmonger*	la gaceta	*gazette*
la gentecilla	*riffraff, rabble*	la gente	*people*
las hablillas [PL.]	*gossip, foolish talk*	la habla	*speech, language*
la mentirilla	*white lie*	la mentira	*lie*
la mujercilla	*hussy, slut, strumpet*	la mujer	*woman*
la personilla	*ridiculous little person*	la persona	*person*

EJERCICIO
86·1

¿Qué o quién es esto? *Provide the correct noun(s) (including the article) for each description.*

1. algo de poco (o no) valor

   _____

2. una persona que siempre sabe la malas noticias de otras y a quien le encanta pasar la información a todo el mundo

   _____

3. la hembra que flirtea con cualquier hombre, especialmente los hombres casados

   _____

4. el grupo de la población que tiene malas maneras y es grosero y ruidoso

   _____

5. el extremo del cigarrillo después de fumarlo

   _____

6. lo que te sientes cuando no crees totalmente lo que alguien te dice

   _____

7. lo que le dices a otra persona para proteger los sentimientos, pero no es exactamente la verdad

   _____

8. los contenidos de las revistas *The Enquirer, Hello!* y *OK!*

   _____

9. un hombre o una mujer que es insignificante o ridículo

   _____

   _____

87 ◆ -illo/-illa

MEANING	Diminutive; depreciative
ENGLISH EQUIVALENT	—
PART OF SPEECH	Noun
GENDER	Masculine/feminine

The widely used suffix **-illo** (feminine: **-illa**) denotes diminution, usually physical, of the base noun. In the following chart, however, the nouns reflect decreased status or a figurative reduction of some type. Note that if the base noun ends in **-r**, a **c** is added to the noun before the suffix (for example, **el doctor** *doctor* yields **el doctorcillo** *third-rate doctor, "quack"*). Several of these nouns, especially those that refer to people and their respective professions, can be downright malicious.

Since the following nouns ending in **-illo** refer to persons, the suffix becomes **-illa** if the person is female: **el mediquillo** ~ **la mediquilla** *third-rate physician, "quack."*

NOUN ENDING IN -illo	ENGLISH EQUIVALENT	BASE WORD	ENGLISH EQUIVALENT
el abogadillo	*third-rate lawyer*	el abogado	*lawyer*
el autorcillo	*third-rate author*	el autor	*author*
el cieguillo	*poor little blind person*	el ciego	*blind person*
el doctorcillo	*third-rate doctor, "quack"*	el doctor	*doctor*
el escritorcillo	*third-rate writer, "hack"*	el escritor	*writer*
el estudiantillo	*wretched student*	el estudiante	*student*
el hombrecillo	*miserable little man*	el hombre	*man*
el ladroncillo	*petty thief*	el ladrón	*thief*
el licenciadillo	*wretched lawyer*	el licenciado	*lawyer*
el maridillo	*pitiful husband*	el marido	*husband*
el mediquillo	*third-rate physician, "quack"*	el médico	*doctor, physician*
el sabidillo	*know-it-all*	el sabio	*wise, learned person*

EJERCICIO 87·1

¿Quién es esto? *Provide the appropriate noun(s) for each description.*

1. el que constantemente recibe malas notas en la escuela _____

2. el que "siempre" tiene razón _____

3. el esposo miserable _____

4. el que persigue la ambulancia _____

_____

5. el "wannabe" a Shakespeare _____

_____

6. el pobrecito que no puede ver nada _____

7. el "wannabe" a Robin Hood o a Blackbeard _____

8. el "wannabe" al mandamás (*big shot*) del hospital _____

_____

9. el varón patético _____

The following nouns ending in **-illo** refer to animals, places, things, and abstractions.

NOUN ENDING IN -illo	ENGLISH EQUIVALENT	BASE WORD	ENGLISH EQUIVALENT
el amorcillo	*passing fancy, flirtation*	el amor	*love, affection*
el animalillo	*wretched little animal*	el animal	*animal*
el baratillo	*heap of junk*	el barato	*cheap merchandise*
el brocadillo	*brocade of inferior quality*	el brocado	*brocade*
el disgustillo	*minor or petty upset*	el disgusto	*displeasure, upset*
el estanquillo	*shabby store or kiosk*	el estanco	*store, shop*
el geniecillo	*sharp temper*	el genio	*temperament, mood*
el pajarillo	*miserable or frail bird*	el pájaro	*bird*

▶

NOUN ENDING IN **-illo**	ENGLISH EQUIVALENT	BASE WORD	ENGLISH EQUIVALENT
el papelillo	*scrap of paper*	el papel	*paper*
los trabajillos [PL.]	*odd jobs*	el trabajo	*work, job, labor*
el veranillo	*late/untimely summer*	el verano	*summer*
el vinillo	*weak wine*	el vino	*wine*

¿Qué es esto? *Provide the appropriate noun for each description.*

1. un pedacito de una carta, una tarjeta o una página de un cuaderno destinado a la basura _____

2. una tienda pequeña, a veces miserable, que vende varias cosas no costosas _____

3. un montón de cosas de poco valor _____

4. un perro sarnoso, un coyote rabioso o una rata enferma _____

5. un Cabernet Sauvignon o un Chardonnay débil _____

6. el encaprichamiento o el enamoramiento de alguien _____

7. un canario enfermo o un águila miserable _____

8. los días, usualmente en septiembre u octubre, cuando el clima está extemporáneamente cálido _____

9. un problema de menor importancia que, sin embargo, te hace loco _____

10. el mal genio crónico _____

11. la broca de baja calidad _____

12. varios empleos por aquí y por allá a tiempo parcial _____

88 ◆ -ito/-ita

MEANING	Relating to, like
ENGLISH EQUIVALENT	*-ite, -it*
PART OF SPEECH	Adjective
GENDER	Masculine/feminine

The suffix **-ito** (feminine: **-ita**) is used to form nouns in a variety of contexts: as a diminutive (Nos. 34 and 35), as a chemical or mineral (No. 136), and as the result of an action. In this section, **-ito/-ita** is an adjectival ending that denotes a similarity to the base word. The base words, whether nouns, verbs, or adjectives, are often derived from Latin. Since many of the suffixed words have English cognates, they tend to be easily recognized and used.

ADJECTIVE ENDING IN -ito	ENGLISH EQUIVALENT	BASE WORD	ENGLISH EQUIVALENT
bendito	*blessed, holy*	bendecir	*to bless*
contrito	*contrite*	contritus [LAT.]	*ground to pieces*
decrépito	*decrepit*	decrepitus [LAT.]	*very old, infirm*
emérito	*emeritus, retired*	emeritus [LAT.]	*past service*
erudito	*erudite, scholarly*	ex- + rudis [LAT.]	*out + unskilled*
explícito	*explicit*	explicitus [LAT.]	*unobstructed*
exquisito	*exquisite, carefully sought*	exquisitus [LAT.]	*carefully sought out, choice*
favorito	*favorite*	el favor	*favor*
finito	*finite*	el fin	*end*
gratuito	*free, gratuitous*	gratuitus [LAT.]	*voluntary*

EJERCICIO

88·1

Sinónimos *Provide a synonym for each group of words.*

1. preferido, elegido, favorecido _____

2. fino, espléndido, excepcional _____

3. intelectual, sapiente, entendido _____

4. santificado, consagrado, santo _____

5. limitado, determinado, definido _____

6. directo, franco, manifiesto _____

7. ruinoso, arruinado, débil, frágil _____

8. lamentoso, compungido, pesaroso _____

9. jubilado, retirado _____

10. gratis, regalado, libre de costos _____

ADJECTIVE ENDING IN -ito	ENGLISH EQUIVALENT	BASE WORD	ENGLISH EQUIVALENT
ilícito	*illicit*	in- + licitus [LAT.]	*not + lawful*
implícito	*implicit, understood*	implicare [LAT.]	*to connect closely*
infinito	*infinite*	infinitus [LAT.]	*unbounded, infinite*
inhóspito	*inhospitable*	inhospitalis [LAT.]	*inhospitable*
lícito	*licit, legal*	licere [LAT.]	*to be lawful*
pretérito	*past, preterit*	praeterire [LAT.]	*to go by, go past*
recóndito	*hidden, secret*	recondere [LAT.]	*to hide, conceal*
sólito	*usual, customary*	soler	*to usually do*
súbito	*sudden*	subire [LAT.]	*to go up on stealthily*
tácito	*tacit, understood*	tacitus [LAT.]	*silent, assumed as a matter of course*

Sinónimos *Provide the appropriate synonym(s) for each group of words.*

1. habitual, cotidiano, acostumbrado, normal _____

2. ilimitado, incalculable, vasto, inmenso _____

3. legal, autorizado, legítimo, permitido _____

4. ilegal, antisocial, contra la ley _____

5. escondido, oculto, guardado _____

6. pasado, ocurrido, sucedido, antiguo _____

7. desagradable, hostil, inhospitable _____

8. inmediato, repentino, inesperado _____

9. entendido, callado, obvio, evidente _____

_____

89 ▸ -izar

MEANING	To make (like)
ENGLISH EQUIVALENT	*-ize, -yze*
PART OF SPEECH	Verb

Spanish has quite a few verbs whose infinitives end in **-izar**. This regular **-ar** verb, which means *to make (like)*, is formed from a base noun or adjective and the suffix **-izar**. Since many of these verbs have English cognates, they tend to be easily recognized and used.

In the following chart, the verbs ending in **-izar** have adjectives as their base words.

VERB ENDING IN **-izar**	ENGLISH EQUIVALENT	BASE WORD	ENGLISH EQUIVALENT
amenizar	*to make pleasant, liven up*	ameno	*pleasant, agreeable*
esterilizar	*to sterilize*	estéril	*sterile*
familiarizar	*to familiarize*	familiar	*familiar*
fertilizar	*to fertilize*	fértil	*fertile*
finalizar	*to finalize*	final	*final*
legalizar	*to legalize*	legal	*legal*
neutralizar	*to neutralize*	neutral	*neutral*
realizar	*to realize, accomplish*	real	*real*
suavizar	*to make smooth*	suave	*smooth*
tranquilizar	*to tranquilize*	tranquilo	*tranquil*
utilizar	*to utilize, make use of*	útil	*useful*
vocalizar	*to vocalize, articulate (music)*	vocal	*vocal*

Complete each sentence with the appropriate verb.

1. Eres médico y quieres calmar a un paciente muy agitado. Necesitas

   _____lo.

2. Eres granjero y quieres preparar la tierra para cultivar las cosechas. Debes

   _____la.

3. Muchos dermatólogos recomiendan Botox para _____ las líneas
   y arrugas de la cara.

4. Muchas personas quieren _____ el cultivo, la venta y el uso
   recreativo de la marihuana.

5. Antes de dar un discurso sobre México, necesitas _____te con el
   país.

6. Una persona muy ambiciosa quiere _____ mucho durante su vida.

7. Si estás en la cocina o en el garaje, necesitas _____ la herramienta
   correcta para la tarea.

8. En la Nochevieja (el 31 de diciembre), hay fuegos artificiales para

   _____ las fiestas.

9. El Secretario de Estado visita a varios líderes del mundo con el propósito de

   _____ los conflictos y cualquier hostilidad entre los países.

10. Es importante _____ un proyecto antes de comenzar otro.

11. La vasectomía es una cirugía para _____ a un hombre.

In the following chart, the verbs ending in **-izar** have nouns as their base words.

VERB ENDING IN **-izar**	ENGLISH EQUIVALENT	BASE WORD	ENGLISH EQUIVALENT
alfabetizar	*to alphabetize*	el alfabeto	*alphabet*
analizar	*to analyze*	el análisis	*analysis*
arborizar	*to plant trees*	el árbol	*tree*
climatizar	*to air-condition*	el clima	*climate, air conditioner*
memorizar	*to memorize*	la memoria	*memory*
organizar	*to organize*	el órgano	*organ, part*
paralizar	*to paralyze*	la parálisis	*paralysis*
polemizar	*to engage in argument*	la polémica	*polemics, dispute*
psicoanalizar	*to psychoanalyze*	el psicoanálisis	*psychoanalysis*
pulverizar	*to pulverize*	el polvo	*powder, dust*
ruborizar	*to make blush*	el rubor	*blush, flush*
valorizar	*to make more valuable*	el valor	*value, worth*

EJERCICIO
89·2

Complete each sentence with the appropriate verb.

1. Cuando hablas ante una audiencia, necesitas _____ tu discurso—
o al menos los puntos principales.

2. Tienes que ordenar una lista de varias palabras de A hasta Z. Necesitas

_____ las palabras.

3. Eres discípulo de Sigmund Freud y tienes un cliente con muchos problemas. Necesitas

_____lo.

4. Eres estadístico y necesitas preparar un informe. Hay que _____
los datos y otra información pertinente.

5. Eres una persona cruel y quieres avergonzar a otra persona hasta el punto que su cara

esté roja. Quieres _____lo.

6. Vives en los trópicos donde hace muchísimo calor todo el tiempo. Necesitas

_____ la casa.

7. Quieres vender tu casa, pero para venderla a un precio que representa tus esperanzas,

necesitas hacer muchas mejoras para _____la.

8. Te gusta disputar con los vecinos. Para ti, es divertido _____ con
otros.

9. Estás enfermo y necesitas tomar varias píldoras durante el día, pero te duele tanto la

garganta que primero necesitas _____ las píldoras.

10. Eres jardinero extraordinario y tienes mucha tierra donde quieres tener un verdadero

bosque. Necesitas _____ la tierra.

11. Se usa un anestésico para _____ los músculos antes de la cirugía.

12. Es importante _____ los resúmenes de banco y otros documentos
importantes antes de encontrarse con el asesor fiscal.

90 ◆ -mano/-mana

MEANING	Crazy/obsessed person
ENGLISH EQUIVALENT	-maniac
PART OF SPEECH	Noun
GENDER	Masculine/feminine

Since many nouns ending in **-mano** (feminine: **-mana**) have English cognates, they tend to be easily recognized and used. These suffixed nouns cover a wide range, encompassing many forms of lunacy and obsession.

NOUN ENDING IN **-mano/-mana**	ENGLISH EQUIVALENT	BASE WORD	ENGLISH EQUIVALENT
el anglómano	*Anglomaniac*	Anglii [LAT.]	*the English*
el bibliómano	*bibliomaniac*	biblion [GRK.]	*book*
el cleptómano	*kleptomaniac*	kleptes [GRK.]	*thief*
el erotómano	*sex addict*	Eros	*Eros (god of love)*
el megalómano	*megalomaniac*	megas [GRK.]	*great, mighty*
el melómano	*music fanatic*	melos [GRK.]	*song, melody*
el monómano	*monomaniac*	monos [GRK.]	*one, single*
la ninfómana	*nymphomaniac*	la ninfa	*nymph, young lady*
el pirómano	*pyromaniac*	la pira	*pyre*
el toxicómano	*drug addict*	el tóxico	*poison*

EJERCICIO
90·1

Provide the correct noun (including its article) to describe the person having an obsession with the items mentioned.

1. los libros _____

2. la música _____

3. Gran Bretaña _____

4. la cocaína, la heroína, la metanfetamina _____

5. las relaciones sexuales con cualquier hombre _____

6. el robo _____

7. el incendio, la hoguera, la fogata _____

8. las relaciones sexuales con cualquier persona _____

9. una idea o un tópico _____

10. los delirios de grandeza, riqueza y poder _____

91 ◆ -miento

MEANING	Action, result of an action, state
ENGLISH EQUIVALENT	*-ment*
PART OF SPEECH	Noun
GENDER	Masculine

The suffix **-miento** denotes achievement of an action. The base word for these suffixed nouns is a verb. For **-ar** verbs, the **a** of the infinitive ending is retained before the suffix is added (for example, **tratar** *to treat* yields **tratamiento** *treatment*). For **-er** verbs, the **e** of the infinitive ending becomes **i** before the suffix is added (for example, **envolver** *to envelop* yields **envolvimiento** *wrapping, involvement*). For **-ir** verbs, the **i** of the infinitive ending is retained before the suffix is added (for example, **sentir** *to feel, sense* yields **sentimiento** *sentiment, feeling*).

NOUN ENDING IN **-miento**	ENGLISH EQUIVALENT	BASE WORD	ENGLISH EQUIVALENT
el abatimiento	*depression*	abatir	*to bring down*
el agrandamiento	*enlargement*	agrandar	*to enlarge*
el amillaramiento	*tax assessment*	amillarar	*to assess (tax)*
el aplazamiento	*postponement*	aplazar	*to postpone*
el aquietamiento	*appeasement*	aquietar	*to ease, appease*
el aturdimiento	*bewilderment, daze*	aturdir	*to bewilder, daze, stun*
el avasallamiento	*subjugation*	avasallar	*to subjugate*
el confinamiento	*confinement*	confinar	*to confine*
el embellecimiento	*embellishment*	embellecer	*to embellish*
el empobrecimiento	*impoverishment*	empobrecer	*to impoverish*

EJERCICIO
91·1

Complete each sentence with the correct form of the appropriate noun.

1. Un zombi anda por las calles en un estado del _____.

2. Cuando una madre ofrece chocolates a un niño llorando, es un acto de

   _____.

3. Amnesty Internacional protesta el _____ de muchas minorías en el mundo entero.

4. Muchos hombres, después de cumplir sesenta años, sufren de un

   _____ de la próstata.

5. Trágicamente, el _____ de millones de habitantes de los países del tercer mundo ocurre sin alivio.

6. La tristeza, la apatía y la depresión son estados emocionales del

   _____.

7. Los prisioneros en el corredor de la muerte están en _____ casi todo el día.

8. Cuando nadie está listo para discutir nada, un jefe sabio recomienda un

   _____ de la reunión.

9. Los dueños de casa siempre odian recibir la noticia desagradable que el

   _____ de su propiedad será incrementado y por eso, el impuesto

   será mayor.

10. El _____ de la casa ocurre en muchas vecindades en los días previos
    de la Navidad, pero siempre hay los que creen "más es mejor" e intentan iluminar el
    mundo.

NOUN ENDING IN -miento	ENGLISH EQUIVALENT	BASE WORD	ENGLISH EQUIVALENT
el encantamiento	*enchantment*	encantar	*to enchant*
el encarcelamiento	*imprisonment*	encarcelar	*to imprison*
el encarecimiento	*rise in price*	encarecer	*to raise the price*
el enriquecimiento	*enrichment*	enriquecer	*to enrich*
el entretenimiento	*entertainment*	entretener	*to entertain*
el envilecimiento	*degradation*	envilecer	*to degrade*
el envolvimiento	*wrapping, involvement*	envolver	*to envelop, involve*
el esclarecimiento	*clarification*	esclarecer	*to clarify, clear up*
el establecimiento	*establishment*	establecer	*to establish*
el limpiamiento	*cleaning*	limpiar	*to clean*

EJERCICIO
91·2

¿Verdadero o falso? *Indicate whether each statement is true or false, using* **V** *for* **verdadero** *true or* **F** *for* **falso** *false.*

1. _____ El encarecimiento del petróleo es una situación difícil para los individuales y para
   los gobiernos del mundo entero.

2. _____ El limpiamiento de la cara es importante para todos, pero especialmente para las
   personas que usan mucho maquillaje.

3. _____ El envolvimiento de los padres en la educación de los niños no es importante.

4. _____ El arte del encantamiento es importante para los brujas y los magos.

5. _____ El establecimiento del ejército no es importante para la mayoría de los países del
   mundo.

6. _____ El encarcelamiento puede incluir el uso de un escáner de cuerpo completo para
   detectar algo oculto bajo la ropa.

7. _____ Hay cárceles en algunas partes del mundo en que torturan y humillan a los
   prisioneros hasta realizar su envilecimiento total.

8. _____ El entretenimiento no es importante en la industria del cine.

9. _____ Cuando se estudia un idioma extranjero, el enriquecimiento del vocabulario es de suma importancia.

10. _____ El esclarecimiento del caso y toda la evidencia es de suma importancia para un buen abogado.

NOUN ENDING IN -miento	ENGLISH EQUIVALENT	BASE WORD	ENGLISH EQUIVALENT
el mejoramiento	*improvement*	mejorar	*to improve*
el movimiento	*movement*	mover	*to move*
el nombramiento	*appointment*	nombrar	*to appoint, name*
el ofrecimiento	*offer*	ofrecer	*to offer*
el pagamiento	*payment*	pagar	*to pay*
el pensamiento	*thought*	pensar	*to think*
el reclutamiento	*recruitment*	reclutar	*to recruit*
el seguimiento	*pursuit, chase*	seguir	*to follow*
el sentimiento	*sentiment, feeling*	sentir	*to feel, sense*
el tratamiento	*treatment*	tratar	*to treat*

EJERCICIO
91·3

¿Sí o no? *Answer each of the following questions with* **Sí** *yes or* **No** *no.*

1. _____ ¿Es de suma importancia a los líderes de un culto el reclutamiento de nuevos miembros?

2. _____ El movimiento del dedo del pie, ¿es de suma importancia para una persona después de una herida de la médula espinal?

3. _____ El pagamiento de la renta a tiempo cada mes, ¿es de poco interés al propietario del apartamento?

4. _____ Para un psicólogo, ¿es de suma importancia el tratamiento de los sentimientos de los clientes?

5. _____ Si un coche nuevo cuesta $35,000, ¿es razonable el ofrecimiento de $20,000 al concesionario de coches?

6. _____ ¿Es absurdo el nombramiento a una posición financiera de una persona que no puede calcular nada sin calculadora electrónica?

7. _____ La calidad de los pensamientos, ¿es de poca importancia para los filósofos?

8. _____ Para un hombre ambicioso o una mujer ambiciosa, ¿es de suma importancia el seguimiento de los sueños y el mejoramiento de sí mismo?

92 ◆ -ón/-ona

MEANING	(Person) tending/given to
ENGLISH EQUIVALENT	—
PART OF SPEECH	Adjective, noun
GENDER	Masculine/feminine

All words with the suffix **-ón** (feminine: **-ona**) function as adjectives; several may also function as nouns, representing persons with the tendencies embodied in the adjectives: **El cincuentón es tragón** *The 50-year-old man is greedy* and **La cuarentona es preguntona** *The 40-year-old woman is nosy*. The masculine plural form ends in **-ones**; the feminine plural form ends in **-onas**.

In the following chart, the words ending in **-ón/-ona** function only as adjectives.

ADJECTIVE ENDING IN -ón	ENGLISH EQUIVALENT	BASE WORD	ENGLISH EQUIVALENT
abusón	*given to taking advantage of*	abusar	*to abuse, take advantage of*
calentón	*unpleasantly warm*	calentar	*to heat*
gordón	*very fat, corpulent*	gordo	*fat*
gritón	*vociferous*	gritar	*to shout, scream*
guapetón	*very handsome, dashing*	guapo	*handsome*
holgachón	*fond of ease and little work*	holgar	*to rest, be idle*
juguetón	*playful, frolicsome*	jugar	*to play (a game)*
peleón	*given to fighting*	pelear	*to fight*
politicón	*keen on politics*	la política	*politics*
regalón	*generous, fond of giving presents*	el regalo	*gift, present*
replicón	*argumentative*	replicar	*to answer (back)*
reservón	*very reserved, secretive*	reservar	*to reserve, keep secret*
respondón	*cheeky, saucy, insolent*	responder	*to answer, reply*
temblón	*shaky, trembling*	temblar	*to shake, tremble*
vomitón	*given to vomiting*	vomitar	*to vomit*

EJERCICIO 92·1

Provide the correct form of the appropriate adjective(s) for each description.

1. un hombre muy perezoso _____

2. un chico que habla siempre con voz muy alta _____

3. una madrina que da muchos juguetes a su ahijado _____

4. un gatito o un cachorro _____

5. Adonis, James Bond, Clark Gable _____

6. Death Valley, un desierto en pleno día _____

7. una persona que sufre de bulimia _____

8. el estafador, el artista del fraude _____

9. el boxeador, el guerrero _____

10. una mujer que no revela nada a nadie   _____

11. el presidente, el senador o el representante   _____

12. Santa Claus, el rey Enrique VIII   _____

13. una persona con las manos que tiritan   _____

14. una persona que se niega a aceptar la palabra "no"   _____

                                                _____

In the following chart, the words ending in **-ón/-ona** may function both as adjectives and as nouns.

NOUN/ADJECTIVE ENDING IN **-ón**	ENGLISH EQUIVALENT	BASE WORD	ENGLISH EQUIVALENT
(el) adulón	*fawning (person)*	adular	*to flatter, dote on*
(el) barbullón	*babbling (person)*	barbullar	*to babble*
(el) besucón	*kissing (person)*	besar	*to kiss*
(el) bocón	*wide-mouthed (person)*	la boca	*mouth*
(el) burlón	*(person) given to mocking*	burlar	*to mock, laugh at*
(el) cabezón	*egocentric (person)*	la cabeza	*head*
(el) cincuentón	*fifty-year-old (person)*	cincuenta	*fifty*
(el) comilón	*gluttonous (person), glutton*	comer	*to eat*
(el) criticón	*faultfinding (person)*	criticar	*to criticize*
(el) cuarentón	*forty-year-old (person)*	cuarenta	*forty*
(el) llorón	*weepy (person), crybaby*	llorar	*to cry*
(el) mandón	*domineering (person)*	mandar	*to order, command*
(el) mirón	*gawking (person), gawker*	mirar	*to look at, watch*
(el) narizón	*big-nosed (person)*	la nariz	*nose*
(el) orejón	*big-eared (person)*	la oreja	*ear (external)*
(el) pidón	*greedy (person)*	pedir	*to request, ask for*
(el) preguntón	*nosy (person)*	preguntar	*to ask a question*
(el) tragón	*gluttonous (person), glutton*	tragar	*to swallow, gulp*

EJERCICIO
92·2

¿Verdadero o falso? *Indicate whether each statement is true or false, using* **V** *for* **verdadero** *true or* **F** *for* **falso** *false.*

1. _____ Un llorón es el alma de la fiesta.

2. _____ Muchas personas quieren decirle al barbullón, "¡Cállate!"

3. _____ Es difícil vivir con un criticón.

4. _____ Con frecuencia el cincuentón tiene el pelo gris.

5. _____ Un bocón tiene más de ochenta dientes.

6. _____ Después de un accidente en la autopista, típicamente hay muchos mirones.

7. _____ Dumbo el elefante es orejón.

8. _____ Los besucones son completamente apropiados durante un servicio en la iglesia.

9. _____ Cuando tu jefe es un mandón, la oficina está muy relajada.

10. _____ A veces un burlón está cómico y a veces está cruel.

11. _____ El tragón y el comilón tienen mucho en común.

12. _____ Muchas cuarentonas se preocupan mucho de su belleza.

13. _____ Los pidones son muy generosos.

14. _____ Pinocho es narizona.

15. _____ El cabezón está feliz en presencia del adulón.

16. _____ Es divertido vivir al lado de un preguntón.

93 ◆ -orio

MEANING	Area, place
ENGLISH EQUIVALENT	*-ory*
PART OF SPEECH	Noun
GENDER	Masculine

The suffix -**orio** denotes an area or place where the action of the base word, which is nearly always a verb, takes place. Since many of these suffixed nouns have English cognates, they tend to be easily recognized and used.

NOUN ENDING IN **-orio**	ENGLISH EQUIVALENT	BASE WORD	ENGLISH EQUIVALENT
el adoratorio	*ancient Indian temple*	adorar	*to adore*
el auditorio	*auditorium*	auditar	*to audit, examine*
el conservatorio	*conservatory*	conservar	*to conserve*
el convictorio	*Jesuit students' quarters*	el convictor	*boarder, pensioner*
el crematorio	*crematorium*	cremar	*to cremate*
el dedicatorio	*dedication, inscription*	dedicar	*to dedicate*
el directorio	*directory*	dirigir	*to direct*
el divisorio	*geological divide*	dividir	*to divide*
el dormitorio	*bedroom, dormitory*	dormir	*to sleep*
el escritorio	*desk, office*	escribir	*to write*
el laboratorio	*laboratory*	laborar	*to labor, work*

EJERCICIO
93·1

Respond in Spanish to each of the following questions.

1. Eres científico. ¿Dónde trabajas? _____

2. Eres seminario y quieres ser sacerdote jesuita. _____
   ¿Dónde vives?

3. Estás en la zona comercial y buscas una tienda en particular. ¿Qué consultas? _____

4. Un miembro de tu familia muere, pero no quiere un funeral tradicional. ¿Adónde se transporta el cuerpo? _____

5. Eres miembro de una banda. ¿Dónde tocas la música durante un concierto? _____

6. Eres estudiante de la universidad. ¿Dónde duermes? _____

7. Eres inca o azteca y quieres tener una ceremonia religiosa. ¿Adónde vas? _____

8. Eres estudiante y, por supuesto, necesitas estudiar. ¿Adónde vas? _____

9. Eres escritor, acabas de terminar tu nuevo libro y ahora quieres mencionar a una persona en particular en las páginas preliminares. ¿Dónde se coloca esta mención? _____

10. Eres maestro de música y quieres enseñar en una institución que se especializa en las artes como la música. ¿Adónde solicitas trabajo? _____

11. Estás en la frontera entre dos áreas de tierra distinta. ¿Dónde estás? _____

NOUN ENDING IN -orio	ENGLISH EQUIVALENT	BASE WORD	ENGLISH EQUIVALENT
el lavatorio	*lavatory, washroom*	lavar	*to wash*
el observatorio	*observatory*	observar	*to observe*
el oratorio	*private place for prayer*	orar	*to pray*
el parlatorio	*parlor, place to visit*	parlar	*to talk, chatter*
el promontorio	*promontory, headland*	prominente	*prominent*
el purgatorio	*purgatory*	purgar	*to purge, cleanse*
el reformatorio	*reformatory*	reformar	*to reform, amend*
el repositorio	*repository*	reponer	*to replace*
el sanatorio	*sanatorium*	sanar	*to heal, cure*
el territorio	*territory*	la tierra	*land, earth, ground*
el vomitorio	*exit passage, vomitorium*	vomitar	*to vomit, spew forth*

EJERCICIO
93·2

Respond in Spanish to each of the following questions.

1. ¿Adónde van los católicos antes de ir al cielo? _____

2. ¿Adónde vas para mirar las estrellas? _____

3. ¿Adónde va una persona para curarse? _____

4. ¿Adónde vas para orar en privado? _____

5. ¿Cómo se llama una región que tiene su propio gobierno? _____

6. ¿Dónde se colocan las cosas que no caben en la casa? _____

7. ¿Adónde vas para lavarte las manos? _____

8. ¿Adónde vas para charlar y visitar con otra persona? _____

9. ¿Adónde va un delincuente juvenil en lugar de ir a
una prisión? _____

10. ¿Cómo se llama el pasaje por el cual se puede salir
rápidamente de un edificio? _____

11. ¿Cómo se llama un área de tierra alta? _____

94 ◆ -ote

MEANING	Augmentative; depreciative
ENGLISH EQUIVALENT	—
PART OF SPEECH	Noun
GENDER	Masculine

The suffix **-ote** serves as an augmentative that sometimes has a negative connotation.
The following nouns ending in **-ote** denote a physical enlargement of the base noun.

NOUN ENDING IN **-ote**	ENGLISH EQUIVALENT	BASE WORD	ENGLISH EQUIVALENT
el angelote	*large angel on an altar*	el ángel	*angel*
el animalote	*big animal*	el animal	*animal*
el barcote	*big boat*	el barco	*boat*
el barrote	*thick iron bar*	el bar	*bar*
el camarote	*ship's cabin, stateroom*	la cámara	*chamber, room*
el cerote	*shoemaker's wax*	la cera	*wax*
el chicote	*husky youngster*	el chico	*boy, youngster*
el gatote	*big cat*	el gato	*cat*
el librote	*huge book, tome*	el libro	*book*
el muchachote	*hefty lad*	el muchacho	*boy, lad*
el papalote	*kite*	el papel	*paper*
el perrote	*big dog*	el perro	*dog*
el pipote	*keg*	la pipa	*barrel, cask*

EJERCICIO 94·1

Provide the correct noun(s) (including the article) for each description.

1. la novela *Guerra y paz* por León Tolstói _____

2. un crucero, un yate _____

3. donde se duerme en un crucero o en un yate _____

4. lo que usa un zapatero _____

5. el león, el tigre, el chita, el jaguar _____

6. un joven grande _____

_____

7. una figura de San Miguel el Arcángel en la catedral _____

8. un elefante, un bisonte, un mastodonte, un dinosaurio _____

9. un rottweiler, un pastor alemán, un gran danés _____

10. lo que contiene la cerveza para las fiestas de fraternidad _____

11. lo que protege el guardia de los prisioneros peligrosos _____

12. lo que se vuela en el parque cuando hay mucho viento _____

In the following chart, the nouns ending in **-ote** convey a figurative, often pejorative, nuance. Some of the words in this chart also appear in the preceding chart, where they serve as physical augmentatives (for example, **el animalote** *big animal* and **el librote** *huge book, tome*). In this chart, they are wondrously snippy (meaning *ignorant person* and *terrible book*, respectively).

NOUN ENDING IN **-ote**	ENGLISH EQUIVALENT	BASE WORD	ENGLISH EQUIVALENT
el amigote	*pal, buddy, crony*	el amigo	*friend*
el angelote	*chubby child*	el ángel	*angel*
el animalote	*ignorant person*	el animal	*animal*
el bobote	*great idiot, simpleton*	el bobo	*fool, dimwit*
el borricote	*utter ass*	el borrico	*ass*
el bravote	*bully, braggart*	bravo	*brave, valiant, manly*
el caballerote	*loutish knight*	el caballero	*knight, gentleman*
el librote	*terrible book*	el libro	*book*
el lugarote	*sprawling village*	el lugar	*place, village, spot*
el machote	*he-man, tough guy*	el macho	*male*
el pegote	*sticky mess*	pegar	*to glue, stick together*
el villanote	*awful villain*	el villano	*villain*

EJERCICIO
94·2

Antónimos *Provide the appropriate antonym(s) for each group of words.*

1. una persona muy humilde y amable hacia todos _____

2. un chiquito flaquísimo, casi esquelético _____

3. una novela corta y fabulosa _____

4. una carretera cubierta de hielo _____

5. un héroe, alguien amado por todos _____

6. una persona súper inteligente _____

_____

7. tu peor enemigo   _____

8. una aldea pequeña y muy linda   _____

9. El Cid, Sir Galahad, Ricardo Corazón de León   _____

10. un hombre muy elegante que siempre dice y hace lo que es correcto   _____

11. un hombre completamente desprovisto de músculos que es un cobarde   _____

95 ▶ -tad

MEANING	State; abstract concept
ENGLISH EQUIVALENT	*-ty*
PART OF SPEECH	Noun
GENDER	Feminine

The suffix **-tad** is relatively uncommon in Spanish. A noun with this suffix represents an abstract or intangible quality (for example **la lealtad** *loyalty*, from the adjective **leal** *loyal, faithful*). An **s** is added before the suffix in some of these words.

NOUN ENDING IN **-tad**	ENGLISH EQUIVALENT	BASE WORD	ENGLISH EQUIVALENT
la amistad	*friendship, amity*	el amigo	*friend*
la dificultad	*difficulty*	difícil	*difficult*
la enemistad	*hatred, enmity*	el enemigo	*enemy*
la facultad	*faculty, school, power*	facultas [LAT.]	*power, ability*
la lealtad	*loyalty*	leal	*loyal, faithful*
la libertad	*liberty, freedom*	libre	*free, unencumbered*
la majestad	*majesty*	majo	*boasting, blustering*
la voluntad	*will, willpower*	voluntas [LAT.]	*will, wish*

EJERCICIO 95·1

Citas *Complete each quotation with the correct form of the appropriate noun.*

1. Una _____ sin confianza es una flor sin perfume. (Laure Conan, el seudónimo de Marie-Louise-Félitité Angers)

2. Evita igualmente la amistad del enemigo y la _____ del amigo. (Nicolae lorga)

3. En el centro de las _____ estriba la oportunidad. (Bruce Lee)

4. Quien conserva la _____ de ver la belleza no envejece. (Franz Kafka)

5. Los que niegan la _____ a los demás no se la merecen ellos mismos. (Abraham Lincoln)

6. Hay cierta _____ en la simplicidad que es por encima de todo la singularidad de ingenio. (Alexander Pope)

7. Los caminos de la _____ son siempre rectos. (Charles Dickens)

8. Quien tiene la _____ tiene la fuerza. (Menandro de Atenas)

96 ▸ -tono/-tona

MEANING   Tone, sound
ENGLISH EQUIVALENT   *-tone*
PART OF SPEECH   Noun, adjective
GENDER   Masculine/feminine

Music lovers, this one's for you! Almost all Spanish words with the suffix -**tono** (feminine: -**tona**) denote a tone or sound, whether spoken or sung. While this suffix is not common in everyday speech, it is widely used in certain contexts, for instance, in discussing voice or music. Words with this suffix are typically nouns, rarely adjectives.

NOUN/ADJECTIVE ENDING IN -**tono**	ENGLISH EQUIVALENT	BASE TERM	ENGLISH EQUIVALENT
átono	*atonic, unstressed, lifeless*	a- [GRK.]	*not*
el barítono	*baritone, male singing voice*	baros [GRK.]	*weight*
el desentono	*rudeness, rude tone of voice*	des- + en- [GRK.]	*not + in*
el dítono	*interval of two tones, ditone, major third (music)*	di- [GRK.]	*two*
el entono	*intonation, being or singing in tune*	en- [GRK.]	*in*
monótono	*monotonous*	mono- [GRK.]	*one*
el semidítono	*semiditone, minor third (music)*	semi- + di- [GRK.]	*half + two*
el semitono	*semitone, half step, half tone (music)*	semi- [GRK.]	*half*
el tritono	*tritone, an interval of three tones (music)*	tri- [GRK.]	*three*

EJERCICIO
96·1

¿A o B? *Choose the best completion for each sentence.*

1. _____ El dítono es un intervalo de

     a. tres tonos   b. dos tonos

2. _____ El barítono canta en una voz

     a. grave   b. alta

3. _____ El tritono es un intervalo de

    a. tres tonos   b. cuatro tonos

4. _____ El desentono se refiere a

    a. la cortesía   b. la grosería

5. _____ Una cadencia átona no está

    a. áspera   b. suave

6. _____ El semitono es un intervalo de

    a. medio tono   b. cuarto de tono

7. _____ El entono se refiere a estar

    a. afinado   b. desafinado

8. _____ La voz monótona suena

    a. vibrante y animada   b. lenta y tediosa

9. _____ El semidítono se refiere a

    a. la tercera menor   b. la tercera mayor

97 ◆ -ucho/-ucha

MEANING	Pejorative
ENGLISH EQUIVALENT	—
PART OF SPEECH	Noun
GENDER	Masculine/feminine

The suffix **-ucho** (feminine: **-ucha**) denotes a strong pejorative, bordering at times on snarky. If you don't like someone or something, you can add **-ucho** or **-ucha** to a base noun to create a stinging description; for example, **el abogaducho** is a lousy lawyer and **el profesorucho** is the professor no one can stand. All the nouns in the following chart, however, can be found in the dictionary.

NOUN ENDING IN -ucho/-ucha	ENGLISH EQUIVALENT	BASE WORD	ENGLISH EQUIVALENT
el animalucho	*ugly/hideous animal*	el animal	*animal*
el avechucho	*wretched or ugly bird*	el ave [F.]	*bird*
el cafetucho	*wretched café, dump, dive*	el café	*café*
el calducho	*tasteless soup or stock*	el caldo	*broth, clear soup*
la camucha	*wretched little bed*	la cama	*bed*
el capirucho	*dunce cap*	el capirote	*academic hood*
el carrucho	*wretched little cart*	el carro	*cart, car*
la casucha	*hovel, dump*	la casa	*house*

▶

NOUN ENDING IN -ucho/-ucha	ENGLISH EQUIVALENT	BASE WORD	ENGLISH EQUIVALENT
el cuartucho	*hovel, poky little room*	el cuarto	*room*
el debilucho	*wimp*	el débil	*weak person*
el medicucho	*third-rate doctor, "quack"*	el médico	*doctor, physician*
el papelucho	*scrap of paper, rubbish*	el papel	*paper*
el periodicucho	*tabloid, "rag"*	el periódico	*newspaper*
el perrucho	*hound, cur, mutt*	el perro	*dog*
el pingucho	*ragamuffin, urchin*	el pingo	*rag*
el santucho	*hypocrite*	el santo	*saint*
la tenducha	*wretched shop, "dump"*	la tienda	*store, shop*

EJERCICIO

97·1

Provide the correct noun (including its article) for each description.

1. una sopa terrible _____

2. el sombrero para una persona tonta _____

3. *The Enquirer, Star, The Sun, Daily Mirror* _____

4. una persona que dice una cosa pero hace otra _____

5. donde vive una persona muy pobre _____

6. donde se vende chatarra _____

7. una bestia fea y horrorosa _____

8. la última persona que quieres ver en la sala de emergencia _____

9. donde se duerme en un dormitorio horrible _____

10. un perro sin raza _____

11. un pájaro muy feo _____

12. el personaje principal de la película *Oliver* _____

13. la basura en una sala de clase _____

14. una sala horrible en una casa _____

15. un restaurante pequeño y horrible _____

16. un vagón horrible _____

17. una persona sin fuerza emocional o moral _____

EJERCICIO
97·2

¿Verdadero o falso? *Indicate whether each statement is true or false, using* **V** *for* **verdadero** *true or* **F** *for* **falso** *false.*

1. _____ Muchas novias prefieren registrarse para regalos en una tenducha.

2. _____ En las prisiones hay muchas camuchas.

3. _____ La Magna Carta de Inglaterra es un papelucho.

4. _____ Beverly Hills, California, es famosa por sus casuchas.

5. _____ Hay muchos perruchos en las calles de las ciudades en países del tercer mundo.

6. _____ Woodstock, el amiguito de Snoopy, es un avechucho.

7. _____ Los escolares de las mejores universidades llevan el capirucho con orgullo.

8. _____ Con frecuencia, los pinguchos piden dinero de los turistas.

9. _____ Se sirve un calducho al rey y le gusta muchísimo.

10. _____ Los medicuchos con frecuencia prescriben los narcóticos y las drogas ilegales.

11. _____ Muchas novias prefieren tener la recepción de boda en un cafetucho.

12. _____ Antes de casarse con el príncipe, Cenicienta duerme en una camucha en un cuartucho.

13. _____ Muchas personas creen que el jabalí, el murciélago, la rata y el cóndor son animaluchos.

14. _____ Un carrucho es un regalo fabuloso para un chófer.

15. _____ Un santucho, de una forma u otra, es muy mentiroso.

16. _____ El debilucho es muy macho.

17. _____ Los periodicuchos reportan solamente la pura verdad.

98 ▶ -uo/-ua

MEANING	Relating to, like
ENGLISH EQUIVALENT	*-uous*
PART OF SPEECH	Adjective
GENDER	Masculine/feminine

Nearly all Spanish adjectives with the suffix **-uo** (feminine: **-ua**) have English cognates with the suffix *-uous*. The base words in the following charts are Latin adjectives, with the exception of **ubique**, which is an adverb.

ADJECTIVE ENDING IN -uo	ENGLISH EQUIVALENT	BASE WORD	ENGLISH EQUIVALENT
arduo	*arduous*	arduus [LAT.]	*steep, high, difficult*
contiguo	*contiguous, next*	contiguus [LAT.]	*touching, bordering*
continuo	*continuous*	continuus [LAT.]	*uninterrupted*
discontinuo	*discontinuous*	dis- + continuus [LAT.]	*not + continuous*
estrenuo	*strenuous*	strenuus [LAT.]	*brisk, vigorous*
fatuo	*fatuous, foolish, inane*	fatuus [LAT.]	*silly, foolish*
individuo	*individual, indivisible*	individuus [LAT.]	*indivisible*
ingenuo	*ingenuous*	ingenuus [LAT.]	*native, frank, candid*
menstruo	*menstrual*	menstrualis [LAT.]	*monthly*
oblicuo	*oblique*	obliquus [LAT.]	*slanting, indirect*
perpetuo	*perpetual, everlasting*	perpetuus [LAT.]	*continuous*
precipuo	*principal, chief*	praecipuus [LAT.]	*excellent, special*
promiscuo	*promiscuous*	promiscuus [LAT.]	*indiscriminate, mixed*
ubicuo	*ubiquitous, omnipresent*	ubique [LAT.]	*everywhere*
vacuo	*vacuous, shallow*	vacuus [LAT.]	*empty*

EJERCICIO
98·1

Sinónimos *Provide the adjective that is most closely related to each group of words.*

1. individual, personal, singular, característico _____

2. adyacente, yuxtapuesto, próximo, lindante _____

3. eterno, interminable, perenne, continuo _____

4. ininterrumpido, continuado, constante, perpetuo _____

5. intermitente, irregular, interrumpido, variable _____

6. omnipresente, difundido, extendido, propagado _____

7. principal, notable, destacado, señalado _____

8. vacante, vacío, desocupado, superficial _____

9. libertino, indecente, mezclado, impuro _____

10. mensual, menstrual, periódico _____

11. estúpido, necio, tonto, imbécil _____

12. diagonal, inclinado, sesgado, torcido _____

13. difícil, complicado, penoso, estrenuo _____

14. hercúleo, exigente, exhaustivo, arduo _____

15. inocente, candoroso, franco, cándido _____

The following adjectives ending in **-uo/-ua** are derived from Latin verbs.

ADJECTIVE ENDING IN **-uo**	ENGLISH EQUIVALENT	BASE WORD	ENGLISH EQUIVALENT
ambiguo	*ambiguous*	ambiguus [LAT.]	*having a double meaning*
congruo	*congruous*	congruus [LAT.]	*fit, suitable*
conspicuo	*conspicuous*	conspicuus [LAT.]	*visible, striking*
incongruo	*incongruous*	incongruus [LAT.]	*inconsistent*
inocuo	*innocuous, harmless*	innocuus [LAT.]	*harmless*
melifluo	*mellifluous*	mellifluus [LAT.]	*flowing with honey*
occiduo	*occidental*	occidentalis [LAT.]	*western*
somnílocuo	*talking in sleep*	somnus + loquus [LAT.]	*sleep + speaking*
superfluo	*superfluous*	superfluus [LAT.]	*unnecessary*

Complete each sentence with the correct form of the appropriate adjective.

1. Típicamente, las tarjetas del día de San Valentín están llenas de palabras

   _____ .

2. Thorstein Veblen, economista y sociólogo americano, acuñó el término "el consumo

   _____" para describir la adquisición de bienes para provocar

   la envidia de otros.

3. Keith Richards, guitarrista de la banda de rock The Rolling Stones, dijo, "Busco la

   ambigüedad cuando escribo porque la vida es _____."

4. Para ahorrar dinero, muchas empresas grandes despiden a los "trabajadores

   _____."

5. Muchas personas creen que el cannabis es una droga peligrosa, mientras que otros creen

   que el cannabis es _____ .

6. Una persona _____ habla en voz alta durante el sueño.

99 ◆ -ura

MEANING	State, abstract concept
ENGLISH EQUIVALENT	*-ness*
PART OF SPEECH	Noun
GENDER	Feminine

All of these Spanish nouns with the suffix **-ura** are derived from adjectives, many of which you probably already know. The suffix **-ura** forms an abstract noun that represents a state or quality of the base adjective.

The following nouns ending in **-ura** represent visual or emotional states.

NOUN ENDING IN **-ura**	ENGLISH EQUIVALENT	BASE WORD	ENGLISH EQUIVALENT
la albura	*whiteness*	albo	*snow white*
la amargura	*bitterness*	amargo	*bitter*
la blancura	*whiteness*	blanco	*white*
la bravura	*courage, fierceness*	bravo	*brave, fierce*
la dulzura	*sweetness*	dulce	*sweet*
la grisura	*grayness, dullness*	gris	*gray*
la grosura	*grossness, coarseness*	grosero	*gross, coarse*
la hermosura	*beauty*	hermoso	*beautiful*
la lindura	*loveliness*	lindo	*lovely*
la listura	*smartness, quickness*	listo	*smart, quick*
la locura	*madness, insanity*	loco	*mad, insane*
la negrura	*blackness*	negro	*black*
la rojura	*redness*	rojo	*red*
la secura	*dryness*	seco	*dry*
la ternura	*tenderness*	tierno	*tender*
la verdura	*greenness*	verde	*green*

EJERCICIO
99·1

¡Resuélvelo! *Provide the correct form of the appropriate noun(s) to describe each of the following items or groups.*

1. el chocolate _____

2. el traje de Santa Claus _____

3. el amor de una madre _____

4. la nieve _____

5. el limón, la toronja, el chocolate sin azúcar _____

6. el traje de Darth Vader _____

7. Miss Universo _____

   _____

8. el soldado, el guerrero, el caballero _____

9. la persona que ha perdido las facultades mentales _____

10. la lechuga, el apio, el brócoli   _____

11. el elefante   _____

12. un concursante en el programa *Jeopardy*   _____

13. el desierto   _____

14. el vestido de boda   _____

15. la persona que se comporta sin cortesía   _____

The following nouns ending in **-ura** represent physical features or textures.

NOUN ENDING IN -ura	ENGLISH EQUIVALENT	BASE WORD	ENGLISH EQUIVALENT
la altura	*height*	alto	*high, tall*
la anchura	*width*	ancho	*wide*
la bajura	*shortness, lowness*	bajo	*short, low*
la blandura	*softness*	blando	*soft*
la espesura	*thickness*	espeso	*thick*
la estrechura	*narrowness*	estrecho	*narrow*
la finura	*fineness*	fino	*fine*
la flacura	*thinness*	flaco	*thin*
la gordura	*fatness, obesity*	gordo	*fat*
la hondura	*depth*	hondo	*deep*
la largura	*length*	largo	*long*
la lisura	*smoothness*	liso	*smooth*
la llanura	*flatness, evenness*	llano	*flat, even*
la soltura	*looseness*	suelto	*loose*
la tersura	*smoothness*	terso	*smooth*
la tiesura	*stiffness*	tieso	*stiff*

EJERCICIO
99·2

¡Resuélvelo! *Provide the correct form of the appropriate noun(s) to describe each of the following items or groups.*

1. la calculación del área de un rectángulo   _____ ✕

    _____

2. una persona obesa   _____

3. la ropa súper confortable   _____

4. una camisa planchada con mucho almidón   _____

5. el Monte Everest   _____

6. una persona que sufre de la anorexia nervosa   _____

7. un enano   _____

8. la piel de un bebé   _____

    _____

9. un callejón muy pequeño _____

10. la piel del elefante _____

11. el papel higiénico, una bola de algodón _____

12. el centro del océano _____

13. un crepe, la pampa de Argentina, el terreno de Kansas _____

14. una cadena de puro oro _____

 **-ura**

MEANING	State, result of an action
ENGLISH EQUIVALENT	*-ure*
PART OF SPEECH	Noun
GENDER	Feminine

Almost all of these Spanish nouns with the suffix **-ura** are derived from verbs; compare these nouns to those in No. 99, which are derived from adjectives. Since nearly all of these Spanish nouns have English cognates with the suffix *-ure*, they are easily recognized and used.

NOUN ENDING IN **-ura**	ENGLISH EQUIVALENT	BASE WORD	ENGLISH EQUIVALENT
la apertura	*opening* [FIG.], *kickoff*	abrir	*to open*
la aventura	*adventure*	aventurar	*to risk, venture*
la cura	*cure*	curar	*to cure, heal, care for*
la escultura	*sculpture*	esculpir	*to sculpt, carve*
la estatura	*stature, natural height*	estar	*to be, stay*
la literatura	*literature*	literatura [LAT.]	*learning, writing*
la manicura	*manicure*	mano + curar	*hand + to care for*
la pedicura	*pedicure*	pes/pedis [LAT.] + curar	*foot + to care for*
la pintura	*painting, picture*	pintar	*to paint*
la postura	*position, stance, posture*	poner	*to place, put, posit*
la temperatura	*temperature*	temperar	*to temper, regulate*

 EJERCICIO
100·1

Complete each sentence with the correct form of the appropriate noun(s).

1. Se necesita un termómetro para tomar la _____ de una persona.

2. A pesar del progreso de la medicina moderna, todavía no hay _____ para el resfriado común.

3. *Las* _____ *de Huckleberry Finn* es el libro más popular y más conocido de Mark Twain.

4. Se puede decir que la _____ más famosa en el Museo del Louvre es la *Mona Lisa*.

5. *El beso* del escultor francés Auguste Rodin es una de las _____ más famosas del mundo.

6. Es imposible ignorar las obras—los dramas, la poesía y los sonetos—de William

Shakespeare al estudiar la _____ inglesa.

7. Siempre se incluye la verificación del peso y de la _____ del paciente en cada reconocimiento físico.

8. La escoliosis es una deformación de la columna vertebral, pero no se debe confundir con

la mala _____ .

9. En la _____ de una película de horror, la escena incluye frecuentemente el asesinato de una víctima inocente en una casa embrujada.

10. Antes de la boda u otro evento especial, es común que mujeres visiten el salón de belleza

para una _____ y una _____ .

NOUN ENDING IN **-ura**	ENGLISH EQUIVALENT	BASE WORD	ENGLISH EQUIVALENT
la abertura	*opening*	abrir	*to open*
la captura	*capture*	capturar	*to capture, seize*
la caricatura	*caricature*	caricaturar	*to represent by caricature*
la censura	*censure*	censurar	*to censor*
la criatura	*creature, child*	criar	*to raise, grow*
la cultura	*culture*	culturar	*to cultivate*
la estructura	*structure*	estructurar	*to structure*
la fractura	*fracture*	fracturar	*to fracture*
la lectura	*reading*	leer	*to read*
la pastura	*pasture, pastureland*	apasturar	*to pasture, forage*
la signatura	*signature*	signar	*to sign*

EJERCICIO
100·2

Sinónimos *Provide a synonym for each group of words.*

1. el niño, el muchacho, el párvulo, el bebé _____

2. la firma, el autógrafo, la rúbrica _____

3. la detención, la aprehensión, el arresto, el apresamiento _____

4. la leída, la disertación, la exposición, la lección _____

5. el dibujo, la viñeta, la exageración, la parodia _____

6. el orificio, la rendija, la entrada, el agujero _____

7. la rotura, la fisura, la quebradura, la fragmentación _____

8. el cultivo, la civilización, el refinamiento, la urbanidad _____

9. la reprobación, la condena, el reproche   _____

10. el pasto, el pastizal, la tierra de pastoreo   _____

11. la configuración, la organización, el armazón   _____

Advanced suffixes

This section presents suffixes and words that you are likely to encounter at advanced levels of instruction, literature, and conversation. Many of these suffixes have very specific meanings, for example, those denoting plants, diseases, and scientific terms.

While the adjectival suffixes frequently denote *relating to, like,* the words presented here allow you to achieve a higher level of sophistication than that found in the two previous sections.

Numerous Latin and Greek words serve as base words for the suffixes in this chapter. You will easily recognize many base words and determine their origins, whether the source is Latin, Greek, Spanish, or another language.

The exercises following the charts are also advanced and assume an increased facility with the Spanish language.

It is important to remember that the lists of words in the charts are not exhaustive. The words included are sufficient to familiarize you with the suffix and its meaning, so that you can recognize the suffix of an unfamiliar word and determine its meaning without turning to the dictionary. This is the major goal of the book and certainly one of yours as you study this beautiful language.

101 ◆ -acho, -acha

MEANING	Augmentative; pejorative
ENGLISH EQUIVALENT	—
PART OF SPEECH	Noun
GENDER	Masculine/feminine

Spanish nouns with the suffix **-acho** (feminine: **-acha**) generally denote an exaggeration of the base word, often with a pejorative connotation. For example, **el rico** is simply *rich man*, while **el ricacho** is *moneybags*—an extremely rich person. Words with this powerful but uncommon suffix should be used with discretion. If the noun refers to a woman, **-acho** becomes **-acha**: **el amigacho** ~ **la amigacha**.

NOUN ENDING IN **-acho, -acha**	ENGLISH EQUIVALENT	BASE WORD	ENGLISH EQUIVALENT
la aguacha	*foul or stagnant water*	el agua [F.]	*water*
el amigacho	*chum, crony, pal*	el amigo	*friend*
el barbicacho	*ribbon tied under the chin*	la barba	*chin*
la bocacha	*bigmouth*	la boca	*mouth*
el cocacho	*rap on the head*	la coca [COLLOQ.]	*head*
el dicharacho	*coarse or vulgar expression*	el dicho	*saying*
la hilacha	*shred, frayed thread*	el hilo	*thread*
el hornacho	*furnace for melting statues*	el horno	*oven, kiln*
el marimacho	*tomboy, mannish woman*	marido	*husband*
el poblacho	*run-down town*	el pueblo	*town*
el populacho	*mob, rabble*	populus [LAT.]	*people*
el riacho	*small and/or dirty river*	el río	*river*
el ricacho	*moneybags* [COLLOQ.]	el rico	*rich individual*
el terminacho	*nasty or rude word*	el término	*term, word*
el verdacho	*gritty green earth*	el verde	*the color green*
el vulgacho	*mob, rabble*	el vulgo	*common people*

EJERCICIO

101·1

Provide the correct form of the appropriate noun(s) (including the article) for each description.

1. un pueblo fantasma donde la población actual es mucho menor de lo que era _____

2. una persona obstinada que habla muy alto _____

3. lo que sale con frecuencia de la boca de una persona repugnante y grosera _____

_____

4. un individual con mucho dinero que habla mucho de su abundancia _____

5. lo que tú no quieres beber nunca _____

6. una mujer que tiene manierismos masculinos _____

7. un cuerpo de agua que está contaminada con basura, suciedad y varias sustancias tóxicas

8. un compañero leal e inseparable

9. lo que se usa para la fundición de metales y estatuas

10. lo que se ve en la manga de una camisa gastada

11. un grupo con quien los esnobs nunca quieren asociarse

12. lo que puede recibir un estudiante durmiente como disciplina de su maestro

13. la tierra arenosa que es del color típico de la hierba

14. la cinta con que haces un lazo para prevenir que el sombrero se vaya volando

 **-acia**

MEANING	State, abstract concept
ENGLISH EQUIVALENT	-acity
PART OF SPEECH	Noun
GENDER	Feminine

Nearly all Spanish nouns with the suffix **-acia** have an adjective as the base word. Many of these base adjectives end in **-az**, a suffix itself (see No. 110). The suffix **-acia** denotes an abstraction of the base word, with one exception: **la farmacia** *pharmacy, drugstore.*

NOUN ENDING IN **-acia**	ENGLISH EQUIVALENT	BASE WORD	ENGLISH EQUIVALENT
la audacia	*audacity, boldness*	audaz	*audacious, bold*
la contumacia	*stubbornness, obstinacy*	contumaz	*stubborn, obstinate*
la eficacia	*efficacy, efficiency*	eficaz	*effective, efficient*
la falacia	*fallacy, deceit*	falaz	*fallacious*
la farmacia	*pharmacy, drugstore*	pharmakon [GRK.]	*drug, poison*
la gracia	*grace, elegance*	gratia [LAT.]	*favor, esteem*
la ineficacia	*ineffectiveness, inefficiency*	in- + eficaz	*not + effective*
la malacia	*pica, abnormal desire to eat non-food items*	malo	*bad*
la perspicacia	*perspicacity, clear-sightedness*	perspicaz	*clear-eyed, insightful*
la pertinacia	*pertinence, stubbornness*	pertinaz	*stubborn, persistent*
la suspicacia	*suspicion, mistrust*	suspicaz	*suspicious*

Provide the correct form of the appropriate noun(s) (including the article) for each description.

1. una falta de confianza _____

2. una disposición de asumir riesgos _____

3. una falsa noción _____

4. el estado de elegancia, simpatía y cordialidad _____

5. el estado de efectividad, eficiencia y utilidad _____

6. el estado de incapacidad, inacción e inutilidad _____

7. el estado de agudeza, intuición y sagacidad _____

8. una droguería, una botica _____

9. la perversión del apetito que consiste en el deseo de comer cosas tales como el yeso, el carbón, la arena, la tierra u otras cosas _____

10. el estado de obstinación, rebeldía y tenacidad _____

103 ◆ -aje

MEANING	Collection, set; abstract concept
ENGLISH EQUIVALENT	*-age*
PART OF SPEECH	Noun
GENDER	Masculine

The suffix **-aje** may denote a grouping or integration of the base word. For example, **la vela** *sail* yields **el velaje** *set of sails* and **el ancla** *anchor* yields **el anclaje** *anchorage, moorings*. In the first example, a single sail becomes a grouping; in the second example, an anchor becomes a place where anchors are used, or even an abstraction signifying the means of securing something.

NOUN ENDING IN **-aje**	ENGLISH EQUIVALENT	BASE WORD	ENGLISH EQUIVALENT
el alambraje	*wiring*	el alambre	*wire*
el almacenaje	*storage, warehouse*	el almacén	*store, warehouse*
el anclaje	*anchorage, moorings*	el ancla [F.]	*anchor*
el andamiaje	*scaffolding*	el andamio	*scaffold, platform*
el camionaje	*trucking, truckage*	el camión	*truck*
el caudillaje	*leadership*	el caudillo	*chief, leader*
el hembraje	*female herd, "womenfolk"*	la hembra	*female*
el herbaje	*herbage, pasture*	la hierba	*grass, herb*
el herraje	*ironwork*	el hierro	*iron*
el lenguaje	*language*	la lengua	*tongue*

¿Qué es esto? *Provide the correct form of the appropriate noun (including its article) for each description.*

1. un grupo de mujeres _____

2. el reunir y guardar cosas en cantidad _____

3. el objetivo del presidente _____

4. el sistema de la instalación eléctrica de un edificio _____

5. una colección de productos de hierro _____

6. el comercio del transporte de cargamento por camión _____

7. la vegetación para animales herbíveros _____

8. lo que se necesita para comunicar _____

9. una plataforma temporal _____

NOUN ENDING IN -aje	ENGLISH EQUIVALENT	BASE WORD	ENGLISH EQUIVALENT
el linaje	*lineage*	la línea	*line*
el maderaje	*woodwork*	la madera	*wood*
el marinaje	*group of sailors*	el marino	*sailor*
el monedaje	*coins, coinage*	la moneda	*coin*
el mueblaje	*furniture*	el mueble	*piece of furniture*
el paisanaje	*civilian population*	el paisano	*countryman, peasant*
el peonaje	*group of laborers*	el peón	*laborer*
el plantaje	*collection of plants*	la planta	*plant*
el plumaje	*plumage, feathers*	la pluma	*feather*
el porcentaje	*percentage*	por ciento	*percent*

¿Qué es esto? *Provide the correct form of the appropriate noun (including its article) for each description.*

1. un grupo de trabajadores _____

2. una colección de sillas, mesas, camas y sofás _____

3. un grupo de hombres de mar _____

4. una colección de arboles, arbustos y flores _____

5. lo que recubre a los aves _____

6. la población que vive en el campo _____

7. una colección de dinero hecho de metal   _____

8. el interés del genealogista   _____

9. el interés del carpintero   _____

10. lo que indica el signo "%"   _____

NOUN ENDING IN **-aje**	ENGLISH EQUIVALENT	BASE WORD	ENGLISH EQUIVALENT
el ramaje	*mass of branches*	la rama	*branch*
el rendaje	*set of reins*	la rienda	*rein*
el rodaje	*set of wheels*	la rueda	*wheel*
el ropaje	*collection of robes or clothing*	la ropa	*clothes*
el ultraje	*outrage, affront*	ultra [LAT.]	*beyond*
el varillaje	*set of ribs (umbrella)*	la varilla	*rib, rod*
el vataje	*wattage*	el vato	*watt*
el velaje	*set of sails*	la vela	*sail*
el vendaje	*bandaging*	la venda	*bandage*
el ventanaje	*row of windows*	la ventana	*window*

EJERCICIO
103·3

¿Qué es esto? *Provide the correct form of the appropriate noun (including its article) for each description.*

1. lo que permite el movimiento de un vehículo   _____

2. lo que permite el movimiento por el viento de un barco   _____

3. un árbol enorme produce esto   _____

4. una persona que compra una bombilla quiere saber esto   _____

5. un insulto enorme   _____

6. una colección de vestidos, pantalones, camisas y faldas   _____

7. la estructura interior de un paraguas   _____

8. lo que provee una vista fabulosa de su casa   _____

9. lo que el vaquero necesita para controlar su caballo   _____

10. lo que la enfermera necesita para tratar una herida abierta   _____

-aje

MEANING	Fee, toll, rent, dues
ENGLISH EQUIVALENT	—
PART OF SPEECH	Noun
GENDER	Masculine

The suffix **-aje** may denote a fee, toll, rent, or dues for a service rendered or an object acquired. The service or object is expressed by the base noun.

NOUN ENDING IN -aje	ENGLISH EQUIVALENT	BASE WORD	ENGLISH EQUIVALENT
el agiotaje	*money exchange*	el agio	*exchange rate*
el almacenaje	*warehouse rent*	el almacén	*warehouse, store*
el barcaje	*boat fare*	el barco	*boat*
el bodegaje	*warehouse dues*	la bodega	*warehouse*
el caballaje	*stud service*	el caballo	*horse*
el cabestraje	*fee paid to a drover*	el cabestro	*leading ox, bell-ox*
el cabotaje	*coastal trade*	el cabo	*cape, coast*
el carneraje	*tax or duty on sheep*	el carnero	*sheep*
el carretaje	*carting fee*	la carreta	*wagon*
el castillaje	*tax or toll on a castle*	el castillo	*castle*
el herbaje	*pasturage fee*	la hierba	*grass*

EJERCICIO
104·1

¿Verdadero o falso? *Indicate whether each statement is true or false, using* **V** *for* **verdadero** *true or* **F** *for* **falso** *false.*

1. _____ Al rey le interesa el castillaje.

2. _____ Al rey le interesa el carretaje.

3. _____ Al comerciante no le interesa el almacenaje.

4. _____ Al comerciante le interesa el bodegaje.

5. _____ Al financiero le interesa el agiotaje.

6. _____ Al ecuestre le interesa el carneraje.

7. _____ Al ecuestre le interesa el caballaje.

8. _____ Al marinero le interesa el barcaje.

9. _____ Al marinero le interesa el cabotaje.

10. _____ Al granjero no le interesa el herbaje.

11. _____ Al ganadero le interesa el cabestraje.

NOUN ENDING IN **-aje**	ENGLISH EQUIVALENT	BASE WORD	ENGLISH EQUIVALENT
el hornaje	*fee for baking bread*	el horno	*bread oven*
el hospedaje	*lodging, board*	el huésped	*overnight guest*
el muellaje	*port fees*	el muelle	*pier, dock, wharf*
el pasaje	*ticket fare*	el paso	*passage, walk*
el pasturaje	*duty for grazing cattle*	la pastura	*pasture, fodder*
el pedaje	*toll*	pes/pedis [LAT.]	*foot*
el pontaje	*bridge toll*	el puente	*bridge*
el recuaje	*duty for cattle passing*	la recua	*drove of cattle*
el terraje	*rent paid for land*	la tierra	*land*
el vareaje	*retail trade, selling by the yard*	la vara	*yardstick*
el vasallaje	*vassalage, liege money*	el vasallo	*vassal, subject*

EJERCICIO

104·2

¿Verdadero o falso? *Indicate whether each statement is true or false, using* **V** *for* **verdadero** *true or* **F** *for* **falso** *false.*

1. _____ Al marinero le interesa el muellaje.

2. _____ Al marinero le interesa el recuaje.

3. _____ Al panadero le interesa el hornaje.

4. _____ Al panadero le interesa el pontaje.

5. _____ Al terrateniente le interesa el terraje.

6. _____ Al terrateniente le interesa el vasallaje.

7. _____ Al comerciante le interesa el pedaje.

8. _____ Al comerciante le interesa el vareaje.

9. _____ Al agente de viajes le interesa el pasaje.

10. _____ Al agente de viajes le interesa el hospedaje.

11. _____ Al granjero le interesa el pasturaje.

◆105◆ -ajo

MEANING	Diminutive; perjorative
ENGLISH EQUIVALENT	—
PART OF SPEECH	Noun
GENDER	Masculine

The suffix **-ajo** often conveys a particularly unpleasant, even nasty, connotation. The nouns in the following chart should be used with caution.

NOUN ENDING IN **-ajo**	ENGLISH EQUIVALENT	BASE WORD	ENGLISH EQUIVALENT
el bebistrajo	*concoction, bad drink*	la bebida	*drink, beverage*
el camistrajo	*pallet, horrid bed*	la cama	*bed*
el cintajo	*tawdry old ribbon*	la cinta	*ribbon*
el comistrajo	*hodgepodge of awful food*	la comistión	*mixture (of food)*
el escobajo	*remains of an old broom*	la escoba	*broom*
el guanajo	*simpleton, dolt*	el guano	*guano, bird dung*
el latinajo	*pig Latin*	el latín	*Latin*
el pingajo	*shred, tatter, patch*	el pingo	*rag*
el tendajo	*dumpy little shop*	la tienda	*store, shop*
el terminajo	*crude word or phrase*	el término	*term*
el trapajo	*old rag, tatter*	el trapo	*rag*

EJERCICIO
105·1

¿Qué dirías por lo bajini? *What would you say under your breath?* *Provide the correct noun in the ¡Qué! expression for each of the following situations.*

1. Tu habitación en el hotel está bastante horrible, pero cuando te acuestas, ¡ay Dios mío!

   ¡Qué _____!

2. Entras en una boutique en la zona comercial en la cual parece que todo vino directamente de la basura.

   ¡Qué _____!

3. Asistes a una conferencia y el orador principal no sabe nada del tema.

   ¡Qué _____!

4. Le haces una pregunta normal a una persona, pero él te responde con una conglomeración de palabras de las letras mezcladas.

   ¡Qué _____!

5. El barman te sirve un cóctel de jugo de naranja, Coca Cola y vino rojo.

   ¡Qué _____!

6. Cenicienta necesita limpiar los suelos de la casa de su madrastra, pero el utensilio que necesita está destruido.

   ¡Qué _____!

7. Quieres decorar el pelo de una niña, pero la única cosa que tienes para hacerlo es vieja, fea y huele mal.

¡Qué _____!

8. Asistes a una recepción de bodas en un hotel muy elegante, pero encuentras que la selección de comida incluye galletas con Cheez Whiz, lentejas crudas y una variedad de cereales de desayuno.

¡Qué _____!

9. Estás durmiendo y en tu sueño estás hablando con el famoso filósofo Aristóteles, de quien esperas una oración profundísima. En vez de esto, él dice, "Oooga Boooga."

¡Qué _____!

10. Eres la sirvienta principal en el Palacio de Buckingham y estás a cargo de pulir la plata de la reina. Prefieres hacer la tarea utilizando sólo tela de algodón bien fino, pero en la cesta de suministros encuentras solamente productos que consideras inferiores.

¡Qué _____! o ¡Qué _____!

In the following chart, the nouns ending in **-ajo** do not have the nasty connotation of those in the preceding chart; instead, they denote a diminution, physical or figurative, of the base word. Note that some of these suffixed nouns are derived from nouns, while others are derived from verbs.

NOUN ENDING IN **-ajo**	ENGLISH EQUIVALENT	BASE WORD	ENGLISH EQUIVALENT
el arrendajo	*mockingbird*	arrendar	*to mimic, imitate nastily*
el colgajo	*flapping rag*	colgar	*to hang, suspend*
el escupitajo	*gob of spit*	escupir	*to spit*
el espantajo	*scarecrow*	espantar	*fright, terror*
el espumarajo	*froth, foam (of mouth)*	la espuma	*foam, lather*
el hatajo	*small herd of cattle*	el hato	*herd of cattle*
el lagunajo	*puddle, pool*	la laguna	*small lake, lagoon*
el lavajo	*watering hole for cattle*	lavar	*to wash*
el sombrajo	*hut for protection from the sun*	la sombra	*shadow*
el tiznajo	*soot, smudge, stain*	la tizna	*blackening, lampblack*
el zancajo	*heel, heel bone of the foot*	el zanco	*stilt*

EJERCICIO
105·2

Provide the correct noun (including its article) to answer each of the following questions.

1. ¿Qué puedes encontrar dentro de la chimenea? _____

2. ¿Qué puedes encontrar en la yarda donde beben las vacas? _____

3. ¿Qué puedes encontrar en la boca de un perro rabioso? _____

4. ¿Qué puedes encontrar en un árbol imitando a los otros pájaros? _____

5. ¿Qué puedes encontrar en el montículo del lanzador de béisbol? _____

6. ¿Qué puedes encontrar en el pie? _____

7. ¿Qué puedes encontrar soplando en el viento del tendedero (*clothesline*) después de un día arduo de limpiar la casa? _____

8. ¿Qué puedes encontrar después de la lluvia? _____

9. ¿Qué puedes encontrar en el corral de una granja pequeña? _____

10. ¿Qué puedes encontrar en el campo de maíz de un granjero muy enfadado con los cuervos? _____

11. ¿Qué puedes encontrar en algunas playas para prevenir la quemadura del sol? _____

106 -al

MEANING	Augmentative; place
ENGLISH EQUIVALENT	—
PART OF SPEECH	Noun
GENDER	Masculine

The suffix **-al** often denotes an enlargement of the base noun. The enlargement may be physical (for example, **el ventanal** *large window*, from **la ventana** *window*). However, **-al** frequently denotes an extension of the base noun (for example, **el dedal** *thimble*, from **el dedo** *finger*). An augmentative ending in **-al** may even enlarge or expand on the base noun so that it signifies an entire place (for example, **el riscal** *site of many cliffs*, from **el risco** *cliff, crag*).

The following nouns with the suffix **-al** denote a physical or figurative enlargement of the base noun.

NOUN ENDING IN **-al**	ENGLISH EQUIVALENT	BASE WORD	ENGLISH EQUIVALENT
el dineral	*fortune*	el dinero	*money*
el festival	*festival*	la fiesta	*party, holiday*
el lodazal	*quagmire, morass*	el lodo	*mud, mire*
el nidal	*hangout*	el nido	*nest*
el parral	*large earthen jar*	la parra	*earthen jar*
el platal	*great wealth*	la plata	*silver, money*
el ritual	*ritual*	el rito	*rite*
el soportal	*portico, arcade*	el soporte	*support, stand, bracket*
el varal [COLLOQ.]	*tall and slender person*	la vara	*pole, rod, staff, stick*
el ventanal	*large window*	la ventana	*window*

Provide the correct noun(s) (including the article) for each description.

1. una celebración enorme que ocurre frecuentemente en las   _____
   calles o en un parque

2. las ganancias de una lotería Mega Millions   _____

   _____

3. la celebración de una confirmación o un bar mitzvah en   _____
   la vida de una persona

4. un hombre alto y muy delgado   _____

5. un camino o pasaje cubierto   _____

6. un lugar donde los adolescentes pasan el tiempo fuera de   _____
   la vista vigilante de sus padres

7. un frasco o tarro grande para la miel, unos líquidos o   _____
   unas comidas

8. un sitio lleno de barro que es difícil atravesar   _____

9. lo que deja pasar la luz en un edificio grande   _____

The following nouns ending in **-al** denote a more figurative expansion of the base noun.

NOUN ENDING IN **-al**	ENGLISH EQUIVALENT	BASE WORD	ENGLISH EQUIVALENT
el bancal	*bench cover*	el banco	*bench, pew*
el cabezal	*small pillow*	la cabeza	*head*
el dedal	*thimble*	el dedo	*finger*
el misal	*missal, book of the mass*	la misa	*(Catholic) Mass*
el ojal	*buttonhole*	el ojo	*eye*
el ostral	*oyster bed*	la ostra	*oyster*
el peñascal	*rocky hill*	la peña	*rock, crag, boulder*
el portal	*front door, doorway*	la puerta	*door*
el pozal	*covering for a well*	el pozo	*well*
el rectoral	*rectory*	el rector	*rector*
el riscal	*site of many cliffs*	el risco	*cliff, crag*
el santoral	*book of saints' lives*	el santo	*saint*
el secadal	*barren ground*	la seca	*dry season*
el semental	*stud horse*	el semen	*semen, sperm*
el tribunal	*court, tribunal*	el tribuno	*tribune, magistrate*
el vitral	*stained glass window*	vitrum [LAT.]	*glass*

Provide the correct noun (including its article) for each description.

1. la entrada de la casa   _____

2. el cubierto para el asiento en una iglesia   _____

3. un tipo de ventana que se encuentra frecuentemente
   en un catedral   _____

4. una almohada pequeña   _____

5. un caballo cuyo trabajo consiste en engendrar numerosos
   potrillos   _____

6. un libro de las biografías de varias personas beatas   _____

7. lo que protege el dedo del sastre   _____

8. donde se pone el botón para cerrar un artículo de ropa   _____

9. el cubierto para un hoyo profundo en la tierra   _____

10. donde trabaja el juez   _____

11. donde viven los moluscos bivalvos   _____

12. donde vive el sacerdote o ministro   _____

13. un sitio muy árido   _____

14. una colina rocosa o pedregosa   _____

15. un sitio donde hay muchos precipicios   _____

16. el libro que se consulta durante el servicio católico   _____

107 ▸ -al

MEANING	Field, orchard, grove, patch, plantation; plant, tree
ENGLISH EQUIVALENT	—
PART OF SPEECH	Noun
GENDER	Masculine

The adjective suffix **-al** is common in Spanish (see No. 5). As a noun suffix, **-al** may denote a type of field, orchard, grove, or plant that produces the base word. Although several of the base nouns are feminine, nouns with the suffix **-al** are always masculine.

The base noun of each of the following nouns is a fruit or vegetable.

NOUN ENDING IN -al	ENGLISH EQUIVALENT	BASE WORD	ENGLISH EQUIVALENT
el alcachofal	*artichoke field*	la alcachofa	*artichoke*
el bananal	*banana plantation*	la banana	*banana*
el berenjenal	*eggplant field*	la berenjena	*eggplant*
el berzal	*cabbage patch*	la berza	*cabbage*
el cerezal	*cherry orchard*	la cereza	*cherry*
el fresal	*strawberry patch*	la fresa	*strawberry*
el frutal	*fruit-bearing tree*	la fruta	*fruit*
el guisantal	*pea field*	el guisante	*pea*
el maizal	*corn field, maize field*	el maíz	*corn, maize*
el manzanal	*apple orchard*	la manzana	*apple*
el naranjal	*orange grove*	la naranja	*orange*
el patatal	*potato field*	la patata	*potato*
el peral	*pear tree*	la pera	*pear*
el pimental	*pepper patch*	el pimiento	*pepper*
el piñal	*pineapple plantation*	la piña	*pineapple*
el platanal	*banana plantation*	el plátano	*banana*
el rabanal	*radish patch*	el rábano	*radish*
el tomatal	*tomato field*	el tomate	*tomato*

EJERCICIO

107·1

Provide the correct base word (including its article) to name the product that comes from each of the following fields, groves, or trees.

1. el naranjal _____

2. el tomatal _____

3. el guisantal _____

4. el piñal _____

5. el cerezal _____

6. el pimental _____

7. el patatal _____

8. el alcachofal _____

9. el maizal _____

10. el rabanal _____

11. el bananal _____

12. el frutal _____

13. el berenjenal _____

14. el peral _____

15. el berzal _____

16. el manzanal _____

17. el platanal _____

18. el fresal _____

The base noun of each of the following nouns is a nut, grain, or other plant.

NOUN ENDING IN -al	ENGLISH EQUIVALENT	BASE WORD	ENGLISH EQUIVALENT
el alcornocal	*plantation of cork trees*	el alcornoque	*cork tree*
el alfalfal	*alfalfa field*	la alfalfa	*alfalfa*
el almendral	*almond grove*	la almendra	*almond*
el arrozal	*rice field*	el arroz	*rice*
el avenal	*oat field*	la avena	*oat*
el cafetal	*coffee plantation*	el café	*coffee*
el cauchal	*rubber plantation*	el caucho	*rubber*
el cebadal	*barley field*	la cebada	*barley*
el pinal	*pine grove*	el pino	*pine tree*
el robledal	*oak grove*	el roble	*oak tree*
el rosal	*rose garden*	la rosa	*rose*
el trigal	*wheat field*	el trigo	*wheat*

EJERCICIO
107·2

Provide the correct base word (including its article) to name the product associated with each description. Then provide the correct noun ending in -al to name the field or grove from which it comes.

	BASE WORD	NOUN ENDING IN -al
1. un árbol de Navidad	_____	_____
2. la flor clásica del día de San Valentín	_____	_____
3. el principal ingrediente del mazapán	_____	_____
4. la suela de un zapato deportivo	_____	_____
5. el tapón para una botella de vino	_____	_____
6. una madera muy dura	_____	_____
7. la bebida principal de Starbucks	_____	_____
8. un alimento básico que se sirve con el sushi	_____	_____
9. un ingrediente básico en la cerveza	_____	_____
10. una comida deliciosa para las vacas	_____	_____
11. una comida favorita de los caballos	_____	_____
12. el gluten	_____	_____

108 ▸ -ato, -ado

MEANING	Office, position, domain
ENGLISH EQUIVALENT	*-ship, -ate*
PART OF SPEECH	Noun
GENDER	Masculine

The suffix **-ato** (less commonly, **-ado**) denotes the office or domain of the base noun, which is almost always a person: **el cancelario** *the chancellor* has his office or domain in **el cancelariato** *the chancellorship.* Many of the suffixed nouns relate to politics and religion.

The following nouns ending in **-ato** or **-ado** represent positions of power in the church and state.

NOUN ENDING IN **-ato, -ado**	ENGLISH EQUIVALENT	BASE WORD	ENGLISH EQUIVALENT
el cancelariato	*chancellorship*	el cancelario	*chancellor*
el canonicato	*canonry*	el canon	*canon*
el cardenalato	*cardinalate*	el cardenal	*cardinal*
el clericato	*priesthood, clergy*	el clérigo	*priest, clergyman*
el colonato	*group of colonies*	la colonia	*colony*
el consulado	*consulate*	el cónsul	*consul*
el diaconato	*deaconship*	el diácono	*deacon*
el generalato	*generalship*	el general	*general*
el juzgado	*tribunal, court of justice*	el juez	*judge*
el liderato	*leadership*	el líder	*leader, ruler*
el obispado	*bishopric, diocese*	el obispo	*bishop*
el priorato	*priory*	el prior	*prior, head monk*
el reinado	*term of a king's reign*	el rey	*king*
el secretariado	*office of the secretary*	el secretario	*secretary*
el sultanato	*sultanate*	el sultán	*sultan*
el superiorato	*office of the superior*	el superior	*superior*

EJERCICIO
108·1

Provide the correct noun (including its article) to name the office, domain, or position of each of the following persons.

1. el cardenal _____

2. el diácono _____

3. el prior _____

4. el clérigo _____

5. el obispo _____

6. el canon _____

7. el superior _____

8. el cancelario _____

9. el cónsul _____

10. el general   _____

11. el líder   _____

12. el rey   _____

13. el sultán   _____

14. la colonia   _____

15. el secretario   _____

16. el juez   _____

The following nouns ending in **-ato** or **-ado** relate to academics, society, and sex.

NOUN ENDING IN -ato, -ado	ENGLISH EQUIVALENT	BASE WORD	ENGLISH EQUIVALENT
el bachillerato	*baccalaureate*	el bachiller	*high school graduate*
el caballerato	*privileges of a gentleman*	el caballero	*gentleman*
el campeonato	*championship*	el campeón	*champion*
el celibato	*celibacy, bachelorhood*	el célibe	*celibate, bachelor*
el concubinato	*concubinage*	la concubina	*concubine*
el doctorado	*doctorate, Ph.D.*	el doctor	*doctor*
el economato	*guardianship, trusteeship*	el ecónomo	*guardian, trustee*
el notariato	*notary title*	el notario	*notary (public)*
el noviciado	*novitiate, apprenticeship*	el novicio	*novice, beginner*
el orfanato	*orphanage*	el huérfano	*orphan*
el procerato	*exalted station*	el prócer	*nobleman, dignitary*
el profesorado	*professorship, faculty*	el profesor	*professor*

EJERCICIO
108·2

Provide the correct noun (including its article) to name the office, domain, or position of each of the following persons.

1. el profesor   _____

2. el doctor   _____

3. el bachiller   _____

4. el ecónomo   _____

5. el prócer   _____

6. el notario   _____

7. el caballero   _____

8. el campeón   _____

9. el novicio   _____

10. el huérfano   _____

11. el célibe   _____

12. la concubina   _____

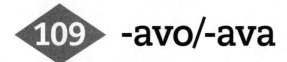 **-avo/-ava**

MEANING	Denominator (of a fraction)
ENGLISH EQUIVALENT	*-th*
PART OF SPEECH	Noun
GENDER	Masculine/feminine

The suffix **-avo** (feminine: **-ava**) denotes a denominator (the number below the line in a fraction); examples are **Yo leí un seisavo del libro** *I read one-sixth of the book* and **Yo comí una octava (parte) de la pizza** *I ate an eighth of the pizza.* If the denominator refers to a feminine noun, **-avo** becomes **-ava**.

NOUN ENDING IN **-avo**	ENGLISH EQUIVALENT	BASE WORD	ENGLISH EQUIVALENT
seisavo	*sixth*	seis	*six*
octavo	*eighth*	octo [LAT.]	*eight*
onceavo	*eleventh*	once	*eleven*
doceavo	*twelfth*	doce	*twelve*
treceavo	*thirteenth*	trece	*thirteen*
catorceavo	*fourteenth*	catorce	*fourteen*
quinceavo	*fifteenth*	quince	*fifteen*
dieciseisavo	*sixteenth*	dieciséis	*sixteen*
diecisieteavo	*seventeenth*	diecisiete	*seventeen*
decimoctavo	*eighteenth*	decem + octo [LAT.]	*eighteen*
diecinueveavo	*nineteenth*	diecinueve	*nineteen*
veintavo	*twentieth*	veinte	*twenty*
veintiunavo	*twenty-first*	veintiuno	*twenty-one*
treintavo	*thirtieth*	treinta	*thirty*
cuarentavo	*fortieth*	cuarenta	*forty*
cincuentavo	*fiftieth*	cincuenta	*fifty*
sesentavo	*sixtieth*	sesenta	*sixty*
setentavo	*seventieth*	setenta	*seventy*
ochentavo	*eightieth*	ochenta	*eighty*
noventavo	*ninetieth*	noventa	*ninety*
centavo	*hundredth*	cien, ciento	*one hundred*

Provide the correct form for each fraction in numbers, according to the example.

EJEMPLO   tres octavos   *3/8*

1. seis onceavos   _____

2. dos treceavos   _____

3. dos quinceavos   _____

4. ocho treintavos   _____

5. siete cuarentavos   _____

6. nueve catorceavos   _____

7. tres diecisieteavos   _____

8. un sesentavo   _____

9. tres dieciseisavos   _____

10. siete veintavos   _____

11. veinte noventavos   _____

12. tres cincuentavos   _____

13. cinco doceavos   _____

14. un setentavo   _____

15. cinco seisavos   _____

16. un decimoctavo   _____

17. tres ochentavos   _____

18. un centavo   _____

19. dos diecinueveavos   _____

20. cinco veintiunavos   _____

Translate the following sentences into Spanish.

1. *We have to read five-sixths of the book by tomorrow.*

   _____

2. *Each person can eat one-fifteenth of the pizza.*

   _____

3. *One-twelfth of a dozen of eggs is one egg.*

   _____

4. *No one can eat one-twentieth of an elephant.*

5. *One-fiftieth of three hundred is six.*

6. *One-fifteenth of sixty is four.*

7. *If only one-thirtieth of the class understands the lesson, there are problems.*

8. *One-fortieth of two hundred is five.*

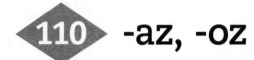

110 -az, -oz

MEANING	Abounding in
ENGLISH EQUIVALENT	*-acious, -ocious*
PART OF SPEECH	Adjective
GENDER	Masculine/feminine

Many Spanish adjectives with the suffix **-az** or, less commonly, **-oz** have English cognates ending in, respectively, *-acious* or *-ocious*. In both languages, the suffix indicates that the person or thing described abounds in an attribute of the base noun. Many of these suffixed adjectives have Latin words as their bases, and in Spanish, English, and Latin, the similarities are legion.

All of the adjectives in the following chart end in **-az**.

ADJECTIVE ENDING IN **-az**	ENGLISH EQUIVALENT	BASE WORD	ENGLISH EQUIVALENT
capaz	*capable*	capax [LAT.]	*able to hold much, roomy*
eficaz	*efficacious, effective*	efficax [LAT.]	*effective, efficient*
feraz	*fertile, fecund*	ferax [LAT.]	*fertile, fruitful*
incapaz	*incapable*	in- + capaz	*not + capable*
lenguaz	*loquacious, talkative*	la lengua	*tongue, language*
locuaz	*loquacious, talkative*	loquax [LAT.]	*talkative*
mendaz	*mendacious, untruthful*	mendax [LAT.]	*lying, deceitful*
montaraz	*wild, untamed, coarse*	el monte	*hill, mountain*
pertinaz	*persistent*	la pertinacia	*persistence, doggedness*
rapaz	*greedy*	rapax [LAT.]	*grasping*
suspicaz	*suspicious, distrustful*	suspicax [LAT.]	*exciting suspicion*
tenaz	*tenacious, persistent*	tenax [LAT.]	*holding fast*
veraz	*veracious, truthful*	verax [LAT.]	*truthful*
vivaz	*vivacious, lively*	vivax [LAT.]	*lively, vigorous*
voraz	*voracious, ravenous*	vorax [LAT.]	*gluttonous, voracious*

Sinónimos *Provide the correct synonym(s) for each group of words.*

1. mentiroso, deshonesto, fraudulento _____

2. honesto, sincero, recto _____

3. efectivo, eficiente, operativo _____

4. vivo, animado, alegre _____

5. fértil, fecundo, abundante _____

6. sospechoso, desconfiado, receloso _____

7. competente, apto, hábil _____

8. incompetente, inepto, inhábil _____

9. salvaje, silvestre, feral _____

10. codicioso, insaciable, glotón _____

_____

11. persistente, determinado, resuelto _____

_____

12. hablador, conversador, parlanchín _____

_____

Although most of the adjectives in the following chart end in **-az**, four use the less common suffix **-oz**.

ADJECTIVE ENDING IN **-az, -oz**	ENGLISH EQUIVALENT	BASE WORD	ENGLISH EQUIVALENT
atroz	*atrocious*	atrox [LAT.]	*fierce, savage, cruel*
audaz	*audacious, reckless*	audax [LAT.]	*brave, bold, daring*
contumaz	*obstinate, stubborn*	la contumacia	*stubbornness, obstinacy*
falaz	*fallacious, false*	la falacia	*fallacy*
feroz	*ferocious*	ferox [LAT.]	*fierce, wild-looking*
mordaz	*biting, corrosive*	morder	*to bite*
perspicaz	*perspicacious, perceptive*	perspicax [LAT.]	*sharp-sighted*
precoz	*precocious, premature*	praecox [LAT.]	*maturing early*
pugnaz	*pugnacious, quarrelsome*	pugnax [LAT.]	*combative*
sagaz	*sagacious, clever*	sagax [LAT.]	*acute, clever*
salaz	*salacious, wanton, lustful*	salax [LAT.]	*lustful*
veloz	*swift, fast, quick*	velox [LAT.]	*swift*

EJERCICIO
110·2

Sinónimos *Provide the correct synonym for each group of words.*

1. ilusorio, falso, engañoso _____

2. rápido, pronto, acelerado _____

3. combativo, belicoso, agresivo _____

4. lascivo, libidinoso, disoluto _____

5. obstinado, inflexible, porfiado _____

6. mordiente, corrosivo, acre _____

7. cruel, terrible, pésimo _____

8. prematuro, adelantado, talentoso _____

9. salvaje, predador, fiero _____

10. perceptivo, agudo, penetrante _____

11. atrevido, temerario, imprudente _____

12. juicioso, avisado, entendido _____

 **-azgo**

MEANING	Office, post; relationship; fee
ENGLISH EQUIVALENT	*-ship*
PART OF SPEECH	Noun
GENDER	Masculine

The suffix **-azgo** usually denotes an office or post. In this sense, **-azgo** is similar in meaning and function to the endings **-ato** and **-ado** (see No. 108). The suffix can also denote a particular relationship (for example, **el primazgo** *cousinship*, from **el primo** *cousin*) or a tariff or fee (for example, **el terrazgo** *land rent*, from **la tierra** *land*).

The following nouns ending in **-azgo** represent posts, relationships, or fees.

NOUN ENDING IN **-azgo**	ENGLISH EQUIVALENT	BASE WORD	ENGLISH EQUIVALENT
el albaceazgo	*executorship*	el albacea	*executor*
el cillazgo	*storehouse fees*	la cilla	*granary*
el comadrazgo	*relationship between parents and godmother*	la comadre	*godmother*
el compadrazgo	*relationship between parents and godfather*	el compadre	*godfather*
el liderazgo	*leadership*	el líder	*leader, ruler* ▶

NOUN ENDING IN -**azgo**	ENGLISH EQUIVALENT	BASE WORD	ENGLISH EQUIVALENT
◀ el madrinazgo	*title or charge of godmother*	la madrina	*godmother*
el mayorazgo	*primogeniture, entailed estate*	el mayor	*the eldest male*
el mecenazgo	*patronage*	el mecenas	*patron of the arts*
el noviazgo	*engagement*	el novio	*boyfriend, fiancé*
el padrinazgo	*title or charge of godfather*	el padrino	*godfather*
el papazgo	*papacy, pontificate*	el Papa	*the Pope*
el pontazgo	*bridge toll, portage*	el puente	*bridge*
el primazgo	*cousinship*	el primo	*cousin*
el sobrinazgo	*relationship of nephew or niece*	el sobrino	*nephew*
el terrazgo	*land rent*	la tierra	*land*

EJERCICIO

111·1

Provide the correct noun (including its article) for each description.

1. la relación entre los padres y la madrina _____

2. la relación entre los padres y el padrino _____

3. el período de tiempo antes de la boda _____

4. el título o cargo de la madrina _____

5. el título o cargo del padrino _____

6. el título o cargo del Papa _____

7. el título o cargo del albacea _____

8. el título o cargo del líder _____

9. el título o cargo del mecenas _____

10. el cargo del hijo mayor _____

11. el parentesco que tienen entre sí los primos _____

12. el parentesco que tienen entre sí los sobrinos y las sobrinas _____

13. los derechos que se pagan por los puentes _____

14. los derechos que se pagan por la tierra _____

15. los derechos que se pagan por el almacén _____

The following nouns ending in -**azgo** represent offices or official positions.

NOUN ENDING IN -**azgo**	ENGLISH EQUIVALENT	BASE WORD	ENGLISH EQUIVALENT
el alaminazgo	*office of the surveyor*	el alamín	*surveyor*
el alarifazgo	*office of the architect or builder*	el alarife	*architect, builder*
el alferazgo	*honorific of an ensign*	el alférez	*ensign, second lieutenant* ▶

NOUN ENDING IN -**azgo**	ENGLISH EQUIVALENT	BASE WORD	ENGLISH EQUIVALENT
el alguacilazgo	*office of the constable*	el alguacil	*constable, sheriff*
el almirantazgo	*admiralship, admiralty*	el almirante	*admiral*
el almotacenazgo	*office of the inspector*	el almotacén	*inspector of weights*
el cacicazgo	*honorific of a political boss*	el cacique	*political boss*
el tenientazgo	*office of the lieutenant*	el teniente	*lieutenant*
el vicealmirantazgo	*vice-admiralship*	el vicealmirante	*vice-admiral*

EJERCICIO
111·2

Provide the correct noun (including its article) for each description.

1. el oficio del alguacil   _____

2. el oficio del alamín   _____

3. el oficio del teniente   _____

4. el oficio del alarife   _____

5. el oficio del almotacén   _____

6. la dignidad del cacique   _____

7. la dignidad del alférez   _____

8. el empleo del almirante   _____

9. el empleo del vicealmirante   _____

112 ▸ -cracia

MEANING	Type of rule, government
ENGLISH EQUIVALENT	*-cracy*
PART OF SPEECH	Noun
GENDER	Feminine

The suffix -**cracia** comes from the Greek word **kratos** *rule, power.* Since most of the Spanish words with this suffix have English cognates with the suffix *-cracy,* they tend to be easily recognized and used. The majority of base words are Greek in origin, and the suffixed nouns denote a type of rule or government. Of particular interest is **la tecnocracia** *technocracy,* from **techne**, the Greek word for *skill.* The word has evolved to encompass not just skill, but the idea of technology. To one degree or another, we all live in a technocratic world, and most people think of computers and modern technology when they hear the word *technocracy.*

NOUN ENDING IN -cracia	ENGLISH EQUIVALENT	BASE WORD	ENGLISH EQUIVALENT
la acracia	*anarchy*	a- [GRK.]	*without*
la aristocracia	*aristocracy*	aristos [GRK.]	*best*
la autocracia	*autocracy*	auto- [GRK.]	*self*
la bancocracia	*abusive influence by bankers*	el banco	*bank*
la burocracia	*bureaucracy*	bureau [FR.]	*office*
la democracia	*democracy*	demos [GRK.]	*people*
la falocracia	*male chauvinism*	phallos [GRK.]	*penis*
la gerontocracia	*gerontocracy*	geron [GRK.]	*old man*
la ginecocracia	*gynocracy*	gyne [GRK.]	*woman*
la meritocracia	*meritocracy*	meritum [LAT.]	*merit*
la mesocracia	*government by middle class*	mesos [GRK.]	*middle*
la oclocracia	*government by multitude*	ochlos [GRK.]	*mob*
la plutocracia	*plutocracy*	ploutos [GRK.]	*wealth*
la tecnocracia	*technocracy*	techne [GRK.]	*skill*
la teocracia	*theocracy*	theos [GRK.]	*god*
la timocracia	*rule by honor*	time [GRK.]	*honor*

EJERCICIO 112·1

¿Qué tipo de gobierno es esto? *Provide the correct noun (including its article) for each description.*

1. el gobierno de la gente _____

2. el gobierno de Dios y los religiosos _____

3. el gobierno de los banqueros _____

4. el gobierno de la multitud _____

5. el gobierno de los machos _____

6. el gobierno de las mujeres _____

7. el gobierno de los ricos _____

8. el gobierno de la élite _____

9. el gobierno de los funcionarios públicos _____

10. el gobierno de los "techies" _____

11. el gobierno del honor _____

12. el gobierno de los ancianos _____

13. el gobierno de la clase media _____

14. el gobierno de una sola persona _____

15. el gobierno de las personas con base en sus habilidades _____

16. el gobierno sin líder _____

113 ◆ -dizo/-diza

MEANING	Relating to, like; tending to
ENGLISH EQUIVALENT	—
PART OF SPEECH	Adjective
GENDER	Masculine/feminine

The suffix **-dizo** (feminine: **-diza**) denotes a characteristic of the base word, which is always a verb. If the base word is an **-ar** verb, the **a** of the infinitive ending is retained before the suffix is added (for example, **acomodar** *to accommodate* yields **acomodadizo** *accommodating, easygoing*). The formation is similar for **-er** verbs (for example, **beber** *to drink* yields **bebedizo** *drinkable*). Some **-ir** verbs retain the **i** of the infinitive ending (for example, **escurrir** *to slip/sneak away* yields **escurridizo** *slippery, elusive*), but some change the **i** to **e** (for example, **salir** *to leave, go out* yields **saledizo** *jutting, salient*).

The following adjectives ending in **-dizo** are often applied to people.

ADJECTIVE ENDING IN **-dizo**	ENGLISH EQUIVALENT	BASE WORD	ENGLISH EQUIVALENT
acomodadizo	*accommodating, easygoing*	acomodar	*to accommodate*
apartadizo	*antisocial, standoffish*	apartar	*to separate, turn aside*
asustadizo	*easily frightened or scared*	asustar	*to frighten, scare*
cambiadizo	*changeable, fickle*	cambiar	*to change, alter*
enojadizo	*irritable, easily annoyed*	enojar	*to anger, vex, irritate*
erradizo	*wandering*	errar	*to wander, miss, err*
olvidadizo	*forgetful*	olvidar	*to forget*
tornadizo	*fickle, changeable*	tornar	*to turn, come back*

EJERCICIO
113·1

Complete each sentence with the correct form of the appropriate adjective(s).

1. Una persona que tiene dificultad con recordar nombres, fechas y números de teléfono es
_____.

2. Un hombre a quien no le importa si vamos al cine o si simplemente nos quedamos en casa
es un hombre _____.

3. Carlito, quien es muy miedoso, es un niño _____.

4. Una mujer que está enamorada de Juan un día y de Jorge el próximo día es una mujer
_____ o _____.

5. Un adolescente que siempre está frustrado con todo y con todos es un chico
_____.

6. Pablo no quiere pasar tiempo con otras personas ni tiene interés en otras personas y por
eso es considerado _____.

7. Un vagabundo es un hombre _____.

The following adjectives ending in -**dizo** are often applied to people or things in a home.

ADJECTIVE ENDING IN -**dizo**	ENGLISH EQUIVALENT	BASE WORD	ENGLISH EQUIVALENT
apagadizo	*tending to go out easily*	apagar	*to turn off, extinguish*
bebedizo	*drinkable*	beber	*to drink*
cogedizo	*easily collected*	coger	*to pick up, collect*
corredizo	*sliding, easily untied*	correr	*to run, flow*
enviadizo	*regularly sent*	enviar	*to send*
escurridizo	*slippery, elusive*	escurrir	*to slip/sneak away*
levadizo	*able to be lifted or raised*	levantar	*to lift, raise*
manchadizo	*easily stained or soiled*	manchar	*to stain, soil, spot*
movedizo	*movable*	mover	*to move*
pegadizo	*catchy (music)*	pegar	*to glue, stick to*
resbaladizo	*slippery*	resbalar	*to slip, slide*
traedizo	*portable*	traer	*to bring, carry*

EJERCICIO

113·2

¿Verdadero o falso? *Indicate whether each statement is true or false, using* **V** *for* **verdadero** *true or* **F** *for* **falso** *false.*

1. _____ A veces hay agua bebediza en una cloaca.

2. _____ Una televisión traediza pesa más de quinientas libras.

3. _____ Un lápiz es levadizo.

4. _____ Los caminos están resbaladizos durante una tormenta de nieve.

5. _____ Afortunadamente, el "spam" es enviadizo por el correo electrónico.

6. _____ Las luces apagadizas típicamente no son deseables.

7. _____ Un mentiroso, un estafador y un tramposo son ejemplos de personas escurridizas.

8. _____ A veces se encuentra una puerta corrediza como separación entre la casa y un patio.

9. _____ Un traje completamente en blanco es práctico porque no es manchadizo y siempre parece nuevo.

10. _____ La sintonía de muchos anuncios de televisión es pegadiza.

11. _____ Los impuestos son cogedizos de estafadores y tramposos.

The following adjectives ending in -**dizo** are often applied to things or situations outside the home.

ADJECTIVE ENDING IN -**dizo**	ENGLISH EQUIVALENT	BASE WORD	ENGLISH EQUIVALENT
anegadizo	*subject to flooding*	anegar	*to flood, inundate*
apretadizo	*easily compressed*	apretar	*to press, tighten*
arrojadizo	*made for throwing*	arrojar	*to throw, hurl*
borneadizo	*pliant, flexible*	bornear	*to bend, turn, twist*
caedizo	*ready to fall*	caer	*to fall*
clavadizo	*nail-studded*	clavar	*to nail*
heladizo	*easily frozen*	helar	*to freeze, congeal*
llovedizo	*leaky*	llover	*to rain*
rajadizo	*easily split*	rajar	*to split, slash*
saledizo	*jutting, salient*	salir	*to leave, go out*

EJERCICIO

113·3

Provide the correct form of the appropriate adjective for each description.

1. un techo que está mal construido _____

2. una flecha _____

3. un área cerca de un dique mal construido _____

4. la fruta excesivamente madura, colgando de un árbol _____

5. un promontorio de tierra o roca _____

6. el agua en las aceras cuando hace mucho frío _____

7. una sandía _____

8. algo muy suave y maleable _____

9. los artículos de ropa de moda "heavy metal" _____

10. una almohada de plumas _____

114 ▸ -dura

MEANING	Action, result of an action, object
ENGLISH EQUIVALENT	*-ing*
PART OF SPEECH	Noun
GENDER	Feminine

Nouns with the suffix -**dura** are derived from verbs and denote the action of a verb (for example, **la mascadura** *chewing*, from **mascar** *to chew*) or the physical object related to a verb (for example, **la bordadura** *embroidery*, from **bordar** *to embroider*). The suffixed nouns retain the characteristic vowel of the infinitive (-**adura**, -**edura**, -**idura**), with the rare exception **la tosidura** *coughing*, which is derived from **toser** *to cough*.

NOUN ENDING IN -dura	ENGLISH EQUIVALENT	BASE WORD	ENGLISH EQUIVALENT
la alisadura	*planing, smoothing*	alisar	*to plane, smooth*
la arrodilladura	*kneeling*	arrodillar(se)	*to kneel (down)*
la lamedura	*lick, licking*	lamer	*to lick, lap*
la limpiadura	*cleaning*	limpiar	*to clean*
la mascadura	*chewing*	mascar	*to chew*
la mecedura	*rocking*	mecer	*to rock*
la peladura	*stripping, peeling*	pelar	*to strip, peel, skin*
la raspadura	*abrasion, scrape*	raspar	*to file, scrape*
la retozadura	*friskiness*	retozar	*to frolic, romp*
la rociadura	*sprinkling*	rociar	*to sprinkle*
la rompedura	*breakage, breaking*	romper	*to break*
la teñidura	*art of dying or staining*	teñir	*to dye, stain, tinge*
la tosidura	*coughing*	toser	*to cough*
la tropezadura	*stumbling*	tropezar	*to stumble, trip up*

EJERCICIO
114·1

Provide the correct noun (including its article) to name the action related to each of the following situations.

1. en la iglesia _____

2. en la sala de tuberculosis del hospital _____

3. en la boca de un chico con un paquete enorme de chicle _____

4. en las sillas de la unidad neonatal _____

5. en la rodilla del chico típico _____

6. entre un grupo de chicos con conos de helado _____

7. en un cuarto lleno de varios gatitos _____

8. en una cacharrería con el proverbial elefante _____

9. en la calle enfrente de un bar a la hora de cierre _____

10. en la fábrica que prepara los colores para la tela _____

11. en el proceso de aplicar las pesticidas a las cosechas _____

12. en el proceso de ordenar y arreglar la casa _____

13. en el proceso de quitar la piel de una manzana u otra fruta _____

14. en el taller de un carpintero _____

NOUN ENDING IN -dura	ENGLISH EQUIVALENT	BASE WORD	ENGLISH EQUIVALENT
la añadidura	*addition, extra measure*	añadir	*to add, increase*
la armadura	*armor, armature*	armar	*to arm*
la bordadura	*embroidery*	bordar	*to embroider*
la cabalgadura	*horse*	cabalgar	*to ride a horse*

NOUN ENDING IN -dura	ENGLISH EQUIVALENT	BASE WORD	ENGLISH EQUIVALENT
la cerradura	*lock, closure*	cerrar	*to close, shut, lock*
la escocedura	*burning pain*	escocer	*to sting, smart*
la ligadura	*ligature, tie, cord*	ligar	*to bind, tie*
la picadura	*bite, prick, sting*	picar	*to prick, pierce*
la quemadura	*burn, scald*	quemar	*to burn, scald, scorch*
la rapadura	*close haircut*	rapar	*to shave or crop hair*
las vestiduras [PL.]	*vestments, robes of distinction*	vestir(se)	*to dress (oneself)*

EJERCICIO
114·2

Provide the correct form of the appropriate noun (including its article) for each description.

1. lo que monta el vaquero _____

2. lo que los reclutas reciben del barbero militar _____

3. lo que lleva el guerrero en la Edad Media _____

4. lo que se necesita en la puerta para prevenir robos _____

5. lo que recibes de una abeja enojada _____

6. lo que lleva el sacerdote cuando celebra la misa _____

7. un arte textil _____

8. lo que se siente después de sumergirse la mano en agua herviente _____

9. el tipo de herido después de sumergirse la mano en agua herviente _____

10. un ingrediente extra (frecuentemente "el amor" cuando la abuela hace galletas) _____

11. un procedimiento ginecológico que consiste en la constricción de las trompas de Falopio para prevenir el embarazo _____

115 ▸ -ecto/-ecta

MEANING	Relating to, like
ENGLISH EQUIVALENT	*-ect*
PART OF SPEECH	Adjective
GENDER	Masculine/feminine

Many Spanish adjectives with the suffix **-ecto** (feminine: **-ecta**) have English cognates ending in *-ect*, which makes these words easy to recognize and use. Base words are usually verbs, and many have Latin or Greek roots. Some of these suffixed adjectives may also function as nouns (see No. 68).

ADJECTIVE ENDING IN -ecto	ENGLISH EQUIVALENT	BASE WORD	ENGLISH EQUIVALENT
abyecto	*abject, despicable*	abiectus [LAT.]	*thrown away*
correcto	*correct*	correctus [LAT.]	*corrected*
dilecto	*loved, beloved*	dilectus [LAT.]	*loved*
directo	*direct*	directus [LAT.]	*set straight*
electo	*elect, elected*	electus [LAT.]	*picked out, chosen*
infecto	*infected, putrid, foul*	infectus [LAT.]	*spoiled, stained*
perfecto	*perfect*	perfectus [LAT.]	*finished, completed*
pluscuamperfecto	*pluperfect*	plus quam perfectum [LAT.]	*more than perfect*
recto	*straight, upright, true*	rectus [LAT.]	*straightened*

EJERCICIO
115·1

¿Verdadero o falso? *Indicate whether each statement is true or false, using* **V** *for* **verdadero** *true or* **F** *for* **falso** *false.*

1. _____ Una herida infectada frecuentemente huele mal.

2. _____ El presidente electo asume el nuevo puesto el día después de las elecciones.

3. _____ El tiempo pluscuamperfecto es el mismo que el tiempo futuro.

4. _____ En un examen perfecto cada respuesta es correcta.

5. _____ Una persona recta no tiene integridad.

6. _____ Para muchas personas, un día perfecto incluye tiempo con sus amigos dilectos.

7. _____ La violación de una mujer o de un niño es un crimen abyecto.

8. _____ La distancia más corta entre dos puntos es una ruta directa.

ADJECTIVE ENDING IN -ecto	ENGLISH EQUIVALENT	BASE WORD	ENGLISH EQUIVALENT
circunspecto	*circumspect, cautious*	circumspectus [LAT.]	*considered carefully*
desafecto	*hostile, disaffected*	des- + afectar	*not + to affect*
erecto	*erect*	erectus [LAT.]	*put up*
imperfecto	*imperfect*	in- + perfectus [LAT.]	*not + finished or completed*
incorrecto	*incorrect, wrong*	in- + correctus [LAT.]	*not + corrected*
indirecto	*indirect*	in- + directus [LAT.]	*not + set straight*
insurrecto	*rebellious*	insurrectus [LAT.]	*risen up against*
selecto	*select, choice, excellent*	selectus [LAT.]	*chosen, singled out*

Sinónimos *Provide a synonym for each group of words.*

1. incompleto, incorrecto, inexacto, deficiente   _____

2. escogido, distinguido, excelente, seleccionado   _____

3. inexacto, errado, equivocado, falso   _____

4. prudente, discreto, juicioso, cauteloso   _____

5. erguido, firme, rígido, tieso   _____

6. hostil, opuesto, contrario, animoso   _____

7. revoltoso, rebelde, sedicioso, insubordinado   _____

8. sinuoso, laberíntico, transversal, oblicuo   _____

116 ▶ -edad

MEANING	State; abstract concept
ENGLISH EQUIVALENT	*-ness*
PART OF SPEECH	Noun
GENDER	Feminine

The suffix **-edad** denotes a state or abstract concept associated with the base word, which is always an adjective. The formation consists in omitting the final vowel of the base adjective and adding **-edad**; if the adjective ends in a consonant, **-edad** is added directly to the base adjective. There may be a spelling change to maintain the pronunciation of the last consonant of the adjective (for example, **brusco** *sudden, curt* yields **brusquedad** *suddenness, bluntness*).

NOUN ENDING IN **-edad**	ENGLISH EQUIVALENT	BASE WORD	ENGLISH EQUIVALENT
la brevedad	*briefness, brevity*	breve	*brief*
la brusquedad	*suddenness, bluntness*	brusco	*sudden, curt*
la ceguedad	*blindness*	ciego	*blind*
la chatedad	*flatness (nose)*	chato	*flat, snub*
la contrariedad	*opposition, setback*	contrario	*contrary*
la cortedad	*shortness*	corto	*short (length)*
la ebriedad	*drunkenness*	ebrio	*drunk, intoxicated*
la enfermedad	*sickness, disease*	enfermo	*sick*
la humedad	*humidity, dampness*	húmedo	*humid*
la impiedad	*impiety, impiousness*	impío	*impious, irreligious*
la levedad	*lightness, levity*	leve	*light, slight, trifling*
la mesmedad	*nature, actuality*	mismo	*same*

¿Verdadero o falso? *Indicate whether each statement is true or false, using* **V** *for* **verdadero** *true or* **F** *for* **falso** *false.*

1. _____ Stevie Wonder, Ray Charles y Helen Keller sufren (o sufrieron) de la ceguedad.

2. _____ No hay mucha humedad en las ciudades cerca del ecuador.

3. _____ El bulldog es muy conocido por la chatedad de su nariz.

4. _____ Desgraciadamente, la diabetes es una enfermedad que no tiene cura.

5. _____ El Papa y los cardenales siempre viven una vida de impiedad.

6. _____ El congreso siempre pasa las leyes a la mayor brevedad posible.

7. _____ Muchos políticos demuestran una cortedad de miras.

8. _____ Nadie conduce el coche en estado de ebriedad porque es ilegal.

9. _____ La mesmedad es un tema de varios filósofos.

10. _____ Las damas elegantes son famosas por su brusquedad.

11. _____ Cuando hay un conflicto de intereses, un abogado debe recusarse.

NOUN ENDING IN **-edad**	ENGLISH EQUIVALENT	BASE WORD	ENGLISH EQUIVALENT
la novedad	*newness, novelty*	nuevo	*new*
la sequedad	*dryness*	seco	*dry*
la seriedad	*seriousness*	serio	*serious*
la sobriedad	*sobriety*	sobrio	*sober*
la soledad	*solitude, loneliness*	solo	*alone, lonely, solitary*
la tochedad	*rusticity, coarseness*	tocho	*unpolished, coarse*
la tosquedad	*coarseness, crudeness*	tosco	*coarse, crude*
la turbiedad	*murkiness, muddiness*	turbio	*turbid, muddy*
la vastedad	*vastness*	vasto	*vast, huge*
la viudedad	*widowhood*	viudo	*widowed*
la voluntariedad	*volition, voluntary nature*	voluntario	*voluntary*
la zafiedad	*boorishness*	zafio	*boorish, uncouth*

Provide the correct noun(s) (including the article) related to each description or item.

1. una persona que absolutamente nunca toma una bebida   _____
   alcohólica

2. los desiertos de Gobi, Sahara y Kalahari   _____

3. el Gran Cañón   _____

4. algo muy oscuro y/u opaco   _____

5. una persona sin familia, sin amigos, sin compañeros _____

6. la pérdida del esposo _____

7. una persona grosera, brusca y sin educación _____

_____

_____

8. la motivación o deseo de hacer algo _____

9. lo contrario de algo viejo, antiguo o usado _____

10. la gravedad, la sobriedad, sin humor _____

117 ◆ -engo/-enga

MEANING	Relating to, like
ENGLISH EQUIVALENT	—
PART OF SPEECH	Adjective
GENDER	Masculine/feminine

The uncommon suffix **-engo** (feminine: **-enga**) is one of several suffixes denoting *relating to* or *like*. The suffixed adjective describes someone or something with a characteristic of the base word. Of interest is **realengo**, whose base word is **el real** *royalty* and which originally referred to ownerless property or property owned by the king but granted to another person without permanent ownership; in Latin America, **realengo** now means *ownerless* and may refer to, for instance, an animal that has no owner.

ADJECTIVE ENDING IN -engo	ENGLISH EQUIVALENT	BASE WORD	ENGLISH EQUIVALENT
abadengo	*pertaining to an abbey*	el abad	*abbot*
barbiluengo	*long-bearded*	la barba	*beard*
frailengo	*monkish*	el fraile	*friar, monk*
luengo [ARCHAIC]	*long*	longus [LAT.]	*long*
mujerengo	*effeminate*	la mujer	*woman*
peciluengo	*long-stalked (fruit)*	el pezón	*stalk, stem*
realengo	*ownerless (property)*	el real	*royalty*

EJERCICIO
117·1

Sinónimos *Provide the noun that is related to each group of words or description. Include its article.*

1. largo, alargado, aumentado, ampliado _____

2. barbado, barbudo, con barba _____

3. afeminado, mujeril, femenino _____

4. concerniendo al monasterio o la abadía _____

5. concerniendo a propiedad que pertenece a la familia real _____

6. concerniendo al tallo de una planta _____

7. monacal, monástico, frailuno _____

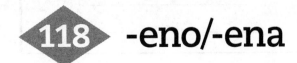

118 ◆ -eno/-ena

MEANING	Ordinal number
ENGLISH EQUIVALENT	*-th*
PART OF SPEECH	Adjective
GENDER	Masculine/feminine

The suffix **-eno** (feminine: **-ena**) is a relatively uncommon suffix denoting an ordinal number (see also No. 126, **-(és)imo/-(és)ima**). Adjectives with this suffix may also be used as a noun, with the referent noun understood. For example, **noveno** is used as an adjective in **El noveno hombre en la fila es mi primo** *The ninth man in line is my cousin*; it is a noun substitute in **El noveno en la fila es mi primo** *The ninth (one) in line is my cousin*. Because adjectives with the suffix **-eno/-ena** are quantitative adjectives, they precede the noun they modify: **el doceno chico** *the twelfth boy*, **la docena chica** *the twelfth girl*.

ADJECTIVE ENDING IN **-eno**	ENGLISH EQUIVALENT	BASE WORD	ENGLISH EQUIVALENT
seiseno	*sixth*	seis	*six*
septeno	*seventh*	septem [LAT.]	*seven*
noveno	*ninth*	nueve	*nine*
deceno	*tenth*	decem [LAT.]	*ten*
onceno	*eleventh*	once	*eleven*
doceno	*twelfth*	doce	*twelve*
treceno	*thirteenth*	trece	*thirteen*
catorceno	*fourteenth*	catorce	*fourteen*
quinceno	*fifteenth*	quince	*fifteen*
dieciocheno	*eighteenth*	dieciocho	*eighteen*
veinteno	*twentieth*	veinte	*twenty*
treinteno	*thirtieth*	treinta	*thirty*
cincuenteno	*fiftieth*	cincuenta	*fifty*
ochenteno	*eightieth*	ochenta	*eighty*
centeno	*hundredth*	cien	*one hundred*

Provide the correct adjective for the ordinal number of each of the following numbers.

1. 10 _____

2. 9 _____

3. 13 _____

4. 7 _____

5. 80 _____

6. 15 _____

7. 6 _____

8. 50 _____

9. 11 _____

10. 20 _____

11. 18 _____

12. 100 _____

13. 14 _____

14. 30 _____

15. 12 _____

Translate the following phrases into Spanish.

1. *the ninth boy* _____

2. *the seventh girl* _____

3. *the fifteenth book* _____

4. *the hundredth day* _____

5. *the fourteenth mile* _____

6. *the twelfth night* _____

7. *the sixth month* _____

8. *the fiftieth person* _____

9. *the eighteenth year* _____

10. *the tenth anniversary* _____

11. *the thirtieth car* _____

12. *the thirteenth egg* _____

13. *the twentieth house* _____

14. *the eleventh horse* _____

15. *the eightieth table* _____

 **-ense**

MEANING	Citizen, native; relating to, like
ENGLISH EQUIVALENT	—
PART OF SPEECH	Noun, adjective
GENDER	Masculine/feminine

The suffix **-ense** is one of several endings that denote geographical origin (see also No. 7, **-ano/-ana**, No. 72, **-eño/-eña**, No. 75, **-és/-esa**, and No. 133, **-ino/-ina**). The suffixed word may function as a noun or adjective, depending on context: **La canadiense lee el periódico nicaragüense** *The Canadian (woman) reads the Nicaraguan newspaper.* Unlike their English counterparts, these suffixed words are not capitalized. The plural form of the suffix is **-enses** (for example, **el parisiense ~ los parisienses**).

NOUN/ADJECTIVE ENDING IN **-ense**	ENGLISH EQUIVALENT	BASE WORD	ENGLISH EQUIVALENT
(el) ateniense	*Athenian*	Atenas	*Athens*
(el) bonaerense	*(native) of Buenos Aires*	Buenos Aires	*Buenos Aires*
(el) bruselense	*(native) of Brussels*	Bruselas	*Brussels*
(el) canadiense	*Canadian*	Canadá	*Canada*
(el) cartaginense	*Carthaginian*	Cartago	*Carthage*
(el) costarricense	*Costa Rican*	Costa Rica	*Costa Rica*
(el) cretense	*(native) of Crete*	Creta	*Crete*
(el) estadounidense	*(native) of the United States*	Estados Unidos	*United States*
(el) lisbonense	*(native) of Lisbon*	Lisboa	*Lisbon*
(el) londinense	*(native) of London*	Londres	*London*
(el) manilense	*(native) of Manila*	Manila	*Manila*
(el) matritense	*(native) of Madrid*	Madrid	*Madrid*
(el) nicaragüense	*(native) of Nicaragua*	Nicaragua	*Nicaragua*
(el) parisiense	*Parisian*	París	*Paris*
(el) peloponense	*Peloponnesian*	Peloponeso	*Peloponnesus*

Complete each sentence with the correct form of the appropriate adjective.

1. Una persona que nace en la capital de Portugal es _____.

2. Imelda Marcos, la política filipina y viuda del ex-presidente de las Filipinas, nació en la

   capital de este país. Ella es _____.

3. Celine Dion, Avril Lavigne, Jim Carrey y Stephen Harper son _____.

4. Una persona que nace en la capital de España es _____.

5. El presidente Daniel Ortega vive en Managua. Él es _____.

6. Una guerra de la Antigua Grecia que duró 27 años (431–404 a.C.) fue principalmente entre

   la liga de Delos (conducida por Atenas) y la liga _____ de Esparta.

7. Marie Antoinette, Coco Chanel y Simone de Beauvoir eran _____.

8. David Bowie, Daniel Day-Lewis y David Beckham son _____.

9. Soy de la capital de Argentina. Soy _____.

10. El famoso filósofo greco, Sócrates, nació en la capital del país. Él era

    _____.

11. Una persona que nace en la capital de Bélgica es _____.

12. Las personas que nacen en la ciudad capital de San José (en Centroamérica) son

    _____.

13. Aunque El Greco vivió por muchos años en Toledo (España), nació en la isla más grande

    de Grecia. Por eso, El Greco era _____.

14. Las personas que nacen en Cartago, cerca de la ciudad capital del país Túnez, son

    _____.

15. El presidente Barack Obama y el empresario Bill Gates son _____.

120 ▸ -eo/-ea

MEANING	Relating to, like; possessing a characteristic
ENGLISH EQUIVALENT	*-eous*
PART OF SPEECH	Adjective
GENDER	Masculine/feminine

The adjectival suffix **-eo** (feminine: **-ea**) indicates that someone or something has a characteristic of the base noun. The suffix is always preceded by a consonant (often **c**, **n**, or **r**) that follows an accented vowel. Many of the suffixed adjectives refer to aspects of nature or colors.

ADJECTIVE ENDING IN -eo	ENGLISH EQUIVALENT	BASE WORD	ENGLISH EQUIVALENT
arbóreo	*arboreal*	el árbol	*tree*
arenáceo	*sandy*	la arena	*sand*
aveníceo	*oat-like*	la avena	*oat*
broncíneo	*of bronze, bronze-like*	el bronce	*bronze*
cetáceo	*cetacean*	cetus [LAT.]	*large sea creature*
contemporáneo	*contemporary*	con + el tiempo	*with + time*
férreo	*ferrous, made of iron, strong*	el fierro [LAT. AM.]	*iron*
plúmeo	*having feathers*	la pluma	*feather*
purpúreo	*purple-colored*	la púrpura	*the color purple*
róseo	*rosy, roseate*	la rosa	*the color pink/rose*
rúbeo	*ruby-colored, reddish*	el rubí	*ruby*
temporáneo	*temporary*	el tiempo	*time*
virgíneo	*virginal*	la virgen	*virgin*

EJERCICIO 120·1

¿Verdadero o falso? *Indicate whether each statement is true or false, using* **V** *for* **verdadero** *true or* **F** *for* **falso** *false.*

1. _____ Un déspota tiene un control férreo del poder.

2. _____ Una colección de arte contemporáneo incluye obras de Rembrandt, John Singer Sargent y El Greco.

3. _____ Muchos cereales para desayuno son aveníceos.

4. _____ Una esmeralda es rúbea.

5. _____ Un pájaro es plúmeo.

6. _____ Las túnicas reales del rey o de la reina son purpúreas.

7. _____ Hay una extensa capa de terreno arbóreo en el desierto.

8. _____ La nariz de un gato tiene un aspecto róseo.

9. _____ *El pensador* de Auguste Rodin es una famosa estatua broncínea.

10. _____ La playa no es arenácea.

11. _____ Una ballena es cetácea.

12. _____ Según la Biblia, María, la madre de Jesucristo, es virgínea.

13. _____ Un hotel es un hogar temporáneo para los turistas, los negociantes y otros visitantes.

ADJECTIVE ENDING IN -eo	ENGLISH EQUIVALENT	BASE WORD	ENGLISH EQUIVALENT
aéreo	*aerial, of the air*	el aire	*air*
ceráceo	*waxy*	la cera	*wax*
cesáreo	*Caesarean, like Caesar*	César	*Caesar*
coriáceo	*pertaining to leather*	el cuero	*leather*
corpóreo	*corporeal*	el cuerpo	*body*
etéreo	*ethereal*	el éter	*ether*
grisáceo	*grayish*	el gris	*the color gray*
rosáceo	*rosaceous*	la rosa	*the color pink/rose*
violáceo	*violet-colored*	la violeta	*violet (botany)*
zafíreo	*sapphire-colored*	el zafiro	*sapphire*

EJERCICIO
120·2

Complete each sentence with the correct form of the appropriate adjective.

1. A veces, la madre tiene una operación _____ para dar a luz a su bebé.

2. El transporte _____ es por avión.

3. Una vela o una candela es _____.

4. Algo _____ no es de nuestra tierra.

5. El anillo de compromiso de la princesa Diana (y treinta años después, de Kate Middleton) es _____.

6. La berenjena es _____.

7. La piel de un elefante es _____.

8. Muchos zapatos y botas contienen materiales _____.

9. Según la Biblia, durante su estancia en la tierra Jesucristo tiene una vida _____.

121 ◆ -ería

MEANING	Abstract concept; place
ENGLISH EQUIVALENT	*-ness, -ry*
PART OF SPEECH	Noun
GENDER	Feminine

The suffix **-ería** may denote an abstraction of the base word (for example, **el estante** *shelf* yields **la estantería** *shelving, shelves in general*). This suffix may also denote a shop or store (see also No. 16, **-ería**). These two meanings may overlap: a store contains a collection of specific items, making it a type of abstraction. For this reason, a gray area is represented by some of these suffixed nouns; for example, **la relojería** (from **el reloj** *clock, watch*) may mean *clock shop* or *clockmaking, watchmaking*.

NOUN ENDING IN -ería	ENGLISH EQUIVALENT	BASE WORD	ENGLISH EQUIVALENT
la armería	*armory, arsenal*	el arma [F.]	*arm, weapon*
la carcelería	*imprisonment*	la cárcel	*jail, prison*
la cohetería	*rocketry*	el cohete	*rocket*
la estantería	*shelving, shelves in general*	el estante	*shelf*
la galantería	*gallantry, politeness*	galante	*courtly, elegant*
la ganadería	*cattle ranching*	el ganado	*cattle*
la gansería	*folly, stupidity*	el ganso	*goose, idiot, fool*
la gitanería	*wiliness, craftiness*	el gitano	*gypsy*
la golfería	*loutish behavior, loafing*	el golfo	*lout, rogue*
la grosería	*grossness, rudeness, swear word*	groso	*coarse*
la hotelería	*hotel trade/business*	el hotel	*hotel*
la lanería	*woolen goods*	la lana	*wool*
la palabrería	*verbiage, "hot air"*	la palabra	*word*
la pobretería	*poverty, indigence*	pobre	*poor*
la porquería	*filth, nastiness*	el puerco	*pig*

Complete each sentence with the correct form of the appropriate noun.

1. Las familias Hilton y Marriott se ocupan con la _____.

2. Wile E. Coyote, el archienemigo del popular personaje de dibujos animados Roadrunner,

   es conocido por su _____.

3. La Biblioteca del Congreso de Estados Unidos tiene más o menos 838 millas de

   _____ para exhibir los libros.

4. Una de las especialidades de NASA es la _____.

5. Una pocilga (*pigsty*) es conocida por su _____.

6. Muchos políticos que hablan mucho pero no hacen nada son conocidos por su

   _____.

7. Los tres chiflados (*stooges*) son conocidos por su _____.

8. Los granjeros y vaqueros son conocidos por su _____.

9. Un hombre bien educado y cortés que trata a una mujer como si fuera una reina es

   conocido por su _____.

10. Haití, con su alta tasa de analfabetismo y desempleo, especialmente después del terremoto

    de 2010, es conocido por su _____.

11. Es ingenuo pensar que la _____ de criminales pone fin a los
    crímenes.

12. Es una _____ escribir palabrotas en la muralla.

13. El lugar donde se almacenan pistolas, rifles, escopetas, carabinas y granadas de mano

es una _____.

14. Donde hay ovejas, ciertamente hay tiendas que se especializan en la

_____.

15. Desgraciadamente, muchos adolescentes que abandonan la escuela secundaria pasan

sus días en la _____.

NOUN ENDING IN -ería	ENGLISH EQUIVALENT	BASE WORD	ENGLISH EQUIVALENT
la porrería	*stupidity, obstinacy*	porro	*dull, stupid, ignorant*
la ratería	*pilfering, petty thieving*	el rata	*sneaky thief*
la relojería	*clockmaking, watchmaking, clock shop*	el reloj	*clock, watch*
la roñería	*stinginess, meanness*	el roña	*stingy person*
la tesorería	*treasury*	el tesoro	*treasure*
la tontería	*tomfoolery*	el tonto	*clown, idiot*
la torería	*bullfighting world*	el toro	*bull*
la tubería	*tubing, piping*	el tubo	*tube*
la tunantería	*debauchery, vagrancy*	el tunante	*rogue, lazy slug*
la versería	*compilation of verses or poetry*	el verso	*verse*
la vidriería	*glassworks, glassware*	el vidrio	*glass*
la vinatería	*wine trade*	el vino	*wine*
la vocería	*clamor, outcry*	la voz	*voice*
la yesería	*plasterwork*	el yeso	*plaster*
la zapatería	*shoemaking trade*	el zapato	*shoe*

EJERCICIO
121·2

¿Qué le interesa? *Provide the correct form of the appropriate noun (including its article) to name the particular interest of the persons mentioned.*

1. la persona que trabaja con el cristal _____

2. Robert Frost, Emily Dickinson y Pablo Neruda _____

3. los que producen el Chardonnay y el champán _____

4. los que fabrican los productos de Rolex, Timex y Casio _____

5. el matador, el picador y el banderillero _____

6. los que fabrican los productos de Jimmy Choo, Adidas y Reebok _____

7. el hombre que repara el daño en las paredes de casas viejas _____

8. el plomero que instala el sistema de drenaje de cualquier edificio _____

9. los gritadores a medianoche de la Nochevieja _____

10. la persona encargada de las finanzas de una organización _____

11. el idiota, el tonto, el imbécil _____

12. el tacaño, el avaro, Scrooge _____

13. el borracho, el seductor, el baboso _____

14. el bromista, el chistoso, el payaso _____

15. el ladrón que roba su billetera _____

◆ 122 ◆ -erizo/-eriza

MEANING	Herder
ENGLISH EQUIVALENT	-herd
PART OF SPEECH	Noun
GENDER	Masculine/feminine

The suffix **-erizo** (feminine: **-eriza**) is highly specialized, and, as a result, few Spanish words have this ending. The base word is the name of an animal that is tended or herded, and the suffixed noun identifies the person doing the tending or herding.

NOUN ENDING IN **-erizo**	ENGLISH EQUIVALENT	BASE WORD	ENGLISH EQUIVALENT
el boyerizo	*oxherd, ox driver*	el buey	*ox*
el caballerizo	*head groom (of a stable)*	el caballo	*horse*
el cabrerizo	*goatherd*	la cabra	*goat*
el porquerizo	*swineherd*	el puerco	*pig, hog*
el vaquerizo	*herdsman*	la vaca	*cow*
el yegüerizo	*keeper of mares*	la yegua	*mare*

EJERCICIO
122·1

¿Quién guarda los animales? *Provide the correct noun (including its article) to name the herder or tender for each group.*

1. Trigger, Seabiscuit y Secretariat _____

2. Wilbur (*La telaraña de Charlotte*), Babe y Hamm _____

3. Flicka y sus amigas _____

4. Babe (el famoso animal azul de Paul Bunyan) y sus amigos _____

5. Bessie, Elsie y Flossie _____

6. Pan (el sátiro mitológico) y sus amigos _____

123 ◆ -ero, -era

MEANING	Plant; place where plants grow
ENGLISH EQUIVALENT	—
PART OF SPEECH	Noun
GENDER	Masculine; feminine

The suffix **-ero** (less commonly, **-era**) may denote the name of a tree or other plant, or a place where plants grow. The base noun is usually the name of the fruit, nut, vegetable, or product that the plant produces. Generally, if the base noun ends in a vowel, the vowel is omitted before the suffix is added; if the base noun ends in a consonant, the suffix is added directly to the base noun. There is no rhyme or reason as to which nouns have the masculine suffix (**-ero**) and which have the feminine suffix (**-era**); the form and gender of each must be memorized.

The nouns in the following chart end in **-ero** and are masculine.

NOUN ENDING IN **-ero**	ENGLISH EQUIVALENT	BASE WORD	ENGLISH EQUIVALENT
el aguacatero	*avocado tree*	el aguacate	*avocado*
el albaricoquero	*apricot tree*	el albaricoque	*apricot*
el alcachofero	*artichoke plant*	la alcachofa	*artichoke*
el algodonero	*cotton plant*	el algodón	*cotton*
el clavero	*clove tree*	el clavo	*clove*
el limero	*lime tree*	la lima	*lime*
el limonero	*lemon tree*	el limón	*lemon*
el melocotonero	*peach tree*	el melocotón	*peach*
el pimentero	*pepper plant*	el pimiento	*pepper*
el semillero	*seedbed*	la semilla	*seed*
el vivero	*plant nursery*	los vivos	*the living*

EJERCICIO
123·1

Choose the noun naming a tree, plant, or place where plants grow in the second column that best matches the English equivalent of its product in the first column.

1. _____ *artichoke*   a. el pimentero

2. _____ *lemon*   b. el clavero

3. _____ *pepper*   c. el limonero

4. _____ *apricot*   d. el aguacatero

5. _____ *clove*   e. el vivero

6. _____ *seed*   f. el algodonero

7. _____ *lime*   g. el albaricoquero

8. _____ *peach*   h. el semillero

9. _____ *the living*   i. el limero

10. _____ *cotton*   j. el melocotonero

11. _____ *avocado*   k. el alcachofero

The nouns in the following chart end in **-era** and are feminine.

NOUN ENDING IN **-era**	ENGLISH EQUIVALENT	BASE WORD	ENGLISH EQUIVALENT
la avellanera	*hazel tree, filbert tree*	la avellana	*hazelnut, filbert*
la datilera	*date palm tree*	el dátil	*date*
la higuera	*fig tree*	el higo	*fig*
la noguera	*walnut tree*	el nogal	*walnut*
la tomatera	*tomato plant*	el tomate	*tomato*

EJERCICIO
123·2

Choose the noun naming a tree or plant in the second column that best matches the English equivalent of its product in the first column.

1. _____ *date*   a. la noguera

2. _____ *fig*   b. la datilera

3. _____ *hazelnut, filbert*   c. la tomatera

4. _____ *tomato*   d. la higuera

5. _____ *walnut*   e. la avellanera

124 -érrimo/-érrima

MEANING	Superlative
ENGLISH EQUIVALENT	—
PART OF SPEECH	Adjective
GENDER	Masculine/feminine

The suffix **-érrimo** (feminine: **-érrima**) is extremely uncommon and therefore often unrecognized. The suffix has exactly the same function and meaning as the superlative suffix **-ísimo/ -ísima** (No. 31), but it is used with one very strict condition: The final consonant of the base adjective must be **r**. Otherwise, the suffix **-ísimo** is used.

ADJECTIVE ENDING IN **-érrimo**	ENGLISH EQUIVALENT	BASE WORD	ENGLISH EQUIVALENT
acérrimo	*extremely bitter or sour*	acre	*acrid, bitter, sour*
aspérrimo	*extremely rough or harsh*	áspero	*rough, harsh*
celebérrimo	*extremely famous*	célebre	*celebrated, famous*
integérrimo	*most honest or upright*	íntegro	*integral, upright, honest*
libérrimo	*extremely free*	libre	*free, detached*
misérrimo	*extremely miserable*	mísero	*miserable, wretched*
nigérrimo	*extremely black*	negro	*black*

▶

ADJECTIVE ENDING IN **-érrimo**	ENGLISH EQUIVALENT	BASE WORD	ENGLISH EQUIVALENT
paupérrimo	*extremely poor*	pauper [LAT.]	*poor*
salubérrimo	*most salubrious*	salubre	*salubrious, healthy*
ubérrimo	*extremely fertile*	uber [LAT.]	*fertile*

EJERCICIO
124·1

Complete each sentence with the correct form of the appropriate adjective.

1. Los vegetarianos estrictos consideran que su régimen es _____.

2. Esta limonada necesita más azúcar. No puedo beberla porque está

   _____.

3. Beyoncé, George Clooney y Mick Jagger son _____.

4. Cuando el prisionero es liberado después de muchos años tras las rejas, él se siente

   _____ al inhalar el aire fresco.

5. Un chico que no tiene ni un solo centavo es considerado _____.

6. El papel de lija (*sandpaper*) que el carpintero utiliza para alisar madera es

   _____.

7. Una mujer que no tiene ni familia ni esperanza está _____.

8. Un hombre _____ siempre dice la verdad y nunca le miente a nadie.

9. En una zona _____, las plantas producen muchas flores y mucha
   comida.

10. Una noche sin luna ni estrellas está _____.

125 ▸ -esco/-esca

MEANING	Characterized by a manner/style; relating to
ENGLISH EQUIVALENT	*-esque*
PART OF SPEECH	Adjective
GENDER	Masculine/feminine

The suffix **-esco** (feminine: **-esca**) is one of several Spanish suffixes that mean *relating to* or *like*. This adjectival suffix, however, is the strongest, since it often captures the essence (and not just an attribute) of the base noun. This is clearly seen in **quijotesco** and **jemsbondesco**, where the base nouns are the two famous literary characters Don Quixote and James Bond, respectively. Each of these characters is known for a focused set of personality traits. This suffix can be applied to almost any person or thing that evokes specific images and/or feelings.

The following adjectives ending in **-esco/-esca** cover a wide semantic range.

ADJECTIVE ENDING IN **-esco**	ENGLISH EQUIVALENT	BASE WORD	ENGLISH EQUIVALENT
brujesco	*relating to witchcraft*	la bruja	*witch*
bufonesco	*buffoonish, clownish*	el bufón	*buffoon, jester*
caballeresco	*chivalrous, knightly*	el caballero	*gentleman, knight*
carnavalesco	*carnival-like*	el carnaval	*carnival*
gatesco	*feline, catlike*	el gato	*cat*
germanesco	*relating to jargon or slang*	la germanía	*thieves' slang*
gigantesco	*gigantic*	el gigante	*giant*
gitanesco	*gypsy-like, wily, sly*	el gitano	*gypsy*
libresco	*bookish*	el libro	*book*
marinesco	*like a sailor*	el marino	*sailor*
monesco	*like a monkey*	el mono	*monkey*
oficinesco	*bureaucratic, clerical*	la oficina	*office*
pedantesco	*absurdly pedantic*	el pedante	*pedant*
soldadesco	*like a soldier*	el soldado	*soldier*
trovadoresco	*like a troubadour*	el trovador	*troubadour*

EJERCICIO
125·1

Complete each sentence with the correct form of the appropriate adjective.

1. Un chico que es un ratón de biblioteca (*bookworm*) es _____.

2. Un hombre que trata a una mujer como una reina es _____.

3. Un miembro de la fuerza naval es _____.

4. Un hombre que actúa como un miembro del ejército es _____.

5. Una mujer que tiene mucho interés en conjuros y encantamientos es

   _____.

6. Una persona que les informa a todos de sus conocimientos es

   _____.

7. Paul Bunyan, Goliath y el monstruo de Frankenstein son _____.

8. Un chico que actúa como una gorila, un chimpancé o un mono es

   _____.

9. Una chica que actúa como un león, un tigre o un gatito es _____.

10. La palabrería de una persona que siempre usa una jerga común es

   _____.

11. Las celebraciones de Mardi Gras son _____.

12. El payaso de la clase es _____.

13. Los músicos de hoy que imitan el estilo de los músicos de la Edad Media son

   _____.

14. Un funcionario público a quien le encanta trabajar en un cubículo es

    _____.

15. Una persona furtiva, tramposa, engañosa y artera es _____.

The following adjectives ending in **-esco/-esca** describe specific people (real or literary), personality types, and places.

ADJECTIVE ENDING IN **-esco**	ENGLISH EQUIVALENT	BASE WORD	ENGLISH EQUIVALENT
arabesco	*arabesque*	Arabia	*Arabia*
burlesco	*burlesque, funny, comic*	la burla	*joke, hoax*
cervantesco	*in the style of Cervantes*	Cervantes	*(Miguel de) Cervantes*
chinesco	*Chinese, relating to China*	China	*China*
dantesco	*Dantesque, nightmarish*	Dante	*(Alighieri) Dante*
goyesco	*in the style of Goya*	Goya	*(Francisco) Goya*
grotesco	*grotesque*	groso	*coarse*
guitarresco	*relating to the guitar*	la guitarra	*guitar*
jemsbondesco	*like James Bond, glamorous*	James Bond	*James Bond*
picaresco	*roguish, rascally picaresque*	el pícaro	*rogue, sly person*
pintoresco	*picturesque, colorful*	pintura	*painting, picture*
quijotesco	*quixotic, like Don Quixote*	Quijote	*(Don) Quixote*
romanesco	*Roman, Romanesque*	Roma	*Rome*
rufianesco	*villainous, scoundrel-like*	el rufián	*villain, ruffian*
sanchopancesco	*like Sancho Panza, compliant*	Sancho Panza	*Sancho Panza*
truhanesco	*dishonest, crooked*	el truhan	*crook, rogue*
villanesco	*rustic, rude, boorish*	el villano	*villain*

EJERCICIO
125·2

¿Verdadero o falso? *Indicate whether each statement is true or false, using* **V** *for* **verdadero** *true or* **F** *for* **falso** *false.*

1. _____ Los abanicos, las linternas y las serpientes son decoraciones chinescas tradicionales para el Año Nuevo chino.

2. _____ La arquitectura arabesca es muy sencilla y desadornada.

3. _____ En Praga, llamada "la ciudad de oro" o "la ciudad de mil agujas," se encuentran los estilos góticos, romanescos, renacentistas y barrocos.

4. _____ Un libro cervantesco es corto, no-ficción y se ocupa de la historia de México.

5. _____ Un espía muy elegante, atractivo y mujeriego es jemsbondesco.

6. _____ Una persona quijotesca es idealista y está en las nubes.

7. _____ Una pintura goyesca tiene colores oscuros y contenido sombrío.

8. _____ Una escena dantesca es macabra, inquietante y grotesca.

9. _____ Un personaje sanchopancesco es obediente, amistoso y servil.

10. _____ Se encuentran varios pueblos pintorescos en Provenza (Francia) y en la campaña inglesa.

11. _____ Las películas de Mel Brooks y Woody Allen son más burlescas que aquellas de Ismail Merchant y James Ivory.

12. _____ La vihuela mexicana y el charango andina son instrumentos guitarrescos.

13. _____ Los estudiantes truhanescos, rufianescos, picarescos y villanescos siempre son los estudiantes favoritos de cualquier maestro.

126 ▷ -(és)imo/-(és)ima

MEANING	Ordinal number
ENGLISH EQUIVALENT	*-th*
PART OF SPEECH	Adjective
GENDER	Masculine/feminine

The suffix **-(és)imo** (feminine: **-(és)ima**) changes cardinal numbers to ordinal numbers. The base words are Latin roots, with the exception of those signifying one thousand and above. An unusual feature of the shortened suffix **-imo/-ima** is that it may be used as an *infix*, a lexical element inserted into a word, not at the beginning or end (for example, **decimoquinto** *fifteenth*). Most of the adjectives with these suffixes have accents.

To form ordinal numbers in English, *-th* is typically added to the cardinal number (for example, *seven* yields *seventh* and *ten* yields *tenth*). Adjectives with the suffix **-ésimo** or suffix/infix **-imo** mark ordinal numbers in Spanish.

ADJECTIVE ENDING IN **-(és)imo**	ENGLISH EQUIVALENT	BASE WORD	ENGLISH EQUIVALENT
séptimo	*seventh*	septem [LAT.]	*seven*
décimo	*tenth*	decem [LAT.]	*ten*
undécimo	*eleventh*	undecim [LAT.]	*eleven*
duodécimo	*twelfth*	duodecim [LAT.]	*twelve*
decimocuarto	*fourteenth*	decem + quattuor [LAT.]	*fourteen*
decimoquinto	*fifteenth*	decem + quinque [LAT.]	*fifteen*
decimosexto	*sixteenth*	decem + sex [LAT.]	*sixteen*
decimoséptimo	*seventeenth*	decem + septem [LAT.]	*seventeen*
decimoctavo	*eighteenth*	decem + octo [LAT.]	*eighteen*
decimonoveno	*nineteenth*	decem + novem [LAT.]	*nineteen*
vigésimo	*twentieth*	viginti [LAT.]	*twenty*
trigésimo	*thirtieth*	triginta [LAT.]	*thirty*
cuadragésimo	*fortieth*	quadraginta [LAT.]	*forty*
quincuagésimo	*fiftieth*	quinquaginta [LAT.]	*fifty*
sexagésimo	*sixtieth*	sexaginta [LAT.]	*sixty*
septuagésimo	*seventieth*	septuaginta [LAT.]	*seventy*
octogésimo	*eightieth*	octoginta [LAT.]	*eighty*
nonagésimo	*ninetieth*	nonaginta [LAT.]	*ninety*

Provide the correct Spanish adjective for each ordinal number.

1. *10th* _____

2. *20th* _____

3. *50th* _____

4. *7th* _____

5. *17th* _____

6. *18th* _____

7. *12th* _____

8. *14th* _____

9. *16th* _____

10. *40th* _____

11. *60th* _____

12. *80th* _____

13. *11th* _____

14. *15th* _____

15. *19th* _____

16. *30th* _____

17. *70th* _____

18. *90th* _____

ADJECTIVE ENDING IN -(és)imo	ENGLISH EQUIVALENT	BASE WORD	ENGLISH EQUIVALENT
centésimo	*one hundredth*	centum [LAT.]	*one hundred*
ducentésimo	*two hundredth*	ducenti [LAT.]	*two hundred*
tricentésimo	*three hundredth*	trecenti [LAT.]	*three hundred*
cuadringentésimo	*four hundredth*	quadringenti [LAT.]	*four hundred*
quingentésimo	*five hundredth*	quingenti [LAT.]	*five hundred*
sexcentésimo	*six hundredth*	sescenti [LAT.]	*six hundred*
septingentésimo	*seven hundredth*	septingenti [LAT.]	*seven hundred*
octingentésimo	*eight hundredth*	octingenti [LAT.]	*eight hundred*
noningentésimo	*nine hundredth*	nongenti [LAT.]	*nine hundred*
milésimo	*one thousandth*	mil	*one thousand*
dosmilésimo	*two thousandth*	dos mil	*two thousand*
tresmilésimo	*three thousandth*	tres mil	*three thousand*
millonésimo	*millionth*	millón	*million*
milmillonésimo	*billionth*	mil millones	*billion*
billonésimo	*trillionth*	billón	*trillion*

Provide the correct Spanish adjective for each ordinal number.

1. *100th*　　　　_____

2. *500th*　　　　_____

3. *1,000th*　　　_____

4. *1,000,000th*　_____

5. *1,000,000,000th*　_____

6. *1,000,000,000,000th*　_____

7. *200th*　　　　_____

8. *400th*　　　　_____

9. *600th*　　　　_____

10. *800th*　　　_____

11. *300th*　　　_____

12. *700th*　　　_____

13. *900th*　　　_____

14. *2,000th*　　_____

15. *3,000th*　　_____

127 ▸ -ez

MEANING	State; abstract concept
ENGLISH EQUIVALENT	*-ity, -ness*
PART OF SPEECH	Noun
GENDER	Feminine

The suffix **-ez** denotes a state or abstract quality relating to the base word, which is nearly always an adjective. Generally, if the base word ends in a vowel, the vowel is omitted before the suffix is added; if the base word ends in a consonant, the suffix is added directly to the base word. A related suffix, **-eza** (No. 21), is similar in meaning.

The following nouns ending in **-ez** generally represent color, age, or mental state.

NOUN ENDING IN -ez	ENGLISH EQUIVALENT	BASE WORD	ENGLISH EQUIVALENT
la adultez	*adulthood*	adulto	*adult*
la amarillez	*yellowness (body)*	amarillo	*yellow*
la estupidez	*stupidity*	estúpido	*stupid*
la languidez	*listlessness, disinterest*	lánguido	*languid*
la lucidez	*lucidity, clarity*	lúcido	*lucid*
la madurez	*maturity, ripeness*	maduro	*mature, ripe*
la mentecatez	*dim-wittedness*	mentecato	*simple, foolish*
la muchachez	*childhood, boyhood*	el muchacho	*boy, lad*
la niñez	*childhood, infancy*	niño	*young*
la rojez	*redness*	rojo	*red*
la salvajez	*savagery, the wild*	salvaje	*savage, barbarous*
la sensatez	*good sense, wisdom*	sensato	*sensible, level-headed*
la timidez	*timidity, shyness*	tímido	*timid, shy*
la vejez	*old age*	viejo	*old*

EJERCICIO 127·1

Complete each sentence with the correct form of the appropriate noun(s).

1. Un síntoma de la vergüenza es la _____ facial.

2. Un síntoma de la ictericia (*jaundice*), es la _____ de la piel.

3. Un bebé típicamente pasa los primeros meses de su _____ casi exclusivamente con su madre y padre.

4. Tom Sawyer, el protagonista de la novela clásica de Mark Twain, *Las aventuras de Tom Sawyer,* pasa su _____ en la ciudad ficticia de St. Petersburg, Missouri.

5. Un signo importante de la _____ es la habilidad de posponer las recompensas.

6. La adolescencia es un tiempo del paso complicado de la niñez a la

   _____ .

7. La mayoría de las personas quieren vivir hasta la _____ .

8. Un buen juez necesita una combinación de la _____ y la

   _____ para tomar decisiones con justicia y misericordia.

9. Un niño que crece en la _____ casi siempre va a tener problemas sociales al llegar a la adultez.

10. La curiosidad es antónimo de la _____ .

11. Muchos adultos sientan _____ al hablar ante una audiencia.

12. La necedad y la tontería, junto con la _____ y la

    _____ , son como una sentencia de muerte al solicitar ingreso a una universidad.

The following nouns ending in **-ez** generally represent a physical state, physical surroundings, or a miscellaneous quality.

NOUN ENDING IN **-ez**	ENGLISH EQUIVALENT	BASE WORD	ENGLISH EQUIVALENT
la aridez	*dryness, aridness*	árido	*dry, arid*
la delgadez	*slenderness, slimness*	delgado	*thin, slim, slender*
la escasez	*scarcity*	escaso	*scarce*
la flacidez	*flabbiness, flaccidity*	flácido	*flaccid, flabby*
la lobreguez	*darkness, gloominess*	lóbrego	*dark, gloomy*
la marchitez	*withered state, fading condition*	marchito	*withered, faded*
la nitidez	*sharpness, clarity*	nítido	*sharp, clear, precise*
la pequeñez	*smallness, littleness*	pequeño	*small, little*
la pesadez	*heaviness, sluggishness*	pesado	*heavy, sluggish*
la putridez	*rottenness*	pútrido	*putrid, rotten*
la rapidez	*rapidity, swiftness, speed*	rápido	*rapid, swift, fast*
la robustez	*robustness, ruggedness*	robusto	*robust, hardy*
la sencillez	*simplicity*	sencillo	*simple*
la validez	*validity*	válido	*valid*

EJERCICIO

127·2

¿En qué se destaca? *What's this noted for?* *Provide the correct noun for each description.*

1. Una tonelada de ladrillos se destaca por su _____.

2. Las supermodelos se destacan por su _____.

3. Un buen examen se destaca por su _____.

4. Una persona obesa se destaca por su _____.

5. El desierto del Sahara se destaca por su _____.

6. El átomo se destaca por su _____.

7. El olor de un huevo viejo se destaca por su _____.

8. En el otoño, las hojas de muchos árboles se destacan por su _____.

9. La chita se destaca por su _____.

10. Un hombre muy macho se destaca por su _____.

11. El desierto de Atacama es el desierto más árido del planeta y se destaca por su

    _____ de agua.

12. De los tres órdenes arquitectónicos clásicos (dórico, jónico y corintio), el orden dórico es

    el más primitivo y menos orientado y se destaca por su _____.

13. El nombre "Debbie Downer" o "Danny Downer" se refiere a una persona que se destaca por su perspectiva de miseria, desolación y _____.

14. Las mejores televisiones digitales se destacan por su _____.

 **-icia**

MEANING	State; abstract concept
ENGLISH EQUIVALENT	*-ice*
PART OF SPEECH	Noun
GENDER	Feminine

The suffix **-icia** denotes a state or abstract quality. Base words may be verbs or adjectives and may derive from Latin or Greek roots. Some of the suffixed words occupy a relatively high register and are, therefore, not frequently used.

NOUN ENDING IN **-icia**	ENGLISH EQUIVALENT	BASE WORD	ENGLISH EQUIVALENT
la ardicia	*ardent desire for something*	arder	*to burn*
la avaricia	*avarice*	avaro	*avaricious, miserly*
la blandicia	*flattery, adulation*	blando	*soft, indulgent, easy-going*
la caricia	*caress*	acariciar	*to stroke, caress*
la estulticia	*stupidity, folly*	estulto	*stupid, foolish*
la ictericia	*jaundice*	ikteros [GRK.]	*jaundice*
la impericia	*lack of skill*	im- + peritia [LAT.]	*not + skill*
la impudicia	*immodesty, shamelessness*	im- + pudicus [LAT.]	*not + chaste, not + modest*

EJERCICIO
128·1

Sinónimos *Provide the noun that is related to each group of words. Include its article.*

1. la estupidez, la tontería, la idiotez _____

2. la incompetencia, la ineptitud, la incapacidad _____

3. el cariño, el contacto, el toque _____

4. la codicia, la tacañería, la cicatería _____

5. la indecencia, la impureza, la desvergüenza _____

6. la biliosidad, la piel amarillenta _____

7. la adulación, el halago, la coba _____

8. el deseo, el anhelo, la ansia _____

NOUN ENDING IN -icia	ENGLISH EQUIVALENT	BASE WORD	ENGLISH EQUIVALENT
la injusticia	*injustice*	in- + justo	*not + just*
la inmundicia	*dirt, filth*	inmundo	*filthy, dirty*
la justicia	*justice*	justo	*fair, just, right*
la malicia	*malice, perversity*	malo	*bad*
la mesticia	*affliction, sadness, sorrow*	maestitia [LAT.]	*sadness, sorrow*
la noticia	*piece of news*	la nota	*note*
la pericia	*skill, knowledge, expertise*	peritia [LAT.]	*skill*
la primicia	*novelty, scoop*	primo	*prime, first*
la pudicia	*virtuous, honest*	pudicus [LAT.]	*chaste, modest, pure*

Sinónimos *Provide the noun that is related to each group of words. Include its article.*

1. la melancolía, la tristeza, el desconsuelo _____

2. la jurisprudencia, la equidad, la imparcialidad _____

3. la parcialidad, el abuso, el improcedencia _____

4. la malignidad, la perversidad, la ruindad _____

5. el anuncio, el informe, la comunicación _____

6. la exclusividad, la novedad, la exclusiva _____

7. la virtud, la honradez, la honestidad _____

8. la competencia, la aptitud, la habilidad _____

9. la suciedad, la porquería, la mugre _____

129 ▶ -ido

MEANING	Action, result/recipient of an action; sound
ENGLISH EQUIVALENT	—
PART OF SPEECH	Noun
GENDER	Masculine

Nouns with the suffix **-ido** are derived from verbs and have much the same meaning as a related suffix, **-ida** (No. 81). Both suffixes denote an action or the result of an action. However, **-ido** is unique in that it is the suffix of choice in naming sounds, in particular those made by animals.

The following nouns ending in **-ido** represent specific sounds, often made by an animal.

NOUN ENDING IN **-ido**	ENGLISH EQUIVALENT	BASE WORD	ENGLISH EQUIVALENT
el aullido	*howl, call of distress*	aullar	*to howl*
el chillido	*scream, shriek*	chillar	*to scream, shriek*
el crujido	*creak, crackle, rustle*	crujir	*to rustle, creak, rustle*
el gruñido	*growl, pig grunt*	gruñir	*to grunt, growl*
el ladrido	*bark*	ladrar	*to bark*
el maullido	*mew, meow*	maullar	*to mew, meow*
el mugido	*moo, mooing*	mugir	*to moo*
el resoplido	*puffing, pant, snort*	resoplar	*to puff, pant*
el roznido	*braying*	roznar	*to bray*
el rugido	*roar*	rugir	*to roar*
el silbido	*whistle, boo (theater)*	silbar	*to whistle, boo*
el sonido	*sound, ring (telephone)*	sonar	*to sound, ring*
el tañido	*strumming (guitar), ring (bell)*	tañer	*to strum, ring*
el tronido	*thunderclap*	tronar	*to thunder*
el zumbido	*buzz, buzzing*	zumbar	*to buzz*

EJERCICIO
129·1

Provide the correct noun (including its article) for the sound produced by each animal or thing mentioned.

1. el perro _____

2. la vaca _____

3. la abeja _____

4. el burro _____

5. el gato _____

6. el león _____

7. el cerdo _____

8. la guitarra _____

9. las hojas en el árbol _____

10. una mujer débil al descubrir un ratón en la casa _____

11. la tormenta eléctrica _____

12. el velocista después de una carrera de cien metros _____

13. un miembro de la audiencia de un drama terrible _____

14. el teléfono _____

15. la dama (*damsel*) en apuros _____

The following nouns ending in **-ido** do not represent sounds. Several of these nouns represent people and thus have both masculine (**-ido**) and feminine (**-ida**) forms.

NOUN ENDING IN **-ido**	ENGLISH EQUIVALENT	BASE WORD	ENGLISH EQUIVALENT
el aparecido	*ghost, specter*	aparecer	*to appear, show up*
el apellido	*surname, last name*	apellidar	*to name, call*
el cocido	*stew*	cocer	*to cook, boil, bake*
el contenido	*contents*	contener	*to contain, comprise*
el desagradecido	*ungrateful person*	desagradecer	*to be ungrateful*
el herido	*injured or hurt person*	herir	*to injure, hurt, wound*
el marido	*married man, husband*	maridar	*to marry*
el mordido	*person bitten*	morder	*to bite*
el nacido	*living human being*	nacer	*to be born*
el oído	*ear (interior)*	oír	*to hear*
el pedido	*commercial order, request*	pedir	*to order, request, ask for*
el prometido	*fiancé, betrothed*	prometer	*to promise*
el sentido	*sense*	sentir	*to sense, feel*
el vestido	*dress, garments, clothing*	vestir	*to dress*

EJERCICIO
129·2

Complete each sentence with the correct form of the appropriate noun.

1. Los cinco _____ son el oído, el gusto, el tacto, el olfato y la vista.

2. Un sinónimo para "el fantasma" es el _____.

3. Durante los meses antes del veintinueve de abril, 2011, el príncipe William era el

   _____ de Kate Middleton.

4. Desde del veintinueve de abril, 2011, el príncipe William es el _____
   de Catalina, la duquesa de Cambridge.

5. El _____ del príncipe William es Mountbatten-Windsor.

6. Para la boda, Catalina, la duquesa de Cambridge llevó un _____
   diseñado por Sarah Burton, la directora creativa de la marca Alexander McQueen.

7. Un _____ absolutamente nunca le dice "gracias" a nadie.

8. Cuando un perro con la rabia muerde a un hombre, el _____
   necesita una serie de inyecciones diarias de vacuna antirrábica.

9. Los ingredientes de un _____ básico incluyen los vegetales (como
   las zanahorias, las patatas, los guisantes y los frijoles) y trozos de carne de ganado, de
   pollo, de frutos de mar o de pescado cocinados en una olla.

10. El tinnitus consiste en notar un sonido o un zumbido en el _____
    y es causado por una infección.

11. Un bebé es considerado como un recién _____ en las primeras
    semanas de la vida.

12. La responsabilidad básica de una cajera en McDonald's es simplemente tomar el

_____, cobrar el dinero del cliente y tener cambio disponible para darle el vuelto.

13. Cuidado con lo que subes a Internet: El _____ de tus mensajes y fotos, si te gusta esto o no, es la propiedad del mundo.

14. Después de ser atracado y golpeado violentamente, _____ sufre frecuentemente del trastorno por estrés postraumático.

 130 ## -iego/-iega

MEANING	Relating to, like; fond of
ENGLISH EQUIVALENT	—
PART OF SPEECH	Adjective
GENDER	Masculine/feminine

Like several other adjectival suffixes, the relatively uncommon suffix **-iego** (feminine: **-iega**) means *relating to* or *like*. This suffix may also mean *fond of* (for example, **mujeriego** *fond of women, womanizing*). If the base word's last consonant is **ñ**, the **i** of the suffix is omitted for purposes of assimilation (for example, **el rebaño** *flock, herd* yields **rebañego** *sheeplike, easily led*). Several of these suffixed adjectives are very specific; this means that they are not often used—but when they are, they pack an impressive punch.

ADJECTIVE ENDING IN -iego	ENGLISH EQUIVALENT	BASE WORD	ENGLISH EQUIVALENT
andariego	*fond of travelling, restless*	el andar	*gait, walk*
asperiego	*sour (like a tart apple)*	áspero	*sour*
moriego	*Moorish*	el moro	*Moor*
mujeriego	*fond of women, womanizing*	la mujer	*woman*
nocherniego	*nocturnal, like a night owl*	la noche	*night*
palaciego	*of the palace/court*	el palacio	*palace*
paniego	*bread-loving*	el pan	*bread*
pinariego	*relating to pines*	el pino	*pine tree*
veraniego	*relating to summer*	el verano	*summer*

EJERCICIO
130·1

Complete each sentence with the correct form of the appropriate adjective.

1. El nómada es _____.

2. Hugh Hefner refleja el estilo de vida _____.

3. Una persona adicta a los carbohidratos es _____.

4. Las manzanas como la Granny Smith son _____.

5. A finales de mayo, la mayoría de los estudiantes en las escuelas primarias y secundarias esperan con impaciencia el descanso _____.

6. Las personas que venden árboles de Navidad trabajan en la industria

_____.

7. La Alhambra es una fortaleza originalmente construida en 899. Con sus varios edificios y palacios, es un rico complejo _____.

8. La Alhambra es uno de los mejores ejemplos de la arquitectura _____.

9. El murciélago, el ratón, la luciérnaga y el mapache son animales

_____.

ADJECTIVE ENDING IN -iego	ENGLISH EQUIVALENT	BASE WORD	ENGLISH EQUIVALENT
aldeaniego	*relating to a village, rustic*	la aldea	*small village*
alijariego	*relating to wastelands*	el alijar	*uncultivated ground*
cadañego	*perennial, yearly (plant)*	cada + año	*each + year*
palomariega	*relating to domestic pigeons*	la paloma	*pigeon, dove*
piariego	*owning a herd of pigs or mules*	la piara	*herd of swine, mules*
rapiego	*rapacious, ravenous*	rapar	*to shave, shave close*
rebañego	*sheeplike, easily led*	el rebaño	*flock, herd*
riberiego	*grazing on the banks of rivers*	la ribera	*riverbank*
serraniego	*relating to a mountain range*	la sierra	*mountain range*
solariego	*ancestral, of the manor house*	el solar	*ancestral home*

EJERCICIO
130·2

¿**Verdadero o falso?** *Indicate whether each statement is true or false, using* **V** *for* **verdadero** *true or* **F** *for* **falso** *false.*

1. _____ Highclere Castle, la casa solariega de la familia Herbert, Condes de Carnarvon, es utilizado para rodar la serie británica *Downton Abbey*.

2. _____ Las plantas que florecen año tras año son cadañegas.

3. _____ El centro de Paris es alijariego.

4. _____ Los miembros de un culto son rebañegos.

5. _____ Los pájaros en el Parque Central de Nueva York son palomas palomariegas.

6. _____ El centro de Tokio es aldeaniego.

7. _____ Una persona rapiega quiere intensamente tenerlo todo.

8. _____ El Mar Muerto, situado a 416.5 metros bajo el nivel del mar entre Israel, Cisjordania y Jordania, es serraniego.

9. _____ Los animales riberiegos pastan por la orilla del río.

10. _____ Una mujer que tiene cerdos y mulas es piariega.

131 ▶ -iento/-ienta

MEANING	Possessing a human characteristic/condition
ENGLISH EQUIVALENT	—
PART OF SPEECH	Adjective
GENDER	Masculine/feminine

The Spanish suffix **-iento/-ienta** has roughly the semantic range of the English suffixes *-ish* and *-y*. The suffix denotes that a human being or an object possesses a particular characteristic, state, or condition of the base noun.

The following adjectives with the suffix **-iento** refer to human characteristics or conditions; for adjectives with the suffix **-iento** that refer to characteristics of objects, see No. 132.

ADJECTIVE ENDING IN **-iento**	ENGLISH EQUIVALENT	BASE WORD	ENGLISH EQUIVALENT
achaquiento	*frail, chronically ill*	el achaque	*ailment*
alharaquiento	*demonstrative, highly emotional*	la alharaca	*overreaction*
avariento	*avaricious, miserly*	el avaro	*miser*
calenturiento	*feverish*	la calentura	*fever*
camariento	*troubled with diarrhea*	la cámara	*stool*
catarriento	*afflicted with a cold*	el catarro	*cold (illness)*
gargajiento	*spitting frequently*	el gargajo	*spit*
granujiento	*pimply*	el granujo [COLLOQ.]	*pimple*
guiñapiento	*ragged, tattered*	el guiñapo	*rag, tatter*
hambriento	*hungry, starving*	el hambre	*hunger*
harapiento	*ragged, tattered*	el harapo	*rag, tatter*
soñoliento	*sleepy, drowsy*	el sueño	*dream, sleep*
sudoriento	*sweaty*	el sudor	*sweat, perspiration*
trapiento	*raggedy, in rags*	el trapo	*rag*
zancajiento	*bowlegged*	la zanca	*shank, long leg*

EJERCICIO
131·1

Provide the correct form of the appropriate adjective(s) to describe the people mentioned in each item.

1. un chico con una superabundancia de saliva, a quien le gusta escupir en todas direcciones   _____

2. una mujer que no ha dormido en veinticuatro horas   _____

3. los vaqueros, después de montar a caballo día tras día tras día   _____

4. un hombre muy tacaño que no quiere compartir nada con nadie   _____

5. dos muchachas que tienen fiebre   _____

6. una persona que expresa con gran vehemencia sus sentimientos   _____

7. un muchacho que tiene dolor de cabeza y de garganta y que estornuda mucho   _____

8. los adolescentes afligidos del acné _____

9. un prisionero que no come nada por tres días _____

10. una mujer, con frecuencia muy vieja, que sufre de la indisposición o dolencia crónica _____

11. un atleta que trabaja duro y no usa el antitranspirante _____

12. la condición típica de la ropa de un mendigo o de las personas muy pobres y sin hogar _____

_____

13. una condición de la enfermedad gastrointestinal _____

132 ▸ -iento/-ienta

MEANING	Relating to, like; possessing a characteristic
ENGLISH EQUIVALENT	*-ish, -y*
PART OF SPEECH	Adjective
GENDER	Masculine/feminine

The Spanish suffix **-iento/-ienta** has roughly the semantic range of the English suffixes *-ish* and *-y*. The suffix denotes that a human being or an object possesses a particular characteristic, state, or condition of the base noun. Some of the suffixed adjectives reflect a less pleasant side of life (for example, **holliniento** *sooty*), that is, they describe "icky" things. Note that the **i** of **-iento** is omitted for ease of pronunciation if the last consonant of the base word is **ll** (for example, **amarillento** *yellowish*, from **el amarillo** *the color yellow*).

The following adjectives with the suffix **-iento** refer to characteristics of objects; for adjectives with the suffix **-iento** that refer to human characteristics or conditions, see No. 131.

ADJECTIVE ENDING IN -iento	ENGLISH EQUIVALENT	BASE WORD	ENGLISH EQUIVALENT
amarillento	*yellowish*	el amarillo	*the color yellow*
cascarriento	*dirty, filthy*	la cascarria	*dirt, filth*
ceniciento	*ashen, ash-gray*	la ceniza	*ash*
ferrugiento	*ferrous, containing iron*	el fierro [LAT. AM.]	*iron*
grasiento	*greasy, oily*	la grasa	*grease, fat*
gusaniento	*worm-eaten, maggot-ridden*	el gusano	*worm, maggot*
herrugiento	*ferrous, containing iron*	el hierro	*iron*
holliniento	*sooty*	el hollín	*soot*
mugriento	*filthy, grimy*	la mugre	*filth, grime*
oriniento	*rusty*	el orín	*rust*
pizmiento	*pitch-colored*	la pez	*pitch, tar*
polvoriento	*dusty*	el polvo	*dust*
sangriento	*bloody, blood-stained*	la sangre	*blood*
zarriento	*spattered with mud*	la zarria	*splash of mud*
zumiento	*juicy*	el zumo	*juice*

Provide the correct form of the appropriate adjective(s) for each description.

1. el interior de una chimenea sucia   _____

2. la superficie de las cosas ignoradas por muchos años en el desván   _____

3. el escenario del crimen después de un ataque con una navaja   _____

4. la condición de un coche viejo que ha estado muchos años afuera en el tiempo lluvioso

   _____

   _____

   _____

5. la condición de la carcasa (el cuerpo de un animal muerto) cuando hace calor y es muy húmedo   _____

6. la condición de los zapatos de una persona que se mete en un charco de barro   _____

7. el suelo sucio en una casa abandonada   _____

   _____

8. la naranja, la toronja, el limón, el melocotón y las uvas   _____

9. la piel de una persona que sufre de la ictericia   _____

10. el pelo de una persona que no lo ha lavado desde hace un mes   _____

11. el polvo de origen volcánico   _____

133 ▸ -ino/-ina

MEANING	Relating to, like; citizen, native
ENGLISH EQUIVALENT	*-ine*
PART OF SPEECH	Adjective, noun
GENDER	Masculine/feminine

The suffix **-ino** (feminine: **-ina**) means *relating to* and *like*; it also denotes geographical origin. Like words with other suffixes denoting origin (see also No. 7, **-ano/-ana**, No. 72, **-eño/-eña**, No. 75, **-és/-esa**, and No. 119, **-ense**)—words with the suffix **-ino** may function both as adjectives and as nouns: **El florentino sirve café argentino a la neoyorquina** *The man from Florence serves Argentine coffee to the (female) New Yorker.* Unlike English, Spanish does not capitalize words denoting origin.

The following words ending in -**ino**/-**ina** function only as adjectives.

ADJECTIVE ENDING IN -**ino**	ENGLISH EQUIVALENT	BASE WORD	ENGLISH EQUIVALENT
alpino	*Alpine*	los Alpes	*the Alps*
ambarino	*relating to amber*	el ámbar	*amber*
azulino	*bluish*	azul	*blue*
blanquecino	*off-white, whitish*	blanco	*white*
canino	*canine, relating to dogs*	canis [LAT.]	*dog*
cedrino	*made of or relating to cedar*	el cedro	*cedar*
corderino	*resembling or relating to lambs*	el cordero	*lamb*
cristalino	*crystalline*	el cristal	*crystal*
dañino	*harmful, noxious*	el daño	*damage, harm*
elefantino	*elephantine, huge*	el elefante	*elephant*
esmeraldino	*green (like an emerald)*	la esmeralda	*emerald*
ferino	*wild, savage*	fera [LAT.]	*wild animal*
mortecino	*dying, faint*	la muerte	*death*
purpurino	*purplish*	la púrpura	*the color purple*
repentino	*sudden*	el repente	*sudden movement, start*
septembrino	*relating to September*	septiembre	*September*
serpentino	*serpentine, winding, snakelike*	la serpiente	*serpent, snake*
zucarino	*sugary*	el azúcar	*sugar*

Complete each sentence with the correct form of the appropriate adjective.

1. Algo del color del cielo claro es _____.

2. Algo del color verde brillante es _____.

3. Algo absolutamente enorme es _____.

4. Algo muy dulce es _____.

5. Algo de vidrio muy frágil es _____.

6. Algo venenoso o tóxico es _____.

7. Un animal que ladra es _____.

8. El vestido de novia es frecuentemente _____.

9. Algo como una culebra es _____.

10. Mucha madera de Líbano es _____.

11. Un animal silvestre y salvaje es _____.

12. Las túnicas reales (del rey y de la reina) son _____.

13. Las montañas entre Austria y Francia son _____.

14. Al fin del día se ve el sol _____.

15. La lana de una oveja joven es _____.

16. Para casi toda persona, el terremoto es un choque _____.

17. La miel es de color _____.

18. Cuando hace fresco y las hojas caen de los árboles, se puede decir que es

_____.

The following words ending in **-ino/-ina** may function both as adjectives and as nouns.

ADJECTIVE/NOUN ENDING IN **-ino**	ENGLISH EQUIVALENT	BASE WORD	ENGLISH EQUIVALENT
(el) andino	*Andean, native of the Andes*	los Andes	*the Andes*
(el) argelino	*Algerian*	Argelia	*Algiers*
(el) argentino	*Argentine, Argentinian*	Argentina	*Argentina*
(el) campesino	*of the country, peasant*	el campo	*country, countryside*
(el) florentino	*Florentine, native of Florence*	Florencia	*Florence*
(el) granadino	*(native) of Granada*	Granada	*Granada*
(el) neoyorquino	*of New York, New Yorker*	Nueva York	*New York*
(el) salmantino	*(native) of Salamanca*	Salamanca	*Salamanca*
(el) santiaguino	*(native) of Santiago*	Santiago	*Santiago*
(el) tangerino	*(native) of Tangiers*	Tánger	*Tangier*
(el) tunecino	*Tunisian*	Túnez	*Tunisia, Tunis*

EJERCICIO
133·2

Complete each sentence with the correct form of the appropriate adjective.

1. Un nativo de la capital de Chile es _____.

2. Una nativa de Buenos Aires es _____.

3. Los nativos de Brooklyn y Manhattan son _____.

4. Una nativa de la ciudad en Italia que es la capital de la región de Toscana es

_____.

5. Un nativo de la capital de la provincia de Andalucía donde está situada La Alhambra es

_____.

6. Las nativas de Argel, la capital de Argelia, son _____.

7. Los nativos de la capital del país más pequeño de África del Norte son

_____.

8. Un nativo de la ciudad española que alberga la universidad más antigua de España es

_____.

9. La nativa de una ciudad en el norte de Marruecos es _____.

10. Los nativos de la cadena de montañas de América del Sur que atraviesa Argentina, Bolivia,

Chile, Colombia, Ecuador, Perú y parte de Venezuela son _____.

11. Los nativos de áreas rurales y lugares apartados son de origen

_____.

134 -isco/-isca

MEANING	Relating to, like; result of an action
ENGLISH EQUIVALENT	—
PART OF SPEECH	Adjective, noun
GENDER	Masculine (-isco); feminine (-isca)

An adjective with the uncommon suffix **-isco/-isca** denotes a person or thing that possesses a characteristic of the base word. A noun with this suffix denotes the result of the base verb's action. Since a suffixed noun may be masculine (**-isco**) or feminine (**-isca**), its form and gender must be memorized.

ADJECTIVE/NOUN ENDING IN **-isco/-isca**	ENGLISH EQUIVALENT	BASE WORD	ENGLISH EQUIVALENT
alemanisco	*Germanic, made in Germany*	Alemania	*Germany*
la arenisca	*sandstone*	la arena	*sand*
arisco	*unfriendly, surly*	ariscarse	*to make suspicious*
jalisco [COLLOQ.]	*plastered, stoned*	jalar [COLLOQ.]	*to guzzle, to get drunk*
levantisco	*restless, turbulent*	Levante	*easterly wind of the Mediterranean Sea*
el mordisco	*bite, love bite, hickey*	morder	*to bite*
morisco	*Moorish*	el moro	*Moor*
olisco	*smelly, stinky*	el olor	*odor*
el pedrisco	*hail, hailstone*	apedrear	*to stone, throw stones at*
la ventisca	*strong wind, snowstorm*	el viento	*wind*

EJERCICIO
134·1

Complete each sentence with the correct form of the appropriate noun or adjective.

1. Un hombre antisocial frecuentemente está _____.

2. Los calcetines sucios de un atleta están _____.

3. La palabra española para *sandstone* es la _____.

4. Algo hecho en Berlín, Múnich, Hamburgo o Fráncfort es _____.

5. La Alhambra, que está situada en Granada, España, es un ejemplo magnífico de la

arquitectura _____.

6. Un disturbio social o político siempre comienza con una multitud

_____.

7. Después de tomar media botella de tequila, un hombre está _____.

8. A veces los adolescentes amorosos se dan un _____ en las horas de la noche.

9. Los _____ pueden causar mucho daño en el techo de un coche o una casa.

10. Es peligroso conducir un coche durante una _____.

◆135◆ -itis

MEANING	Inflammation
ENGLISH EQUIVALENT	-itis
PART OF SPEECH	Noun
GENDER	Feminine

Words with the suffix **-itis** are usually medical words that indicate inflammation of the base word. Since nearly all of these Spanish words have English cognates ending in *-itis*, they are easily recognized and used. Many of the base words are Greek roots.

The following nouns ending in **-itis** represent common conditions.

NOUN ENDING IN **-itis**	ENGLISH EQUIVALENT	BASE WORD	ENGLISH EQUIVALENT
la amigdalitis	*tonsillitis*	la amígdala	*tonsil*
la apendicitis	*appendicitis*	el apéndice	*appendix*
la artritis	*arthritis*	arthron [GRK.]	*joint*
la bronquitis	*bronchitis*	bronchos [GRK.]	*windpipe*
la celulitis	*cellulitis*	la célula	*cell, cellule*
la conjuntivitis	*conjunctivitis*	la conjuntiva	*conjunctiva*
la gastritis	*gastritis*	gaster [GRK.]	*belly*
la gingivitis	*gingivitis*	gingiva [LAT.]	*gums*
la hepatitis	*hepatitis*	hepar [GRK.]	*liver*
la laringitis	*laryngitis*	la laringe	*larynx*
la nefritis	*nephritis*	nephros [GRK.]	*kidney*
la otitis	*otitis*	ous/otos [GRK.]	*ear*
la rinitis	*rhinitis*	rhis/rhinos [GRK.]	*nose*
la tendinitis	*tendonitis*	el tendón	*tendon*
la timpanitis	*tympanitis*	tympanon [GRK.]	*drum*

EJERCICIO

135·1

Provide the correct noun(s) (including the article) to name the correct diagnosis or diagnoses for each set of symptoms listed.

1. congestión nasal, nariz mocosa, estornudos _____

2. dolor recurrente o crónico de la garganta _____

3. dificultades del habla, ronquera _____

4. inflamación del oído medio _____

5. pus en el ojo, el ojo rosado _____

6. encías hinchadas, halitosis _____

7. indigestión o acidez estomacal _____

8. dolores y deformidad de las articulaciones _____

9. pérdida del apetito, fatiga, fiebre leve, posible inflamación del hígado _____

10. sangre en la orina, nausea y vómitos, aumento o disminución en la producción de orina, problemas con los riñones _____

11. tos persistente que produce moco, molestia en el pecho, fatiga, fiebre leve _____

12. dolor y sensibilidad, especialmente con el movimiento o la actividad, frecuentemente en el manguito rotatorio, cerca de la rodilla o en la articulación del tobillo _____

13. dolor abdominal, fiebre, escalofríos, estreñimiento, diarrea, nauseas, vómitos, temblores, dolor en la espalda _____

14. enrojecimiento de la piel, inflamación y sensibilidad, a veces fiebre, escalofríos y/o inflamación de los ganglios linfáticos _____

NOUN ENDING IN **-itis**	ENGLISH EQUIVALENT	BASE WORD	ENGLISH EQUIVALENT
la colitis	*colitis*	el colon	*colon*
la dermatitis	*dermatitis*	la dermis	*dermis, layer of skin*
la encefalitis	*encephalitis*	enkephalos [GRK.]	*brain*
la estomatitis	*stomatitis*	stoma [GRK.]	*mouth*
la flebitis	*phlebitis*	phleps [GRK.]	*vein*
la glositis	*glossitis*	glossa [GRK.]	*tongue*
la meningitis	*meningitis*	meninx [GRK.]	*membrane*
la neuritis	*neuritis*	neuron [GRK.]	*nerve*
la oftalmitas	*opthalmitis*	ophthalmos [GRK.]	*eye*
la pancreatitis	*pancreatitis*	el páncreas	*pancreas*

▶

NOUN ENDING IN **-itis**	ENGLISH EQUIVALENT	BASE WORD	ENGLISH EQUIVALENT
◀ la pericarditis	*pericarditis*	peri + kardia [GRK.]	*around + heart*
la queratitis	*inflammation of the cornea*	keras [GRK.]	*horn*
la vaginitis	*vaginitis*	la vagina	*vagina*

◆ EJERCICIO
135·2

¡Juguemos al doctor! *Provide the correct noun(s) (including the article) for the diagnosis or diagnoses that each doctor named would make.*

1. el dermatólogo _____

2. el cardiólogo _____

3. el ginecólogo _____

4. el oftalmólogo _____

   _____

5. el otorrinolaringólogo _____

   _____

6. el gastroenterólogo _____

   _____

7. el internista _____

8. el neurólogo _____

   _____

   _____

136 ◆ -ito/-ita

MEANING	Chemical, mineral
ENGLISH EQUIVALENT	*-ite*
PART OF SPEECH	Noun
GENDER	Masculine/feminine

Chemists and geologists, this one's for you! The suffix **-ito/-ita** is commonly used to form the names of chemicals and minerals. Most of the base nouns are of Latin and Greek origin. There is no obvious explanation why some of these nouns end in **-ito** and are masculine, while others end in **-ita** and are feminine.

NOUN ENDING IN -ito/-ita	ENGLISH EQUIVALENT	BASE WORD	ENGLISH EQUIVALENT
el acónito	*aconite (poisonous plant)*	aconit [FR.]	*aconite*
la amonita	*ammonite, fossil mollusk*	Ammonis [LAT.]	*horn of Ammon*
el arsenito	*arsenite, salt of arsenious acid*	arsenicon [GRK.]	*arsenic*
la bauxita	*bauxite (aluminum ore)*	bauxite [FR.]	*bauxite*
la dinamita	*dynamite*	dynamis [GRK.]	*power*
la estalactita	*stalactite*	stalaktos [GRK.]	*dripping*
la estalagmita	*stalagmite*	stalagmos [GRK.]	*a dropping*
el grafito	*graphite*	graphein [GRK.]	*to write*
el granito	*granite*	el grano	*grain*
la hematita	*hematite*	haima [GRK.]	*blood*
el meteorito	*meteorite*	el meteoro	*meteor*
el nitrito	*nitrite*	nitron [GRK.]	*sodium carbonate*
la pirita	*pyrite*	pyrites lithos [GRK.]	*stone of fire, flint*
la saponita	*soapstone*	sapo [LAT.]	*soap*
el sulfito	*salt from sulfurous acid*	sulfur [LAT.]	*sulfur*

EJERCICIO

136·1

Provide the correct noun (including its article) for each description.

1. el interior de un lápiz común _____

2. un material popular para las superficies de la cocina _____

3. un material explosivo similar a TNT _____

4. una masa de materia que cae a la superficie de la Tierra desde el espacio exterior _____

5. un material con la raíz etimológica del fuego _____

6. un material con la raíz etimológica de la sangre _____

7. un silicato con una masa jabonosa _____

8. un ácido con la raíz etimológica del arsénico _____

9. la concreción calcárea que cuelga del techo de las cavernas _____

10. la concreción calcárea que nace en el suelo de las cavernas, con la punta hacia arriba _____

11. el éster del ácido nitroso _____

12. la base de hidrato de alúmina _____

13. una planta venenosa _____

14. el fósil del molusco _____

15. un ácido con la raíz etimológica del azufre _____

137 ◆ -itud

MEANING	State, condition
ENGLISH EQUIVALENT	*-tude*
PART OF SPEECH	Noun
GENDER	Feminine

The suffix **-itud** denotes a state or condition relating to the base word, which is usually an adjective; for example, **la ineptitud** *ineptitude, incompetency* is the state of being **inepto** *inept, incompetent*. A few of these suffixed words are derived from nouns (for example, **la actitud** *attitude*, from **el acto** *act, deed*).

The formation of these terms is regular: if the base word ends in **-o**, the **o** is omitted before adding **-itud**; otherwise, **-itud** is added directly to the base word.

NOUN ENDING IN **-itud**	ENGLISH EQUIVALENT	BASE WORD	ENGLISH EQUIVALENT
la actitud	*attitude*	el acto	*act, deed*
la amplitud	*amplitude, roominess*	amplio	*ample, roomy*
la aptitud	*aptitude, ability*	apto	*able, apt, competent*
la beatitud	*beatitude, blessedness*	beato	*blessed*
la decrepitud	*decrepitude*	decrépito	*decrepit, in decay*
la esclavitud	*slavery, bondage*	el esclavo	*slave*
la exactitud	*exactitude, accuracy*	exacto	*exact, accurate*
la excelsitud	*loftiness*	excelso	*lofty, sublime*
la habitud	*convention, practice*	el hábito	*habit*
la ilicitud	*illicitness, criminal nature*	ilícito	*illicit*
la ineptitud	*ineptitude, incompetency*	inepto	*inept, incompetent*
la inexactitud	*inexactness, inaccuracy*	inexacto	*inexact, inaccurate*
la inverosimilitud	*unlikelihood*	inverosímil	*unlikely*
la lasitud	*lassitude, weariness*	laso	*weary, languid*

EJERCICIO
137·1

¿Verdadero o falso? *Indicate whether each statement is true or false, using* **V** *for* **verdadero** *true or* **F** *for* **falso** *false.*

1. _____ Cada religión proclama la excelsitud de su Dios.

2. _____ La actitud de un candidato por un puesto en una empresa es importante.

3. _____ La ineptitud es una buena calidad de un candidato por un puesto.

4. _____ Desgraciadamente, hay mucha decrepitud en el centro de muchas ciudades grandes.

5. _____ La amplitud de una casa nunca es una indicación del precio.

6. _____ La exactitud no es importante en carreras como la arquitectura o la carpintería.

7. _____ Un buen examen mide la aptitud de una persona en un área en particular.

8. _____ La inverosimilitud del testimonio de un testigo indica gran credibilidad.

9. _____ La habitud de mentir es un problema para Pinocho.

10. _____ La lasitud de los padres resulta frecuentemente en los niños malcriados.

11. _____ El estado de beatitud es uno de serenidad, paz espiritual y felicidad.

12. _____ El Jefe de Policía está a favor de la ilicitud de varios actos.

13. _____ La esclavitud de cualquier persona es terrible y un delito contra la naturaleza.

14. _____ La inexactitud del testimonio de un testigo de un delito no importa mucho.

NOUN ENDING IN -itud	ENGLISH EQUIVALENT	BASE WORD	ENGLISH EQUIVALENT
la latitud	*latitude, breadth, width*	lato	*broad, wide, large*
la laxitud	*laxness, laxity*	laxo	*lax, slack*
la lentitud	*slowness*	lento	*slow*
la licitud	*legality, lawfulness*	lícito	*lawful*
la longitud	*longitude*	luengo	*long*
la magnitud	*magnitude*	magno	*great*
la plenitud	*plenitude, fullness*	pleno	*full*
la prontitud	*promptness*	pronto	*prompt, soon*
la pulcritud	*neatness, tidiness*	pulcro	*neat, tidy*
la rectitud	*rectitude, honesty*	recto	*right, upright*
la similitud	*similitude, similarity*	símil	*similar*
la solicitud	*solicitude, attentiveness*	solícito	*solicitous, obliging*
la verosimilitud	*verisimilitude, plausibility*	verosímil	*likely, probable*
la vicisitud	*vicissitude, sudden change*	vicis [LAT.]	*turn, change*

EJERCICIO
137·2

Sinónimos *Provide the noun that is related to each group of words. Include its article.*

1. algo muy grande, enorme o vasto _____

2. la puntualidad, algo que ocurre rápido o en poco tiempo _____

3. la honestidad, la veracidad, la moralidad _____

4. muchos cambios, las altas y bajas, los altibajos _____

5. la tortuga, el caracol, la melaza, el glaciar _____

6. el cuidado, la minuciosidad, la escrupulosidad _____

7. la abundancia, la cornucopia, la generosidad _____

8. la pereza, el liberalismo, la facilidad _____

9. la atención, la consideración, la vigilancia, la preocupación _____

10. la largura, la distancia, la extensión _____

11. la anchura, la extensión, la gama, la margen _____

12. la legalidad, la justicia, la legitimidad _____

13. la representación, la semejanza, la réplica, el parecido _____

14. la plausibilidad, la credibilidad, la probabilidad, _____
    la fiabilidad

138 ▸ -izo/-iza

MEANING	Relating to, like; made of
ENGLISH EQUIVALENT	—
PART OF SPEECH	Adjective
GENDER	Masculine/feminine

Of the many Spanish suffixes meaning *relating to* and *like*, the suffix **-izo/-iza** is relatively uncommon. However, **-izo** may also mean *made of* (for example, **el cobre** *copper* yields **cobrizo** *made of copper, coppery*). Adjectives ending in **-izo** may be derived from nouns or adjectives.

ADJECTIVE ENDING IN -izo	ENGLISH EQUIVALENT	BASE WORD	ENGLISH EQUIVALENT
agostizo	*born in August*	agosto	*August*
banderizo	*factionalist, fiery*	la bandera	*flag, banner*
enfermizo	*sickly, unhealthy*	enfermo	*sick, ill*
estadizo	*stagnant, stale, unmoving*	estar	*to be*
mellizo	*twin*	gemellus [LAT.]	*twin*
mestizo	*of mixed race, crossbred*	mixtus [LAT.]	*mixed*
otoñizo	*autumnal, of the autumn*	el otoño	*autumn, fall*
primerizo	*first-time, inexperienced*	primero	*first*
rojizo	*reddish*	rojo	*red*
sequizo	*dry, dried (fruit)*	seco	*dry*

EJERCICIO 138·1

Complete each sentence with the correct form of the appropriate adjective.

1. Es comprensible cuando los padres _____ están nerviosos y no saben cómo responder a algunas situaciones.

2. Astrológicamente, la mayoría de las personas que nacen bajo el signo de Leo son

   _____ .

3. A un hipocondríaco, le gusta estar _____ por la atención que puede recibir de los médicos, los enfermeros y el resto del mundo.

4. Las mejillas _____ pueden indicar o la buena salud o la vergüenza.

5. Los hermanos _____ frecuentemente se parecen mucho.

6. En septiembre y octubre, durante el tiempo _____, hace fresco y las hojas se tiñen de tonalidades amarillas y naranjas.

7. Una persona cuyos padres son de razas distintas es _____.

8. Se puede decir que un hombre _____ es súper patriótico.

9. Un sinónimo de "deshidratado" es _____.

10. Un sinónimo de "estancado" es _____.

ADJECTIVE ENDING IN -izo	ENGLISH EQUIVALENT	BASE WORD	ENGLISH EQUIVALENT
cabrerizo	*goatish, like a goat*	la cabra	*goat*
calverizo	*of land without vegetation*	calvo	*bald, bare (land)*
cenizo	*ash-colored*	la ceniza	*ash*
cobrizo	*made of copper, coppery*	el cobre	*copper*
ferrizo	*made of iron, ferrous*	el fierro [LAT. AM.]	*iron*
fronterizo	*of a border or frontier*	la frontera	*border, frontier*
macizo	*solid, massive*	la masa	*mass*
pajizo	*straw-colored, made of straw*	la paja	*straw*
plomizo	*lead-colored, made of lead*	el plomo	*lead*
terrizo	*earthy, earthen*	la tierra	*earth, land*

EJERCICIO
138·2

¿**Verdadero o falso?** *Indicate whether each statement is true or false, using* **V** *for* **verdadero** *true or* **F** *for* **falso** *false.*

1. _____ Una estructura de acero macizo es muy fuerte.

2. _____ Se encuentran caminos terrizos en el centro de una ciudad metropolitana.

3. _____ Un cielo plomizo es común antes de una tormenta.

4. _____ Una de las casas en el cuento de "Los tres cochinitos" es pajiza.

5. _____ Los símbolos del signo astrológico Capricornio son cabrerizos.

6. _____ Muchos clavos y cabezas de martillos son ferrizos.

7. _____ Muchas ollas y sartenes son cobrizas.

8. _____ Los agentes del control fronterizo no tienen interés en los pasaportes de viajeros internacionales.

9. _____ La tierra calveriza es el placer de un jardinero.

10. _____ Durante una sequía, las plantas no pueden crecer en la tierra ceniza.

139 ◆ -o

MEANING	Plant
ENGLISH EQUIVALENT	—
PART OF SPEECH	Noun
GENDER	Masculine

Plant lovers, this one's for you! The suffix **-o** denotes trees and bushes. The name of the fruit, nut, leaf, or wood that a tree or bush produces often ends in **-a**; the suffix **-o** simply replaces the **-a**. The plant is masculine and its product is feminine; for example, **el cerezo** *cherry tree* produces **la cereza** *cherry.* An exception is **el cafeto** *coffee tree*, from **el café** *coffee.*

The following nouns ending in **-o** represent trees and bushes that bear sweet and citrus fruits.

NOUN ENDING IN **-o**	ENGLISH EQUIVALENT	BASE WORD	ENGLISH EQUIVALENT
el banano	*banana tree*	la banana	*banana*
el bergamoto	*bergamot tree*	la bergamota	*bergamot*
el cerezo	*cherry tree*	la cereza	*cherry*
el ciruelo	*plum tree*	la ciruela	*plum*
el frambueso	*raspberry bush*	la frambuesa	*raspberry*
el granado	*pomegranate tree*	la granada	*pomegranate*
el manzano	*apple tree*	la manzana	*apple*
el naranjo	*orange tree*	la naranja	*orange*
el pero	*pear tree*	la pera	*pear*
el toronjo	*grapefruit tree*	la toronja	*grapefruit*

EJERCICIO
139·1

Provide the correct nouns (including their articles) to name (a) the fruit and (b) the plant that produces it for the description in each item.

1. Esta fruta es redonda y anaranjada, del tamaño aproximado de un béisbol. Es parte de la familia de los cítricos. Es la base de un jugo muy popular.

   a. _____ b. _____

2. Esta fruta es amarilla, larga y curvada, una favorita de los monos. Se cultiva esta fruta en todo el mundo, principalmente en los terrenos de climas más calurosos.

   a. _____ b. _____

3. Esta fruta es roja y pequeña. El árbol tiene su origen en las zonas occidentales de Asia y es parte de la leyenda de George Washington.

   a. _____ b. _____

4. Esta fruta es amarilla, anaranjada o rosada y es muy agria. Es del tamaño aproximado de un softball. Es parte de la familia de los cítricos.

   a. _____ b. _____

5. Esta fruta es morada, del tamaño aproximado de una pelota de tenis. En su forma seca, se usa esta fruta como laxante.

   a. _____ b. _____

6. Esta fruta es nombrada por su ciudad de origen en Italia y es parte de la familia de los cítricos. Es una fruta pequeña que es popular por el aceite esencial que se extrae de su corteza.

   a. _____ b. _____

7. Esta fruta es roja o verde. Se dice que si una persona come una porción de esta fruta cada día, se puede distanciarse del médico.

   a. _____ b. _____

8. Esta fruta es una baya de muchas semillas, de cáscara gruesa y del tamaño aproximado de una naranja.

   a. _____ b. _____

9. Esta fruta típicamente es roja, pero hay variedades del color morado y negro. La fruta no crece en un árbol, sino en un arbusto.

   a. _____ b. _____

10. Esta fruta es verde o amarilla. Hay muchas variedades y las más conocidas son la Bartlett y la Bosc. China es el primer productor mundial de esta fruta.

   a. _____ b. _____

The following nouns ending in **-o** represent trees and plants that produce nuts, squash, and other fruits.

NOUN ENDING IN **-o**	ENGLISH EQUIVALENT	BASE WORD	ENGLISH EQUIVALENT
el aceituno	*olive tree*	la aceituna	*olive*
el almendro	*almond tree*	la almendra	*almond*
el cafeto	*coffee tree*	el café	*coffee*
el calabazo	*pumpkin plant*	la calabaza	*pumpkin*
el canelo	*cinnamon tree*	la canela	*cinnamon*
el castaño	*chestnut tree*	la castaña	*chestnut*
el cedro	*cedar tree*	la cedria	*resin from the cedar*
el jícaro	*calabash tree*	la jícara	*bottle gourd*
el majuelo	*white hawthorn tree*	la majuela	*white hawthorn fruit*
el olivo	*olive tree*	la oliva	*olive*

Provide the correct nouns (including their articles) to name (a) the fruit and (b) the plant that produces it for the description in each item.

1. En una canción popular de la Navidad, esta nuez está tostándose en un fuego abierto (Jack Frost pellizcándote la nariz...).

   a. _____   b. _____

2. Starbucks, Juan Valdez, Folgers, Casa Maxwell: la bebida más importante para millones de personas cada mañana. El producto del árbol es un grano.

   a. _____   b. _____

3. El árbol es conífero (pinoso) y de gran tamaño. La madera es olorosa y los árboles son muy utilizados para ornamentación de parques. El país Líbano es famoso por este árbol.

   a. _____   b. _____

4. Esta planta se lleva a cabo en el mes de octubre. Es el símbolo del Halloween y también el ingrediente más popular en las tartas del día de Acción de Gracias en los Estados Unidos.

   a. _____   b. _____

5. Este arbolillo es de la familia Rosácea (la rosa) y suele alcanzar los 5 metros de altura. Tiene flores blancas en mayo, seguidas de bayas rojas. Pierde las hojas para pasar el invierno.

   a. _____   b. _____

6. Esta nuez es considerada uno de los primeros alimentos cultivados en el mundo. California produce el 80% del suministro mundial de esta nuez. Esta nuez es una excelente fuente de la vitamina E y el magnesio y también de proteínas y el potasio.

   a. _____   b. _____

7. Esta especia viene de la corteza interior de un árbol de laurel originario de Sri Lanka. Típicamente se pulveriza la corteza para usar en la comida. También es muy popular en el té.

   a. _____   b. _____

8. Se usa la corteza de esta fruta para hacer vasijas para bebidas o comidas. Otros productos que vienen de este árbol son las semillas, que son ricas en aceite comestible, y la pulpa fibrosa junto a las semillas, que tiene efectos laxantes y eméticos.

   a. _____   b. _____

9. Este árbol produce una fruta que se come o en su forma original o como parte de un aderezo de ensalada, mezclado con el vinagre.

   a. _____   b. _____

   a. _____   b. _____

 **-ón**

MEANING	Sudden/intense action
ENGLISH EQUIVALENT	—
PART OF SPEECH	Noun
GENDER	Masculine

The relatively uncommon suffix **-ón** may denote a sudden movement or action. The base word is always a verb, which often represents an intense or violent action.

The following nouns ending in **-ón** represent specific, often extreme situations.

NOUN ENDING IN -ón	ENGLISH EQUIVALENT	BASE WORD	ENGLISH EQUIVALENT
el acelerón	*acceleration, burst of speed*	acelerar	*to accelerate*
el apagón	*blackout*	apagar	*to extinguish, turn off (light)*
el atracón	*gluttony, stuffing*	atracarse	*to stuff oneself*
el baldón	*insult, affront*	baldonar	*to insult abusively*
el bebezón	*drunken spree*	beber	*to drink*
el chapuzón	*dip (in a pool, lake)*	chapuzar	*to duck, dip down*
el hinchazón	*swelling, pomposity*	hinchar	*to swell, inflate*
el nevazón	*snowstorm*	nevar	*to snow*
el pregón	*proclamation*	pregonar	*to announce, proclaim*
el relumbrón	*flash of light*	relumbrar	*to shine brightly*
el restregón	*hard scrubbing*	restregar	*to scrub, rub*
el retortijón	*twisting, stomach cramp*	retortijar	*to twist, curl*
el reventón	*burst, blowout*	reventar	*to burst, explode*
el tachón	*erasure, crossing out*	tachar	*to cross out, delete*
el turbión	*downpour, squall*	turbar	*to disturb, stir up*

EJERCICIO
140·1

Sinónimos *Provide the noun that is related to each group of words. Include its article.*

1. un rayo de luz _____

2. comer compulsivamente _____

3. una tormenta de nieve _____

4. una tormenta de lluvia _____

5. una noche de borrachera _____

6. la explosión de un neumático _____

7. la eliminación de algo escrito _____

8. una aspersión o un insulto horrible _____

9. fregar o lavar con presión _____

10. extinguir todas las luces _____

11. un refrescante baño en el río o la piscina _____

12. una declaración o proclamación oficial   _____

13. el aumento o inflamación de una parte del cuerpo   _____

14. un calambre o molestia abdominal   _____

15. un aumento en la velocidad   _____

The following nouns ending in **-ón** represent physical actions or experiences.

NOUN ENDING IN **-ón**	ENGLISH EQUIVALENT	BASE WORD	ENGLISH EQUIVALENT
el aguijón	*sting, pinch, goad*	aguijar	*to goad, incite*
el apretón	*handshake, squeeze*	apretar	*to squeeze, press*
el empujón	*hard push, boost*	empujar	*to push*
el encontrón	*unexpected meeting, collision*	encontrarse	*to meet, collide with*
el estirón	*growth spurt*	estirar	*to pull, stretch*
el hurgón	*thrust (fencing)*	hurgar	*to poke, jab*
el jalón	*pull, tug, jerk*	jalar	*to pull*
el lametón	*hard and/or strong lick*	lamer	*to lick*
el picazón	*itch, itching*	picar	*to sting, bite, peck*
el remesón	*plucking out of hair*	remesar	*to pluck hair*
el repelón	*tug or yank on hair*	repelar	*to pull hair*

¿Verdadero o falso? *Indicate whether each statement is true or false, using **V** for* **verdadero** *true or* **F** *for* **falso** *false.*

1. _____ La picadura de un mosquito puede provocar el picazón.

2. _____ Muchas madres sienten un jalón en su falda de un niño que quiere su atención.

3. _____ Cuando un muchacho de repente crece en altura, no indica un estirón.

4. _____ Es común darle un apretón de manos al conocer a una persona.

5. _____ El aguijón de una abeja es una experiencia divertida.

6. _____ Un trastorno del arrancamiento del cabello se refiere a una compulsión que resulta en el remesón.

7. _____ Al conocer a la reina de Inglaterra, es cortés darle un empujón.

8. _____ Es común recibir un lametón de un perro muy amistoso.

9. _____ El repelón puede doler mucho.

10. _____ Un encontrón es un encuentro sorprendente o inesperado.

11. _____ El hurgón es un movimiento en el deporte de la esgrima (*fencing*).

141 ◆ -orio/-oria

MEANING	Relating to, like
ENGLISH EQUIVALENT	*-ory*
PART OF SPEECH	Adjective
GENDER	Masculine/feminine

The suffix **-orio** (feminine: **-oria**) is one of several adjectival suffixes that mean *relating to* and *like*. Adjectives with the suffix **-orio** are derived from verbs, nearly all of which are **-ar** verbs. If the base word is an **-ar** verb, the infinitive ending is replaced by **-at-** before **-orio** is added; for example, **circular** *to circulate* yields **circulatorio** *circulatory*. Formation of these adjectives from **-er** and **-ir** verbs is irregular.

ADJECTIVE ENDING IN **-orio**	ENGLISH EQUIVALENT	BASE WORD	ENGLISH EQUIVALENT
acusatorio	*accusatory*	acusar	*to accuse*
circulatorio	*circulatory*	circular	*to circulate*
congratulatorio	*congratulatory*	congratular	*to congratulate*
depilatorio	*depilatory*	depilar	*to remove hair*
discriminatorio	*discriminatory*	discriminar	*to discriminate*
giratorio	*rotating, swivel*	girar	*to rotate, revolve*
ilusorio	*illusory, unrealistic*	ilusionar	*to excite, cause illusions*
inflamatorio	*inflammatory*	inflamar	*to inflame, set afire*
mortuorio	*of the dead*	morir	*to die*
obligatorio	*obligatory*	obligar	*to oblige, force*

EJERCICIO
141·1

Complete each sentence with the correct form of the appropriate adjective.

1. La sangre fluye por el sistema _____.

2. Ejemplos del lenguaje _____ son las referencias a las mujeres como débiles y tontas.

3. Para quitarse el pelo se necesita una crema _____.

4. Es _____ imaginarse un mundo sin problemas.

5. Típicamente hay una silla _____ para cada escritorio en una oficina.

6. Es _____ que casi cada trabajador pague los impuestos.

7. Después de hacer ejercicio, los atletas quieren prevenir los efectos

   _____, así que usan el hielo para reducir la posibilidad de lesiones.

8. Una funeraria es un edificio _____.

9. Al ganar las elecciones presidenciales, el nuevo líder recibe muchos mensajes

   _____.

10. Durante un juicio penal, el fiscal (abogado de la acusación) habla en un tono

   _____.

ADJECTIVE ENDING IN -orio	ENGLISH EQUIVALENT	BASE WORD	ENGLISH EQUIVALENT
aclaratorio	*explanatory*	aclarar	*to make clear, explain*
aprobatorio	*approving, approbatory*	aprobar	*to approve*
conciliatorio	*conciliatory, peacemaking*	conciliar	*to reconcile*
decisorio	*decisive*	decidir	*to decide*
declamatorio	*declamatory, emphatic*	declamar	*to speak passionately*
meritorio	*meritorious, worthy*	merecer	*to deserve, merit*
ondulatorio	*wavelike*	ondear	*to undulate, wave*
operatorio	*operative, operating*	operar	*to operate, run*
promisorio	*promissory*	prometer	*to promise*
satisfactorio	*satisfactory, satisfying*	satisfacer	*to satisfy*

EJERCICIO

141·2

¿Verdadero o falso? *Indicate whether each statement is true or false, using* **V** *for* **verdadero** *true or* **F** *for* **falso** *false.*

1. _____ Se ve el movimiento ondulatorio en el océano.

2. _____ Típicamente se ve un párrafo aclaratorio en la contraportada de un libro.

3. _____ Una nota promisoria es igual a un recibo por pago.

4. _____ Antes de recibir el doctorado, el estudiante necesita ser aprobado por un proceso aprobatorio.

5. _____ Una calificación del 40% indica un nivel satisfactorio.

6. _____ El trabajo del Secretario de Estado tiene un componente conciliatorio y de diplomacia medioambiental.

7. _____ Después de una cirugía, el paciente recibe instrucciones de cuidado post-operatorio.

8. _____ Un filibustero acelera el proceso decisorio.

9. _____ El desarrollo de una educación equilibrada es un objetivo meritorio.

10. _____ Los sermones de un ministro apasionado nunca son declamatorios.

142 ·osis

MEANING	Process; condition, disease
ENGLISH EQUIVALENT	*-osis*
PART OF SPEECH	Noun
GENDER	Feminine

Nouns with the suffix **-osis** denote a process, condition, or disease. Since they have English cognates with the suffix *-osis*, they are easily recognized and used. Many of the suffixed words are common, but not all refer to a disease; **la ósmosis** *osmosis, assimilation*, for example, is a process. Nearly all of these suffixed words are derived from Greek or Latin roots, which also have English cognates.

NOUN ENDING IN **-osis**	ENGLISH EQUIVALENT	BASE WORD	ENGLISH EQUIVALENT
la acidosis	*acidosis*	acidus [LAT.]	*sour*
la alcalosis	*alkalosis*	el álcali	*alkali*
la amaurosis	*amaurosis, blindness*	amauros [GRK.]	*dim*
la cirrosis	*cirrhosis*	kirrhos [GRK.]	*orange-colored*
la endometriosis	*endometriosis*	endon + metra [GRK.]	*within + uterus*
la halitosis	*halitosis, bad breath*	halitus [LAT.]	*breath*
la hematosis	*hematosis*	haima [GRK.]	*blood*
la melanosis	*melanosis, dark pigmentation*	melas [GRK.]	*black*
la miosis	*miosis, pupil constriction*	meoiosis [GRK.]	*diminution*
la mononucleosis	*mononucleosis*	monos [GRK.] + nucleus [LAT.]	*single + nucleus*
la nefrosis	*nephrosis*	nephros [GRK.]	*kidney*
la neurosis	*neurosis*	neuron [GRK.]	*nerve*
la queratosis	*keratosis, wart*	keras [GRK.]	*horn*
la silicosis	*silicosis, lung disease*	silex [LAT.]	*flint*
la triquinosis	*trichinosis*	trichonos [GRK.]	*hair-like*

EJERCICIO

142·1

¿Cuál es la enfermedad o condición? *Provide the correct form of the appropriate noun (including its article) to name each illness or condition.*

1. la enfermedad del riñón _____

2. la enfermedad del hígado _____

3. la enfermedad del pulmón _____

4. la "enfermedad del beso" _____

5. la enfermedad de la sangre _____

6. la enfermedad de los ciegos _____

7. la enfermedad que incluye las verrugas _____

8. la enfermedad causada por carne mala _____

9. la enfermedad del útero   _____

10. la condición de tener demasiado ácido   _____

11. la condición de tener mal aliento   _____

12. la condición de tener demasiado álcali   _____

13. la condición de tener demasiado melanina   _____

14. la condición de constricción excesiva de la pupila   _____

15. la enfermedad mental como la ansiedad o la fobia   _____

NOUN ENDING IN -osis	ENGLISH EQUIVALENT	BASE WORD	ENGLISH EQUIVALENT
la arteriosclerosis	*arteriosclerosis*	arteria [LAT.] + skleros [GRK.]	*artery + hard*
la esclerosis	*sclerosis*	skleros [GRK.]	*hard*
la estenosis	*stenosis*	stenos [GRK.]	*narrow*
la fibrosis	*fibrosis, scarring of connective tissue*	fibra [LAT.]	*fiber*
la hipnosis	*hypnosis*	hypnos [GRK.]	*sleep*
la metamorfosis	*metamorphosis*	meta + morphe [GRK.]	*beyond + form*
la necrosis	*necrosis, death of cells*	nekros [GRK.]	*dead body*
la ósmosis	*osmosis, assimilation*	osmos [GRK.]	*impulse*
la psicosis	*psychosis*	psyche [GRK.]	*the mind*
la simbiosis	*symbiosis*	syn + bios [GRK.]	*with + life*
la trombosis	*thrombosis, blood clot*	thrombos [GRK.]	*clot*
la tuberculosis	*tuberculosis*	tuberculum [LAT.]	*small swelling*

EJERCICIO

142·2

¿Verdadero o falso? *Indicate whether each statement is true or false, using* **V** *for* **verdadero** *true or* **F** *for* **falso** *false.*

1. _____ Franz Anton Mesmer—de quien tenemos la palabra inglesa *mesmerized*— es considerado por muchas personas como "el padre de la hipnosis."

2. _____ La arteriosclerosis es una enfermedad de los jóvenes.

3. _____ La necrosis es la muerte del tejido en una parte del cuerpo.

4. _____ La tuberculosis usualmente ataca los pulmones.

5. _____ La esclerosis múltiple es una enfermedad del sistema nervioso central.

6. _____ La psicosis es un término que se refiere a la pérdida de contacto con la realidad.

7. _____ La trombosis no tiene nada que ver con la sangre.

8. _____ La estenosis denote una constricción o estrechamiento de un orificio o conducto corporal.

9. _____ La ósmosis ocurre solamente cuando una persona está durmiendo.

10. _____ La simbiosis se refiere a una relación mutualista entre dos o más individuos.

11. _____ La fibrosis quística (*cystic*) es una enfermedad genética que afecta principalmente los pulmones.

12. _____ La metamorfosis es un proceso biológico por el cual un animal se desarrolla por medio de cambios drásticos y fisiológicos.

143 ▶ -scopio

MEANING	Tool for viewing/observing
ENGLISH EQUIVALENT	—
PART OF SPEECH	Noun
GENDER	Masculine

Scientists, this one's for you! The Spanish suffix **-scopio** and English suffix *-scope* are derived from the Greek verb **skopein** *to look at.* Like its English counterpart, the Spanish suffix **-scopio** denotes a tool used to view very large or very small objects or phenomena, as well as objects or phenomena that are ordinarily not directly observable. Almost all nouns with this suffix have Greek base words; one exception is **el espectroscopio** *spectroscope*, from Latin **spectrum** *apparition.*

NOUN ENDING IN -scopio	ENGLISH EQUIVALENT	BASE WORD	ENGLISH EQUIVALENT
el anemoscopio	*anemoscope*	anemos [GRK.]	*wind*
el calidoscopio	*kaleidoscope*	kalos [GRK.]	*beautiful*
el cistoscopio	*cystoscope*	kystis [GRK.]	*bladder*
el electroscopio	*electroscope*	elektron [GRK.]	*amber*
el endoscopio	*endoscope*	endon [GRK.]	*within*
el espectroscopio	*spectroscope*	spectrum [LAT.]	*apparition*
el estetoscopio	*stethoscope*	stethos [GRK.]	*chest*
el giroscopio	*gyroscope*	gyros [GRK.]	*circle*
el helioscopio	*helioscope*	helios [GRK.]	*sun*
el higroscopio	*hygroscope*	hygros [GRK.]	*fluid*
el laringoscopio	*laryngoscope*	larynx [GRK.]	*larynx*
el microscopio	*microscope*	micros [GRK.]	*small*
el oftalmoscopio	*ophthalmoscope*	ophthalmos [GRK.]	*eye*
el otoscopio	*otoscope*	ous/otos [GRK.]	*ear*
el periscopio	*periscope*	peri [GRK.]	*around*
el telescopio	*telescope*	tele- [GRK.]	*far*

Provide the correct noun (including its article) to name the instrument used for each purpose mentioned.

1. para inspeccionar el oído   _____

2. para inspeccionar la retina y otras partes del ojo   _____

3. para escuchar los latidos del corazón   _____

4. para inspeccionar la laringe   _____

5. para examinar la vejiga urinaria   _____

6. para inspeccionar las partes internas del cuerpo   _____

7. para determinar la dirección del viento   _____

8. para determinar la humedad en el aire   _____

9. para ver objetos muy pequeños como las células
   animales o vegetales   _____

10. para ver las estrellas y otros objetos astronómicos   _____

11. para observar el sol y las manchas solares   _____

12. para saber si algo está cargado eléctricamente   _____

13. para observar desde un lugar oculto o sumergido, como
    un submarino   _____

14. para ver colores y unas formas hermosas y diferentes,
    cuyas imágenes se ven multiplicadas simétricamente   _____

15. para mantener la orientación durante el movimiento de
    un vehículo u otro objeto   _____

 **-uco, -uca**

MEANING	Diminutive; depreciative
ENGLISH EQUIVALENT	—
PART OF SPEECH	Noun
GENDER	Masculine, feminine

The suffix **-uco** (feminine: **-uca**) is one of several diminutive and/or depreciative suffixes in Spanish. This rare suffix may convey a very negative connotation; for example, **el hermanuco**, a derisive name given to laymen by snobbish religious. Another example is **el bazuco**, a cocaine-based street drug, derived from **la bazuca** *bazooka*.

NOUN ENDING IN **-uco**, **-uca**	ENGLISH EQUIVALENT	BASE WORD	ENGLISH EQUIVALENT
el abejaruco	*bee-eater*	la abeja	*bee*
el almendruco	*green almond*	la almendra	*almond*
el bazuco [COLLOQ.]	*mix of cocaine and heroin*	la bazuca	*bazooka*
el carruco	*small cart*	el carro	*car*
la casuca	*hovel, shack*	la casa	*house*
el frailuco	*despicable friar*	el fraile	*friar, monk*
el hermanuco	*name of contempt given to lay brothers by ecclesiastics*	el hermano	*brother*
el patuco	*bootee*	la pata	*foot (animal), paw*
la peluca	*wig*	el pelo	*hair*
el ventanuco	*little window*	la ventana	*window*

EJERCICIO 144·1

Complete each sentence with the correct form of the appropriate noun.

1. Un bebé lleva los _____ en los pies para mantener el calor.

2. Un animal que come las avispas y otros insectos que pican es un

_____.

3. Se puede decir que un monje despreciable es un _____.

4. Para drogarse muchísimo, unos drogadictos consideran el _____ la droga de elección.

5. Una designación que unos sacerdotes usan en secreto para referirse despectivamente a los

laicos de la iglesia es "_____."

6. En una casa muy pequeña, se puede ver los pájaros y los arboles por el

_____.

7. Se usa un _____ en una mina para transportar los minerales.

8. Una almendra inmadura es un _____.

9. Unas personas calvas o que sufren de alopecia llevan una _____ para esconder la calvicie.

10. La mayoría de las personas optan por vivir en una casa, pero otras—como los personajes en la película clásica *Deliverance*—no desean otra cosa que vivir en una

_____ en el bosque con el whisky y un banjo.

145 ◆ -ulo, -ula

MEANING	Diminutive; result of an action
ENGLISH EQUIVALENT	*-ule*
PART OF SPEECH	Noun
GENDER	Masculine, feminine

The suffix **-ulo** (less commonly, **-ula**) often denotes a very small form of the base noun (for example, **el animálculo** *animalcule, microscopic animal*, from **el animal** *animal*). Many of the suffixed nouns are taken directly from Latin. The suffix **-ulo** may also denote the result of an action represented by the base verb (for example, **el discípulo** *disciple*, from the Latin verb **discere** *to learn*). Note that the antepenultimate syllable is accented in each of these suffixed words.

NOUN ENDING IN **-ulo**, **-ula**	ENGLISH EQUIVALENT	BASE WORD	ENGLISH EQUIVALENT
el animálculo	*animalcule, microscopic animal*	el animal	*animal*
el capítulo	*chapter*	caput/capitis [LAT.]	*head*
la cápsula	*capsule*	capsa [LAT.]	*box, case, chest*
el discípulo	*disciple*	discere [LAT.]	*to learn*
la pápula	*papule, lesion, pimple*	papolstan [O.E.]	*pebble, stone*
el párvulo	*infant, small child*	parvo	*small*
la pústula	*pustule, pimple*	pustula [LAT.]	*blister, pimple*
el vestíbulo	*vestibule, entrance hall*	vestibulum [LAT.]	*forecourt, entrance*

EJERCICIO
145·1

Provide the correct noun(s) (including the article) for each description.

1. una división principal de un libro u otra obra escrita _____

2. un niño muy joven _____

3. una persona que sigue la opinión de un maestro _____

4. la entrada de una iglesia u otro edificio _____

5. un organismo microscopio, como una ameba _____

6. un compartimento de las naves espaciales en que viajan los astronautas _____

7. dos síntomas del acné _____

_____

NOUN ENDING IN -ulo, -ula	ENGLISH EQUIVALENT	BASE WORD	ENGLISH EQUIVALENT
la célula	*cell (biology)*	cella [LAT.]	*cell*
la fístula	*fistula, abnormal passageway (medical)*	fistula [LAT.]	*pipe, ulcer*
el glóbulo	*globule, blood cell*	globus [LAT.]	*globe*
el gránulo	*granule*	el grano	*grain, seed*
el módulo	*module, unit*	el modo	*mode, way, manner*
el nódulo	*nodule*	nodus [LAT.]	*knot*
el péndulo	*pendulum*	pendere [LAT.]	*to hang*
la válvula	*valve, opening, aperture*	valvae [LAT.]	*folding doors*

¿Verdadero o falso? *Indicate whether each statement is true or false, using* **V** *for* **verdadero** *true or* **F** *for* **falso** *false.*

1. _____ Se encuentra un péndulo en un reloj de pie (*grandfather clock*).

2. _____ Muchos peces en un acuario comen alimento en gránulos.

3. _____ Una conexión o canal anormal entre órganos, vasos o tubos es una fístula.

4. _____ Un sofá módulo tiene exactamente una parte.

5. _____ Un nódulo es una pequeña inflamación o agregación de células en el cuerpo.

6. _____ Tenemos glóbulos rojos y blancos en la sangre.

7. _____ El mecanismo que regula el flujo de la comunicación entre dos partes de una máquina o sistema es una válvula.

146 ▸ -umbre

MEANING	Abstract concept
ENGLISH EQUIVALENT	*-ness, -tude*
PART OF SPEECH	Noun
GENDER	Feminine

The relatively uncommon suffix **-umbre** denotes an abstract concept associated with the base word. If the base word ends in a vowel, **d** is inserted before the suffix for pronunciation purposes.

NOUN ENDING IN **-umbre**	ENGLISH EQUIVALENT	BASE WORD	ENGLISH EQUIVALENT
la certidumbre	*certainty, certitude*	cierto	*certain*
la dulcedumbre	*sweetness*	dulce	*sweet*
la herrumbre	*rust, taste of iron*	el hierro	*iron*
la incertidumbre	*uncertainty*	incierto	*uncertain*
la mansedumbre	*meekness, gentleness*	manso	*meek, docile*
la muchedumbre	*crowd, multitude*	mucho	*much, a lot*
la pesadumbre	*grief, sorrow*	el peso	*weight*
la podredumbre	*rottenness, corruption*	la podre	*pus*
la quejumbre	*moan*	la queja	*complaint*
la salsedumbre	*saltiness*	la sal	*salt*
la servidumbre	*servitude*	servir	*to serve*
la techumbre	*roofing material*	el techo	*roof*

EJERCICIO
146·1

Complete each sentence with the correct form of the appropriate noun.

1. Durante un funeral hay un ambiente de _____.

2. Muchas frutas tienen una _____ natural y son ideales para un postre bajo en calorías.

3. El platino y el oro son dos metales que no son susceptibles a la

   _____.

4. Los fanáticos religiosos afirman tener _____ absoluta.

5. La esclavitud es la _____ sin pago, sin derechos y sin respeto.

6. En *Hamlet* por Shakespeare, el oficial Marcelo proclama que hay

   _____ en el estado de Dinamarca.

7. En las islas tropicales, las cabañas frecuentemente tienen _____ de paja.

8. El narcisista nunca experimenta la sensación de humildad o _____.

9. Nadie quiere escuchar la _____ incesante de una persona que siempre está miserable.

10. En Times Square en Nueva York, siempre hay una gran _____ en la Nochevieja.

147 ▸ -undo/-unda

MEANING	Relating to, like
ENGLISH EQUIVALENT	*-und*
PART OF SPEECH	Adjective
GENDER	Masculine/feminine

The suffix **-undo** (feminine: **-unda**) denotes that a person or thing has a characteristic of the base word, which may be a noun, verb, or adjective. Many of these suffixed adjectives come directly from Latin. If the base word is Spanish, a consonant is often inserted between the base word and **-undo**; most commonly, that consonant is **b** (for example, **la nausea** *nausea* yields **nauseabundo** *nauseating, loathesome*).

ADJECTIVE ENDING IN **-undo**	ENGLISH EQUIVALENT	BASE WORD	ENGLISH EQUIVALENT
cogitabundo	*pensive, thoughtful*	cogitar	*to reflect, meditate*
fecundo	*fecund, fertile*	fecundare [LAT.]	*to fertilize*
furibundo	*furious, raging*	la furia	*fury, rage*
inmundo	*filthy*	in- + mundus [LAT.]	*not + clean*
iracundo	*wrathful, ireful*	la ira	*ire, wrath*
jocundo	*placid, agreeable*	iocus [LAT.]	*joke*
meditabundo	*thoughtful, pensive*	meditar	*to meditate*
rotundo	*rotund, round, definitive*	rotundus [LAT.]	*round, rotund*
rubicundo	*rubicund, red, rosy*	el rubí	*ruby*
tremebundo	*terrifying, dreadful*	tremebundus [LAT.]	*trembling*

EJERCICIO
147·1

Sinónimos *Provide the correct synonym(s) for each group of words.*

1. sucio, puerco, cochambroso _____

2. redondo, esférico, circular _____

3. rojizo, pelirrojo, colorado _____

4. fértil, prolífico, feraz, copioso _____

5. terrible, espantoso, aterrador, horroroso _____

6. alegre, plácido, agradable, jocoso _____

7. irritable, furioso, colérico, rabioso _____

   _____

8. pensativo, ensimismado _____

   _____

ADJECTIVE ENDING IN **-undo**	ENGLISH EQUIVALENT	BASE WORD	ENGLISH EQUIVALENT
errabundo	*wandering, strolling about*	errar	*to wander, be mistaken*
facundo	*eloquent*	facundus [LAT.]	*eloquent*
gemebundo	*groaning, moaning*	gemir	*to groan, moan, whine*
moribundo	*moribund, dying*	morir	*to die*
nauseabundo	*nauseating, loathsome*	la nausea	*nausea*
oriundo	*native (of)*	oriundus [LAT.]	*arising, springing from*
profundo	*profound*	profundus [LAT.]	*deep, profound*
pudibundo	*prudish, modest*	el pudor	*modesty, shyness*
segundo	*second*	secundus [LAT.]	*second, next*
vagabundo	*vagabond, vagrant, stray*	vagar	*to wander, roam*

EJERCICIO
147·2

Sinónimos *Provide the correct synonym(s) for each group of words.*

1. originario, nativo, congénito _____

2. hondo, penetrante, interior _____

3. próximo, siguiente, adyacente _____

4. repugnante, asqueroso, fétido, repulsivo _____

5. verboso, locuaz, elocuente, hablador _____

6. quejumbroso, llorón, lastimero, plañidero _____

7. expirante, muriendo, semidifunto, desahuciado _____

8. puritano, mojigato, remilgado _____

9. errante, ambulante, nómada, inestable _____

_____

148 ⬥ -usco/-usca

MEANING	Relating to, like
ENGLISH EQUIVALENT	—
PART OF SPEECH	Adjective
GENDER	Masculine/feminine

The uncommon suffix **-usco** (feminine: **-usca**) means *relating to* and *like*. The base word, which may be Latin or Spanish, may represent a color or a way of behaving.

ADJECTIVE ENDING IN **-usco**	ENGLISH EQUIVALENT	BASE WORD	ENGLISH EQUIVALENT
amusco	*brown*	muscus [LAT.]	*moss*
chusco	*funny, droll*	el chiste	*joke*
etrusco	*Etruscan*	Etruria	*Etruria (region of central Italy)*
fusco	*brown, of a dark color*	fuscus [LAT.]	*dark, swarthy*
lusco	*one-eyed, cross-eyed*	luscus [LAT.]	*one-eyed*
musco	*brown*	muscus [LAT.]	*moss*
pardusco	*olive drab, grayish-brown*	pardo	*grayish-brown, black*
rusco	*rude, peevish, forward*	ruscum [LAT.]	*butcher's broom*
tusco	*Tuscan*	Toscana	*Tuscany*
verdusco	*greenish*	verde	*the color green*

EJERCICIO

148·1

Complete each sentence with the correct form of the appropriate adjective(s).

1. Un hombre de Etruria es _____.

2. Una mujer de Toscana es _____.

3. Algo chistoso, cómico o gracioso también es _____.

4. Una mujer tuerta (con un ojo) es _____.

5. Un hombre crudo es _____.

6. Algo que tiene un color verdoso es _____.

7. Se puede decir que algo café es _____,

   _____, _____ o

   _____.

149 ▸ -uto/-uta

MEANING	Relating to, like; result of an action
ENGLISH EQUIVALENT	*-ute*
PART OF SPEECH	Adjective, noun
GENDER	Masculine/feminine

A Spanish word with the suffix **-uto** (feminine: **-uta**) often has an English cognate ending in *-ute*. These suffixed words may function as adjectives or nouns; as a noun suffix, **-uto** is more common than **-uta**. Nearly all Spanish adjectives with the suffix **-uto** have a Latin base word, while most nouns have a Spanish base word. Note that **minuto** may function as either an adjective (**minuto** *small, minute, trifling*) or a noun (**el minuto** *minute*); the derivation is the same for both formed words—Latin **minutus** *small*.

The following words ending in **-uto/-uta** are adjectives.

ADJECTIVE ENDING IN -uto	ENGLISH EQUIVALENT	BASE WORD	ENGLISH EQUIVALENT
absoluto	*absolute*	absolver	*to absolve, set free*
astuto	*astute*	astutus [LAT.]	*shrewd, discerning*
bruto	*brutish, coarse*	brutus [LAT.]	*dull, insensible*
diminuto	*tiny, diminutive*	disminuir	*to diminish, lessen*
disoluto	*dissolute, licentious, loose*	disolver	*to dissolve, loosen up*
enjuto	*lean, dried, meatless*	enjutar	*to dry*
hirsuto	*hirsute, hairy*	hirsutus [LAT.]	*hairy*
impoluto	*spotless, pure, unpolluted*	in- + pollutus [LAT.]	*not + polluted*
insoluto	*unpaid, insolvent*	in- + solutus [LAT.]	*not + paid*
irresoluto	*indecisive, unresolved*	in- + resolutus [LAT.]	*not + untied*
minuto	*small, minute, trifling*	minutus [LAT.]	*small*
poluto	*polluted, contaminated*	pollutus [LAT.]	*polluted*
resoluto	*resolute, certain, resolved, determined*	resolutus [LAT.]	*untied*

EJERCICIO
149·1

Antónimos *Provide the correct antonym(s) for each group of words.*

1. enorme, gigantesco   _____

  _____

2. estúpido, lento   _____

3. casto, puro, modesto   _____

4. calvo, sin pelo   _____

5. elegante, cortés   _____

6. puro, no contaminado   _____

7. gordo, grasiento   _____

8. pagado, financieramente sólido   _____

9. inmundo, puerco, asqueroso _____

10. decisivo, conclusivo, terminante _____

11. incierto, inestable, flexible _____

_____

The following words ending in **-uto/-uta** are nouns.

NOUN ENDING IN **-uto/-uta**	ENGLISH EQUIVALENT	BASE WORD	ENGLISH EQUIVALENT
el atributo	*attribute*	atribuir	*to attribute*
la disputa	*dispute*	disputar	*to dispute, argue*
el instituto	*institute*	instituir	*to institute, establish*
el minuto	*minute*	minutus [LAT.]	*small*
la prostituta	*prostitute*	prostituir	*to prostitute*
el sustituto	*substitute*	sustituir	*to substitute, replace*
el tributo	*tribute*	tributar	*to pay tribute*
la voluta	*spiral, smoke ring*	volutare [LAT.]	*to roll*

EJERCICIO
149·2

Sinónimos *Provide a synonym, including its article, for each group of words.*

1. el argumento, la discusión, el conflicto _____

2. el homenaje, el encomio, la alabanza _____

3. el establecimiento, la asociación, el colegio _____

4. el momento, sesenta segundos, poco tiempo _____

5. la característica, la peculiaridad, el rasgo _____

6. la puta, la guarra _____

7. el suplente, la sustitución, el representante _____

8. el espiral, la hélice, el anillo de humo _____

150 ◆ -zuelo, -zuela

MEANING	Diminutive; depreciative
ENGLISH EQUIVALENT	—
PART OF SPEECH	Noun
GENDER	Masculine, feminine

The suffixes -**zuelo** and -**zuela** denote physical smallness. Some of these diminutives are depreciative (for example, **el ladronzuelo** *petty thief, pickpocket*, from **el ladrón** *thief*). Usually, however, the suffix denotes smallness in the physical sense (for example, **el cabezuelo** *small head*, from **la cabeza** *head*). Related suffixes -**uelo** and -**uela** are similar in function. Be sure to note Venezuela's charming derivation in the second chart.

The following nouns end in -**zuelo** and are masculine.

NOUN ENDING IN -zuelo	ENGLISH EQUIVALENT	BASE WORD	ENGLISH EQUIVALENT
el cabezuelo	*small head*	la cabeza	*head*
el cedazuelo	*small sieve or strainer*	el cedazo	*sieve, strainer*
el cornezuelo	*ergot (horn-shaped fungus)*	el cuerno	*horn*
el corpezuelo	*small body*	el cuerpo	*body*
el dentezuelo	*small tooth*	el diente	*tooth*
el escritorzuelo	*wretched writer, hack*	el escritor	*writer*
el garbanzuelo	*small chickpea*	el garbanzo	*chickpea*
el herrezuelo	*light piece/scrap of iron*	el hierro	*iron*
el ladronzuelo	*petty thief, pickpocket*	el ladrón	*thief*
el pobrezuelo	*wretched/poor man*	el pobre	*poor person*
el pontezuelo	*small bridge*	el puente	*bridge*
el puertezuelo	*small port*	el puerto	*port*
el reyezuelo	*petty king/ruler*	el rey	*king*
el vejezuelo	*little old man*	el viejo	*old man*

EJERCICIO 150·1

Complete each sentence with the correct form of the appropriate noun.

1. En la boca de un bebé se encuentra un _____.

2. Una muñeca Barbie tiene un _____ conectado al cuello.

3. Un poni tiene un _____.

4. Para cruzar un río pequeñísimo se camina por un _____.

5. Para preparar un poquito de humus, se puede usar los _____.

6. El _____ puede causar una enfermedad fúngica del centeno y otros cereales.

7. Un barco pequeñísimo atraca en un _____.

8. Para hacer una sartén pequeñísima, se necesita _____.

9. Para tamizar un poquito de harina, se usa un _____.

10. Un hombre pequeño de cien años es un _____ .

11. Un hombre miserable sin dinero es un _____ .

12. Un hombre que roba a turistas y a personas inocentes es un _____ .

13. Un gobernante miserable e insignificante es un _____ .

14. El autor de libros pésimos y terribles es un _____ .

The following nouns end in **-zuela** and are feminine.

NOUN ENDING IN **-zuela**	ENGLISH EQUIVALENT	BASE WORD	ENGLISH EQUIVALENT
la bestezuela	*little beast*	la bestia	*beast*
la cabezuela	*floret (as of cauliflower)*	la cabeza	*head*
la cazuela	*casserole*	el cazo	*saucepan, pot*
la chozuela	*miserable hut/cottage*	la choza	*hut, cottage, hovel*
la fontezuela	*small fountain*	la fontana	*fountain*
la lanzuela	*small lance*	la lanza	*lance*
la lengüezuela	*small tongue*	la lengua	*tongue*
la mujerzuela	*slut, whore*	la mujer	*woman*
la pecezuela	*small piece*	la pieza	*piece, part*
la pobrezuela	*wretched/poor woman*	la pobre	*poor woman*
la pozuela	*small puddle/pond*	el pozo	*well*
la puertezuela	*small door*	la puerta	*door*
las tenazuelas	*tweezers*	la tenaza	*pincers, pliers*
la vejezuela	*little old woman*	la vieja	*old woman*
Venezuela	*Venezuela, little Venice*	Venecia	*Venice*

EJERCICIO

150·2

¿Verdadero o falso? *Indicate whether each statement is true or false, using* **V** *for* **verdadero** *true or* **F** *for* **falso** *false.*

1. _____ El rey de España vive en una chozuela.

2. _____ Caracas es la capital de Venezuela.

3. _____ Se depilan las cejas con las tenazuelas.

4. _____ Se encuentra la lengüezuela en la boquita.

5. _____ El río Misisipi es una pozuela.

6. _____ El caballero pequeñísimo entra en combate con una lanzuela.

7. _____ Una persona pequeñísima entra en la casita por la puertezuela.

8. _____ Las secciones individuas del coliflor o el brócoli son ejemplos de cabezuelas.

9. _____ La famosa Fuente de Trevi en Roma, Italia, es una fontezuela.

10. _____ Una anoréxica frecuentemente come sólo una pecezuela de pan para la cena.

11. _____ Típicamente se encuentra la cazuela en la cocina.

12. _____ Una bestezuela es la mascota perfecta.

13. _____ Una mujerzuela no recibe respeto del público en general.

14. _____ Muchas vejezuelas compitan en las Olimpiadas.

15. _____ Se encuentran varias pobrezuelas en los refugios para personas sin hogar.

APPENDIX A
List of Spanish prefixes

Following is a list of 100 common Spanish prefixes, numbered and arranged alphabetically. Each prefix is given with its meaning and two examples.

1	a-	*Not*	abiótico, anormal
2	a-	*Toward*	alargar, agrupar
3	aero-	*Air*	aeropuerto, aeróbico
4	ambi-	*Both*	ambidextro, ambivalente
5	anglo-	*England, English*	anglohablante, anglófilo
6	ante-	*Before*	anteayer, antecedente
7	anti-	*Against*	antipático, antibiótico
8	antropo-	*Human*	antropología, antropomórfico
9	arbori-	*Tree*	arboricida, arboricultura
10	archi-/arqui-	*Main, chief*	archipiélago, arquitecto
11	astro-	*Celestial body, star*	astrofísica, astrónomo
12	auto-	*Self*	autobiografía, automóvil
13	baro-	*Weight*	barométrico, barógrafo
14	bene-	*Well, good*	beneficio, benevolencia
15	bi-	*Two*	bimensual, bisección
16	biblio-	*Book*	bibliografía, biblioteca
17	bio-	*Life*	biografía, biología
18	bis-	*Twice*	bisabuela, bisnieto
19	cardio-	*Heart*	cardiólogo, cardiovascular
20	centi-	*One hundred*	centiloquio, centímetro
21	ciber-	*Computer*	ciberespacio, ciberterrorismo
22	co-	*With*	cooperar, copiloto
23	con-/com-	*With*	convivir, compadre
24	contra-	*Against*	contrarreforma, contraseña
25	de-	*(Away) from*	decaer, deducción
26	des-	*Not, opposite*	desayunar, desaparecer
27	di-	*Two*	dicromático, disección
28	dia-	*Through*	diafragma, diámetro
29	dis-	*Not, opposite*	disconforme, distraer
30	eco-	*Environment*	ecólogo, ecosistema
31	en-	*In*	enamorar, enrojecer
32	entre-	*Between*	entrelinear, entremés
33	equi-	*Equal*	equidistancia, equilibrar
34	etno-	*People, nation*	etnocéntrico, etnografía
35	ex-	*Former*	ex-marido, ex-presidente
36	extra-	*Outside, beyond*	extraordinario, extraterrestre
37	ferro-	*Iron*	ferrocarril, ferroviario

38	fili-	*Friendship, love*	filiación, filial
39	foto-	*Light*	fotogénico, fotógrafo
40	geo-	*Earth*	geografía, geoquímico
41	helio-	*Sun*	heliocéntrico, heliotropo
42	hemato-	*Blood*	hematología, hematoma
43	hemi-	*Half*	hemiciclo, hemisferio
44	hidro-	*Water*	hidrógeno, hidrotermal
45	hiper-	*Over*	hiperactivo, hipérbole
46	hipo-	*Under*	hipodérmico, hipótesis
47	histo-	*Tissue*	histología, histológico
48	holo-	*Whole*	holocausto, hológrafa
49	homo-	*Same*	homónimo, homosexual
50	ideo-	*Idea*	ideograma, ideológico
51	in-/im-	*Not*	inaceptable, impaciente
52	in-/im-	*In, into*	incorporar, impeler
53	inter-	*Between*	intercomunicación, internacional
54	intra-	*Inside, within*	intramuros, intravenoso
55	iso-	*Equal*	isósceles, isotopo
56	lito-	*Stone*	litografía, litosfera
57	macro-	*Long, large*	macrocosmo, macroeconomía
58	mega-	*Great, large*	megáfono, megalomanía
59	meta-	*Beyond*	metafísico, metáfora
60	micro-	*Small*	microbiológico, microonda
61	mili-	*Thousandth*	miligramo, milisegundo
62	mono-	*Alone, only*	monógamo, monotonía
63	multi-	*Many*	multiplicación, multinacional
64	narco-	*Sleep, stupor*	narcolepsia, narcótico
65	necro-	*Dead*	necrofilia, necrosis
66	neo-	*New, recent*	neoclásico, neologismo
67	neuro-	*Nerve*	neurocirujano, neurólogo
68	orto-	*Straight, correct*	ortodontista, ortografía
69	pan-	*All, every*	panorámico, panteísmo
70	penta-	*Five*	pentágono, pentagrama
71	per-	*Through*	perdonar, perenne
72	peri-	*Around, about*	periférico, periscopio
73	piro-	*Fire*	pirómano, pirotecnia
74	poli-	*Many, much*	polígamo, poligloto
75	pos-	*After*	posfechar, posguerra
76	post-	*After*	postimpresionismo, postmeridiano
77	pre-	*Before*	predestinación, prehistoria
78	primo-	*First*	primogenitura, primordial
79	pro-	*Forward*	proclividad, procrear
80	proto-	*First*	prototipo, protoplasma
81	psico-	*Brain, mind*	psicoanálisis, psicoterapia
82	radio-	*Ray*	radiografía, radiólogo
83	re-	*Again*	reconocer, reconstrucción
84	rect-	*Right, straight*	rectángulo, rectificar
85	rino-	*Nose*	rinoceronte, rinoplastia
86	semi-	*Half*	semicírculo, semiforme
87	sin-	*With, together*	sinfonía, sinónimo
88	sobre-	*Over*	sobresaliente, sobrevivir
89	sub-	*Under*	subgrupo, subterráneo
90	super-	*Above, over*	superfluo, supervisión

91	tele-	*Far*	teléfono, telepatía
92	ten-	*Hold*	tenazas, tenedor
93	trans-/tras-	*Across, beyond*	transcribir, traslación
94	tri-	*Three*	triángulo, triciclo
95	ultra-	*Beyond*	ultrasonido, ultravioleta
96	uni-	*One, single*	unicornio, uniforme
97	vice-	*Deputy, in place of*	viceministro, vicepresidente
98	xeno-	*Foreign, stranger*	xenofilia, xenofobia
99	xilo-	*Wood*	xilófono, xilografía
100	zoo-	*Animal*	zoólogo, zoomorfo

APPENDIX B
List of Spanish suffixes

Each suffix in this book is given with its number reference, meaning, and two examples.

Beginning suffixes

1	-a	*Resulting object/state*	la cocina, la visita
2	-able	*Able to be (acted on)*	adorable, cultivable
3	-ada	*Fullness of a measure or vessel*	la brazada, la cucharada
4	-ado/-ada	*Performer of an action, person on whom an action has been performed; result of an action*	el abogado, el cercado
5	-al	*Relating to, like*	central, cerebral
6	-ancia	*Action, result of an action, state*	la ambulancia, la abundancia
7	-ano/-ana	*Citizen, native; adherent, believer*	(el) boliviano, (el) luterano
8	-ante	*Performer, expert*	el cantante, el estudiante
9	-ario	*Book, printed matter, bound collection*	el diario, el himnario
10	-astro/-astra	*Step relation, diminutive*	la hermanastra, el medicastro
11	-azo	*Augmentative*	el gatazo, el humazo
12	-ción	*Action, result of an action, state*	la conversación, la separación
13	-dor/-dora	*Performer, expert*	el jugador, el conquistador
14	-ente/-enta	*Performer, expert*	el asistente, la presidenta
15	-era	*Container, vessel*	la pecera, la pulsera
16	-ería	*Store, shop*	la cafetería, la droguería
17	-ero	*Container, vessel, collection*	el brasero, el ropero
18	-ero/-era	*Worker, professional*	el banquero, el panadero
19	-eta	*Diminutive*	la camiseta, la opereta
20	-ete	*Diminutive*	el brazalete, el torete
21	-eza	*State, abstract concept*	la belleza, la riqueza
22	-ible	*Able to be (acted on)*	comprensible, movible
23	-ico/-ica	*Relating to, like*	patriótico, fantástico
24	-idad	*State, quality*	la densidad, la humanidad
25	-ificar	*To make (like)*	clasificar, justificar
26	-illa	*Diminutive*	la cocinilla, la manecilla
27	-illo	*Diminutive*	el torillo, el pasillo
28	-ín	*Diminutive*	el calcetín, el violín
29	-ina	*Diminutive; female counterpart*	la filmina, Carolina
30	-ino	*Diminutive; place where*	el michino, el camino
31	-ísimo/-ísima	*Superlative*	felicísimo, poquísimo
32	-ismo	*System, doctrine, attitude, way of life*	el idealismo, el mejicanismo
33	-ista	*Performer, expert*	el dentista, el comunista
34	-ita	*Diminutive*	la chiquita, la notita

35	-ito	*Diminutive*	el abuelito, el momentito
36	-ivo/-iva	*Characterized by a tone/manner*	defensivo, nutritivo
37	-ívoro/-ívora	*Person/animal that eats*	(el) omnívoro, (el) piscívoro
38	-lento/-lenta	*Relating to, like, full of*	corpulento, violento
39	-manía	*Mania, madness*	la bibliomanía, la megalomanía
40	-mente	*In a manner pertaining to*	alegremente, relativamente
41	-o	*Resulting object/action*	el aumento, el vuelo
42	-o/-a	*Performer, professional*	el biólogo, el médico
43	-ón/-ona	*Augmentative; pejorative*	el barcón, el hambrón
44	-or, -ora	*Performer, professional*	el escritor, el lector
45	-oso/-osa	*Possessing, full of*	dudoso, maravilloso
46	-sión	*Action, result of an action, state*	la decisión, la precisión
47	-teca	*Repository*	la biblioteca, la filmoteca
48	-triz	*Female performer/professional*	la actriz, la emperatriz
49	-udo/-uda	*Possessing a great deal of; augmentative*	peludo, zapatudo
50	-uno/-una	*Relating to, like, resembling*	conejuno, machuno

Intermediate suffixes

51	-ada	*Blow, strike, swift movement; resulting action*	la cabezada, la cuchillada
52	-ada	*Group, collection; flock, drove; amount*	la caballada, la década
53	-ado/-ada	*Relating to, like*	colorado, letrado
54	-aje	*Landing*	el alunizaje, el aterrizaje
55	-ante	*Relating to, like; doing*	abundante, parlante
56	-anza	*Quality, state, condition; process*	la alianza, la labranza
57	-arca	*Ruler*	la matriarca, el monarca
58	-ario/-aria	*Relating to, like*	centenario, necesario
59	-ario/-aria	*Person/thing possessing a characteristic*	el adversario, el ordinario
60	-asma, -asmo	*Result of an action, condition; being*	el entusiasmo, el protoplasma
61	-aza	*Augmentative; depreciative*	la bocaza, la sangraza
62	-azo	*Blow, strike, swift movement; resulting action*	el portazo, el pistoletazo
63	-cial	*Relating to, like*	comercial, parcial
64	-cidio	*Murder, killing*	el genocidio, el tiranicidio
65	-culo, -cula	*Diminutive; result of an action*	el cubículo, la molécula
66	-dor	*Device, machine, appliance*	el despertador, el ordenador
67	-dora	*Device, machine, appliance*	la calculadora, la secadora
68	-ecto	*Person; result of an action; abstract concept*	el arquitecto, el dialecto
69	-ejo	*Diminutive; pejorative*	el anillejo, el caballejo
70	-encia	*Result of an action, state*	la obediencia, la opulencia
71	-ente	*Relating to, like; doing*	corriente, residente
72	-eño/-eña	*Relating to, like; citizen, native*	marmoleño, nicaragüeño
73	-eo	*Action*	el blanqueo, el recreo
74	-ero/-era	*Relating to, like; able to be (acted on)*	azucarero, bebedero
75	-és/-esa	*Citizen, native; relating to*	(el) japonés, (el) burgués
76	-estre	*Relating to, like*	alpestre, silvestre
77	-fobia	*Fear, aversion*	la agorafobia, la xenofobia
78	-fono	*Sound*	el megáfono, el saxófono
79	-icio	*Result of an action, attribute, abstract noun*	el edificio, el solsticio
80	-ico	*Diminutive*	el angélico, el ventanico
81	-ida	*Action, result of an action*	la herida, la salida
82	-ido/-ida	*Relating to, like*	cándido, gélido
83	-ífero/-ífera	*Bearing, producing*	florífero, soporífero

84	-iforme	*Shaped, in the form of, like*	aliforme, biforme
85	-il	*Relating to, like; able to be (acted on)*	estudiantil, tornátil
86	-illa	*Diminutive; depreciative*	la figurilla, la mentirilla
87	-illo/-illa	*Diminutive; depreciative*	el vinillo, el autorcillo
88	-ito/-ita	*Relating to, like*	bendito, explícito
89	-izar	*To make (like)*	esterilizar, finalizar
90	-mano/-mana	*Crazy/obsessed person*	el cleptómano, el pirómano
91	-miento	*Action, result of an action, state*	el agrandamiento, el encantamiento
92	-ón/-ona	*(Person) tending/given to*	juguetón, (el) criticón
93	-orio	*Area, place*	el auditorio, el territorio
94	-ote	*Augmentative; depreciative*	el gatote, el caballerote
95	-tad	*State; abstract concept*	la amistad, la voluntad
96	-tono/-tona	*Tone, sound*	el barítono, monótono
97	-ucho/-ucha	*Pejorative*	la camucha, el perrucho
98	-uo/-ua	*Relating to, like*	continuo, melifluo
99	-ura	*State, abstract concept*	la bravura, la verdura
100	-ura	*State, result of an action*	la cura, la literatura

Advanced suffixes

101	-acho, -acha	*Augmentative; pejorative*	el amigacho, el poblacho
102	-acia	*State, abstract concept*	la contumacia, la suspicacia
103	-aje	*Collection, set; abstract concept*	el mueblaje, el lenguaje
104	-aje	*Fee, toll, rent, dues*	el hospedaje, el pontaje
105	-ajo	*Diminutive; perjorative*	el latinajo, el espantajo
106	-al	*Augmentative; place*	el dineral, el portal
107	-al	*Field, orchard, grove, patch, plantation; plant, tree*	el cerezal, el rosal
108	-ato, -ado	*Office, position, domain*	el generalato, el doctorado
109	-avo/-ava	*Denominator (of a fraction)*	octavo, centavo
110	-az, -oz	*Abounding in*	capaz, lenguaz
111	-azgo	*Office, post; relationship; fee*	el liderazgo, el pontazgo
112	-cracia	*Type of rule, government*	la democracia, la plutocracia
113	-dizo/-diza	*Relating to, like; tending to*	olvidadizo, heladizo
114	-dura	*Action, result of an action, object*	la limpiadura, la armadura
115	-ecto/-ecta	*Relating to, like*	correcto, insurrecto
116	-edad	*State; abstract concept*	la brevedad, la humedad
117	-engo/-enga	*Relating to, like*	barbiluengo, mujerengo
118	-eno/-ena	*Ordinal number*	noveno, centeno
119	-ense	*Citizen, native; relating to, like*	(el) canadiense, (el) parisiense
120	-eo/-ea	*Relating to, like; possessing a characteristic*	contemporáneo, rúbeo
121	-ería	*Abstract concept; place*	la galantería, la armería
122	-erizo/-eriza	*Herder*	el cabrerizo, el vaquerizo
123	-ero, -era	*Plant; place where plants grow*	el limonero, la tomatera
124	-érrimo/-érrima	*Superlative*	celebérrimo, paupérrimo
125	-esco/-esca	*Characterized by a manner/style; relating to*	caballeresco, picaresco
126	-(és)imo/-(és)ima	*Ordinal number*	séptimo, septuagésimo
127	-ez	*State; abstract concept*	la muchachez, la rojez
128	-icia	*State; abstract concept*	la avaricia, la noticia
129	-ido	*Action, result/recipient of an action; sound*	el marido, el ladrido
130	-iego/-iega	*Relating to, like; fond of*	asperiego, cadañego
131	-iento/-ienta	*Possessing a human characteristic/condition*	avariento, catarriento

132	-iento/-ienta	*Relating to, like; possessing a characteristic*	ferrugiento, holliniento
133	-ino/-ina	*Relating to, like; citizen, native*	cristalino, (el) neoyorquino
134	-isco/-isca	*Relating to, like; result of an action*	arenisca, olisco
135	-itis	*Inflammation*	la apendicitis, la hepatitis
136	-ito/-ita	*Chemical, mineral*	el arsenito, la hematita
137	-itud	*State, condition*	la aptitud, la magnitud
138	-izo/-iza	*Relating to, like; made of*	enfermizo, plomizo
139	-o	*Plant*	el naranjo, el cedro
140	-ón	*Sudden/intense action*	el apretón, el nevazón
141	-orio/-oria	*Relating to, like*	congratulatorio, operatorio
142	-osis	*Process; condition, disease*	la metamorfosis, la psicosis
143	-scopio	*Tool for viewing/observing*	el giroscopio, el telescopio
144	-uco, -uca	*Diminutive; depreciative*	el carruco, la peluca
145	-ulo, -ula	*Diminutive; result of an action*	la cápsula, el gránulo
146	-umbre	*Abstract concept*	la dulcedumbre, la quejumbre
147	-undo/-unda	*Relating to, like*	iracundo, moribundo
148	-usco/-usca	*Relating to, like*	amusco, verdusco
149	-uto/-uta	*Relating to, like; result of an action*	poluto, el minuto
150	-zuelo/-zuela	*Diminutive; depreciative*	el dentezuelo, la pobrezuela

Answer key

◆ I ◆ BEGINNING SUFFIXES

1·1 1. plantas 2. hipoteca 3. cena 4. cuenta 5. renta 6. ruedas 7. fecha 8. cocina 9. plancha 10. lágrimas 11. causa 12. pruebas 13. noticias 14. copia 15. pregunta

1·2 1. ducha 2. pausa 3. compras 4. subasta 5. obras 6. disciplina 7. espera 8. práctica 9. ayuda 10. caricia 11. guarda 12. busca 13. visita 14. burla

2·1 1. adorable 2. condenable 3. cultivable 4. imputable 5. conservable 6. calculable 7. evitable 8. dudable 9. aplacable 10. falseable 11. acabable 12. compensable

2·2 1. notable 2. vulnerable 3. palpable 4. penable 5. opinable 6. mudable 7. navegable 8. penetrable 9. soportable 10. negable 11. pasable 12. refrenable

3·1 1. dedada 2. calderada 3. pulgadas 4. cestada 5. zurronada 6. ponchada 7. narigada 8. cucharada 9. hornadas 10. cazolada 11. brazada 12. sartenada 13. panzada 14. capada

3·2 1. V 2. F 3. V 4. V 5. V 6. V 7. F 8. V 9. V 10. F

4·1 1. el criado 2. el abogado 3. el encargado 4. el licenciado 5. el delegado 6. el adoptado 7. el enviado 8. el empleado 9. el chalado 10. el enterrado 11. el enamorado 12. el emigrado 13. el ahijado 14. el convidado, el invitado

4·2 1. el tornado 2. el decorado 3. el desagrado 4. el constipado 5. el guisado 6. el adobado 7. el helado 8. el granizado 9. el peinado 10. el cercado 11. el estado 12. el teclado

5·1 1. astral 2. cuaresmal 3. horizontal 4. elemental 5. central 6. codal 7. experimental 8. disciplinal 9. final 10. labial 11. colonial 12. cerebral, intelectual 13. arsenical

5·2 1. otoñal 2. poligonal 3. oriental 4. semanal 5. veinteñal 6. personal 7. papal 8. sacerdotal 9. parroquial 10. mental 11. suplemental 12. Mundial 13. ornamental 14. vecinal 15. terrenal

6·1 1. distancia 2. ambulancia 3. estancia 4. intolerancia 5. infancia 6. vigilancia 7. discrepancia 8. exuberancia 9. redundancia 10. perseverancia 11. relevancia 12. observancia

6·2 1. la repugnancia 2. la abundancia 3. la constancia 4. la importancia 5. la tolerancia 6. la resonancia 7. la vagancia 8. la consonancia 9. la asonancia 10. la disonancia

7·1 1. colombiano 2. mexicana/mejicana 3. venezolano 4. australiana 5. peruana 6. americano 7. cubano 8. boliviano 9. ecuatoriano 10. camboyano 11. paraguayano 12. surcoreana 13. norcoreano 14. jordano 15. italiano

7·2	1. jerosolimitana 2. californiano 3. centroamericanos 4. sudamericanos 5. nuevomexicano 6. tejanos 7. romanas 8. veneciano 9. siberiano 10. siciliano 11. castellano 12. alsaciano 13. aldeanos

7·2 1. jerosolimitana 2. californiano 3. centroamericanos 4. sudamericanos 5. nuevomexicano 6. tejanos 7. romanas 8. veneciano 9. siberiano 10. siciliano 11. castellano 12. alsaciano 13. aldeanos

7·3 1. vegetariano 2. vegano 3. cristiano 4. presbiterianos 5. luteranos 6. puritanos 7. paganos 8. victoriana 9. republicanos 10. mendeliano

8·1 1. las cantantes 2. los danzantes 3. los amantes 4. los ignorantes 5. los negociantes 6. los maleantes 7. los gobernantes 8. los dibujantes 9. el viajante 10. los comandantes

8·2 1. el estudiante 2. el caminante 3. la veraneante 4. el habitante 5. el donante 6. el participante 7. la votante 8. el protestante 9. la debutante 10. el delineante 11. la visitante 12. el navegante 13. la litigante 14. el copiante 15. la solicitante

9·1 1. diario 2. calendario 3. obituario 4. inventario 5. anuario 6. recetario 7. horario 8. glosario 9. diccionario 10. abecedario 11. vocabulario 12. cuestionario 13. noticiario 14. silabario 15. comentario

9·2 1. el recetario 2. el obituario 3. el diario 4. el diccionario 5. el inventario 6. el noticiario 7. el calendario 8. el cuestionario 9. el horario 10. el silabario 11. el abecedario 12. el anuario 13. el vocabulario 14. el glosario 15. el comentario

9·3 1. el epistolario 2. el himnario 3. el devocionario 4. el maitinario

10·1 1. madrastra 2. padrastro 3. hermanastro 4. hermanastra 5. hijastros 6. hijastras 7. abuelastro 8. abuelastra 9. nietastros 10. nietastras

10·2 1. un musicastro 2. un cochastro 3. un pinastro 4. un pollastro 5. un medicastro 6. una pollastra 7. un camastro

11·1 1. el bigotazo 2. el perrazo 3. el playazo 4. el cuerpazo 5. el plumazo 6. el boyazo 7. el zapatazo 8. el copazo 9. el hombrazo 10. el gatazo 11. el animalazo 12. el copazo

11·2 1. g 2. e 3. k 4. b 5. i 6. l 7. a 8. h 9. c 10. f 11. j 12. d

12·1 1. V 2. F 3. V 4. V 5. F 6. V 7. F 8. V 9. V 10. V 11. F 12. F 13. F 14. V 15. V

12·2 1. e 2. d 3. g 4. h 5. f 6. i 7. j 8. a 9. c 10. b

13·1 1. veedores 2. malgastadora 3. cazadores 4. jugador 5. luchadores 6. boxeadores 7. bateadores 8. pateadores 9. escupidor 10. matador, picador, toreador

13·2 1. V 2. V 3. F 4. V 5. F 6. F 7. V 8. V 9. V 10. F 11. V 12. V 13. V

14·1 1. el dependiente 2. el doliente 3. el asistente 4. el adquirente 5. el contribuyente 6. el creyente 7. el correspondiente 8. el compareciente 9. el contendiente 10. el distribuyente

14·2 1. el residente 2. el presidente 3. el oyente 4. el recipiente 5. el sobreviviente 6. el sirviente 7. el respondiente 8. el maldiciente 9. el pretendiente 10. el regente

14·3 1. la dependienta 2. la sirvienta 3. la regenta 4. la presidenta 5. la asistenta

15·1 1. la regadera 2. la leñera 3. la cajonera 4. la pistolera 5. la cartera 6. la gorrinera 7. la pecera 8. la pulsera 9. la salsera 10. la caldera 11. la sopera 12. la carbonera 13. la polvera 14. la escalera 15. la tortera 16. la mantequera

15·2 1. g 2. k 3. i 4. o 5. l 6. s 7. c 8. u 9. q 10. d 11. m 12. a 13. f 14. e 15. v 16. j 17. n 18. h 19. r 20. b 21. t 22. p

16·1 1. la droguería 2. la mueblería 3. la cafetería 4. la pastelería 5. la dulcería 6. la especiería 7. la licorería 8. la pescadería 9. la vaquería 10. la carnicería 11. la verdulería 12. la tabaquería 13. la floristería 14. la juguetería 15. la calcetería 16. la ferretería

16·2 1. g 2. n 3. f 4. j 5. a 6. i 7. c 8. o 9. l 10. k 11. p 12. e 13. d 14. m 15. h 16. b

17·1 1. el salero 2. el pimentero 3. el paragüero 4. el harinero 5. el pastillero 6. el alfiletero 7. el costurero 8. el cenicero 9. el arenero 10. el brasero 11. el hormiguero 12. el servilletero

17·2 1. d 2. f 3. i 4. j 5. c 6. g 7. b 8. l 9. k 10. a 11. e 12. h

18·1   1. el droguero, la droguera   2. el lechero, la lechera   3. el banquero, la banquera   4. el florero, la florera   5. el carnicero, la carnicera   6. el cartero, la cartera   7. el granjero, la granjera   8. el cochero, la cochera   9. el barbero, la barbera   10. el fontanero, la fontanera   11. el guerrero, la guerrera   12. el casero, la casera   13. el cocinero, la cocinera   14. el cervecero, la cervecera   15. el basurero, la basurera   16. el librero, la librera   17. el chispero, la chispera

18·2   1. a   2. b   3. a   4. b   5. b   6. b   7. a   8. b   9. a   10. a   11. b   12. a   13. b   14. a   15. b   16. b

19·1   1. capeta   2. hacheta   3. historietas   4. camioneta   5. coletas   6. avionetas   7. camiseta   8. caseta   9. aleta   10. cazoleta   11. faldeta   12. buseta   13. isleta   14. cuarteta

19·2   1. toalleta   2. lengüeta   3. veleta   4. tarjeta   5. tijereta   6. paleta   7. operetas   8. manteleta   9. tineta   10. papeleta   11. libreta   12. vinagreta   13. peineta

20·1   1. el clarinete   2. la gorrete   3. el caballete   4. el juguete   5. el arete / los aretes   6. el brazalete   7. el colorete   8. el banquete   9. el mollete   10. el barrilete   11. el torete   12. el guantelete   13. el sombrerete   14. el paquete   15. el zaguanete   16. el soplete   17. el tenderete   18. el templete

21·1   1. la graseza   2. la certeza, la agudeza   3. la dureza   4. la presteza   5. la belleza, la lindeza   6. la franqueza, la llaneza   7. la bajeza, la rudeza   8. gentileza, terneza   9. la majeza   10. la sutileza

21·2   1. la tristeza   2. la flaqueza   3. la pureza   4. la pobreza   5. la riqueza   6. la torpeza   7. la maleza   8. la limpieza   9. la grandeza   10. la nobleza   11. la rareza   12. la guapeza   13. la viveza   14. la naturaleza   15. la largueza

22·1   1. comible   2. bebible   3. audible   4. admisibles   5. rompibles   6. convertible   7. vendibles   8. concebible   9. aborrecible   10. comprimibles

22·2   1. V   2. F   3. F   4. V   5. F   6. V   7. V   8. V   9. F   10. F   11. V   12. V   13. F   14. V   15. V   16. V

23·1   1. dramáticas   2. asmáticos   3. patrióticos   4. telefónica   5. pacífico   6. satánico   7. católica   8. tóxicos   9. básicas   10. evangélicos   11. psíquica   12. metálico   13. semíticos   14. sádico   15. panorámica

23·2   1. V   2. F   3. V   4. V   5. V   6. F   7. V   8. F   9. V   10. F   11. V   12. F   13. V   14. V   15. V

24·1   1. infinidad   2. castidad   3. utilidad   4. ferocidad   5. relatividad   6. humanidad   7. probabilidad   8. fecundidad   9. densidad   10. veracidad   11. superioridad   12. virilidad   13. atrocidad   14. mortalidad   15. adversidad, prosperidad

24·2   1. V   2. F   3. V   4. F   5. V   6. V   7. V   8. F   9. V   10. V   11. V   12. V   13. V   14. V   15. V

25·1   1. dosificar   2. pacificar   3. cuantificar   4. orifica   5. cosifica   6. clasificar   7. glorifican   8. calificar   9. santificar   10. gasificar   11. osificar   12. crucifican

25·2   1. simplificar   2. rectificar   3. intensificar   4. falsificar   5. fortificar   6. unificar   7. solidificar   8. beatificar   9. amplificar   10. petrificar   11. certificar   12. purificar   13. diversificar   14. especificar   15. justificar

26·1   1. la frutilla   2. la cocinilla   3. la tortilla   4. la camilla   5. la zapatilla / las zapatillas   6. la cajetilla   7. la saetilla   8. la mesilla   9. la carretilla   10. la mariposilla   11. la gavetilla   12. la escobilla   13. la cortinilla   14. la sabanilla   15. la cadenilla

26·2   1. V   2. F   3. V   4. V   5. F   6. V   7. V   8. V   9. F   10. V   11. V   12. V   13. V   14. V   15. F

27·1   1. jaboncillo   2. cigarrillos   3. torillo   4. cervatillo   5. balconcillo   6. librillo   7. banquillo   8. bolsillo   9. dragoncillo   10. platillo   11. zarandillo   12. plieguecillo   13. cachorrillo, perrillo

27·2   1. V   2. V   3. F   4. V   5. V   6. F   7. V   8. F   9. F   10. V   11. V   12. F   13. V

28·1   1. el botiquín   2. el cajetín   3. el sillín   4. el violín   5. el maletín   6. el calabacín   7. el calcetín   8. el balín   9. el botín   10. el espadín   11. el fajín   12. el banderín   13. el camarín   14. el bolín

28·2   1. i   2. e   3. j   4. d   5. l   6. h   7. o   8. b   9. m   10. f   11. c   12. g   13. k   14. a   15. p   16. n

29·1   1. V   2. F   3. V   4. V   5. F   6. V   7. F   8. V   9. F   10. V   11. V   12. V   13. F

29·2   1. la gallina   2. la bailarina   3. la reina   4. la heroína   5. la madrina   6. Angelina, Serafina   7. Carolina   8. Tomasina   9. Guillermina   10. Cristina   11. Josefina   12. Agustina   13. Geraldina

30·1 1. padrino 2. ansarino 3. palomino 4. michino 5. vellocino 6. colino 7. porrino 8. cebollino
9. pollino 10. camino 11. molino 12. casino

31·1 1. riquísimo 2. felicísima 3. larguísimo 4. venerabilísimo 5. jovencísimo 6. poquísimo
7. ferventísima 8. amabilísima 9. nobilísimo, valentísimo 10. notabilísima 11. probabilísima
12. sucísimo

31·2 1. beatísimo 2. bellísimo 3. buenísimo 4. clarísimo 5. delgadísimo 6. delicadísimo 7. excelentísimo
8. feísimo 9. grandísimo 10. guapísimo 11. hermosísimo 12. ilustrísimo 13. importantísimo
14. limpísimo 15. malísimo 16. muchísimo 17. palidísimo 18. pequeñísimo 19. santísimo
20. tranquilísimo

32·1 1. el tabaquismo 2. el narcotismo 3. el alcoholismo 4. el machismo 5. el materialismo 6. el idiotismo
7. el feísmo 8. el hipnotismo 9. el egoísmo, el narcisismo 10. el esnobismo 11. el terrorismo
12. el vandalismo 13. el idealismo 14. el magnetismo

32·2 1. el españolismo 2. el mejicanismo 3. el argentinismo 4. el despotismo 5. el obrerismo 6. el ateísmo
7. el catolicismo 8. el judaísmo 9. el paganismo 10. el mormonismo 11. el conservadurismo
12. el nacionalismo, el patriotismo 13. el deísmo, el teísmo

33·1 1. el violinista 2. el pianista 3. el percusionista 4. el clarinetista 5. el flautista 6. el florista
7. el licorista 8. el periodista 9. el inversionista 10. el maquinista 11. el dentista 12. el vocabulista
13. el artista 14. el paisajista 15. el acuarelista

33·2 1. el ciclista 2. el optimista 3. el pesimista 4. el carterista 5. el pacifista 6. el budista 7. el andinista
8. el fatalista 9. el comunista 10. el cuentista 11. el bautista 12. el perfeccionista 13. el capitalista
14. el deportista 15. el terrorista

34·1 1. pollita 2. vaquita 3. chiquita 4. señorita 5. viejecita 6. viudita 7. hormiguita 8. trencitas
9. sortijitas 10. patita 11. manecita 12. ramitas

34·2 1. V 2. F 3. V 4. V 5. V 6. F 7. V 8. F 9. V 10. V 11. F 12. V

35·1 1. burrito 2. perrito 3. gatito 4. cerdito 5. caballito 6. conejito 7. patito 8. pajarito 9. halconcito
10. huerfanito 11. hijito 12. abuelito 13. pobrecito 14. viejecito 15. amiguitos

35·2 1. corralito 2. besitos 3. cochecito 4. regalito 5. adiosito 6. granitos 7. pedacitos 8. poquito
9. cajoncitos 10. puentecito 11. saltito 12. momentito 13. ratito 14. traguito 15. corazoncito

36·1 1. declarativa 2. exclamativa 3. digestivo 4. exclusiva 5. evolutivos 6. educativo 7. abusivo
8. defensiva 9. admirativa 10. descriptivo 11. evocativa 12. administrativo, ejecutivo 13. expeditivo

36·2 1. V 2. V 3. F 4. V 5. F 6. V 7. V 8. V 9. V 10. V 11. F 12. F

37·1 1. el frugívero 2. el piscívoro 3. el herbívoro 4. el carnívoro 5. el insectívoro 6. el omnívoro
7. el granívoro

37·2 1. F 2. V 3. V 4. F 5. V 6. V 7. F 8. V 9. V 10. F 11. F 12. V 13. F

38·1 1. friolenta 2. suculenta 3. violento 4. corpulenta 5. purulento 6. fraudulento 7. virulento
8. sanguinolenta 9. flatulenta 10. vinolento 11. pulverulenta 12. virolenta

39·1 1. la bibliomanía 2. la piromanía 3. la melomanía 4. la dipsomanía 5. la toxicomanía
6. la anglomanía 7. la lipemanía 8. le cleptomanía 9. la ninfomanía 10. la erotomanía
11. la megalomanía 12. la monomanía

40·1 1. f 2. c 3. i 4. a 5. j 6. b 7. d 8. e 9. h 10. g

40·2 1. aparentemente 2. elegantemente 3. evidentemente 4. fácilmente 5. finalmente 6. horriblemente
7. mentalmente 8. naturalmente 9. normalmente 10. probablemente 11. tristemente 12. usualmente

40·3 1. k 2. g 3. e 4. l 5. a 6. i 7. b 8. c 9. f 10. d 11. h 12. j

40·4 1. absolutamente 2. claro 3. directamente 4. enfático 5. fabulosamente 6. lento 7. malamente
8. necesario 9. obviamente 10. perfecto 11. precisamente 12. rápido 13. seguramente 14. trágico

41·1 1. el desayuno   2. el almuerzo   3. el silencio   4. el comienzo   5. el cuento   6. el abrigo   7. el pago
8. el aumento   9. el hado   10. el fracaso   11. el voto   12. el vómito   13. el vuelo   14. el juego
15. el ejército   16. el gobierno

41·2 1. grito   2. odio   3. paso   4. ayuno   5. saludos   6. abrazos, besos   7. sueños   8. desarrollo   9. castigo
10. estudio   11. regreso   12. atajo   13. trabajo   14. atraco   15. auxilio

42·1 1. filósofos   2. médicos   3. coreógrafos   4. fotógrafos   5. astrónomos   6. teólogos   7. pornógrafos
8. polígamos   9. psicólogos   10. sociólogos   11. gastrónomos   12. biólogos

42·2 1. el oftalmólogo   2. la astróloga   3. el cartógrafo   4. la mitóloga   5. el bígamo   6. la monógama
7. el radiólogo   8. la ginecóloga   9. el misántropo   10. la neuróloga   11. el patólogo   12. el físico
13. la química   14. el toxicólogo   15. la calígrafa

43·1 1. el barcón   2. el portón   3. el zapatón   4. el culebrón   5. el narigón   6. el balón   7. el cortezón
8. el gigantón   9. el moscón   10. el tazón   11. el camón   12. el rodeón   13. el cortinón   14. el bolsón
15. el hombretón   16. el goterón   17. el platón   18. el cestón   19. el cajón

43·2 1. V   2. V   3. F   4. V   5. F   6. V   7. F   8. V   9. V   10. F   11. V   12. V   13. V   14. V   15. F

44·1 1. el pintor   2. el actor   3. el inventor   4. el compositor   5. el director   6. el escultor   7. el autor,
el escritor   8. el confesor   9. el rector   10. el instructor, el profesor   11. el editor   12. el pastor

44·2 1. la conductora   2. la opositora   3. la consultora   4. la mentora   5. la seductora   6. la expositora
7. la lectora   8. la auditora   9. la ejecutora   10. la contralora

45·1 1. dudoso   2. mocoso   3. temerosa   4. celosa, codiciosa   5. lloroso   6. nervioso   7. gozosa, jubilosa
8. odiosos   9. respetuoso   10. lastimoso   11. rencorosa   12. pomposo

45·2 1. lujosos   2. misteriosas   3. doloroso   4. peligrosa   5. espantosos   6. ventajoso   7. milagrosa
8. escandalosa   9. pegajoso   10. ventosos   11. fabulosas, maravillosas

45·3 1. venenosa   2. mentiroso   3. poderoso   4. mantecoso   5. pulgoso   6. cuidadoso   7. sabrosa
8. carnosas   9. perezoso   10. humosas

46·1 1. la depresión   2. la ascensión   3. la decisión   4. la inversión   5. la confusión   6. la expansión
7. la invasión   8. la aspersión   9. la incisión   10. la distorsión   11. la fusión   12. la accesión

46·2 1. posesión   2. televisión   3. visión   4. extensión   5. percusión   6. propulsión   7. transfusión
8. transmisión   9. persuasión   10. transgresión   11. repulsión   12. progresión   13. suspensión
14. precisión   15. oclusión

47·1 1. la pinacoteca   2. la fototeca   3. la biblioteca   4. la hemeroteca   5. la videoteca   6. la filmoteca
7. la discoteca

48·1 1. c   2. f   3. i   4. g   5. a   6. e   7. b   8. d   9. h

48·2 1. la emperatriz   2. la protectriz   3. la saltatriz   4. la actriz   5. la fregatriz   6. la adoratriz   7. la institutriz
8. la cantatriz   9. la meretriz

49·1 1. h   2. o   3. m   4. l   5. r   6. a   7. n   8. s   9. p   10. g   11. d   12. t   13. q   14. f   15. j   16. i
17. b   18. k   19. c   20. e

49·2 1. el pico, picudo   2. el zanco, zancudo   3. la lana, lanudo   4. el ceño, ceñudo   5. la molla, molletudo
6. la carne, carnudo   7. la toza, tozudo   8. la felpa, felpudo   9. el zapato, zapatudo   10. la teta, tetudo
11. la pata, patudo

50·1 1. el oso, osuno   2. el conejo, conejuno   3. el caballo, caballuno   4. el perro, perruno   5. el lobo, lobuno
6. la oveja, ovejuno   7. el ciervo, cervuno   8. el zorro, zorruno   9. el puerco, porcuno   10. la vaca, vacuno
11. el gato, gatuno   12. el cordero, corderuno

50·2 1. el monte, montuno   2. el bajo, bajuno   3. el moro, moruno   4. la boca + el conejo, boquiconejuno
5. algo, alguno   6. el macho, machuno; el hombre, hombruno

51·1 1. la muchachada 2. la corazonada 3. la puñada 4. la patada, la pernada 5. la palmada, la uñada 6. la morrada, la rodillada 7. la gaznatada 8. la mangonada 9. la zancada 10. la cabezada 11. la gargantada 12. la lengüetada 13. la hombrada 14. la brazada

51·2 1. la escobada 2. la coleada 3. la fumada 4. la palotada 5. la azadada 6. la puñalada 7. la cuchillada 8. la badajada 9. la galopada 10. la tijeretada 11. la mazada

52·1 1. la arañada 2. la caballada 3. la cerdada 4. la boyada 5. la vacada 6. la perrada 7. la gatada 8. la torada 9. la novillada 10. la borregada 11. la pavada 12. la burrada

52·2 1. V 2. F 3. F 4. V 5. V 6. V 7. F 8. V 9. V 10. F 11. V 12. V 13. V 14. F

53·1 1. colorada 2. triangulada 3. cuadrada 4. nublado 5. azafranado 6. limonado 7. irisados 8. ovalado 9. anisados 10. nevada 11. leonado 12. rosado

53·2 1. jorobado 2. rayado 3. cruzado 4. pesado 5. avergonzada 6. estrellada 7. vertebrado 8. frustrada, enojada 9. letrado 10. rizado 11. destinado

54·1 1. alunizaje 2. aterraje 3. aterrizaje 4. arribaje

55·1 1. brillante 2. espumante 3. agravante 4. flagrante 5. ambulante 6. colgante 7. fascinantes 8. abundante 9. aplastante 10. alarmante

55·2 1. participantes 2. flamante 3. interesante 4. saltante 5. vigilante 6. susurrante 7. sobrante 8. triunfante 9. parlante 10. penetrantes 11. vacilante 12. vibrante

56·1 1. cobranza 2. crianza 3. confianza 4. añoranza 5. adivinanza 6. alianzas 7. desesperanza 8. andanzas 9. balanza 10. desemejanza 11. alabanza 12. desconfianza

56·2 1. V 2. F 3. V 4. F 5. V 6. V 7. V 8. V 9. V 10. V 11. F 12. V

57·1 1. matriarca 2. patriarca 3. monarca 4. tetrarca 5. pentarca 6. oligarca 7. jerarca 8. anarca

58·1 1. es 2. no es 3. no es 4. no es 5. son 6. no es 7. es 8. no es 9. es 10. no es 11. son 12. es 13. son 14. no es 15. es

58·2 1. F 2. V 3. F 4. V 5. V 6. V 7. F 8. V 9. V 10. V 11. F 12. V

59·1 1. F 2. V 3. V 4. V 5. V 6. F 7. F 8. V 9. F 10. V 11. F 12. V

59·2 1. es 2. no es 3. es 4. son 5. es 6. es 7. es 8. es 9. es 10. es 11. no son 12. Es

60·1 1. sarcasmo 2. entusiasmo 3. fantasma 4. espasmo 5. orgasmo 6. miasma 7. marasmo 8. plasma 9. protoplasma 10. citoplasma

61·1 1. madraza 2. barbaza 3. hilaza 4. manaza 5. barcaza 6. bocaza 7. sangraza 8. pajaza 9. carnaza 10. terraza 11. pernazas

62·1 1. el chinelazo 2. el alazo, el picazo 3. el tacazo 4. el portazo 5. el tijeretazo 6. el tablazo 7. el pretinazo 8. el timbrazo 9. el palazo 10. el patinazo

62·2 1. el gatillazo 2. el culatazo 3. el pistoletazo 4. el balazo 5. el escopetazo 6. el puñetazo 7. el botonazo 8. el porrazo 9. el estacazo 10. el latigazo 11. el varazo 12. el golpazo

62·3 1. e 2. f 3. a 4. i 5. h 6. c 7. b 8. j 9. g 10. d

63·1 1. palacial 2. artificial 3. crucial, esencial 4. exponencial 5. consecuencial 6. judicial 7. especial 8. penitencial 9. comercial 10. parcial 11. existencial

63·2 1. V 2. F 3. V 4. V 5. F 6. V 7. F 8. V 9. V 10. V 11. F 12. F

64·1 1. el fratricidio 2. el conyugicidio 3. el uxoricidio 4. el infanticidio 5. el feticidio 6. el parricidio 7. el matricidio 8. el filicidio 9. el deicidio 10. el regicidio 11. el tiranicidio 12. el magnicidio 13. el genocidio 14. el homicidio 15. el suicidio 16. el excidio

65·1 1. película 2. círculo 3. edículo 4. artículos 5. versículos 6. pináculo 7. ventrículo 8. cubículo 9. minúsculo 10. tabernáculo 11. molécula 12. testículo 13. folículo 14. signáculo 15. pedículo

65·2 1. el oráculo 2. el vehículo 3. el ridículo 4. el receptáculo 5. el vínculo 6. el obstáculo 7. el tentáculo

66·1 1. el borrador 2. el humidificador 3. el acondicionador 4. el contestador 5. el despertador 6. el calentador 7. el congelador 8. el abridor 9. el destornillador 10. el asador 11. el destripador

66·2 1. el refrigerador 2. el incinerador 3. el ordenador 4. el ordeñador 5. el secador 6. el rallador 7. el tostador 8. el purificador 9. el mezclador 10. el radiador 11. el rociador

67·1 1. la lavadora 2. la segadora de césped 3. la licuadora 4. la grabadora 5. la calculadora 6. la secadora 7. la batidora 8. la máquina expendedora 9. la aspiradora 10. la trilladora 11. la grapadora 12. la cribadora 13. la cultivadora 14. la copiadora 15. la computadora 16. la cosechadora

68·1 1. V 2. F 3. V 4. V 5. F 6. V 7. V 8. V 9. V 10. F

68·2 1. el dialecto 2. el prefecto 3. el desperfecto 4. el insurrecto 5. el proyecto 6. el aspecto 7. el desafecto 8. el trayecto 9. el afecto

69·1 1. el arenalejo 2. el lugarejo 3. el anillejo 4. el zagalejo 5. el azoguejo 6. el librejo 7. el atabalejo 8. el diablejo 9. el animalejo 10. el castillejo 11. el arbolejo

69·2 1. el bozalejo 2. el collarejo 3. el martillejo 4. el telarejo 5. el puñalejo 6. el barrilejo 7. el vallejo 8. el camellejo 9. el marmolejo 10. el caballejo 11. el cordelejo

70·1 1. independencia 2. coincidencia 3. preferencia 4. agencia 5. obediencia 6. evidencia 7. presidencia 8. residencia 9. existencia 10. conciencia 11. deficiencia 12. diferencia

70·2 1. la reverencia 2. la descendencia 3. la tendencia 4. la presencia 5. la divergencia 6. la afluencia 7. la conferencia 8. la dependencia 9. la insistencia 10. la influencia 11. la resistencia 12. la opulencia 13. la deferencia

71·1 1. V 2. V 3. F 4. V 5. F 6. V 7. F 8. V 9. V 10. V 11. F 12. F

71·2 1. rugiente 2. yacente 3. siguiente 4. reincidente 5. viviente 6. resistente 7. reluciente 8. teniente 9. repelente 10. sorprendentes 11. residente 12. luciente

72·1 1. risueña 2. galgueño 3. navideño 4. marfileños 5. hogareña 6. marmoleñas 7. halagüeña 8. costeñas 9. caribeñas 10. roqueñas 11. guijarreños 12. trigueña

72·2 1. madrileño 2. nicaragüeña 3. brasileños 4. hondureñas 5. puertorriqueño 6. salvadoreña 7. panameños 8. guadalajareñas 9. guayaquileños 10. gibraltareño 11. limeña 12. lugareños 13. isleños 14. norteños 15. sureños

73·1 1. el escopeteo 2. el ceceo 3. el blanqueo 4. el devaneo 5. el besuqueo 6. el campaneo 7. el paladeo 8. el cabeceo 9. el empleo 10. el papeleo 11. el careo 12. el fisgoneo 13. el deletreo 14. el lavoteo 15. el bloqueo

73·2 1. recreo 2. pareo 3. salteo 4. parqueo 5. revoloteo 6. tecleo 7. paseo 8. tartamudeo 9. zapateo 10. pataleo 11. repiqueteo 12. traqueteo

74·1 1. faldero 2. hacendera 3. bebederas 4. lastimera 5. llevadera 6. casera 7. aduanero 8. carbonera 9. maderera 10. azucarera 11. bananera 12. caminero 13. guerrera 14. harinero 15. mañanero

74·2 1. V 2. F 3. V 4. V 5. F 6. V 7. F 8. V 9. V 10. V

75·1 1. irlandés 2. portuguesa 3. nepalés 4. polonés 5. francesa 6. danés 7. inglesa 8. libaneses 9. holandés 10. japonesa 11. finlandesa 12. escoceses 13. neozelandesas 14. luxemburguesa 15. tailandés 16. groenlandesa

75·2 1. lisbonés 2. berlinesa 3. pequinesa 4. siamés 5. aragonesas 6. burgueses 7. vienés 8. salamanqués 9. montañés 10. hamburguesa 11. leoneses 12. barcelonés 13. milaneses 14. neoescocesa

76·1 1. silvestre 2. alpestre 3. campestre 4. ecuestre 5. terrestre 6. pedestre

77·1 1. la claustrofobia 2. la hemafobia 3. la fotofobia 4. la androfobia 5. la clerofobia 6. la acrofobia 7. la anglofobia 8. la aerofobia 9. la homofobia 10. la hidrofobia 11. la agorafobia 12. la xenofobia

78·1   1. xilófono   2. saxófono   3. homófono   4. gramófono   5. teléfono   6. micrófono   7. megáfono
8. Dictáfono   9. vibráfono

79·1   1. el novicio   2. el edificio   3. el oficio   4. el beneficio   5. el indicio   6. el perjuicio   7. el juicio
8. el ejercicio

79·2   1. el vicio   2. el prejuicio   3. el servicio   4. el suplicio   5. el precipicio   6. el sacrificio   7. el solsticio
8. el vitalicio

80·1   1. el patico   2. el villancico   3. el asnico   4. el angélico, el santico   5. el zatico   6. el tontico   7. el corecico
8. el sillico   9. el ventanico   10. el corpecico   11. el saltico   12. el liebratico

81·1   1. la comida   2. la huida   3. la mordida   4. la partida   5. la salida   6. la parida   7. la acogida
8. la despedida   9. la herida   10. la bebida   11. la sacudida   12. la corrida

82·1   1. V   2. V   3. F   4. V   5. V   6. F   7. V   8. F   9. V   10. V   11. F   12. V   13. V   14. V   15. V   16. F
17. V

83·1   1. lanífera   2. aurífero   3. fumífera   4. floríferas   5. lactífera   6. coralíferos   7. coníferos   8. conchífera
9. gumífero   10. fructíferos   11. astrífero

83·2   1. V   2. V   3. F   4. V   5. F   6. V   7. F   8. V   9. V   10. F   11. F

84·1   1. cruciforme   2. reniforme   3. cuneiforme   4. coniforme   5. conquiforme   6. pisciforme   7. corniforme
8. aliforme   9. fungiforme   10. cuadriforme   11. lotiforme   12. arboriforme, dendriforme   13. ramiforme

84·2   1. triforme   2. deiforme   3. baciliforme   4. filiforme   5. biforme   6. semiforme   7. coleriforme
8. estratiforme   9. uniforme   10. gaseiforme   11. carniforme

85·1   1. infantil   2. borreguil   3. abogadil   4. becerril   5. estudiantil   6. febril   7. aceitunil   8. femenil
9. concejil   10. juvenil   11. fabril   12. grácil

85·2   1. varonil   2. móvil, portátil   3. monjil   4. servil   5. manzanil   6. muchachil   7. tornátil, versátil
8. libreril   9. mujeril   10. señoril   11. volátil

86·1   1. la cosilla   2. la gacetilla   3. la mujercilla   4. la gentecilla   5. la colilla   6. la dudilla   7. la mentirilla
8. las hablillas   9. la figurilla, la personilla

87·1   1. el estudiantillo   2. el sabidillo   3. el maridillo   4. el abogadillo, el licenciadillo   5. el autorcillo,
el escritorcillo   6. el cieguillo   7. el ladroncillo   8. el doctorcillo, el mediquillo   9. el hombrecillo

87·2   1. el papelillo   2. el estanquillo   3. el baratillo   4. el animalillo   5. el vinillo   6. el amorcillo
7. el pajarillo   8. el veranillo   9. el disgustillo   10. el geniecillo   11. el brocadillo   12. los trabajillos

88·1   1. favorito   2. exquisito   3. erudito   4. bendito   5. finito   6. explícito   7. decrépito   8. contrito
9. emérito   10. gratuito

88·2   1. sólito   2. infinito   3. lícito   4. ilícito   5. recóndito   6. pretérito   7. inhóspito   8. súbito   9. implícito,
tácito

89·1   1. tranquilizar   2. fertilizar   3. suavizar   4. legalizar   5. familiarizar   6. realizar   7. utilizar   8. amenizar
9. neutralizar   10. finalizar   11. esterilizar

89·2   1. memorizar   2. alfabetizar   3. psicoanalizar   4. analizar   5. ruborizar   6. climatizar   7. valorizar
8. polemizar   9. pulverizar   10. arborizar   11. paralizar   12. organizar

90·1   1. el bibliómano   2. el melómano   3. el anglómano   4. el toxicómano   5. la ninfómana   6. el cleptómano
7. el pirómano   8. el erotómano   9. el monómano   10. el megalómano

91·1   1. aturdimiento   2. aquietamiento   3. avasallamiento   4. agrandamiento   5. empobrecimiento
6. abatimiento   7. confinamiento   8. aplazamiento   9. amillaramiento   10. embellecimiento

91·2   1. V   2. V   3. F   4. V   5. F   6. V   7. V   8. F   9. V   10. V

91·3   1. Sí   2. Sí   3. No   4. Sí   5. No   6. Sí   7. No   8. Sí

92·1   1. holgachón   2. gritón   3. regalona   4. juguetón   5. guapetón   6. calentón   7. vomitona   8. abusón
9. peleón   10. reservona   11. politicón   12. gordón   13. temblona   14. replicona, respondona

92·2   1. F   2. V   3. V   4. V   5. F   6. V   7. V   8. F   9. F   10. V   11. V   12. V   13. F   14. V   15. V   16. F

93·1   1. en el laboratorio   2. en el convictorio   3. el directorio   4. al crematorio   5. en el auditorio   6. en el dormitorio   7. al adoratorio   8. al escritorio   9. en el dedicatorio   10. al conservatorio   11. al divisorio

93·2   1. al purgatorio   2. al observatorio   3. al sanatorio   4. al oratorio   5. el territorio   6. el repositorio   7. al lavatorio   8. al parlatorio   9. al reformatorio   10. el vomitorio   11. el promontorio

94·1   1. el librote   2. el barcote   3. el camarote   4. el cerote   5. el gatote   6. el chicote, el muchachote   7. el angelote   8. el animalote   9. el perrote   10. el pipote   11. los barrotes / el barrote   12. el papalote

94·2   1. el bravote   2. el angelote   3. el librote   4. el pegote   5. el villanote   6. el animalote, el bobote   7. el amigote   8. el lugarote   9. el caballerote   10. el borricote   11. el machote

95·1   1. amistad   2. enemistad   3. dificultades   4. facultad   5. libertad   6. majestad   7. lealtad   8. voluntad

96·1   1. b   2. a   3. a   4. b   5. b   6. a   7. a   8. b   9. a

97·1   1. el calducho   2. el capirucho   3. el periodicucho   4. el santucho   5. la casucha   6. la tenducha   7. el animalucho   8. el medicucho   9. la camucha   10. el perrucho   11. el avechucho   12. el pingucho   13. el papelucho   14. el cuartucho   15. el cafetucho   16. el carrucho   17. el debilucho

97·2   1. F   2. V   3. F   4. F   5. V   6. F   7. F   8. V   9. F   10. V   11. F   12. V   13. V   14. F   15. V   16. F   17. F

98·1   1. individuo   2. contiguo   3. perpetuo   4. continuo   5. discontinuo   6. ubicuo   7. precipuo   8. vacuo   9. promiscuo   10. menstruo   11. fatuo   12. oblicuo   13. arduo   14. estrenuo   15. ingenuo

98·2   1. melifluas   2. conspicuo   3. ambigua   4. superfluos   5. inocuo   6. somnílocua

99·1   1. la dulzura   2. la rojura   3. la ternura   4. la albura   5. la amargura   6. la negrura   7. la hermosura, la lindura   8. la bravura   9. la locura   10. la verdura   11. la grisura   12. la listura   13. la secura   14. la blancura   15. la grosura

99·2   1. la largura, la anchura   2. la gordura   3. la soltura   4. la tiesura   5. la altura   6. la flacura   7. la bajura   8. la lisura, la tersura   9. la estrechura   10. la espesura   11. la blandura   12. la hondura   13. la llanura   14. la finura

100·1   1. temperatura   2. cura   3. aventuras   4. pintura   5. esculturas   6. literatura   7. estatura   8. postura   9. apertura   10. manicura, pedicura

100·2   1. la criatura   2. la signatura   3. la captura   4. la lectura   5. la caricatura   6. la abertura   7. la fractura   8. la cultura   9. la censura   10. la pastura   11. la estructura

◆III◆ ADVANCED SUFFIXES

101·1   1. el poblacho   2. la bocacha   3. el dicharacho, el terminacho   4. el ricacho   5. la aguacha   6. el marimacho   7. el riacho   8. el amigacho   9. el hornacho   10. la hilacha   11. el populacho, el vulgacho   12. el cocacho   13. el verdacho   14. el barbicacho

102·1   1. la suspicacia   2. la audacia   3. la falacia   4. la gracia   5. la eficacia   6. la ineficacia   7. la perspicacia   8. la farmacia   9. la malacia   10. la contumacia, la pertinacia

103·1   1. el hembraje   2. el almacenaje   3. el caudillaje   4. el alambraje   5. el herraje   6. el camionaje   7. el herbaje   8. el lenguaje   9. el andamiaje

103·2   1. el peonaje   2. el mueblaje   3. el marinaje   4. el plantaje   5. el plumaje   6. el paisanaje   7. el monedaje   8. el linaje   9. el maderaje   10. el porcentaje

103·3   1. el rodaje   2. el velaje   3. el ramaje   4. el vataje   5. el ultraje   6. el ropaje   7. el varillaje   8. el ventanaje   9. el rendaje   10. el vendaje

104·1   1. V   2. F   3. F   4. V   5. V   6. F   7. V   8. V   9. V   10. F   11. V

104·2   1. V   2. F   3. V   4. F   5. V   6. F   7. F   8. V   9. V   10. V   11. V

105·1   1. camistrajo   2. tendajo   3. guanajo   4. latinajo   5. bebistrajo   6. escobajo   7. cintajo   8. comistrajo   9. terminajo   10. pingajo, trapajo

105·2   1. el tiznajo   2. el lavajo   3. el espumarajo   4. el arrendajo   5. el escupitajo   6. el zancajo   7. el colgajo   8. el lagunajo   9. el hatajo   10. el espantajo   11. el sombrajo

106·1   1. el festival   2. el dineral, el platal   3. el ritual   4. el varal   5. el soportal   6. el nidal   7. el parral   8. el lodazal   9. el ventanal

106·2   1. el portal   2. el bancal   3. el vitral   4. el cabezal   5. el semental   6. el santoral   7. el dedal   8. el ojal   9. el pozal   10. el tribunal   11. el ostral   12. el rectoral   13. el secadal   14. el peñascal   15. el riscal   16. el misal

107·1   1. la naranja   2. el tomate   3. el guisante   4. la piña   5. la cereza   6. el pimiento   7. la patata   8. la alcachofa   9. el maíz   10. el rábano   11. la banana   12. la fruta   13. la berenjena   14. la pera   15. la berza   16. la manzana   17. el plátano   18. la fresa

107·2   1. el pino, el pinal   2. la rosa, el rosal   3. la almendra, el almendral   4. el caucho, el cauchal   5. el alcornoque, el alcornocal   6. el roble, el robledal   7. el café, el cafetal   8. el arroz, el arrozal   9. la cebada, el cebadal   10. la alfalfa, el alfalfal   11. la avena, el avenal   12. el trigo, el trigal

108·1   1. el cardenalato   2. el diaconato   3. el priorato   4. el clericato   5. el obispado   6. el canonicato   7. el superiorato   8. el cancelariato   9. el consulado   10. el generalato   11. el liderato   12. el reinado   13. el sultanato   14. el colonato   15. el secretariado   16. el juzgado

108·2   1. el profesorado   2. el doctorado   3. el bachillerato   4. el economato   5. el procerato   6. el notariato   7. el caballerato   8. el campeonato   9. el noviciado   10. el orfanato   11. el celibato   12. el concubinato

109·1   1. 6/11   2. 2/13   3. 2/15   4. 8/30   5. 7/40   6. 9/14   7. 3/17   8. 1/60   9. 3/16   10. 7/20   11. 20/90   12. 3/50   13. 5/12   14. 1/70   15. 5/6   16. 1/18   17. 3/80   18. 1/100   19. 2/19   20. 5/21

109·2   1. Tenemos que leer cinco seisavos del libro para mañana.   2. Cada persona puede comer una quinceava de la pizza.   3. Una doceava de una docena de huevos es un huevo.   4. Nadie puede comer un veintavo de un elefante.   5. Un cincuentavo de trescientos es seis.   6. Un quinceavo de sesenta es cuatro. 7. Si solamente una treintava de la clase entiende/comprende la lección, hay problemas.   8. Un cuarentavo de doscientos es cinco.

110·1   1. mendaz   2. veraz   3. eficaz   4. vivaz   5. feraz   6. suspicaz   7. capaz   8. incapaz   9. montaraz   10. rapaz, voraz   11. pertinaz, tenaz   12. lenguaz, locuaz

110·2   1. falaz   2. veloz   3. pugnaz   4. salaz   5. contumaz   6. mordaz   7. atroz   8. precoz   9. feroz   10. perspicaz   11. audaz   12. sagaz

111·1   1. el comadrazgo   2. el compadrazgo   3. el noviazgo   4. el madrinazgo   5. el padrinazgo   6. el papazgo   7. el albaceazgo   8. el liderazgo   9. el mecenazgo   10. el mayorazgo   11. el primazgo   12. el sobrinazgo   13. el pontazgo   14. el terrazgo   15. el cillazgo

111·2   1. el alguacilazgo   2. el alaminazgo   3. el tenientazgo   4. el alarifazgo   5. el almotacenazgo   6. el cacicazgo   7. el alferazgo   8. el almirantazgo   9. el vicealmirantazgo

112·1   1. la democracia   2. la teocracia   3. la bancocracia   4. la oclocracia   5. la falocracia   6. la ginecocracia   7. la plutocracia   8. la aristocracia   9. la burocracia   10. la tecnocracia   11. la timocracia   12. la gerontocracia   13. la mesocracia   14. la autocracia   15. la meritocracia   16. la acracia

113·1   1. olvidadiza   2. acomodadizo   3. asustadizo   4. cambiadiza, tornadiza   5. enojadizo   6. apartadizo   7. erradizo

113·2   1. F   2. F   3. V   4. V   5. F   6. V   7. V   8. V   9. F   10. V   11. F

113·3   1. llovedizo   2. arrojadiza   3. anegadiza   4. caediza   5. saledizo   6. heladiza   7. rajadiza   8. borneadizo   9. clavadizos   10. apretadiza

114·1   1. la arrodilladura   2. la tosidura   3. la mascadura   4. la mecedura   5. la raspadura   6. la lamedura   7. la retozadura   8. la rompedura   9. la tropezadura   10. la teñidura   11. la rociadura   12. la limpiadura   13. la peladura   14. la alisadura

114·2   1. la cabalgadura   2. la rapadura   3. la armadura   4. la cerradura   5. la picadura   6. las vestiduras   7. la bordadura   8. la escocedura   9. la quemadura   10. la añadidura   11. la ligadura

115·1   1. V   2. F   3. F   4. V   5. F   6. V   7. V   8. V

115·2   1. imperfecto   2. selecto   3. incorrecto   4. circunspecto   5. erecto   6. desafecto   7. insurrecto   8. indirecto

116·1   1. V   2. F   3. V   4. V   5. F   6. F   7. V   8. F   9. V   10. F   11. V

116·2   1. la sobriedad   2. la sequedad   3. la vastedad   4. la turbiedad   5. la soledad   6. la viudedad   7. la tochedad, la tosquedad, la zafiedad   8. la voluntariedad   9. la novedad   10. la seriedad

117·1   1. luengo   2. barbiluengo   3. mujerengo   4. abadengo   5. realengo   6. peciluengo   7. frailengo

118·1   1. deceno   2. noveno   3. treceno   4. septeno   5. ochenteno   6. quinceno   7. seiseno   8. cincuenteno   9. onceno   10. veinteno   11. dieciocheno   12. centeno   13. catorceno   14. treinteno   15. doceno

118·2   1. el noveno chico   2. la septena chica   3. el quinceno libro   4. el centeno día   5. la catorcena milla   6. la docena noche   7. el seiseno mes   8. la cincuentena persona   9. el dieciocheno año   10. el deceno aniversario   11. el treinteno coche   12. el treceno huevo   13. la veintena casa   14. el onceno caballo   15. la ochentena mesa

119·1   1. lisbonense   2. manilense   3. canadienses   4. matritense   5. nicaragüense   6. peloponense   7. parisienses   8. londinenses   9. bonaerense   10. ateniense   11. bruselense   12. costarricenses   13. cretense   14. cartaginenses   15. estadounidenses

120·1   1. V   2. F   3. V   4. F   5. V   6. V   7. F   8. V   9. V   10. F   11. V   12. V   13. V

120·2   1. cesárea   2. aéreo   3. cerácea   4. etéreo   5. zafíreo   6. violácea   7. griseada   8. coriáceos   9. corpórea

121·1   1. hotelería   2. gitanería   3. estantería   4. cohetería   5. porquería   6. palabrería   7. gansería   8. ganadería   9. galantería   10. pobretería   11. carcelería   12. grosería   13. armería   14. lanería   15. golfería

121·2   1. la vidriería   2. la versería   3. la vinatería   4. la relojería   5. la torería   6. la zapatería   7. la yesería   8. la tubería   9. la vocería   10. la tesorería   11. la porrería   12. la roñería   13. la tunantería   14. la tontería   15. la ratería

122·1   1. el caballerizo   2. el porquerizo   3. el yegüerizo   4. el boyerizo   5. el vaquerizo   6. el cabrerizo

123·1   1. k   2. c   3. a   4. g   5. b   6. h   7. i   8. j   9. e   10. f   11. d

123·2   1. b   2. d   3. e   4. c   5. a

124·1   1. salubérrimo   2. acérrima   3. celebérrimos   4. libérrimo   5. paupérrimo   6. aspérrimo   7. misérrima   8. integérrimo   9. ubérrima   10. nigérrima

125·1   1. libresco   2. caballeresco   3. marinesco   4. soldadesco   5. brujesca   6. pedantesca   7. gigantescos   8. monesco   9. gatesca   10. germanesca   11. carnavalescas   12. bufonesco   13. trovadorescos   14. oficinesco   15. gitanesca

125·2   1. V   2. F   3. V   4. F   5. V   6. V   7. V   8. V   9. V   10. V   11. V   12. V   13. F

126·1   1. décimo   2. vigésimo   3. quincuagésimo   4. séptimo   5. decimoséptimo   6. decimoctavo   7. duodécimo   8. decimocuarto   9. decimosexto   10. cuadragésimo   11. sexagésimo   12. octogésimo   13. undécimo   14. decimoquinto   15. decimonoveno   16. trigésimo   17. septuagésimo   18. nonagésimo

126·2   1. centésimo   2. quingentésimo   3. milésimo   4. millonésimo   5. milmillonésimo   6. billonésimo   7. ducentésimo   8. cuadringentésimo   9. sexcentésimo   10. octingentésimo   11. tricentésimo   12. septingentésimo   13. noningentésimo   14. dosmilésimo   15. tresmilésimo

127·1   1. rojez   2. amarillez   3. niñez   4. muchachez   5. madurez   6. adultez   7. vejez   8. lucidez, sensatez   9. salvajez   10. languidez   11. timidez   12. estupidez, mentecatez

127·2   1. pesadez   2. delgadez   3. validez   4. flacidez   5. aridez   6. pequeñez   7. putridez   8. marchitez   9. rapidez   10. robustez   11. escasez   12. sencillez   13. lobreguez   14. nitidez

128·1   1. la estulticia   2. la impericia   3. la caricia   4. la avaricia   5. la impudicia   6. la ictericia   7. la blandicia   8. la ardicia

128·2   1. la mesticia   2. la justicia   3. la injusticia   4. la malicia   5. la noticia   6. la primicia   7. la pudicia   8. la pericia   9. la inmundicia

129·1   1. el ladrido   2. el mugido   3. el zumbido   4. el roznido   5. el maullido   6. el rugido   7. el gruñido   8. el tañido   9. el crujido   10. el chillido   11. el tronido   12. el resoplido   13. el silbido   14. el sonido   15. el aullido

129·2   1. sentidos   2. aparecido   3. prometido   4. marido   5. apellido   6. vestido   7. desagradecido   8. mordido   9. cocido   10. oído   11. nacido   12. pedido   13. contenido   14. el herido

130·1   1. andariego   2. mujeriego   3. paniega   4. asperiegas   5. veraniego   6. pinariega   7. palaciego   8. moriega   9. nocherniegos

130·2   1. V   2. V   3. F   4. V   5. V   6. F   7. V   8. F   9. V   10. V

131·1   1. gargajiento   2. soñolienta   3. zancajientos   4. avariento   5. calenturientas   6. alharaquienta   7. catarriento   8. granujientos   9. hambriento   10. achaquienta   11. sudoriento   12. guiñopienta, harapienta, trapapienta   13. camariento

132·1   1. holliniento   2. polvorienta   3. sangriento   4. herrugiento, oriniento, ferrugiento   5. gusanienta   6. zarrienta   7. cascarriento, mugriento   8. zumientos   9. amarillenta   10. grasiento   11. ceniciento

133·1   1. azulino   2. esmeraldino   3. elefantino   4. zucarino   5. cristalino   6. dañino   7. canino   8. blanquecino   9. serpentino   10. cedrina   11. ferino   12. purpurinas   13. alpinas   14. mortecino   15. corderina   16. repentino   17. ambarino   18. septembrino

133·2   1. santiaguino   2. argentina   3. neoyorquinos   4. florentina   5. granadino   6. argelinas   7. tunecinos   8. salmantino   9. tangerina   10. andinos   11. campesino

134·1   1. arisco   2. oliscos   3. arenisca   4. alemanisco   5. morisca   6. levantisca   7. jalisco   8. mordisco   9. pedriscos   10. ventisca

135·1   1. la rinitis   2. la amigdalitis   3. la laringitis   4. la otitis, la timpanitis   5. el conjuntivitis   6. la gingivitis   7. la gastritis   8. la artritis   9. la hepatitis   10. la nefritis   11. la bronquitis   12. la tendinitis   13. la apendicitis   14. la celulitis

135·2   1. la dermatitis   2. la pericarditis   3. la vaginitis   4. la oftalmitis, la queratitis   5. la estomatitis, la glositis   6. la colitis, la pancreatitis   7. la flebitis   8. la encefalitis, la meningitis, la neuritis

136·1   1. el grafito   2. el granito   3. la dinamita   4. el meteorito   5. la pirita   6. la hematita   7. la saponita   8. el arsenito   9. la estalactita   10. la estalagmita   11. el nitrito   12. la bauxita   13. el acónito   14. la amonita   15. el sulfito

137·1   1. V   2. V   3. F   4. V   5. F   6. F   7. V   8. F   9. V   10. V   11. V   12. F   13. V   14. F

137·2   1. la magnitud   2. la prontitud   3. la rectitud   4. la vicisitud   5. la lentitud   6. la pulcritud   7. la plenitud   8. la laxitud   9. la solicitud   10. la longitud   11. la latitud   12. la licitud   13. la similitud   14. la verosimilitud

138·1   1. primerizos   2. agostizos   3. enfermizo   4. rojizas   5. mellizos   6. otoñizo   7. mestiza   8. banderizo   9. sequizo   10. estadizo

138·2   1. V   2. F   3. V   4. V   5. V   6. V   7. V   8. F   9. F   10. V

139·1   1. a. la naranja   b. el naranjo   2. a. la banana   b. el banano   3. a. la cereza   b. el cerezo   4. a. la toronja   b. el toronjo   5. a. la ciruela   b. el ciruelo   6. a. la bergamota   b. el bergamoto   7. a. la manzana   b. el manzano   8. a. la granada   b. el granado   9. a. la frambuesa   b. el frambueso   10. a. la pera   b. el pero

139·2 1. a. la castaña b. el castaño   2. a. el café b. el cafeto   3. a. la cedria b. el cedro   4. a. la calabaza b. el calabazo   5. a. la majuela b. el majuelo   6. a. la almendra b. el almendro   7. a. la canela b. el canelo   8. a. la jícara b. el jícaro   9. a. la oliva b. el olivo, a. la aceituna b. el aceituno

140·1 1. el relumbrón   2. el atracón   3. el nevazón   4. el turbión   5. el bebezón   6. el reventón   7. el tachón   8. el baldón   9. el restregón   10. el apagón   11. el chapuzón   12. el pregón   13. el hinchazón   14. el retortijón   15. el acelerón

140·2 1. V   2. V   3. F   4. V   5. F   6. V   7. F   8. V   9. V   10. V   11. V

141·1 1. circulatorio   2. discriminatorio   3. depilatoria   4. ilusorio   5. giratoria   6. obligatorio   7. inflamatorios   8. mortuorio   9. congratulatorios   10. acusatorio

141·2 1. V   2. V   3. F   4. V   5. F   6. V   7. V   8. F   9. V   10. F

142·1 1. la nefrosis   2. la cirrosis   3. la silicosis   4. la mononucleosis   5. la hematosis   6. la amaurosis   7. la queratosis   8. la triquinosis   9. la endometriosis   10. la acidosis   11. la halitosis   12. la alcalosis   13. la melanosis   14. la miosis   15. la neurosis

142·2 1. V   2. F   3. V   4. V   5. V   6. V   7. F   8. V   9. F   10. V   11. V   12. V

143·1 1. el otoscopio   2. el oftalmoscopio   3. el estetoscopio   4. el laringoscopio   5. el cistoscopio   6. el endoscopio   7. el anemoscopio   8. el higroscopio   9. el microscopio   10. el telescopio   11. el helioscopio   12. el electroscopio   13. el periscopio   14. el calidoscopio   15. el giroscopio

144·1 1. patucos   2. abejaruco   3. frailuco   4. bazuco   5. hermanuco   6. ventanuco   7. carruco   8. almendruco   9. peluca   10. casuca

145·1 1. el capítulo   2. el párvulo   3. el discípulo   4. el vestíbulo   5. el animálculo   6. la cápsula   7. la pápula, la pústula

145·2 1. V   2. V   3. V   4. F   5. V   6. V   7. V

146·1 1. pesadumbre   2. dulcedumbre   3. herrumbre   4. certidumbre   5. servidumbre   6. podredumbre   7. techumbre   8. mansedumbre   9. quejumbre   10. muchedumbre

147·1 1. inmundo   2. rotundo   3. rubicundo   4. fecundo   5. tremebundo   6. jocundo   7. furibundo, iracundo   8. cogitabundo, meditabundo

147·2 1. oriundo   2. profundo   3. segundo   4. nauseabundo   5. facundo   6. gemebundo   7. moribundo   8. pudibundo   9. errabundo, vagabundo

148·1 1. etrusco   2. tusca   3. chusco   4. lusca   5. rusco   6. verdusco   7. amusco, fusco, musco, pardusco

149·1 1. diminuto, minuto   2. astuto   3. disoluto   4. hirsuto   5. bruto   6. poluto   7. enjuto   8. insoluto   9. impoluto   10. irresoluto   11. absoluto, resoluto

149·2 1. la disputa   2. el tributo   3. el instituto   4. el minuto   5. el atributo   6. la prostituta   7. el sustituto   8. la voluta

150·1 1. dentezuelo   2. cabezuelo   3. corpezuelo   4. pontezuelo   5. garbanzuelos   6. cornezuelo   7. puertezuelo   8. herrezuelo   9. cedazuelo   10. vejezuelo   11. pobrezuelo   12. ladronzuelo   13. reyezuelo   14. escritorzuelo

150·2 1. F   2. V   3. V   4. V   5. F   6. V   7. V   8. V   9. F   10. V   11. V   12. F   13. V   14. F   15. V